ColdFusion® MX with Dreamweaver® MX

ColdFusion® MX with Dreamweaver® MX

David Golden

www.newriders.com

201 West 103rd Street, Indianapolis, Indiana 46290
An Imprint of Pearson Education
Boston • Indianapolis • London • Munich • New York • San Francisco

ColdFusion® MX with Dreamweaver® MX

Publisher
David Dwyer

Associate Publisher
Stephanie Wall

Production Manager
Gina Kanouse

Acquisitions Editors
Kate Small
Elise Walter

Development Editor
Chris Zahn

Senior Marketing Manager
Tammy Detrich

Publicity Manager
Susan Nixon

Senior Editor
Lori Lyons

Copy Editor
Toni Zuccarini Ackley

Senior Indexer
Cheryl Lenser

Manufacturing Coordinator
Jim Conway

Book Designer
Louisa Adair

Cover Production
Aren Howell

Cover Designer
Brainstorm Design, Inc.

Proofreader
Kelley Thornton

Composition
Gloria Schurick

❖

For Julie, my love.

❖

TABLE OF CONTENTS

About the Author

David Golden writes documentation for Flash and application server integration technologies, including Flash Remoting. He contributed to Ben Forta's *ColdFusion 5 Web Application Construction Kit* and writes articles for the Designer and Developer Center on Macromedia's web site. Born and raised in Arkansas, David now lives and works in Massachusetts.

About the Contributing Author

Greg Kettell has contributed to several books on web application development and HTML. He currently is a senior software engineer for a leading Internet company, using .NET and other cutting-edge technologies. Prior to that, he developed computer games for a living. Greg lives in Arizona with his wife and two children.

About the Technical Reviewers

These reviewers contributed their considerable hands-on expertise to the entire development process for *ColdFusion MX with Dreamweaver MX*. As the book was being written, these dedicated professionals reviewed all the material for technical content, organization, and flow. Their feedback was critical to ensuring that *ColdFusion MX with Dreamweaver MX* fits our reader's need for the highest-quality technical information.

Lon Coley is an IT professional specializing in Internet solutions and the Internet in education. More details are available at `http://www.ariadne-webdeign.co.uk`. She has been working professionally within the Internet sector for five years, working with companies and colleges looking to expand and understand the Internet in the modern working environment. Lon has authored or contributed to a variety of titles, including *How to Use Dreamweaver MX and Fireworks MX, Flash Site Workshop*, and *Special Edition Using Flash MX*.

Anne Groves lives in Columbus, Ohio, where she works as a web developer for The Ohio State University. Anne has edited several titles, including *Mac OS X: Unleashed, FrontPage 2002: Unleashed, Teach Yourself Dreamweaver UltraDev in 21 Days*, and *Mac OS X in 24 Hours*. While Anne enjoys developing web sites, her passion is teaching others how to use today's technology to make their lives easier.

Acknowledgments

Without the patience and guidance from my editors, you would not be reading this book. My sincerest thanks goes out to Chris Zahn, the development editor, and Kate Small, the acquisitions editor. Also, I need to acknowledge the technical editors, who corrected my mistakes and offered invaluable suggestions, greatly improving the quality and scope of this book.

The Macromedia documentation department and management also deserve my thanks for allowing me to pursue this project and offering encouragement along the way.

Most important of all, none of this would have been possible without Julie, whose undying support, encouragement, and support kept me on track and pointed toward my goal. I could not have asked for a better partner in writing a book and in life.

Tell Us What You Think

As the reader of this book, you are the most important critic and commentator. We value your opinion and want to know what we're doing right, what we could do better, what areas you'd like to see us publish in, and any other words of wisdom you're willing to pass our way.

As the Associate Publisher for New Riders Publishing, I welcome your comments. You can fax, email, or write me directly to let me know what you did or didn't like about this book—as well as what we can do to make our books stronger.

Please note that I cannot help you with technical problems related to the topic of this book, and that due to the high volume of mail I receive, I might not be able to reply to every message.

When you write, please be sure to include this book's title and author as well as your name and phone or fax number. I will carefully review your comments and share them with the author and editors who worked on the book.

Fax: 317-581-4663
Email: stephanie.wall@newriders.com
Mail: Stephanie Wall
         Associate Publisher
         201 West 103rd Street
         Indianapolis, IN 46290 USA

Introduction

The latest round of improvements in the Macromedia web development technologies has made a great set of tools even more accessible and powerful. In particular, the integration between ColdFusion MX and Dreamweaver MX now makes it even easier for you to produce sophisticated, database-driven applications. The leap forward that this integration represents is what inspired me to write this book. We have the tools; now with the education provided by this book, you can be off and running, developing the site that you always wanted to create.

Who Should Read This Book?

If you want to learn how to use Dreamweaver MX with ColdFusion, this is your book. The ideal reader would be an individual familiar with the design elements of Dreamweaver with little or no experience in building dynamic web sites with ColdFusion. At the same time, experienced ColdFusion developers who have been using ColdFusion Studio can also learn how to leverage Dreamweaver's visual development capabilities. Also, developers experienced in other web development technologies, such as ASP, PHP, or JSP, can use this book to understand ColdFusion development with Dreamweaver.

This book tries to be as applicable to the daily life of a ColdFusion developer as possible. You won't find in-depth discussions of passing arrays to JavaBeans or instructions about how to create a COM object from CFScript. This book serves as an introduction to visual ColdFusion development, not a blueprint for best design practices and methodologies or ColdFusion administration. In short, this book is designed to get you up and running quickly with the full power of Dreamweaver and ColdFusion.

How to Use This Book

If you want to skip around in this book, you might want to take a moment to decide on a course through the chapters. This book is broken up into segments. Read the following sections to decide which chapter is appropriate to your personal situation.

Part I: The Fundamentals of ColdFusion Development

Chapter 1, " Introducing Dreamweaver MX and ColdFusion MX," provides just that—it introduces you to the two products by giving you a little historical perspective on web development in general and Dreamweaver and ColdFusion specifically.

In Chapter 2, "Introducing ColdFusion MX," you learn about how ColdFusion works and the notion of a ColdFusion application. In addition, you will be introduced to the ColdFusion Administrator, the web-based control console for ColdFusion.

Chapter 3, "Introducing Dreamweaver MX," covers the Dreamweaver development environment. You also set up your site, which will be used throughout the rest of the book.

Chapter 4, "Working with Databases," provides a general overview of databases. You will learn how they work, how ColdFusion interacts with them, and guidelines for choosing the correct database for your application.

Part II: Creating ColdFusion Forms

Chapter 5, "Creating Form and Action Pages," introduces you to creating ColdFusion form and action pages. You will learn the basics of sending information from one page to another and displaying the results.

Chapter 6, "Creating Pages with Dynamic Elements," shows you how to dynamically bind database records to page elements, such as list-box menus or text boxes, using Dreamweaver's Bindings panel.

Chapter 7, "Validating Data and Handling Errors," demonstrates various methods of validating user-entered data in your ColdFusion pages. Data validation is critical to maintaining an accurate database and avoiding errors.

Part III: Displaying Results with ColdFusion

Chapter 8, "Displaying Records in a Dynamic Table," shows you how to build dynamic tables to display the results of database queries. Dynamic tables are an important component of building recordset navigation.

Chapter 9, "Creating Recordset Navigation," demonstrates how to leverage Dreamweaver's server behaviors to build navigation aids for recordset results.

Chapter 10, "Charting Dynamic Data," shows you how to use ColdFusion's built-in charting and graphing engine to create dynamic charts and graphs in your ColdFusion pages.

Part IV: Processing ColdFusion Forms

Chapter 11, "Inserting a Record into the Database," contains directions about inserting records into a database using ColdFusion. The capability to save information over the web is critical to web site interactivity.

Chapter 12, "Updating a Record in the Database," teaches you how to update existing database records. Updating database records lets users maintain records themselves, letting you focus on other matters.

Chapter 13, "Deleting a Record in the Database," offers instructions on deleting database records using ColdFusion.

Part V: Common ColdFusion Programming Techniques

Chapter 14, "Conditional Logic Problems and Solutions," covers ColdFusion logic constructs, including looping and if conditional logic.

Chapter 15, "Debugging and Error Handling," describes how to uncover problems in your ColdFusion applications and fix them. Also, you learn how to build your ColdFusion applications so that, when errors happen, a descriptive message is displayed to the user.

Chapter 16, "Sessions and the Application Variable Scope," teaches you more about ColdFusion session handling, which lets you assign a session to a user and persist information associated with the user across multiple page requests.

Chapter 17, "Building User Authentication," introduces you to ColdFusion security and user authentication. By authenticating users, you provide a measure of security to your ColdFusion application, a necessity when you allow users to make changes to the database.

Chapter 18, "Building a Search Interface," describes how to build a search interface that lets users search the pages of your web site for a certain word or phrase.

Part VI: Advanced ColdFusion Development

Chapter 19, "Using ColdFusion Components," introduces ColdFusion components. ColdFusion components represent a step forward in ColdFusion development by providing a construct to create reusable, self-describing components that support web services, Flash Remoting, and XML.

Chapter 20, "Building Flash Remoting Services," describes building ColdFusion pages and components for Flash movies. Flash offers a number of advantages over HTML, such as vector-based animations and enabling dynamic data and graphics without requiring a new page to load.

Chapter 21, "Using and Creating Web Services," introduces you to using and building web services, an emerging technology that enables you to call functionality on remote servers and use it in your ColdFusion application. In addition, ColdFusion components let you build web services for other developers to use.

Part VII: Customizing Dreamweaver

Chapter 22, "Customizing Dreamweaver for ColdFusion Development," provides information on using Dreamweaver's numerous customization features to tailor the development environment to your liking.

Chapter 23, "Building Custom Server Behaviors," describes how to use Dreamweaver's Server Behavior Builder to create custom server behaviors. Among other things, custom server behaviors can cut development time by automating repetitive tasks.

Chapter 24, "Building Dreamweaver Extensions," introduces you to the Dreamweaver Extension architecture that gives you the tools and application programming interfaces (APIs) to build sophisticated extensions to the Dreamweaver environment.

Part VIII: Appendixes

Appendix A, "Installing ColdFusion MX and Dreamweaver MX," offers instructions on installing ColdFusion and Dreamweaver, as well as configuration options and system requirements.

Appendix B, "ColdFusion MX CFML Tag Reference," contains a comprehensive listing of CFML tags and the corresponding Dreamweaver dialogs.

Appendix C, "Dreamweaver MX Keyboard Shortcuts," contains a listing of keyboard shortcuts in Dreamweaver.

Conventions

This book follows a few typographical conventions:

- A new term is set in *italic* the first time it is introduced.

- Program text, functions, variables, and other "computer language" are set in a fixed-width font—for example, `<cfoutput>`. Placeholders in syntax are set in a fixed-width italic font—for example, name=`"argument name"`.

I

The Fundamentals of ColdFusion Development

1

Introducing Dreamweaver MX and ColdFusion MX

THIS BOOK TEACHES YOU HOW TO DEVELOP ColdFusion MX applications with Dreamweaver MX. ColdFusion is an application server. Application servers process user input, query databases, and generate results to a web browser. Application servers lie at the heart of database-driven web applications, such as content management systems, online shopping, and user registration.

Dreamweaver offers an award-winning visual development environment that lets you click buttons and drop and drag to create dynamic, interactive web pages. Using Dreamweaver's features specifically designed for ColdFusion, you can build sophisticated web applications that leverage emerging technologies, such as XML and web services.

Although the excitement of the Internet gold rush is over, thousands of web developers are working harder than ever to make web sites better and more useful. Application servers and visual design environments have become the norm. In fact, while the dotcom business model—or lack of a business model—proved fatally flawed, the technologies that made the web popular continued to make great strides in both power and ease of use.

Today, ColdFusion MX and Dreamweaver MX represent the best in modern web application development. To appreciate just how far web development has come, a little history is in order.

A Short History of the Web

If you're reading a book on dynamic web development, you've probably been surfing around the Internet for years. If you can remember the very early days of the World Wide Web, you likely remember the novelty of reading web sites from around the world and sending text emails to friends. For many, exchanging information over a computer quickly became as natural as picking up a telephone.

Like many grassroot movements, an exact date and place for the birth of the Internet is hard to pinpoint. In 1969, an early prototype of a distributed network named ARPANET was set up between a small cluster of universities around the United States. Within just a few years, the fledgling Internet was already demonstrating its capability to grow quickly with the rapid addition of campuses from around the world.

During this time, other uses of the underlying network appeared, such as email and newsgroups. In the 1980s, the rise in popularity of networks connected by TCP/IP (Transmission Communications Protocol/Internet Protocol) in concert with the explosion of personal computer ownership provided the setting for the invention the World Wide Web as we know it today.

Much like its use today, the web was originally invented to share information. In 1990, while working at the European High-Speed Particle Physics research center in Switzerland, Tim Berners-Lee proposed three new technologies that used the TCP/IP network: Hypertext Transport Protocol (HTTP), Hypertext Markup Language (HTML), and a specification of a client to view HTML documents over HTTP, commonly known today as a web browser. Berners-Lee's original intention was just to share documents electronically with his fellow scientists.

According to Berners-Lee's specification, computers find each other using IP addresses. IP addresses identify a unique computer on the network. The problem with IP addresses is that they are hard to remember and easy to mistype. The Domain Naming Service (DNS) offered a solution. The IP address of a specific computer remained valid, and a host name was also associated with that IP address or multiple IP addresses. This became the familiar URL names used to locate web sites today. To make the DNS system possible, a special kind of computer, called a router, takes the HTTP request using a DNS host name, such as www.dgolden.net, and matches it to the corresponding IP address.

With the release of the Mosaic browser in 1993, the web was well on its way. By 1994, 10,000 web servers were running around the world. By 2002, more than 20 million servers host tens of millions of web sites. And the web continues to grow. With the spectacular rise in popularity of the web, companies began to appear that built applications for the express purpose of making the creation and maintenance of web sites easier.

Web Development B.C. (Before ColdFusion)

With the exponential growth of the web, people from a broad spectrum of backgrounds began to use the web as an electronic encyclopedia. If you looked hard enough, you could find information on just about anything. However, when the initial excitement of the web began to wear off, something began to become painfully clear to the web developers and web masters of popular web sites: It was impossible to maintain hundreds of HTML pages so that they would contain the latest and most accurate information.

At the same time, web developers started looking for ways to make their web sites more interactive. Although HTML's capability to format text and link to other HTML documents with a click of the mouse lies at the core of the web's usefulness, the promise of processing user-entered information and connecting databases to the web proved even more tantalizing.

Also, the development tools for web development began to adapt to web-specific development tasks. When the web first began, popular text editors of the time were used to write HTML, such as Emacs (as shown in Figure 1.1) and Vi. As web sites evolved and expanded and popularity of the Windows and Macintosh operating systems grew, a new generation of text editors, such as HomeSite and BBEdit, appeared that featured HTML tag support and visual file managers.

Figure 1.1 Emacs, a popular open-source text editor, originated in the Unix world. Although its size and feature set has grown over the years, Emacs remains true to its no-nonsense roots of plain text display.

Back on the server side, the Common Gateway Interface (CGI) removed many of the restraints holding back the web from what it could be. Using CGI, developers could write small programs in a variety of programming languages, such as Perl or C++, that would recognize and accept incoming HTTP requests, process the information, possibly interact with a database, and return the results back over HTTP. CGI instantly proved a hit and continues to be used today.

The popularity of the web and mounting corporate interest translated into an intense demand for developers familiar with web development technologies, especially interactive and database-related technologies. The spike in demand quickly outstripped the pool of available C and Perl developers. One reason that so many web sites appeared at the same time is that HTML, the language used to display format text, was so simple to learn. HTML's elegance and simplicity made it possible for people without a formal education in computer science to build web sites. But it lacked the capability to create dynamic sites, and CGI, although it added that capability, could quickly become overwhelmed by high numbers of requests for pages.

Enter ColdFusion and Dreamweaver

The stage was set for a change. In 1995, Allaire released ColdFusion 1.0, an application server designed from the ground up for building web sites and connecting them to a database. Moreover, ColdFusion built on the skill set of HTML coders with the introduction of the Database Markup Language (DBML). DBML, which shortly became the ColdFusion Markup Language (CFML), offered a simple tag-based syntax that closely resembled HTML. Thus, an experienced programmer could quickly learn the tags necessary to connect to a database and display database records.

Over the next two years, ColdFusion quickly proved to be a runaway hit. Thousands of developers flocked to the application server and away from the inefficiencies that plagued CGI. By 1997, 30,000 developers were using ColdFusion, and the third version of ColdFusion was available. In the same year, Allaire acquired from Bradbury Software Homesite, a widely used and respected text editor, and quickly released ColdFusion Studio, the first development environment intended for ColdFusion development (see Figure 1.2).

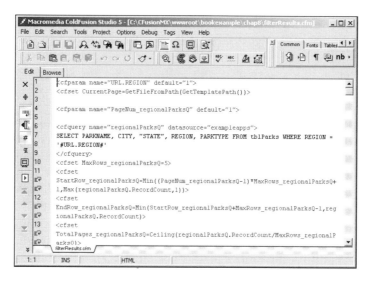

Figure 1.2   ColdFusion Studio, shown here in its fifth version, is a text
editor designed for ColdFusion development. Although it offers more
visual design features than Emacs, ColdFusion Studio remained solidly
entrenched in text editing.

Also in 1997, Macromedia released Dreamweaver 1.0 as one of the first What
You See Is What You Get (WYSIWYG) development environments for professional web site development. WYSIWYG editors let developers design web
site layouts visually by clicking buttons and using the drag-and-drop approach.
Although it still produced HTML under the covers, the initial success of
Dreamweaver showed that many developers would rather not always work
with just the underlying code. Whereas Dreamweaver focused on visual
HTML design, Elemental Software also introduced Drumbeat 1.0 in 1997,
which let developers visually create application server-powered web sites with
little or no hand-coding.

As the popularity of dynamic web sites grew over the next two years,
Macromedia realized the potential of Drumbeat and acquired Elemental
Software in 1999. Although Macromedia did release Drumbeat 2000, it
quickly folded many of Drumbeat's features into a new product, UltraDev.
UltraDev represented the marriage of Drumbeat's application server and
database features with Dreamweaver's visual design capabilities. When

Macromedia released UltraDev 1.0 in 2000, UltraDev supported three application servers: Microsoft's Active Server Pages (ASP), Java Server Pages (JSP), and Allaire's ColdFusion.

The Modern Era of Web Development

A lot can change in a couple of years. In 2001, Macromedia and Allaire merged into one company, keeping the Macromedia banner. ColdFusion 5.0 was released as was UltraDev 4, which skipped version numbers between 1 and 4. Today, ColdFusion MX and Dreamweaver MX offer a rapid application development (RAD) environment to build, test, and deploy ColdFusion applications faster and more easily than ever.

ColdFusion MX marks a significant milestone in ColdFusion's history. Like much of the software industry, the web development community has moved toward standards-based solutions for application servers and web site design. To address this trend and keep ColdFusion on an equal footing with competing technologies, ColdFusion MX has been completely re-engineered in Java, or more accurately, Java 2 Enterprise Edition (J2EE).

Although the significance of this change may be lost on most people, J2EE should provide a standards-based technology platform for ColdFusion to expand and evolve to meet the ever-changing demands of the web development community. With the increased competition from pure J2EE applications servers, the open-source phenomenon of PHP, and the introduction of Microsoft's ambitious and all-encompassing .NET strategy, ColdFusion MX stands poised for battle.

Dreamweaver MX, otherwise known as Dreamweaver 5, now contains all the application server and database connectivity features of UltraDev rolled into one. In addition, Dreamweaver MX integrates closely with ColdFusion MX to produce the most capable and extensible IDE for ColdFusion development ever. Not only can you develop and design web applications visually, you can get your hands dirty in the underlying code as well, as shown in Figure 1.3.

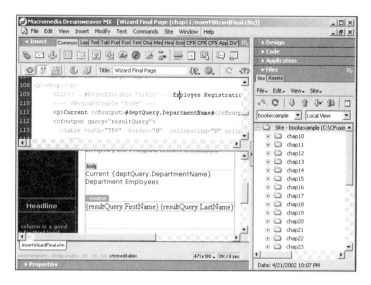

Figure 1.3   Dreamweaver MX offers the best in visual design and code editing capabilities in one integrated package.

The Next Big Thing

The future of dynamic web development, like the rest of the software industry, is in the midst of change. Predicting the future of software development is a tricky, possibly ultimately foolish endeavor. Like any technology, new trends in software development build upon what's gone before it and add additional capabilities.

That's especially true for the web. The web's incredibly wide reach among certain demographics depends on the wide distribution of preinstalled software. For example, TCP/IP is built into most, if not all, modern operating systems. In addition, HTTP support through web browsers, which are present on almost all personal and business computers these days, is required.

From the early beginnings of the Internet, many computer scientists dreamed of a distributed network of computers that could share each other's processing resources to perform greater, more complex tasks. Although today's web services don't fully deliver distributed computing, they do hold promise by allowing web developers to build an application that uses functionality on a remote computer.

Although HTML-based web pages are currently the norm, some developers are exploring the building of Flash-based user interfaces for web sites. Flash offers numerous advantages over traditional HTML, such as no page refreshes, vector-based animation, and a client-side runtime environment. The Flash Player is also supported on a number of wireless devices. ColdFusion contains the Flash Remoting service, which enables you to connect Flash movies to the application server and web services.

Using ColdFusion and Dreamweaver, you can use remote web services or, using ColdFusion components, generate web services for others to consume. One of the promises of web services is that application servers can build business logic functionality that multiple clients can consume. For example, one client type is that of a web browser—it browses web pages and displays HTML.

ColdFusion Development: What Do I Need?

To run any software, you need an operating system. If you want to run Dreamweaver and ColdFusion on the same system, your only choice is Windows. If you can run Dreamweaver on one computer and ColdFusion on another, you have a few more options. For example, ColdFusion supports a number of Linux and Unix distributions in addition to Windows. So, if you run Dreamweaver on a Macintosh and ColdFusion on a Linux or Unix-based server, you can develop ColdFusion applications in a completely non-Windows environment.

As will be explained in Chapter 2, "Introducing ColdFusion MX," you need a web server to serve HTML pages over the web. For development purposes, ColdFusion MX includes its own HTTP web server. This proves very convenient for development purposes if you do not already have a web server installed on your system. For deployment purposes, you will want to use another web server, such as Internet Information Services (IIS) (http://www.microsoft.com) or the Apache Web Server (http://www.apache.org).

Both IIS, which is Windows only, and Apache Web Server offer similar features. You should keep in mind that persistent security problems have plagued IIS. Microsoft issues security fixes quickly when security holes become public, but as the continuing saga shows, hackers will find new ways to attack web sites.

Summary

In this chapter, you learned a bit about the history of the Internet and the web and about how ColdFusion and Dreamweaver fit into that history. You also gained a glimpse into the present capabilities of ColdFusion MX and Dreamweaver MX, as well as the future where technologies like Flash and web services are starting to make a splash. In the next chapter, you will be introduced to ColdFusion MX and learn how modern application servers work.

2

Introducing ColdFusion MX

I N THIS CHAPTER, YOU LEARN HOW COLDFUSION works, including how ColdFusion relates to the web server, how ColdFusion pages use CFML, and how to use the ColdFusion Administrator. If you're not sure how application servers function, read on.

Understanding ColdFusion

ColdFusion is an application server that processes ColdFusion pages or components. ColdFusion pages (*.cfm) typically contain HTML, just like a regular web page, but they also contain ColdFusion tags or CFScript that provides database operations, conditional logic, and so on.

Nondynamic web sites consist of a collection of HTML pages, which might also contain graphics, multimedia, and Java applets. The web server, such as Microsoft's Internet Information Services (IIS) and the Apache Web Server (http://www.apache.org), provides the pages to web browsers. Figure 2.1 shows how a web site works without an application server.

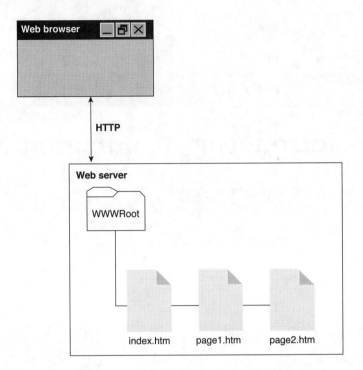

Figure 2.1 Without an application server, a web site consists of a group of HTML pages that the web server serves to web browser requests.

You can also mix HTML pages with ColdFusion pages in a dynamic web site. Web sites can contain a mixture of dynamic and static pages.

Usually, ColdFusion and your web server are installed on the same computer. That's because ColdFusion and web servers work together. HTTP requests contain more information than just the URL. For example, the MIME (Multipurpose Internet Mail Extensions) specifies the type of document being requested. If the MIME type is HTM, then the web server just returns the requested HTML page. However, if the MIME type is CFM, the web server forwards the request to ColdFusion. ColdFusion then returns the processed page to the web server, which returns the result to the calling web browser. Figure 2.2 shows a simplified representation of this process.

Configuring a Web Browser

When you install ColdFusion, you have the option of configuring an installed web server. For more information, see Appendix A, "Installing ColdFusion MX and Dreamweaver MX." ColdFusion supports most popular web servers, including Microsoft IIS 4 and 5, Netscape Enterprise Server 3.6, iPlanet Enterprise Server 4 and 6, and Apache Web Server 1.3.12 to 1.3.22 and 2.0.

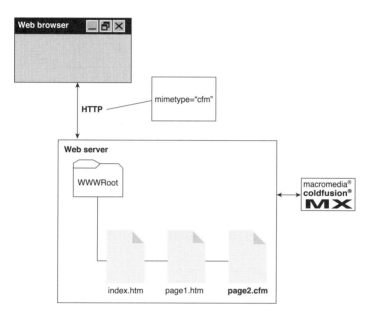

Figure 2.2 When the web server receives an HTTP request with a MIME type of CFM, it forwards the request to ColdFusion, which processes the ColdFusion page and returns the results to the web server.

Understanding CFML

ColdFusion pages contain HTML, just like any other web page. When ColdFusion processes the page, it looks for CFML tags—such as CFQUERY or CFOUTPUT—to process, not HTML tags. However, HTML can be enclosed in ColdFusion tags so that the HTML is repeated or modified in some way. In addition, ColdFusion looks for values enclosed in hash signs (#...#) that signify a ColdFusion variable.

This flexibility lets you use your existing HTML skills to build a web page and just insert ColdFusion tags where you want dynamic content to appear. As the following example shows, you can build on your knowledge of HTML to learn CFML:

```html
<html>
<head>
    <title>Hello World</title>
</head>
<body>
    <cfset var1="Hello, World!">
    <cfloop index="count" from=1 to=5>
        <ul>
            <cfoutput><li>#var1#</li></cfoutput>
        </ul>
    </cfloop>
</body>
</html>
```

In the example, the CFSET tag creates a variable named var1. The var1 variable contains the text, "Hello, World!" The CFLOOP tag repeats the HTML bullet row five times. Notice that the CFLOOP tag has attributes, just like an HTML tag. You use the attributes of CFML tags to set processing options.

In the HTML row tag, `<li>#var1#</li>`, notice that the var1 variable is referenced and bracketed by hash signs. Also notice that CFOUTPUT tags surround the li statement. When ColdFusion is parsing the page and finds a CFOUTPUT tag, it knows that the contents of the CFOUTPUT statement are dynamic.

Note

Appendix B, "ColdFusion MX CFML Tag Reference," contains a full list of CFML tags.

You can also use CFML functions for simple formatting, comparison, and arithmetic processing. As the following example shows, many CFML tags have corresponding CFML functions:

```html
<html>
<head>
    <title>Hello World</title>
</head>
<body>
    <cfset var1="<li>Hello, World!</li>">
    <ul>
        <cfoutput>#RepeatString(var1, 5)#</cfoutput>
    </ul>
</body>
</html>
```

Much like JavaScript and other scripting languages, CFML functions can take any number of arguments. In this case, the RepeatString function, which repeats a string a specified number of times, takes two arguments. The first argument is the string to be repeated, var1. The second argument supplies the number of times to repeat the string.

Notice that opening and closing CFOUTPUT tags surround the RepeatString function as do the hash signs. Hash signs tell ColdFusion to interpret the value, usually a variable, contained within so that it can be displayed in the browser. In the RepeatString function's first argument, no hash signs are used around var1 because it is being used as an argument and is not intended to be displayed.

For a complete listing of all CFML functions, see the CFML function reference in the documentation installed with ColdFusion MX.

Connecting to External Applications with ColdFusion

Although ColdFusion easily performs simple processing tasks like loops, its real power lies in its ability to connect to and interact with external applications or system resources. CFML provides specialized tags according to the application or resource being accessed.

For example, to connect to a database, you use the CFQUERY tag. In the CFQUERY tag's attributes, you specify the data source and the variable to contain the recordset returned. In addition, you use the Structured Query Language (SQL) to create the recordset.

> **Note**
>
> Before you can interact with a database, you must create a ColdFusion data source. For more information, see the "Using the ColdFusion Administrator" section later in this chapter.

The following example shows two CFML tags, CFQUERY and CFOUTPUT, working together to display the contents of a database column:

```
<cfquery name="Recordset1" data source="exampleapps">
    SELECT LastName
    FROM tblEmployees
</cfquery>
<html>
<head>
    <title>Employees' Last Names</title>
</head>
<body>
    <ul>
        <cfoutput query="Recordset1"><li>#Recordset1.LastName#</li></cfoutput>
    </ul>
</body>
</html>
```

In the example, the CFQUERY tag creates a recordset named Recordset1. The CFOUTPUT tag includes the query attribute, which references Recordset1. When ColdFusion processes the CFOUTPUT tag, it repeats the contents—in this case the

LastName column of the database—for each record in the recordset. Notice that the variable referenced between the hash signs specifies the LastName column of the Recordset1 recordset using the dot syntax.

As you will learn in Chapter 4, "Working with Databases," a database consists of tables. Tables are organized by column, much like an HTML table. The table rows represent individual records. The ColdFusion data source represents a group of settings, including database drivers, that ColdFusion uses to connect to a specific database.

Naming Variables

Although Dreamweaver automatically generates recordset variable names that are made up of the recordset name prepended to the column name, such as Recordset1.LastName, it is not required unless more than one CFQUERY statement exists in a ColdFusion page. However, it's usually a good idea to be as specific as possible when writing code to avoid confusion and promote code maintainability.

Figure 2.3 shows a simplified representation of a ColdFusion system.

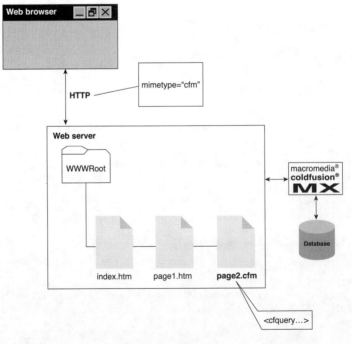

Figure 2.3   ColdFusion can interact with a variety of external applications and systems, including databases. When ColdFusion processes a CFM page that contains a CFQUERY tag, it queries the database according to the parameters supplied to the CFQUERY tag.

ColdFusion isn't limited to just database connectivity, however. You can interact with a wide variety of external applications and systems on your network, as Table 2.1 describes.

Table 2.1   **ColdFusion Connectivity Options**

Connectivity Type	Associated CFML Tags
Databases	CFQUERY, CFQUERYPARAM, CFSTOREDPROC
File Systems	CFFILE, CFDIRECTORY
File Transfer Protocol (FTP)	CFFTP
Other Web Sites	CFHTTP
Email	CFMAIL, CFPOP, CFMAILPARAM
Java and C++ Applications	CFOBJECT
Component Object Model (COM) or Common Object Request Broker Architecture (CORBA)	CFOBJECT
XML	CFXML
Web Services	CFINVOKE, CFCOMPONENT
Lightweight Directory Access Protocol (LDAP) Systems	CFLDAP

Using the ColdFusion Administrator

The ColdFusion Administrator lets you change how ColdFusion works. You access the ColdFusion Administrator using the Windows Start menu (Start, Programs, ColdFusion MX, Administrator) or by entering the Administrator URL in a web browser on the same intranet as the server running ColdFusion.

Depending on your installation, the Administrator URL is usually in the following form:

```
http://localhost/CFIDE/administrator/index.cfm
```

When the Administrator first opens, as shown in Figure 2.4, you are prompted for a password. You set this password when you installed ColdFusion. For more information, see Appendix A, "Installing ColdFusion MX and Dreamweaver MX."

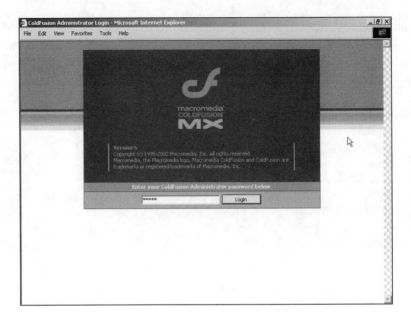

Figure 2.4   The ColdFusion Administrator login page requires the password that you specified in the ColdFusion installation.

After you log in successfully, the Administrator home page loads, as shown in Figure 2.5. The Administrator home page presents you with a plethora of information, including online information resources, documentation, and a navigation bar that lets you select your desired settings page.

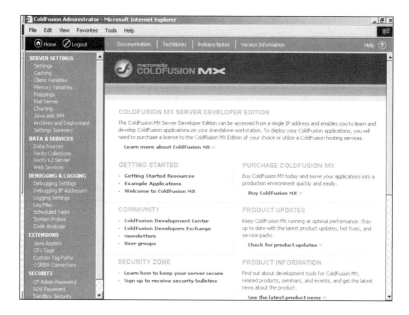

Figure 2.5   The ColdFusion Administrator home page offers a lot of information, including online information resources.

ColdFusion Administrator Settings Pages

As you can see in the Administrator's left navigation bar, the ColdFusion Administrator settings pages are divided into the following categories:

- **Server Settings**. Contains general ColdFusion settings, including memory, variable storage, and mappings.

- **Data & Services**. Contains database, Verity, and web services settings. The Verity search engine is used to index and search your site efficiently.

- **Debugging & Logging**. Contains settings for debugging output. Also contains ColdFusion logs, which provide a detailed transcript of ColdFusion operations.

- **Extensions**. Contains settings to register Java applets, ColdFusion custom tags, and CORBA connections.

- **Security**. Contains settings to change ColdFusion passwords and ColdFusion security settings.

Saving Administrator Settings

After you make any changes to the settings in the Administrator, be sure to click the Submit Changes button. After ColdFusion saves your settings, a success message will appear in the page. If you don't click the Submit Changes button, your settings will not be saved.

Server Settings Pages

The Server Settings pages of the ColdFusion Administrator let you configure general options for ColdFusion, including memory management and URL mappings. To look at a summary of ColdFusion Administrator's current settings, as shown in Figure 2.6, click the Settings Summary link in the navigation bar. Table 2.2 lists the available Server Settings pages, with a brief description of each page.

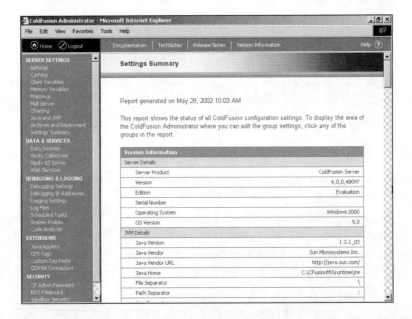

Figure 2.6   The ColdFusion Administrator's Settings Summary displays all of the current settings.

Table 2.2   **Server Settings Pages**

Page	Description
Settings	Contains general ColdFusion settings, including limits on simultaneous requests, whitespace management, and custom error templates.

Page	Description
Caching	Contains settings for ColdFusion's memory caching. Caching lets you cache ColdFusion pages or queries to server memory (RAM), which provides better performance than processing pages every time you request them.
Client Variables	Contains settings to change the client variable storage mechanism. By default, ColdFusion stores client variables in the Registry. You can change that to a database, client cookie, or none.
Memory Variables	Contains settings to change the default settings variable timeout. To preserve memory resources, ColdFusion times out memory variables created during page processing.
Mappings	Contains settings to add ColdFusion mappings. Using the `CFINCLUDE` or `CFMODULE` tags, you can call other ColdFusion pages. You can store those ColdFusion pages in directories outside of the web root if you add a ColdFusion mapping.
Mail Server	Contains settings to register your mail server with ColdFusion to send email from your ColdFusion applications and configure mail logging.
Charting	Contains settings for ColdFusion's built-in charting and graphing engine. You can configure charting cache type, the number of charts to cache, and so on.
Java and JVM	Contains settings for configuring how ColdFusion starts the Java Virtual Machine.
Archives and Deployment	Contains settings for creating and deploying archives of ColdFusion applications. Archiving and deployment provide an easy way to package and deploy your ColdFusion applications.
Settings Summary	Contains a summary of the current set of Administrator settings.

Data & Services Pages

The Data & Services pages of the ColdFusion Administrator let you create and configure ColdFusion data sources, web services, and the Verity search engine. Table 2.3 lists the available pages, with a brief description of each page.

Table 2.3   **Data & Services Pages**

Page	Description
Data Sources	Contains settings to create new ColdFusion data sources and edit existing ones. ColdFusion data sources represent a connection to a database. Data sources must be configured for ColdFusion to connect to a database.
Verity Collections	Contains settings to create new Verity collections and modify existing collections. The Verity search engine lets you quickly build search functionality for your ColdFusion application.

continues

Table 2.3 **Continued**

Page	Description
Verity K2 Server	Contains settings for connecting to a Verity K2 server—which provides high-performance searching—and managing K2-related collections.
Web Services	Contains settings to register web services with ColdFusion. Once you register a web service, you only need to use the name of the web service in your CFML code.

Debugging & Logging Pages

The Debugging & Logging pages of the ColdFusion Administrator lets you configure debugging and logging options, which help you diagnose and fix problems in your ColdFusion applications. In addition, the Scheduled Tasks, System Probes, and Code Analyzer pages let you create recurring ColdFusion tasks, place probes on ColdFusion pages to test for availability and performance, and analyze your CFML code for compatibility with ColdFusion MX. Table 2.4 lists the available pages, with a brief description of each page.

Table 2.4 **Debugging & Logging Pages**

Page	Description
Debugging Settings	Contains settings to enable and configure debugging options. Debugging information contains a wealth of data about ColdFusion processing, which aids in finding and fixing problems.
Debugging IP Addresses	Contains settings to create additional IP addresses to display debugging information. If you enable debugging in the Debugging Settings page, you should restrict debugging output to just your computer or the IP addresses of your development group. If you do not restrict debugging information by IP address, everyone who requests a ColdFusion page will see the debugging information, including site users and customers.
Logging Settings	Contains settings to configure ColdFusion's logging mechanism, which provides a transcript of the ColdFusion processing. This can provide an invaluable reference for locating a problem during ColdFusion processing.
Log Files	Contains facilities to view ColdFusion logs in the Administrator. Logs provide a history, or transcript, of ColdFusion processing that helps you isolate problems quickly.
Scheduled Tasks	Contains facilities to create scheduled events in ColdFusion, which run at intervals that you specify. Scheduled events can do any number of tasks, including Verity collection maintenance and clearing email spools.

Page	Description
System Probes	Contains facilities that let you create a probe in a ColdFusion page that monitors performance and availability. Using system probes, you can create automatic notification emails that alert system administrators when performance or availability slips below a specified level.
Code Analyzer	Contains facilities to analyze a ColdFusion page or a directory of ColdFusion pages for incompatibilities with ColdFusion MX. In addition, you can use the Code Analyzer to validate your CFML code for proper syntax.

Extensions Pages

The Extensions pages of the ColdFusion Administrator let you register and configure Java applets, ColdFusion custom tags, and CORBA connections. Table 2.5 lists the available pages and a brief description.

Table 2.5   **Extensions Pages**

Page	Description
Java Applets	Contains settings to register Java applets that you can then use in your ColdFusion applications with the `CFAPPLET` tag.
CFX Tags	Contains settings to register ColdFusion Java or C++ custom tags to use in your ColdFusion applications.
Custom Tag Paths	Contains settings to create additional custom tag paths, which let you store your ColdFusion custom tags in directories other than the default `[installdrive]:\CFusionMX\CustomTags`.
CORBA Connectors	Contains settings to register CORBA Object Request Brokers (ORBs) ORBs for use in your ColdFusion applications.

Security Pages

The Security pages of the ColdFusion Administrator let you change Administrator and RDS passwords as well as configure ColdFusion sandbox security.

Table 2.6 lists the available pages, with a brief description of each page.

Table 2.6   **Security Pages**

Page	Description
CF Admin Password	Contains settings to change the Administrator password that you specified during the ColdFusion Administrator setup.
RDS Password	Contains settings to change the Remote Development Services password for ColdFusion. Dreamweaver uses this password to connect to ColdFusion data sources.

continues

Table 2.6 **Continued**

Page	Description
Sandbox Security	Contains settings to enable and configure ColdFusion's sandbox security. Sandbox security lets you restrict access to certain directories using CFML security tags, such as `CFLOGIN`. You must build the security functionality into your ColdFusion applications before enabling sandbox security.

Summary

In this chapter, you learned how ColdFusion works, how CFML relates to HTML, and how to use the ColdFusion Administrator. Of course, you don't really need to deal with the CFML code by hand if you use the visual development features of Dreamweaver MX, which are covered in the next chapter.

3

Introducing
Dreamweaver MX

I N THIS CHAPTER, YOU LEARN ABOUT Dreamweaver MX, including an introduction to the Dreamweaver workspace and setting up a ColdFusion site. If you're unfamiliar with Dreamweaver or are interested in the new interface, this chapter is for you.

Understanding the Dreamweaver Workspace

In the grand scheme of this book, Dreamweaver is a visual development environment for ColdFusion applications. Rather than relying on text editing alone, Dreamweaver lets you develop ColdFusion pages as they would be seen in a web browser. At the same time, Dreamweaver lets you work directly with the code with just the click of a mouse button.

When you open Dreamweaver for the first time, a Workspace Setup dialog box displays, as shown in Figure 3.1. When you work in Dreamweaver, you are working within the Dreamweaver workspace. The Dreamweaver workspace represents a specific configuration of the Dreamweaver environment, such as displaying certain panels, document window views, and toolbars.

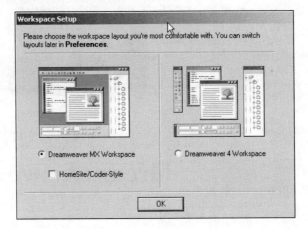

Figure 3.1   The Workspace Setup dialog box appears when you first start Dreamweaver. It lets you select the workspace that best fits your development needs.

Dreamweaver offers three different workspaces: Dreamweaver MX, HomeSite/Coder Style, and Dreamweaver 4. The Dreamweaver MX workspace, which is used in this book, features the latest Dreamweaver interface enhancements, such as an integrated workspace that eliminates the floating windows found in previous versions of Dreamweaver. The HomeSite/Coder Style workspace moves the panel groups to the left side of the workspace and the document window defaults to Code View. The Dreamweaver 4 workspace replicates the floating windows of the previous version of Dreamweaver.

In the Workspace Setup dialog box, select the Dreamweaver MX Workspace radio button and click the OK button.

Change Your Workspace

If you use Windows, you can change your workspace at any time in the Preferences dialog box. To open the Preferences dialog box, select Edit, Preferences. In the Preferences dialog box, click the Workspace Setup button in the General Settings category. This option is not available on the Macintosh.

When the Dreamweaver MX workspace first opens, as shown in Figure 3.2, you are presented with a document window, toolbars, and various panels. In general, the Dreamweaver workspace consists of the following elements:

- Document window
- Toolbar
- Properties Inspector
- Insert bar
- Panel groups

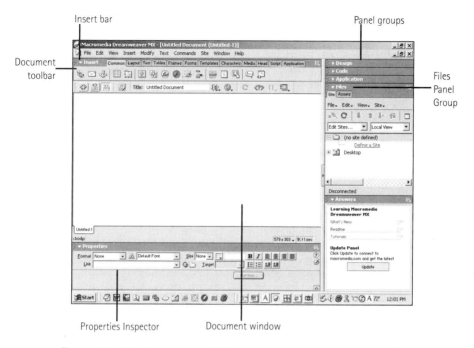

Figure 3.2   The Dreamweaver MX workspace contains a document window, toolbars, and panel groups.

Using the Document Window, Document Toolbar, and Properties Inspector

You use Dreamweaver's document window as your primary interface to the page and the code. The Document toolbar lets you change the display of the document window, such as using Code view, Design view, Code and Design view, Server Debug view, and Live Data view.

The Property Inspector provides a contextual interface to the code underlying a selected page element.

For Windows users, when working with multiple documents, you can use the document tabs that appear at the bottom of the document window, as shown in Figure 3.3. Using the document tabs, you can quickly and easily switch between separate documents without opening a menu or using a keyboard shortcut combination.

Figure 3.3 In Windows, a document tab appears in the document window for each document open in the workspace. Using the tabs, you can see which documents are open and switch to a specific document in just one click.

The document window also contains a status bar at the bottom of the page. As shown in Figure 3.4, the status bar displays the tags used in the page between the HTML <BODY> tags. You can click on the individual tag to select that element in the document window. Also on the status bar, you'll see the dimensions of the HTML page in the document window and an estimation of how long the page will take to download according to connection speed. To change the dimensions or connection speed setting, just double-click on the display.

Tags, Page dimension, Download time

Figure 3.4 The document window's status bar displays the HTML or CFML tags used in the page, the page dimensions, and an estimation of the page size and download time.

Using the Document Toolbar

You change views using the Document toolbar, which sits directly above the document window. As shown in Figure 3.5, the Document toolbar contains controls for the document window, such as changing views, file management, preview in browser, code reference, and page title. To open and close the Document toolbar, select the View menu, Toolbars, Document.

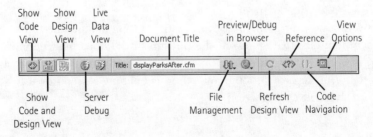

Figure 3.5 The Document toolbar provides control options for the document window, including changing views, previewing in the browser, and view options.

Using the Document Window in Design View

To create and prototype a page quickly, most people prefer to design visually. The Design View can be described as What You See Is What You Get (WYSIWYG). In other words, what you see in Design View is very close to what the page will look like in a web browser.

Although the Design View is intended for visual development, you can also access the underlying code through a variety of mechanisms, including the Quick Tag Editor of the Property Inspector, the Property Inspector itself, and the Code Inspector panel of the Code panel group.

Figure 3.6 shows the document window in Design View.

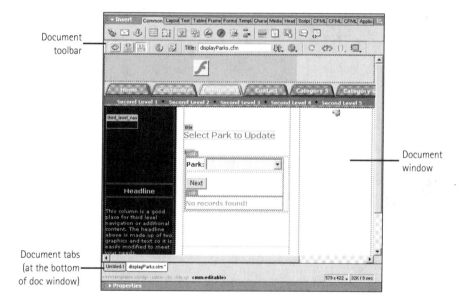

Figure 3.6   In the document window, the Design View lets you see the page as it would look in a web browser.

Using the Document Window in Code View

The Code View is a text editor that lets you work with the source code. Code View offers features to help with hand coding, such as code hints that can automatically generate code for you. For example, when you are defining a color attribute, a color-picker dialog box pops up.

Figure 3.7 shows the document window in Code View.

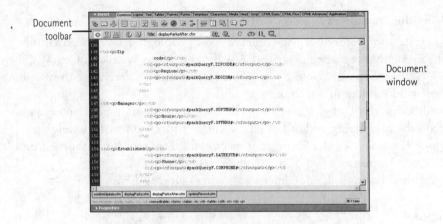

Figure 3.7   In the document window, the Code View lets
you work with the source code directly.

Using the Document Window in Code and Design View

Using the Code and Design View, as shown in Figure 3.8, you can split the
document window to see the source code and the visual page elements at the
same time. The Code and Design View highlights the integration between the
two. For example, when you select a page element, such as a table row or text
box in Design View, the corresponding code is highlighted in Code View.

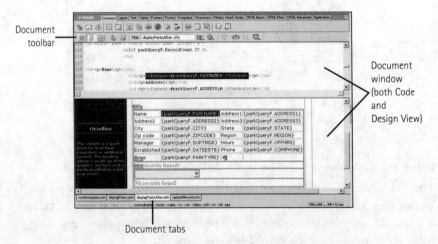

Figure 3.8   In the document window, the Code and Design
View lets you work with the source code directly and also see
the visual design elements.

Using the Property Inspector

The Property Inspector provides a contextual graphic interface to the selected page element in the document window. For example, if you select a table with your cursor in the document window, the Property Inspector changes to show the table's attributes, as shown in Figure 3.9.

When you insert a page element, such as a menu or text field, into the document window, you are creating code, usually HTML or CFML tags. Those tags contain numerous required and optional attributes. You can think of Dreamweaver's Property Inspector as your access point to each tag's attributes.

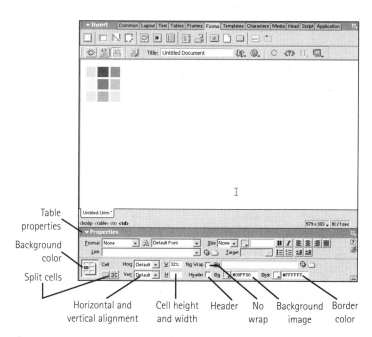

Figure 3.9 The Property Inspector serves as a contextual interface to the code underlying visual page elements, such as tables or form objects.

Using the Insert Bar

As its name implies, you use the Insert bar to insert page elements into the document window. Using a tabular organization, the Insert bar consists of a wide variety of categories, from designing to creating web application elements. As shown in Figure 3.10, the Insert bar includes some of the following categories:

- Common—Contains the most commonly used buttons, such as hyperlinks, tables, images and multimedia objects, horizontal rules, comments, and importation of tabular data.

- Tables—Contains buttons, like the Insert Table button, for creating and editing HTML tables. When using the document window in Code View, you can use the HTML tag buttons for a table, including TABLE, TR, TH, TD, and CAP.

- Forms—Contains buttons for form controls, including text fields, submit buttons, radio buttons, and ??menus.

- Application—Contains buttons for prebuilt application elements like dynamic tables, ??menus, and so on.

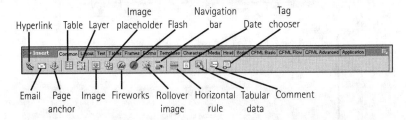

Figure 3.10 The Common tab of the Insert bar provides a wide variety of buttons for everything from designing web pages to inserting dynamic page elements.

When you click on a button in the Insert bar, a dialog box usually appears. In the dialog box, you change the options presented. For example, if you click the Insert Table button, the Insert Table dialog box appears, as shown in Figure 3.11.

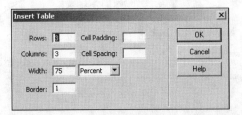

Figure 3.11 Like all other dialog boxes, you use the controls in the Insert Table dialog box to specify the options that you want, and then click the OK button.

Tag Chooser

If you cannot find the control that you want in any of the Insert bar tabs, you can use the Tag Chooser to access all HTML and CFML tags. To open the Tag Chooser, select the Insert menu, Tag, or use the keyboard shortcut Ctrl+E on Windows or Command+E on Macintosh.

When you define a ColdFusion site, three ColdFusion-related tabs—CFML Basic, CFML Flow, and CFML Advanced—appear in the Insert bar. The tabs organize the CFML tags into the following broad categories:

- CFML Basic—As shown in Figure 3.12, the CFML Basic tab contains buttons for server variables (CGI variables), CFQUERY, CFOUTPUT, CFINSERT, CFUPDATE, CFINCLUDE, CFLOCATION, CFSET, CFPARAM, comment (<!--- ... --->), hash signs (# ... #), and CFSCRIPT.

- CFML Flow—As shown in Figure 3.13, the CFML Flow tab contains buttons for CFTRY, CFCATCH, CFTHROW, CFLOCK, CFSWITCH, CFCASE, CFDEFAULTCASE, CFIF, CFELSE, CFELSEIF, CFLOOP, and CFBREAK.

- CFML Advanced—As shown in Figure 3.14, the CFML Advanced tab contains buttons for CFCOOKIE, CFCONTENT, CFHEADER, ColdFusion Page Encoding (CFPROCESSINGDIRECTIVE), CFAPPLICATION, CFERROR, CFDIRECTORY, CFFILE, CFMAIL, CFPOP, CFHTTP, CFHTTPPARAM, CFLDAP, CFFTP, CFSEARCH, CFINDEX, CFMODULE, CFOBJECT, and CFGRAPH.

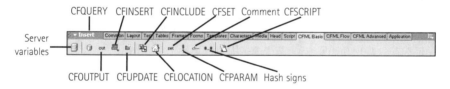

Figure 3.12   The CFML Basic tab of the Insert bar provides easy access to commonly used CFML tags, including CFOUTPUT, CFQUERY, and CFSET.

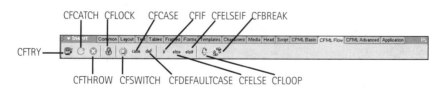

Figure 3.13   The CFML Flow tab of the Insert bar contains buttons for CFML logic, error handling, and page processing, including CFTRY, CFCCATCH, CFTHROW, CFIF, CFELSE, and CFELSEIF.

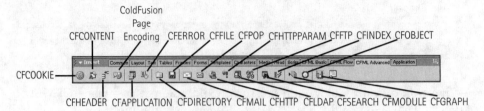

Figure 3.14   The CFML Advanced tab of the Insert bar contains buttons for a wide variety of advanced uses, such as `CFFILE`, `CFDIRECTORY`, and `CFGRAPH`.

To use most of the buttons on the CFML tabs, you must be using the document window in Code View. Also, this book doesn't cover all of the CFML tags. For tag usage and syntax, see Appendix B, "ColdFusion MX CFML Tag Reference."

Using the Panel Groups

Located on the right side of the Dreamweaver MX workspace, panel groups provide a general structure for organizing related panels. Most Dreamweaver panels provide an interface for a specific task, such as creating database queries, applying CSS or HTML styles, or managing site files.

The following panel groups are relevant to ColdFusion development:

- Code—As shown as Figure 3.15, the Code panel group contains the Reference, Snippets, and Tag Inspector panels. The panels provide code access, storage, and reference information.

- Application—As shown as Figure 3.16, the Application panel group contains the Database, Bindings, Server Behaviors, and Component panels. ColdFusion development uses these panels extensively.

- Files—As shown as Figure 3.17, the Files panel group contains the Site and Assets panels. These panels provide file access and management.

After you define a ColdFusion site, the panels in the Application panel group become active.

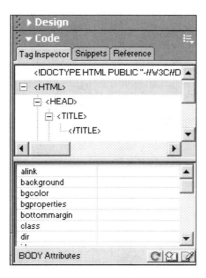

Figure 3.15 The Code panel group contains code-related panels, including the Tag Inspector, Reference, and Snippets panels.

Figure 3.16 The Applications panel group contains application server–related panels, including Database, Bindings, Server Behaviors, and Component.

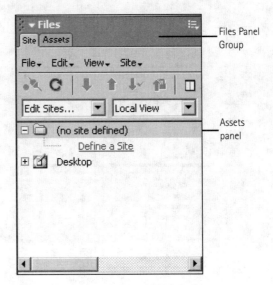

Figure 3.17   The Files panel group contains
file management–related panels, including
the Site and Assets panels.

Using the Code Panel Group

The Code panel group contains three panels: Tag Inspector, Snippets, and
Reference. All three panels are used for code editing tasks. The Tag Inspector,
shown in Figure 3.18, displays the tag structure of the current page. From the
<HTML> tag to a simple paragraph tag (<p>), the Tag Inspector displays all the tags
and their attributes, including CFML tags.

Figure 3.18   The Tag Inspector panel displays
all tags used in the current page, using a
tree-like structure. When you select a tag, its
attributes appear in table form. To make
one of the attributes dynamic, click the
Lighting Bolt button.

You can also use the Tag Inspector to insert new tags, delete old tags, and
modify existing tags. When you modify an existing tag, you simply select a tag
in the tree display, and its attributes appear in the table display below. Using
ColdFusion, you can bind those attributes to database queries or variables passed
from other pages by clicking on the Lightning Bolt button. For more information on using dynamic data, see Chapter 2, "Introducing ColdFusion MX."

New Tag Shortcut

In Windows, you can right-click your mouse inside the Tag Inspector panel to reveal a shortcut menu
that allows you to insert a new tag, edit an existing tag, or remove a selected tag.

In the Snippets panel, shown in Figure 3.19, you can use the existing library of code snippets or create new ones. A snippet is simply a piece of code, including HTML, CFML, JavaScript, CFScript, or anything else, that does one thing, such as creating a page footer or a JavaScript function. Dreamweaver includes a library of snippets, such as JavaScript functions and navigation layouts. To insert a snippet, you click the Insert button on the Snippets panel.

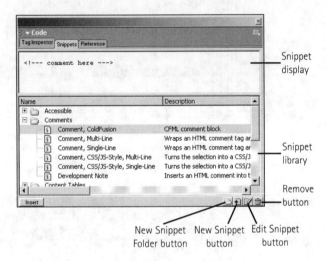

Figure 3.19 The Snippets panel lets you insert pieces of code. You can use the library of snippets included with Dreamweaver or you can create new snippets.

For ColdFusion development, good candidates for snippets would be a CFScript function, a simple CFIF statement, or a dynamic table that you use frequently. You can create a ColdFusion folder by clicking the New Snippets Folder button in the Snippets panel. To add new snippets, you can select code in the document window. When you click the New Snippet button, the Snippet dialog box appears, as shown in Figure 3.20.

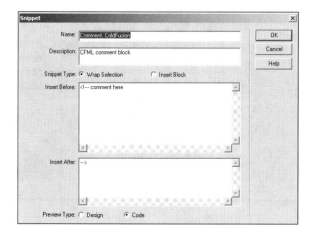

Figure 3.20 The Snippet dialog box lets you modify existing snippets and create new ones. The dialog box provides options to name the snippet, enter a description, edit the snippet code, and so on.

In the Snippet dialog box, you can name the snippet, enter a description, edit the snippet code, choose whether the code should wrap in the document window, or just insert the code, and choose whether to use the snippet in Design View or Code View.

The Reference panel, shown in Figure 3.21, provides quick access to multiple language references, including the CFML Reference, a JavaScript reference, and an HTML reference. You use the menus to select a specific tag and attribute.

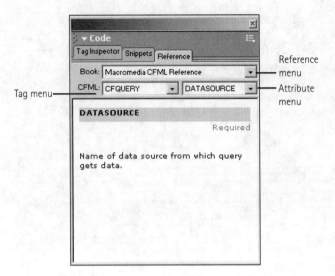

Tag menu

Reference menu

Attribute menu

Figure 3.21 The Reference panel provides easy access to language references, including CFML and HTML. You select individual tags and attributes in the panel menus.

Note

The Files panel group is described in the next section, "Defining and Working with a ColdFusion Site." The Application panel group is described in the context of other chapters, including Chapters 5, 6, and 7.

Defining and Working with a ColdFusion Site

Before you can use any of Dreamweaver's ColdFusion development features, you must define a ColdFusion site. In a nutshell, a Dreamweaver site represents a collection of files, such as HTML and ColdFusion pages, and a set of site characteristics. This section contains the following topics:

- Defining a ColdFusion site
- Troubleshooting a ColdFusion site
- Using the Files panel group

Defining the ColdFusion Site

For this book, you'll define a local site in the wwwroot directory of your ColdFusion installation. ColdFusion MX offers its own web server for development purposes, which lets you develop ColdFusion applications on systems without web servers. To access pages in the ColdFusion web root from a web browser, you specify the domain name (localhost), the port number of the ColdFusion web server, and the file name of the ColdFusion file:

```
http://localhost:8500/hello.cfm
```

Notice that the port number is specified after the host name with a colon. By default, the ColdFusion web server runs on port 8500.

If your installation of ColdFusion uses another web server, such as Microsoft's Internet Information Services (IIS), the URL will be different. Usually, IIS handles HTTP requests directed at the localhost URL, as the following example shows:

```
http://localhost/hello.cfm
```

Which Web Server?

In Windows, the web server used depends on your version of Windows. For Windows 98 and Windows ME, you use the Personal Web Server (PWS). Like ColdFusion's internal web server, PWS is intended for development purposes only and allows a limited number of HTTP connections. Thus, you should not use PWS as a production web server. For Windows NT 4, Windows 2000, and Windows XP, you use IIS, which handles more HTTP connections than PWS and provides security features.

If you're using Dreamweaver on a Macintosh, you must run ColdFusion on another computer running Windows, Linux, Solaris, or HP-UX. Or, you can create an account with a ColdFusion hosting provider and define your site using your hosting account's file directory.

Of course, you'll want to organize your site files using a subdirectory from the web root. For example, if you placed the hello.cfm file in a directory named myApp under the wwwroot directory, you'd use the following URL with ColdFusion's web server:

```
http://localhost:8500/myApp/hello.cfm
```

If you use IIS, the URL would appear like the following example:

```
http://localhost/myApp/hello.cfm
```

Now that you have a basic understanding of the URL syntax, you can build the ColdFusion site used in this book. To create the ColdFusion site, follow these steps:

1. Open the Site Definition wizard by clicking the Create Site link in the Site panel.

2. In the Site Definition wizard, shown in Figure 3.22, the Basic layout takes a multiple-page approach to configuring the necessary options. Using the Basic or Advanced tabs at the top of the dialog box, you can also you use the Advanced layout, shown in Figure 3.23, which provides controls for all·options.

   Although the Advanced layout does not walk you through the site defin-ition process like the Basic layout does, you can access a wide variety of advanced site definition options, such as cloaking, design notes, site map layout, and Site panel display options.

   As its name implies, the Cloaking page lets you hide certain file types and directories so they can't be accessed. Cloaking lets you exclude files of any type, including potential security risks, such as Flash files (*.swf) and database files like Microsoft Access (*.mdb). The Design Notes page lets you enable design notes for a site and choose whether to upload design notes with other files. Design notes let you describe site files, track revision changes, and so on. The Site Map Layout page simply lets you choose a home page for your site, which is required for Dreamweaver to generate a site map. The File View Columns page lets you select what information will be displayed in the Site panel, which is described in the following section.

   The following steps use the Basic layout.

3. In the Editing Files, Part 1 page, shown in Figure 3.24, you name your site. For this book, enter the name **bookexample**. This name lets you identify this particular site in Dreamweaver, so make sure the name is unique. Click Next.

4. In the Editing Files, Part 2 page, shown in Figure 3.25, you choose your server technology. Dreamweaver can detect the ColdFusion system. Ensure that the Yes, I want to use a server technology radio button is selected, and select ColdFusion in the Which server technology? menu. Click Next.

5. In the Editing Files, Part 3 page, shown in Figure 3.26, you decide where you're going to store your site files. Essentially, Dreamweaver needs to know whether you're going to edit the files locally (on your computer) or on a remote server.

   This book assumes you're editing and testing files locally, but you can easily modify that setting to edit files directly on a remote server on the local network or using FTP. You can also edit locally and then upload the files to a remote server for testing. For the purposes of this book, select the Edit and test locally radio button.

You also choose where the site files should be stored on your local computer. Click the folder icon, and the Choose Local Root Folder dialog box appears, as shown in Figure 3.27. Navigate your file system until you arrive at the ColdFusion installation directory, usually C:\CFusionMX. In the CFusionMX directory, select the wwwroot directory (C:\CFusionMX\wwwroot\), which serves as ColdFusion's web root directory. Using the Create Folder button, create a new folder and name it **bookexample**. Make sure you double-click the bookexample directory before you click the OK button. Back in the Site Definition wizard, click Next.

6. In the Testing Files page of the Site Definition wizard, shown in Figure 3.28, you test the URL that Dreamweaver will use for your site, particularly for the Live Data View feature. Usually, Dreamweaver automatically generates a valid URL for your site. Just in case, click the Test URL button. If ColdFusion is running, you will receive a success message. If you receive an error message, make sure that ColdFusion is running and make sure the URL is valid. Click Next.

7. In the Sharing Files page of the Site Definition wizard, shown in Figure 3.29, you specify whether you want to upload your site files to a remote server for testing. Although this book doesn't require this, you might find this option useful if you use a ColdFusion testing server over a local network, virtual private network (VPN), or hosting service. For the purposes of this book, click the No radio button and then click Next.

8. In the Summary page of the Site Definition wizard, shown in Figure 3.30, you review your settings. If everything checks out, click the Done button.

Be advised that, depending on your selections in the Site Definition wizard, the pages might differ from those shown in the following figures. Figure 3.31 shows the Dreamweaver workspace after a ColdFusion site has been defined. Once you have defined your ColdFusion site, a number of features become available, such as the following:

- CFML Basic, CFML Flow, and CFML Advanced tabs in the Insert bar
- Databases, Bindings, Server Behaviors, and Component panels in the Application panel group
- Site controls in the Site panel
- Live Data and Server Debug Views in the document window

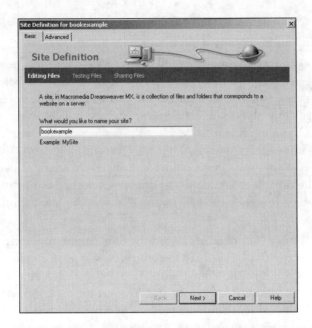

Figure 3.22 Editing Files, Part 1 of the Site Definition wizard lets you name your Dreamweaver site.

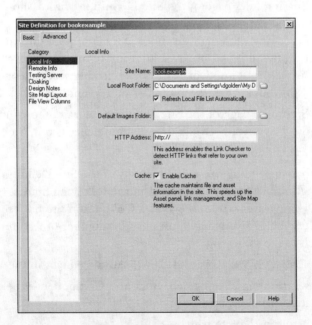

Figure 3.23 The Advanced Layout of the Site Definition wizard lets you access all configuration options.

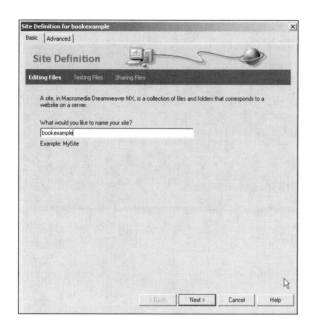

Figure 3.24   Editing Files, Part 1 of the Site Definition wizard
lets you name your site. Make sure the name is unique.

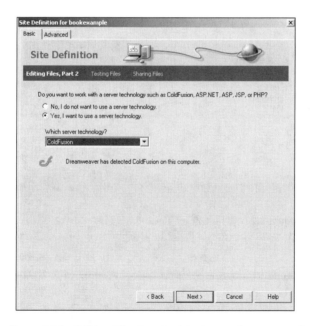

Figure 3.25   Editing Files, Part 2 of the Site Definition wizard
lets you choose the server technology for your site,
such as ColdFusion.

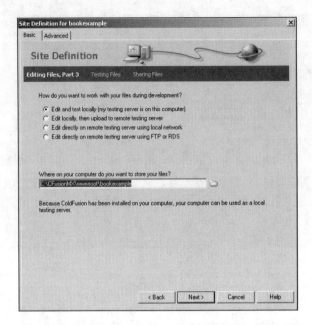

Figure 3.26   Editing Files, Part 3 of the Site Definition wizard
lets you choose whether to store your files locally.

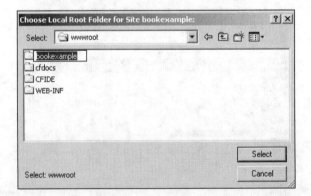

Figure 3.27   The Choose Local Root Folder dialog box lets
you select or create a folder in which to store your site files.

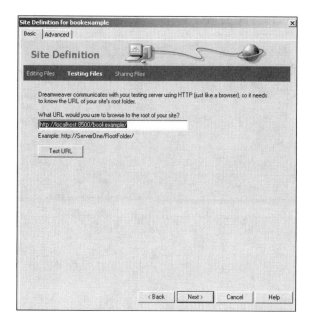

Figure 3.28   The Testing Files page of the Site Definition wizard lets you specify and test the URL for Dreamweaver to use.

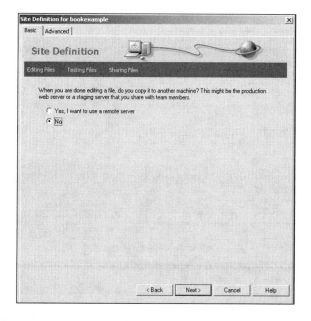

Figure 3.29   The Sharing Files page of the Site Definition wizard lets you choose whether to upload your site files to a remote server automatically.

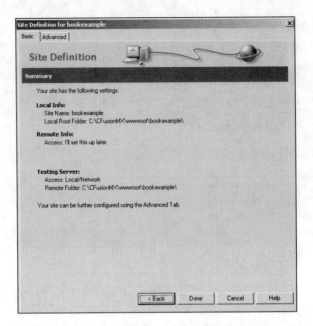

Figure 3.30   The Summary page of the Site Definition wizard
lets you review your settings.

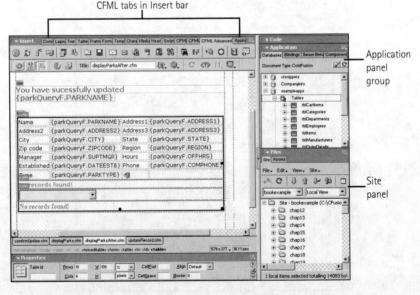

Figure 3.31   Once you define a ColdFusion site, the Dreamweaver workspace
changes, including new CFML tabs in the Insert bar and the activation
of the Files panel group and Application panel group.

Troubleshooting a ColdFusion Site

The site definition process is intended to be as easy as possible, but problems do arise. If you have problems defining a ColdFusion site, keep the following points in mind:

- Many people experience problems getting the site URL right. As was described earlier in this chapter and in other chapters, ColdFusion's internal web server runs on port 8500. Thus, the URL would be `http://localhost:8500/bookexample`. If you're running ColdFusion using IIS, the URL would likely be the same minus the port number: `http://localhost/bookexample`. If you are connecting to a remote ColdFusion installation, such as a hosting provider, you would use the URL supplied to you by the administrator.

- When you define a site, make sure that ColdFusion is running and operating properly. To test ColdFusion, try to open the ColdFusion Administrator. If it opens, ColdFusion is running.

- Create your site directory in the web root of your web server before defining the Dreamweaver site.

- If you're connecting to a remote ColdFusion installation like a shared hosting account, make sure that you get all the FTP connection information right. You might need to contact the hosting provider's customer support for help.

If all else fails, try the Dreamweaver or ColdFusion support centers on the Macromedia web site (`www.macromedia.com`).

Using the Files Panel Group

Once you have defined a ColdFusion site, you can use the Files panel group to perform site-related tasks, such as adding, removing, and moving files; checking hyperlinks site-wide; and managing site assets like image, multimedia, and other files. The Files panel group contains two panels: Site and Asset.

As shown in Figure 3.32, the Site panel serves as your primary interface for administrating your site files and changing site-wide settings. The Site panel's usefulness really shines when you want to make changes in multiple files at once. If you have ever tried to change one link by hand in 10 different pages, you realize that site-management tools are a necessity.

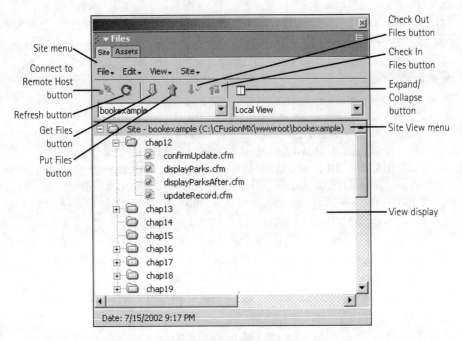

Figure 3.32 The Site panel lets you see and manage the files in your site, including CFML, CFC, HTML, graphics, and multimedia.

The Site panel offers a wide selection of tools, from simple site maps to advanced reporting on HTML validation results. As shown in Figure 3.33, when you click the Expand/Collapse button, the Site panel expands to full-screen.

Remote
View

Local
View

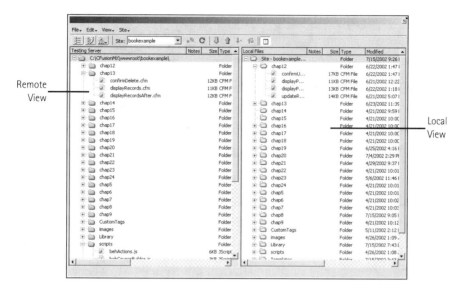

Figure 3.33   When expanded, the Site panel fills your screen with a split
screen that displays two views, such as remote and local. Using the
expanded view, you have more space to see and manage your site's files.

If you use a remote server, you'll likely use the Get File and Put File buttons.
If you use a source-control system, you'll likely use the Check In File and
Check Out File buttons. The Site Map shows a graphical representation of
your site files, including dependencies on other files.

The Assets panel (see Figure 3.34) lets you associate files, URLs, scripts,
templates, and so on within a Dreamweaver site. By associating a file, URL, or
color with a site, you can record, organize, and keep track of frequently used
items for convenient access. Think of the Assets panel as the Dreamweaver
version of your web browser's Favorite menu.

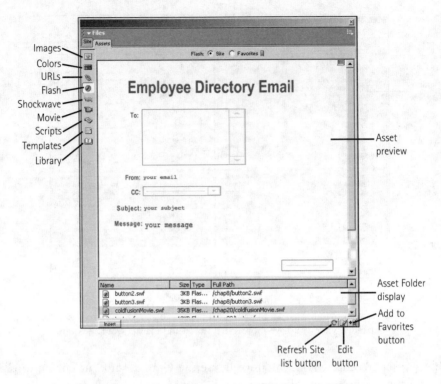

Figure 3.34   The Assets panel lets you view site image, Flash, Shockwave, and movie files, as well as URLs, scripts, and even colors. You can modify existing site assets or create new ones of your own. Shown expanded, the Assets panel can even preview Flash movies/applications without opening the Flash Player.

Creating the Book Template

In certain sections in the following chapters, you are instructed to create a new ColdFusion page from the bookexample template. In this section, you will create that template. A Dreamweaver template, much like a Microsoft Word template, lets you design your page once and then create copies of the template when you need a new page.

In addition to any formatting layouts with layers, frames, tables, or Cascading Style Sheets (CSS) that you apply to the page, Dreamweaver lets you add editable and noneditable regions into an HTML or CFML page. When the template is used to create a page, only the regions set as editable are available for modification. Areas that are locked cannot be modified.

Templates exist in the context of a Dreamweaver site. In fact, you can find the templates associated with a particular site using the Asset panel, described in the previous section. You can also use the New Document dialog box by selecting the File menu, New.

To create the bookexample template, follow these steps:

1. In Dreamweaver, select the File menu, New.

2. In the New Document dialog box that appears, shown in Figure 3.35, select Template Page and ColdFusion Template, and click the Create button. A new, untitled, blank document is created with two editable regions.

3. You can now design the page however you like. The template used in the screenshots throughout this book was created using a set of carefully sized tables, an area map, a few images, a Flash movie, and a few background colors. For the purposes of this book, you only need to create two editable regions, named Title and Body. With its Editable Region button, you can use the Template tab of the Insert bar to create the editable regions. Because it accepts the majority of the content, the editable Body region should be larger than the editable Title region.

4. After you have formatted the page to your liking and created the editable regions, you save the template by clicking the Make Template button.

5. In the Save As Template dialog box, shown in Figure 31.36, select bookexample in the Site menu and enter bookexample in the Save As text box. Click the Save button.

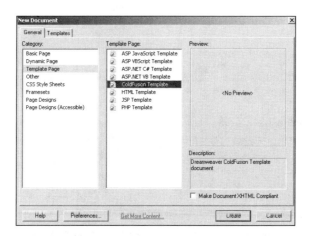

Figure 3.35 In the New Document dialog box, select the Dynamic Page category and ColdFusion. Notice that the Templates tab can be used to create new pages from templates.

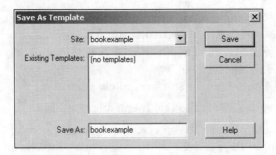

Figure 3.36 The Save As Template dialog box lets you name the template and associate it to a site.

The bookexample template is saved as bookexample.dwt in the Templates folder, which is automatically created in the site root. Once a template has been created, you can use the Templates tab in the New from Template dialog box to create a new page, as shown in Figure 3.37.

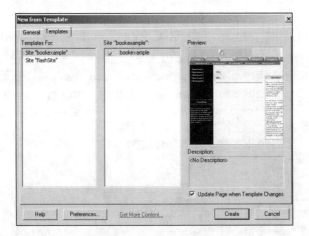

Figure 3.37 In the New from Template dialog box's Templates tab, select the bookexample template and click the Create button to generate a new page from the template.

Summary

In this chapter, you learned about the Dreamweaver MX workspace, how to set up a ColdFusion site, and how to create the Dreamweaver template used in this book. To start creating ColdFusion pages, go on to Chapter 5, "Creating Form and Action Pages." If you want to learn about database fundamentals, read the next chapter about databases and their use in ColdFusion and Dreamweaver.

4

Working with Databases

IN THIS CHAPTER, YOU LEARN THE BASICS of databases, including how they work, how ColdFusion interfaces with a database, and how to create a ColdFusion datasource. If you've been hesitant to try application servers because you're unfamiliar with databases, you should read this chapter.

Understanding Databases

In one form or another, you use databases every day. If you visit any popular web site, you're using a database through a web browser. If you use an ATM, you're using a database. If you use an automated call system to check the arrival time of a flight, you're using a database.

In short, databases are integral to all of our lives because of the enormous amount of information we access on a daily basis. Whatever form they take, databases store related information in an organized manner. This book uses a database installed with ColdFusion. To find the database, browse to the db folder of the CFusionMX directory, such as C:\CFusionMX\db, and find the cfexamples.mdb file.

If you have Microsoft Access installed, you can view the contents of the database file. As you will see as you explore the cfexamples.mdb file, databases store information in tables, which contain rows and columns. As shown in Figure 4.1, the tblEmployees table contains a row for each employee. Columns separate the rows by information category, such as FirstName, LastName, and Title. In the rows, individual pieces of data are stored in fields.

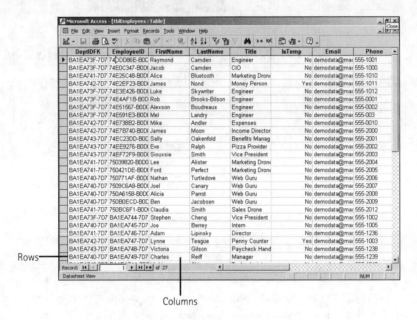

Figure 4.1   The tblEmployee table of the cfexamples database contains information related to employees. Notice that rows and columns organize the table.

Using Database Data Types

For storage efficiency, each column is assigned a data type, such as text, number, date/time, currency, and so on. Just like programming languages, databases use data types to maximize memory usage. Although you could store most information entered in a web browser as characters (text), using different data types increases database performance and promotes data validity.

The tblEmployees database table contains a variety of data types. For example, the FirstName and LastName columns are text data types. The IsTemp column is a Boolean (yes or no) data type, and the StartDate column is a date/time data type. Data types also restrict the information to the specified data type.

Understanding Relational Databases

You probably noticed that the cfexamples database contains multiple tables, including tblDepartments, tblEmployees, and tblParks. That's because the cfexamples database is considered a relational database, meaning that information in multiple tables is related, and the tables have relationships with each other.

Relationships represent links between tables. Usually, primary and foreign keys define relationships. Primary keys, such as the EmployeeID column in the tblEmployees table, identify the record, in this case an employee. The data stored in the primary key field of a record must be unique because other database tables will use this value to identify an employee. Don't worry, most database applications can automatically generate primary keys for you.

A foreign key lets you represent a primary key in another table. For example, the DeptIDFK column in the tblEmployees table contains foreign keys for the primary keys in the DeptID column of the tblDepartments table. Figure 4.2 shows the relationships among the tables of the cfexamples database.

Database Naming

A set of informal database-naming conventions have developed over time. For example, the "tbl" preface to a name indicates that the name refers to a database table. If a column contains primary keys, the column name is prefaced by "PK." If a column contains foreign keys, the column name is suffixed by "FK."

Figure 4.2   You can use Microsoft Access's Relationship feature to view a graphical representation of the relationships between tables. Notice that the links connect primary keys to foreign keys.

Selecting a Database Vendor

Usually, you don't get to choose the database vendor because ColdFusion is frequently used to put existing databases on the web. If you do get the chance to select a database vendor, you must carefully weigh the project requirements against the cost of purchase and maintenance.

If your project consists of creating a database for a company intranet, Microsoft Access is a popular choice, if for no other reason than most companies already own a license for Access through Microsoft Office. However, as a shared-file or desktop database, Access has some significant drawbacks, such as scalability and possible data corruption.

Client/server database programs, such as Microsoft SQL Server or Oracle 9i, provide robust, scalable enterprise database solutions. Client/server databases tightly control access to database information, offer excellent performance, and provide multiple safeguards against data corruption and failure. At the same time, client/server database systems are very expensive and are more difficult to set up and maintain. As an alternative, check out open-source databases, such as MySQL and PostgreSQL.

ColdFusion supports the majority of popular database programs used today, including Microsoft Access and SQL Server, Oracle, Informix, Sybase, IBM DB2, and MySQL. For a complete list of database programs that ColdFusion supports, check the Macromedia web site (www.macromedia.com).

Understanding ColdFusion Data Sources

For ColdFusion to interface with a database, you must create a ColdFusion data source. A data source is a connection to a database management system or database file. Just like a Windows data source, a ColdFusion data source represents a kind of ghost copy of the real database. Because ColdFusion runs as a Java application, it interfaces with a system database through Java Database Connectivity (JDBC), a Java technology for standardizing access to databases.

JDBC uses database drivers to communicate directly with the database. JDBC drivers are specifically designed for a particular database system, so, for example, there is an Oracle driver and a Sybase driver. As Figure 4.3 shows, JDBC provides a level of abstraction that lets you work with multiple databases.

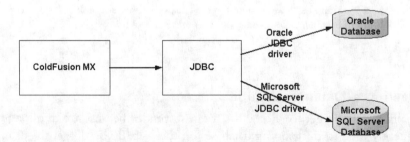

Figure 4.3   ColdFusion uses JDBC, a Java technology, to connect to different databases. JDBC drivers provide direct connections to a specific database type.

The Windows operating system uses Open Database Connectivity (ODBC) for database connections. Because Microsoft Access is a Windows-based application, it uses ODBC as well. If you are running ColdFusion on Windows, you must register the data sources in Windows first before you can use them in ColdFusion. For example, to open the Data Source Administrator in Windows 2000, select the Start menu, Settings, Control Panel, Administrative Tools, (ODBC) Data Sources.

Figure 4.4 shows the ODBC Data Source Administrator.

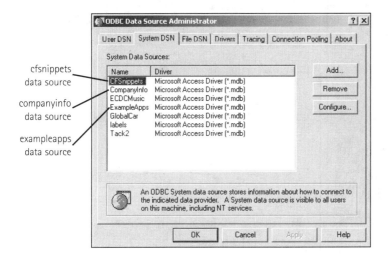

Figure 4.4   In Windows, the ODBC Data Source Administrator lets you review, modify, and create new ODBC data sources. Notice that when you installed ColdFusion, three ODBC data sources were created: CFSnippets, ExampleApps (used in this book), and CompanyInfo.

You might be wondering how ColdFusion, which uses JDBC, works with an ODBC data source like Microsoft Access. ColdFusion contains a database driver named ODBC Socket. The ODBC Socket database driver lets JDBC interface with ODBC to simulate a JDBC connection.

Creating a ColdFusion Data Source

To work with ColdFusion data sources, you use the Data Sources page in the ColdFusion Administrator. You can open the ColdFusion Administrator in Windows by selecting Start, Programs, ColdFusion MX, Administrator. Once you log into the Administrator, click the Data Sources link in the left navigation bar.

In the Data Sources page, shown in Figure 4.5, you see the registered data sources and the driver used for each. To see the details of a data source, click on the Edit icon. This book uses the exampleapps data source, so click on its Edit icon. In the ODBC Socket page that appears, as shown in Figure 4.6, you see the details of the data source, such as the data source name, the database driver, and a description.

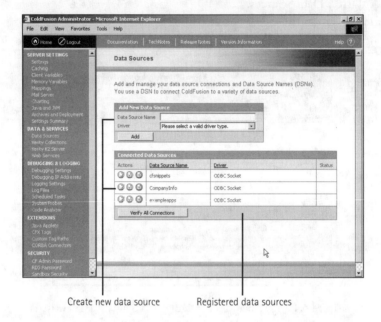

Create new data source   Registered data sources

Figure 4.5   The ColdFusion Administrator's Data Sources page contains the available data sources and the capability to create new data sources.

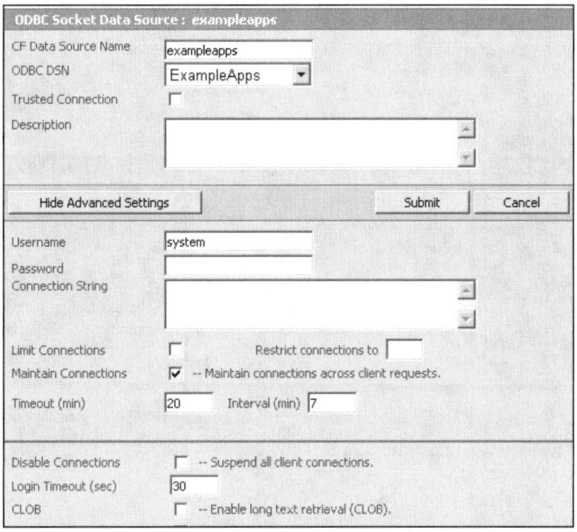

Figure 4.6 The ODBC Socket page lets you see the details of an ODBC Socket data source, such as the ExampleApps data source. Click the Show Advanced Settings button to reveal additional settings.

Although this book uses the ExampleApps data source, the following procedure creates a new data source for the cfexamples.mdb file:

1. In the Data Sources page of the ColdFusion Administrator, enter a name for the data source, such as myDataSource, in the Data Source Name text box. The name that you enter here will be the name used in Dreamweaver and your CFML code.

   In the Driver menu, select a database driver. Because you are using the cfexamples.mdb file (Microsoft Access), select the Microsoft Access driver. Notice that the ODBC socket driver was not used. The Microsoft Access driver in the Data Sources page is a JDBC driver, which provides better performance and stability than the ODBC socket driver.

   Click the Add button.

2. In the Microsoft Access page that appears, as shown in Figure 4.7, click the Browse Server button to the right of the Database File text box. In the Browse Server page, shown in Figure 4.8, browse to the cfexamples.mdb file in the CFusionMX\db directory. Click the Apply button.

3. Make sure the Use Default Username check box is selected, and enter a short description in the Description text box.

4. Click the Submit button.

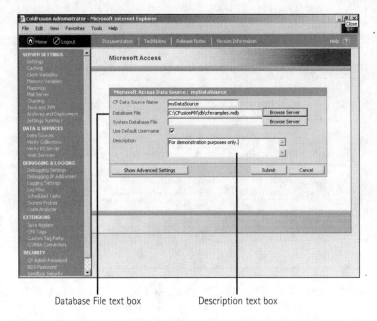

Database File text box   Description text box

Figure 4.7 The Microsoft Access page lets you select the database file as well as enter a description for the data source. If you need additional options, such as security login information, click the Advanced Settings button.

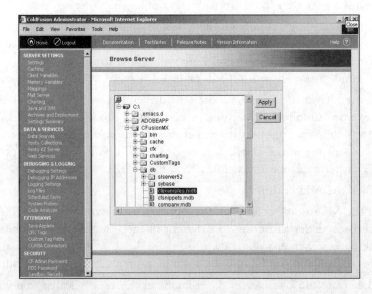

Figure 4.8 The Browse Server page lets you navigate your file system to find the database file. After you click the Apply button, the file path appears in the Database File text box.

> **Duplicate Data Sources**
>
> Avoid creating duplicate data sources for the same database. Duplicate data sources will likely cause confusion or mistakes later.

In the Connected Data Sources table on the Data Sources page, shown in Figure 4.9, you can do more than just see the available data sources. Using the Edit, Verify, and Delete icons in the Actions columns, you can manage your data sources easily. When you verify a data source to make sure it is functioning properly, OK appears in the Status column.

You can also see ColdFusion data sources in the Databases panel of Dreamweaver MX. As shown in Figure 4.9, the Databases panel displays the same list of databases as the Data Sources page in the ColdFusion Administrator. You can also expand and collapse the databases to reveal tables and columns.

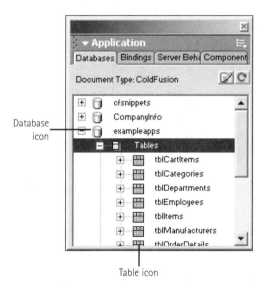

Figure 4.9   The Databases panel of the Application panel group lets you see the registered ColdFusion data sources, their tables, and their table columns.

Querying Databases with SQL

Although storing information is very useful, the true power of databases comes from their capabilities to accept queries and return specific records in a certain order. Queries consist of a communication sent from a program to a database that specifies how a database should search its records. The *de facto* query language supported by almost every database vendor is Structured Query Language (SQL). The database takes the results of the query and creates a recordset, which contains all the records that match the criteria of the SQL query, and passes the recordset back to the program that requested the query.

Understanding SQL

SQL is a query language that uses basic statement syntax. In general, SQL statements consist of the following types:

- SELECT—List of one or more table column names. Must be used with a FROM statement.
- FROM—List of one or more table names. Must be used with a SELECT statement.
- WHERE—A comparison statement to filter the query created in the SELECT and FROM statements.
- ORDER BY—List of one or more column names to sort by. You can also use ASC (ascending) or DESC (descending) to specify which way to sort the records.

You use SELECT and FROM statements to specify one or more table columns from one or more database tables. The following example selects the FirstName column from the tblEmployees table:

```
<cfquery name="Recordset1" datasource="exampleapps">
    SELECT FirstName
    FROM tblEmployees
</cfquery>
```

As you can see, SQL can be very simple. To select more than one table column, simply add a comma and the column name, as the following example shows:

```
<cfquery name="Recordset2" datasource="exampleapps">
    SELECT FirstName, LastName, Email
    FROM tblEmployees
</cfquery>
```

To select all columns in the tblEmployees table, use the asterisk (*), as the following example shows:

```
<cfquery name="Recordset3" datasource="exampleapps">
    SELECT *
    FROM tblEmployees
</cfquery>
```

To filter a query, you use the WHERE statement to filter the records using a comparison statement, such as comparing a record to a value or another record.

The following example compares the ItemCost column to a numeric value:

```
<cfquery name="Recordset3" datasource="exampleapps">
    SELECT ItemCost, ItemName
    FROM tblItems
    WHERE ItemCost > 500
</cfquery>
```

If the value in an ItemCost column cell is greater than the value, the record is kept. If not, the record is removed. If you want to compare against text, you use single quotes (') to surround the comparison value, such as the following example:

```
<cfquery name="Recordset5" datasource="exampleapps">
    SELECT LastName
    FROM tblEmployees
    WHERE LastName = 'Moon'
</cfquery>
```

If you want to compare column values in one table to column values in another, you simply add the table name to the FROM statement and preface the column names in the SELECT statement with their table name, as the following example shows:

```
<cfquery name="Recordset6" datasource="exampleapps">
    SELECT tblEmployees.FirstName, tblEmployees.LastName,
    tblEmployees.Email, tblEmployees.DeptIDFK, tblDepartments.DepartmentID,
    tblDepartments.DepartmentName
    FROM tblEmployees, tblDepartments
    WHERE tblEmployees.DeptIDFK = tblDepartments.DepartmentID
    ORDER BY tblEmployees.LastName ASC
</cfquery>
```

This SQL statement associates a department name with each employee. The tblEmployees table does not contain the department name, but does include a foreign key to the tblDepartments column. By prefacing the column names in the SELECT statement with the table name, you identify the column with a particular table, thereby avoiding errors.

The WHERE clause checks for equivalence between the DeptIDFK column in the tblEmployees table, which contains foreign keys, to the DepartmentID column in the tblDepartments table. Notice that the LastName column is sorted by the ORDER BY statement.

For more information on displaying or manipulating recordsets in ColdFusion pages, see Chapter 6, "Creating Pages with Dynamic Elements" and Chapter 8, "Displaying Records in a Dynamic Table."

> **Note**
>
> All SQL contains SELECT and FROM statements, but you can also use other programming language constructs, such as the AND, OR, and EXISTS operators, or evaluation precedence.

Using Dreamweaver to Build Query Statements

In ColdFusion, you use SQL inside a CFQUERY statement. The CFQUERY tag supplies a name for the recordset created by the SQL statement as well as the ColdFusion data source name for the query. As the following example shows, the CFQUERY tag encapsulates your SQL:

```
<cfquery name="lastNameQuery" datasource="exampleapps">
    SELECT LastName
    FROM tblEmployees
</cfquery>
```

As you can see, the CFQUERY tag creates a name for the recordset created by the SQL, lastNameQuery, and specifies the database to use, exampleapps.

In Dreamweaver MX, you use the Recordset dialog box, accessible from the Bindings or Server Behaviors panel in the Application panel group, to create SQL queries. To open the Recordset dialog box, click the plus (+) button in the Bindings or Database panel. In the submenu that appears, select Recordset (Query).

In the Recordset dialog box, shown in Figure 4.10, you build the query using a set of menus and text boxes. In the Name text box, you specify the name for the recordset, which translates to the name attribute of the CFQUERY tag. In the Data Source menu, you select the ColdFusion data source to use, which translates to the datasource attribute of the CFQUERY tag. If required, the User Name and Password text boxes let you enter security credentials to the database.

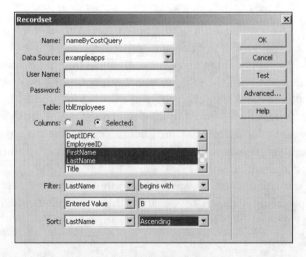

Figure 4.10 The Recordset dialog box lets you create SQL queries using menus and text boxes. You'll notice that what you select in one control dynamically changes the values in other controls.

For more information on displaying recordsets in ColdFusion pages, see Chapter 6.

In the Table menu, you select the table to query, which translates to the FROM SQL statement. In the Columns section, you can select some or all of the columns in a table, which translates to the SELECT SQL statement. The Filter menus and text boxes let you construct simple WHERE statements, and the Sort menu lets you specify a column to sort by.

To test the SQL before you create the recordset, click the Test button. In the Test SQL Statement dialog box, shown in Figure 4.11, Dreamweaver runs the query and displays the results. This feature is especially helpful when developing more complex SQL statements.

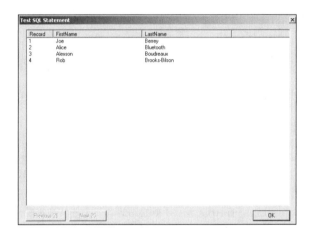

Figure 4.11   The Test SQL Statement dialog box displays the results of your SQL, letting you quickly edit and test SQL statements during development.

To create queries that use multiple tables, you must use the Advanced Recordset dialog box. To switch to the Advanced layout, click the Advanced button in the Recordset dialog box.

In the Advanced Recordset dialog box, shown in Figure 4.12, you can write your SQL by hand in the SQL text box, or you can use the Database Items section and the SELECT, WHERE, and ORDER BY buttons to build the SQL visually.

You can also specify page parameters in your SQL. Parameters are variables passed from external sources, such as other ColdFusion pages, Flash movies, application and session scope variables, and so on. For more information about passing parameters, see Chapter 6.

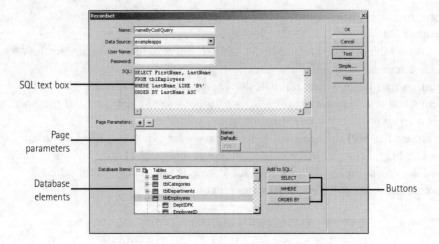

SQL text box

Page parameters

Database elements

Buttons

Figure 4.12   The Recordset dialog in Advanced mode provides controls for writing SQL by hand or building SQL visually using the Database Items tree control and the WHERE, SELECT, and ORDER BY buttons.

Summary

In this chapter, you learned the basics of databases, including terminology, SQL, and database structure. In the next chapter, you jump into ColdFusion development by building simple form and action pages.

Creating ColdFusion Forms

5

Creating Form and Action Pages

I N THIS CHAPTER, YOU WILL LEARN the basics of building ColdFusion form and action pages. Using the Forms panel, you will insert form objects, such as text areas and radio buttons. You will then use the Data Bindings panel to build the action page by creating form variables to display the data passed from the form page.

Creating Form Pages

Form pages gather user information and submit that information to a server-side resource, such as a ColdFusion page or component. Form pages are one of the most common pages on the web. The ability to collect user data, including usernames, passwords, and email addresses, using form pages lies at the heart of web development.

The ColdFusion page that receives and processes the form data is called an action page. Typical action page processing tasks include validating passed information, querying a database, and displaying the passed data for user confirmation.

You build form pages by inserting form objects into a ColdFusion page (.cfm) or HTML page (.htm). In fact, you have probably created HTML form pages before. Form objects use the HTTP methods GET and POST to send data. In HTML code, the FORM tag defines a form page. In the FORM tag, you specify the HTTP method and which file will receive the data.

The GET and POST methods differ in how they pass data. The GET method passes information using name/value pairs in a URL string. For example, the following URL passes a first and last name:

```
http://www.example.com?firstname=john&lastname=doe
```

Notice that the site address is separated from the name/value pairs by a question mark (?). The name/value pairs are separated by ampersands (&). When data is passed using a URL, the web browser copies the information entered in INPUT, SELECT, and TEXTAREA tags into the URL. According to the HTTP protocol, any data in a URL after a question mark is considered a query string consisting of name/value pairs. A URL can contain multiple name/value pairs, which are separated using ampersands.

One significant drawback of the GET method is that URLs can be seen by the end user and over the web. In contrast, when you use the POST method, the data is passed into the HTTP header information, which is invisible to the end user. Deciding whether to use the GET or POST method depends on the user information being passed. If users will be entering sensitive information, such as passwords and credit card numbers, you should use the POST method because the transmitted data is not visible to others.

Figure 5.1 shows a simplified representation of passing data from form pages.

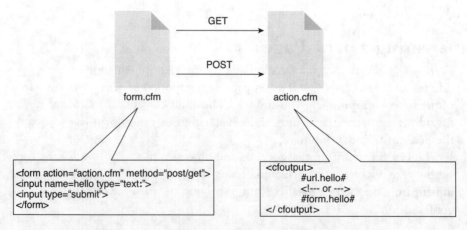

Figure 5.1 Collected information can be passed from form pages using either the GET or POST method.

Creating a Simple Form Page

To create form pages in Dreamweaver, you use the Forms panel of the Insert bar. Make sure that the Insert bar is already open by clicking the Window menu and ensuring a checkmark exists next to Insert. If a checkmark is not beside Insert, click the Insert menu item.

> **Note**
>
> You can also open the Insert bar by typing Ctrl+F2 in Windows or Command+F2 on the Mac. For more information, see Appendix C, "Dreamweaver MX Keyboard Shortcuts."

In this section, you will create a form page that signs up users for an email newsletter, a common user-retention technique. To sign up for an email newsletter, users must do the following:

- Submit email address
- Confirm email address
- Select email newsletter options

Take a moment to examine the information and consider the best form objects for the job. For the first two pieces of information, a user will type his or her email address into a text field. For the final piece of information, users will select from two newsletter options: HTML and plain text. Two radio buttons will be used.

Using the Forms Panel

The Insert bar appears at the top of the Dreamweaver document window, as shown in Figure 5.2. To choose the Forms panel, simply click on the Forms tab. The Forms panel contains common form objects, including input controls, list boxes, and so on.

Figure 5.2   The Insert bar contains the Forms panel, which provides common form objects.

Table 5.1 describes the buttons on the Forms panel used in this chapter.

Table 5.1 **Forms Panel Buttons**

Button	Name	Description	HTML Tag
	Form	Inserts form tag (required)	`<form action="file" method="get/post">`
	Text Field	Inserts text field	`<input type="text">`
	Hidden Field	Inserts hidden text field	`<input type="hidden">`
	Check Box	Inserts check box	`<input type="checkbox">`
	Radio Button	Inserts radio button	`<input type="radio">`
	Radio Group	Inserts group of radio buttons (multiple tags)	`<input type="radio">`

Building a Simple Form Page

To start, create a new page from the book example template, which you created in Chapter 3, "Introducing Dreamweaver MX." Save it as form.cfm in the chap5 directory of your web root. Notice that this is not a ColdFusion page, but an ordinary HTML page. This page demonstrates that you don't need to make the calling pages, also known as clients, dynamic to use them with dynamic applications.

Your page should appear like the one shown in Figure 5.3.

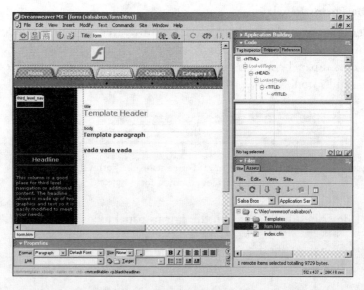

Figure 5.3 The form.cfm page appears with placeholder text. Soon, it will contain a form.

To build the simple form page, complete the following steps:

1. Using the Design view, place the cursor within the editable Body region of the document window.

2. On the Forms panel, click the Form button. A red, broken-line box appears. In the FORM tag's Property Inspector, select the action text field and enter action.cfm.

   The action attribute of the FORM tag specifies the file to receive the passed information. We will create action.cfm in the next section.

   Make sure the Method list box is set to POST.

3. In the Insert bar, click the Common tab.

4. In the Common toolbar, click Table.

5. In the Insert Table dialog, specify three rows with two columns and no border.

6. Using the Forms panel, insert a text box in the upper-left cell of the table. In its Property Inspector, change its name from textbox1 to email1.

7. In the cell below email1, insert another text box, and label it email2.

8. In the cell below email2, insert a radio group. In the Radio Group dialog, change the name to **format**. Create two radio buttons. Label one button **HTML format** and set its value to html. Label the other button **Text format** and set its value to text. To see the configured Radio Group dialog, see Figure 5.4.

9. In the cell to the right of the radio buttons, insert a Submit button and a Reset button. You use the same button on the Forms panel for both.

10. Fill in the text beside the text boxes and in the page heading, as shown in Figure 5.5. When you are done, save your work.

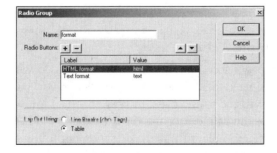

Figure 5.4 The Radio Group dialog lets you easily create and configure multiple radio buttons, a very useful feature for form page development.

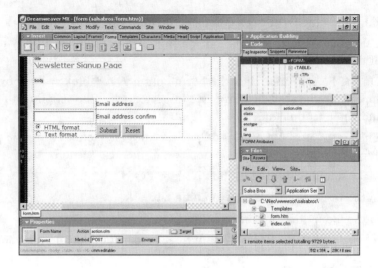

Figure 5.5   The completed form page offers a simple, effective user interface for gathering user information.

Creating Action Pages

Action pages receive external data, process the data and code on the page, and optionally return a value to the calling page. A ColdFusion page that serves as an action page to a form page does not differ from any other ColdFusion page; the ColdFusion server processes the page with its variables and CFML logic.

As you learned in the previous section, form pages can send data using only the HTTP methods GET and POST. Therefore, any information sent to a ColdFusion action page will be available in either the form variable scope or the URL variable scope. The form variable scope receives any data sent from a form using the POST method. The URL variable scope, as the name implies, accepts variables sent using URL strings (through the GET method).

Creating a Simple Action Page

You build action pages according to what you want to do with passed variables. In the action page for the Salsa Bros. newsletter, you will display only the variables that were passed to the page. In later chapters, you will build CFML logic that evaluates the passed data, queries a database, and handles errors.

Even though the example is simple, take a moment to think about what variables are being passed and what you want to display. Three variables are passed:

- The first email text box (email1)
- The confirmation email text box (email2)
- The email format selection (format)

To display those three variables, you use the Data Bindings panel to create three form variables.

Building a Simple Action Page

In the Files bar's Site panel, select the form.cfm page and click your right mouse button. In the contextual menu, select Duplicate. A copy of form.cfm appears. Rename the copy to **action.cfm**. Open action.cfm in Design view. To complete the page, do the following:

1. In the Data Bindings panel, click the Plus (+) button. In the submenu that appears, select Form Variable. In the Form dialog box that appears, enter **email1** and click the OK button. Repeat this step to create the email2 and format form variables.

2. Place your cursor in the editable Body region of the document window above the table containing the form objects. Using the Table button in the Common toolbar, create a table with two columns and three rows with no border.

3. In the left column of table cells enter the text as shown in Figure 5.6.

4. In the right column, drag and drop the `email1`, `email2`, and `format` variables from the Data Bindings panel into the appropriate cell.

5. Save your work.

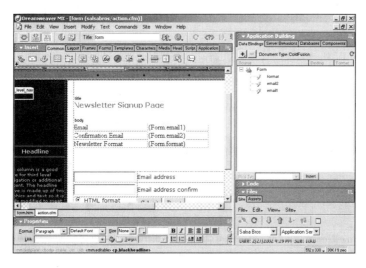

Figure 5.6 In Design view, the form variables inserted from the Data Bindings panel appear as form.email1, form.email2, and form.format.

You also can bind the form variables to the initial values of the email text boxes. When the action page loads in the user's browser, his or her email address will appear again in the text box. Although simple, such small touches give web sites a professional appearance.

To further polish the interface, you can filter the form variable output. For example, the `format` variable will contain either "html" or "email." To transform the words' letters to uppercase when displayed, apply an AlphaCase formatting function, as follows:

1. In Design view, select the first email text box with your cursor.

2. In the text box's Property Inspector, click the Dynamic Data button beside the Init Val text box.

3. In the Dynamic Data dialog, select email1. As shown in Figure 5.7, notice the value of the Code text box:

   ```
   <cfoutput>#Form.email1#</cfoutput>
   ```

   Dreamweaver actually inserts this code into the INPUT tag's `value` attribute. To see for yourself, look at the code in the Code/Design view.

4. Repeat the procedure on the second email text box, substituting the `email2` variable.

5. With your cursor, select the `form.format` variable. In the Data Bindings panel, click the Format column and select AlphaCase and then Upper. As shown in Figure 5.8, the `form.format` variable changes to show "text" in the document window.

6. Save your work.

Note

Changing the display format of a variable does not change its value, only how its value is displayed on the screen.

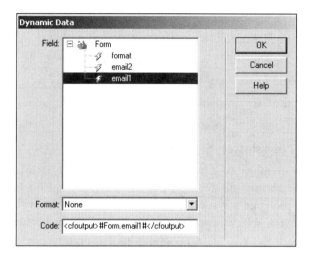

Figure 5.7   In the Dynamic Data dialog box, you select a form variable to bind to the text box.

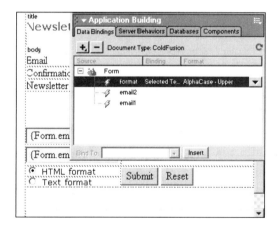

Figure 5.8   In the Data Bindings panel, you select the display format of variables, including form variables.

Testing the Form and Action Pages

Dreamweaver makes testing dynamic pages, especially form pages, easy. Using the Live Data view, you can see an action page at work. For the Salsa Bros. newsletter, you'll actually do it the old-fashioned way: in a web browser.

To test form and action pages, you want to consider what things could go wrong. For example, the following areas are typical problem areas:

- Whether the form data is passed from form.cfm properly
- Whether the form variables are received in action.cfm
- Whether the form variables are handled properly in action.cfm

Testing the Newsletter Signup Page

Put yourself in the place of a user. When a user first arrives at the Newsletter Signup Page, he or she will decide whether or not to sign up. If not interested, the user leaves the page for another. If interested, he or she will type in an email address twice, select a format, and click the Submit button.

1. Open a web browser and enter the following URL:

   ```
   http://localhost/bookexample/chap5/form.cfm
   ```

   The page should look similar to the one displayed in Figure 5.9.

Note

Depending on how you set up ColdFusion, your URL might use a different domain or a port number. For more information, see Chapter 2, "Introducing ColdFusion MX."

2. In the page, enter an email address in both text fields, make a format selection, and click the Submit button.
3. Success! As shown in Figure 5.10, everything seems to be working.

When you receive error messages from ColdFusion, you must fix the problem. As you can see in Figure 5.11, ColdFusion returns the location where the error occurred. This lets you locate the problematic code quickly and make the necessary changes.

Figure 5.9   In a web browser, form.cfm looks like a professional web page. Notice that it does not contain any dynamic elements.

Figure 5.10   The action.cfm page works as you built it. Notice that the same email addresses show up in the email text boxes that you entered in form.cfm.

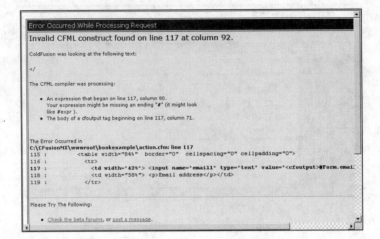

Figure 5.11 The ColdFusion error page lets you know when something goes wrong. In this example, the `form.email` variable is not present.

Summary

In this chapter, you learned the rudimentary concepts of building ColdFusion form and action pages. Using the Forms and Data Bindings panels, you created simple form and action pages. In the next chapter, you will start tapping into the power of ColdFusion by building form and action pages with dynamic elements.

6

Creating Pages with Dynamic Elements

IN THIS CHAPTER, YOU WILL LEARN HOW to create dynamic elements using recordsets, including binding a recordset to a list box menu, prefilling form fields from a recordset, and building form-driven Structured Query Language (SQL) queries.

When a web browser requests a ColdFusion page, ColdFusion processes the page according to the CFML code contained within it. When you bind a recordset to a page element, Dreamweaver generates a CFQUERY statement on the page, which queries the database when ColdFusion processes the page.

In Chapter 4, "Working with Databases," you learned that the SQL code inside CFQUERY statements provides the necessary instructions, or parameters, for ColdFusion to query a specific database table for a specific result.

When the query results return, ColdFusion dynamically places the results within the HTML code on the page. Therefore, when the finished page is loaded in a web browser, the dynamic elements within the page contain the database results. Figure 6.1 shows a simplified representation of ColdFusion processing pages with dynamic elements. This chapter consists of the following sections:

- Creating pages with dynamic elements
- Prefilling form pages dynamically
- Building form-driven queries

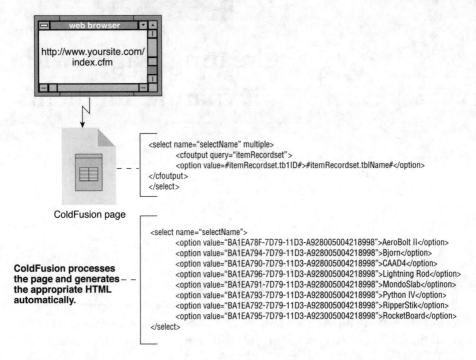

Figure 6.1 When a page that contains a database query is requested, ColdFusion queries the database and dynamically inserts the results into the HTML. The whole process typically takes two or three seconds.

Using Dynamic Elements

Almost every HTML control, including colors, table size and appearance, menus, and the like, can be dynamic. Making HTML controls dynamic can be as simple as binding a text box to the value of a form variable or as complex as binding a Flash movie to a filtered web service.

In this section, you will create a dynamic list box menu that displays the contents of the TblItems table in the exampleapps database. Using Dreamweaver MX's Data Bindings panel, you will create a recordset and bind that recordset to a list box menu. Creating a dynamic list box menu consists of the following steps:

1. Familiarize yourself with the Data Bindings panel.

2. Create the recordset.

3. Bind the recordset to an HTML control.

4. Test the ColdFusion page.

5. Look at the code.

exampleapps Database

The examples in this chapter use one of the databases that is installed with the ColdFusion examples. Before proceeding in this chapter, make sure the exampleapps database is installed and working correctly by opening the ColdFusion Administrator. Select Data Sources and click on the Verify button next to the exampleapps entry. A verification message appears if everything checks out.

Using the Data Bindings Panel

As its name suggests, the Data Bindings panel (see Figure 6.2) lets you bind data sources, including database recordsets and a variety of variable scopes, to HTML controls on a page. When you bind a data source or variable to a page element, Dreamweaver inserts CFML code into the appropriate tag attribute. Table 6.1 describes the data sources available to ColdFusion.

Table 6.1   **Data Bindings Panel Data Sources**

Data Source	Description	CFML Example
Recordset (Query)	Recordsets represent database queries that you define in Dreamweaver.	`<cfquery name="queryName" datasource="exampleapps">`
Stored procedures	Stored procedures represent predefined queries in the database.	Not applicable
CFPARAM	The CFML tag CFPARAM ensures that a parameter of the correct data type is passed.	`<cfparam name="hello" value="hi" type="string">`

continues

Table 6.1 **Continued**

Data Source	Description	CFML Example
Form and URL variables	The form and URL variable scopes access variables passed using HTTP FORM and GET methods.	`<cfoutput> #form.var# #url.var# </cfoutput>`
Session, local, server, and application variables	The session variable scope accesses variables passed as part of ColdFusion session management. The server variable scope is available to all applications running on the server. The local variable scope is available only during the execution of the page. The application variable scope is available to all pages in a ColdFusion application, which is defined in the application.cfm page.	`<cfoutput> #session.var# #server.var# #local.var# #application.var# </cfoutput>`
Cookie, client, and CGI variables	The cookie variable scope references variables stored in small text files on users' computers, also referred to as cookies. The client variable scope references variables stored in the memory of users' web browsers.	`<cfoutput> #cookie.var# #client.var# #cgi.var# </cfoutput>`
Data source name variables	Data source name variables let you create variables of data source names to save you the trouble of retyping the names over and over.	`<cfoutput> #exampleapps# </cfoutput>` With data source: `<cfoutput> variablesexampleapps </cfoutput>`

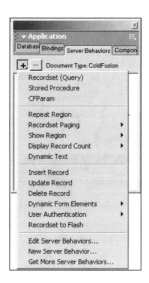

Figure 6.2   The Data Bindings panel serves as your interface to building dynamic page elements, providing access to database queries and various variable scopes.

To bind a data source, you first create a recordset or variable.

Creating a Recordset

A recordset simply consists of a database query that you define. After you have created a recordset, you can apply it to multiple page elements. To create a recordset, on the Data Bindings panel of the Application Building window click the plus (+) button. In the submenu that appears, select Recordset (Query). The Recordset dialog displays, as shown in Figure 6.3.

For this example, you will create a recordset that contains the ItemName column of the tblItems table. Follow these steps:

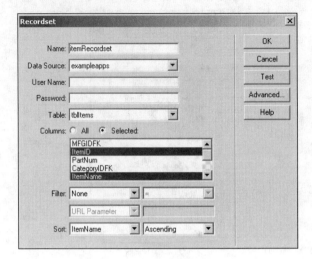

Figure 6.3 You use the Recordset dialog to build recordsets, which are database queries that you define.

1. In the Recordset dialog box, name the recordset **itemRecordset**.

2. Select exampleapps as the Data Source.

3. Leaving the User Name and Password fields blank, select the tblItems table.

4. Select the ItemID and ItemName columns. Click the Selected radio button beside the Columns field so that you can select fields in the table. To select multiple columns, hold down the Ctrl key as you click column names.

5. Sort the query results by ItemName in ascending order.

6. Click the OK button.

Previewing the Recordset

To see the results of a recordset before you create it, click the Test button in the Recordset dialog box. As shown in Figure 6.4, the Test SQL Statement dialog box displays the query results.

After you create a recordset, the columns that can be bound to page elements appear as entries below the recordset name in the Data Bindings panel (see Figure 6.5).

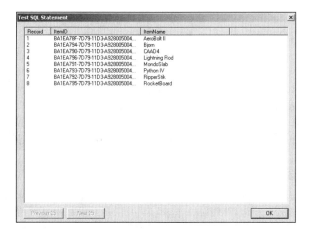

Figure 6.4   You test recordsets in the Test SQL Statement dialog
box. The results of the query display in the output screen.

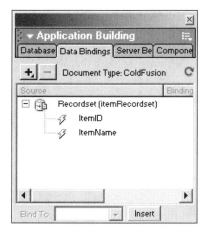

Figure 6.5   After you have created a recordset
it appears, with its database columns,
in the Data Bindings panel.

Binding the Recordset to an HTML Control

When you bind a data source to an HTML control, Dreamweaver inserts
CFML into the HTML control. As shown in Table 6.1, the CFML inserted
into the page depends on the data source used. If you bind a form variable to
a text box, Dreamweaver creates the following code:

```
<input type="text" value=<cfoutput>#form.var#</cfoutput>>
```

Notice that the INPUT tag's value attribute is defined by a CFOUTPUT statement. When processed by ColdFusion, the CFOUTPUT statement displays the value of a form variable in the text box.

When you bind a recordset to a list box menu, the CFML becomes a little more complicated because a recordset contains a potential number of records. That means you cannot determine ahead of time how many records will be in a recordset. For example, a recordset can contain all columns in a table and consist of hundreds of entries, or, using filtering, it can consist of a single record.

A list box menu is created using the SELECT and OPTION HTML tags. Each entry in a list box menu requires an OPTION tag. When the list box menu is to display the contents of a recordset, each record requires an OPTION tag. Because recordsets can contain different numbers of records, an OPTION tag must be dynamically generated for every record. The following example shows a typical static SELECT statement:

```
<select name="selectName" multiple>
    <option value="helloMessage">Hello</option>
    <option value="byeMessage">Bye</option>
</select>
```

To make the list box menu dynamic, you wrap the OPTION tag with CFOUTPUT tags. Using the CFOUTPUT tag's QUERY attribute, you specify the recordset to display. In the value attribute between the opening and closing OPTION tags, you use variable notation to specify the query columns to display. The following example shows a dynamic SELECT statement:

```
<select name="selectName" multiple>
    <cfoutput query="itemRecordset">
    <option value=#itemRecordset.tblID#>#itemRecordset.tblName#</option>
    </cfoutput>
</select>
```

Of course, Dreamweaver makes this process much easier. The following steps demonstrate how to bind a recordset to a list box menu:

1. Using the Site panel, create a new ColdFusion page from the bookexample template and name it dynamicForm.cfm.

2. Place your cursor in the editable Body region in Design view.

3. In the Forms panel of the Insert bar, click the Form button. A red broken-line box appears, representing the FORM tag. Make sure your cursor is inside the red box.

4. In the Common panel of the Insert bar, click the Table button. In the Table dialog box, create a table with one row and three columns with no border. Click the OK button. The table appears.

5. In the left table cell, type a description for the list box menu, such as "Select the product." In the Property Inspector, apply the Paragraph format to the text.

6. In the middle table cell, using the Forms panel of the Insert bar, click the List/Menu button. A list box menu appears.

7. In the list box menu's Property Inspector, click the Dynamic button. The Dynamic List/Menu dialog box appears, as shown in Figure 6.6.

8. In the Dynamic List/Menu dialog, select itemRecordset in the Options From Recordset list box menu. In the Values list box menu, select ItemID. In the Labels list box menu, select ItemName.

9. Click the OK button. The list box menu (see Figure 6.7) on the page changes color to light blue.

10. In the right table cell, using the Forms panel of the Insert bar, create a Submit button.

11. In the button's Property Inspector, change its label to "Go!".

12. Save your work.

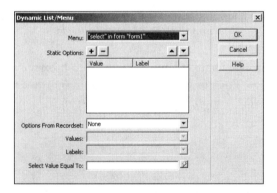

Figure 6.6   Using the Dynamic List/Menu dialog box, you can bind menu attributes to recordset values.

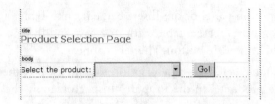

Figure 6.7   In Design view, the list box menu, which is
bound to a recordset, appears light blue.

Testing the ColdFusion Page

When you are ready to test dynamicForm.cfm, you want to ensure that the
list box menu is populated by ColdFusion when processed. To test this, use the
Preview in Browser button located on the Document toolbar, as shown in
Figure 6.8. You can also use the keyboard shortcut F12 to preview the
ColdFusion page in a browser.

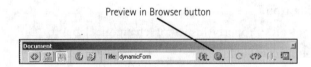

Figure 6.8   The Preview in Browser button launches a web
browser displaying dynamicForm.cfm.

The Preview in Browser button launches your web browser and directs it to
the appropriate page. Therefore, as shown in Figure 6.9, you see the same page
as site visitors would.

Figure 6.9   The list box menu is populated with the ItemName column
and displays as it would in a visitor's web browser.

Viewing the Real Thing

By default, when you click the Preview in Browser button, Dreamweaver makes a copy of the ColdFusion
page and displays it in a web browser. If you want to see the actual page that you're working on, select
the Edit menu, Preferences. In the Preferences dialog box, select the Preview in Browser category and
uncheck the Previewing Using Temporary File checkbox. For more information, see Chapter 22,
"Customizing Dreamweaver for ColdFusion Development."

If you completed all of the steps in the previous section without receiving an
error, the ColdFusion application should work. However, if you receive an
error or if the page doesn't display correctly, check the following areas:

- Make sure that you saved the file.
- Make sure that ColdFusion is running by opening the ColdFusion
  Administrator. If it displays, ColdFusion is working.
- Check the Server Behaviors panel for exclamation points next to the list
  of inserted behaviors. If you see an exclamation point, double-click that
  behavior and fix the problem.
- Verify the exampleapps data source in the ColdFusion Administrator's
  Data Sources page. You should receive a verification message.

Looking at the Code

Dreamweaver provides a number of tools that you can use to access the code underlying the ColdFusion pages that you create in Design view. For example, the Code and Design view lets you work in Design view while seeing the code at the same time. Table 6.2 describes Dreamweaver's code viewing and editing tools.

Table 6.2   **Dreamweaver Code Access Tools**

Tool	Description	Location
Code and Design View	Splits the Document window to show Code and Design view	Document toolbar button
Code View	Changes the document view to only code	Document toolbar button
Quick Tag Editor	Provides access to single tag code	Windows, Properties
Tag Inspector	Opens a separate window that provides basic text editing	Windows, Others, Code Inspector
External Text Editor	Launches a separate application to edit the code	Edit, Edit in External Editor

Prefilling Form Pages Dynamically

In Chapter 4, you built an action page that prefilled text boxes by binding form variables. In this chapter, you will go one step further by creating an action page that queries a database using form-driven queries and prefills text boxes dynamically. Form-driven queries simply consist of a CFQUERY statement that contains one or more form variables in SQL.

You will use dynamicForm.cfm, created in the previous section, as the form page. When a user selects a product in the dynamic list box menu, the page sends a form request to the page specified in its FORM tag. In the action page, you create a number of text boxes to display the contents of a recordset. Using the form variable passed to it, the query filters the recordset.

Essentially, you will be creating an "edit" page, such as those used in any kind of web content management system. In the following procedure, you will insert a Save button into the page. In this chapter, this is solely for cosmetic purposes. For more information, refer to "Inserting Records" in Chapter 11, "Inserting a Record into the Database."

Building an action page that prefills text boxes consists of the following steps:

1. Set the FORM tag's action attribute in dynamicForm.cfm.

2. Create the action page interface, including the text boxes.

3. Create the recordset.

4. Bind the recordset to the text boxes.

5. Test the page.

Preparing the Form Page

To prepare dynamicForm.cfm, you must set the value of the FORM tag's action attribute to the location of the action page. In addition, you will use the GET HTTP method. As previously described, the GET method passes information using the URL. Follow these steps:

1. Open dynamicForm.cfm.

2. Open the Tag Inspector by selecting Window, Tag Inspector. The Tag Inspector displays, as shown in Figure 6.10.

3. In the Document window, use your mouse to click near the broken red line, which represents the HTML FORM tag.

4. If the Tag Inspector does not change to the FORM tag immediately, click the <form> entry on the Document window's status bar.

5. In the Tag Inspector, the FORM tag's attributes display in a table below the tag tree view. Click the table cell next to the action attribute. Type "dynamicAction.cfm". In the method attribute, select GET. Set the name attribute to ItemID.

6. Also using the Tag Inspector, change the value of the SELECT statement to ItemID.

7. Save your work.

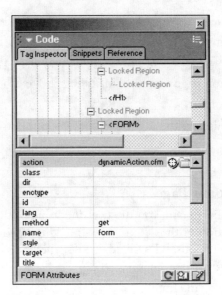

Figure 6.10   The Tag Inspector provides
convenient access to both HTML and
CFML tag attributes, which saves you
from going directly to the code.

Creating the Action Page Interface

The action page interface essentially consists of multiple text boxes. Other
than binding the text boxes to the recordset, this page does not contain any
dynamic elements. To a large extent, the lack of dynamic display elements can
be attributed to the fact that the query will only return a single record. To
create the action page interface, follow these steps:

1. Create a new ColdFusion page from the bookexample template, and
   name it dynamicForm.cfm.
2. Place your cursor inside the editable Body region of the page.
3. Using the Forms panel in the Insert bar, click the Form button. A
   red broken-line box appears. Ensure that your cursor is resting inside
   the box.
4. Using the Common panel in the Insert bar, click the Table button.
   Create a table with two columns and nine rows with no border.
5. Insert text boxes and a text area, as shown in Figure 6.11.

6. In the bottom row, merge the table cells and insert a Reset button and a Submit button labeled "Save". As described before, this page will not actually save any information to the database.

7. Save your work.

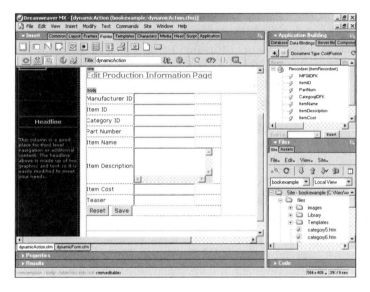

Figure 6.11 The Edit Product Information Page consists of multiple text boxes. This page is typically part of a web content management system, such as a bulletin board application.

Creating the Recordset

To create the recordset for dynamicForm.cfm, you use an URL variable to filter the database results. The URL variable is passed from dynamicForm.cfm. Follow these steps to create the recordset:

1. Open dynamicForm.cfm.

2. In the Data Bindings panel, click the plus (+) button. In the submenu that displays, select Recordset (Query).

3. In the Recordset dialog box, name the recordset **editRecordset**. In the Data Source list box menu, select exampleapps. In the Table list box menu, select tblItems. Ensure that the All Columns radio button is selected.

   Set the Filter for ItemID to equal the URL variable `itemSelection`, as shown in Figure 6.12.

4. Click the OK button.

You now have a recordset that is filtered by the URL variable `itemSelection`. You specified that the ItemID column must equal the URL variable and that the ItemID column contains an identification number.

Remember that you bound the same column to the `value` attribute of the list box menu's `SELECT` statement. That means it will always send an identification number. So, the editRecordset recordset always returns one number.

When you specify a filter, Dreamweaver automatically generates a `CFPARAM` tag. The `CFPARAM` tag lets you test for the presence of a variable, and if the variable is not present, it can supply a default value. For example, the following `CFPARAM` tag supplies a default value for a URL variable:

```
<cfparam name="URL.var" default="1">
```

If the variable is not passed, the number one (1) is supplied. `CFPARAM` tags are always a good idea for action pages that require a passed variable to process properly.

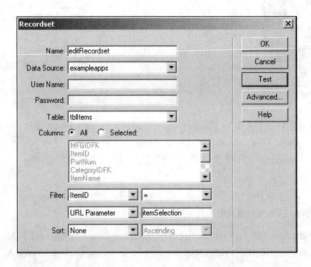

Figure 6.12   In the Recordset dialog box, you can filter query results using a variety of variable scopes, including URL, form, session, and application scopes.

Binding a Recordset to Multiple Text Boxes

In dynamicAction.cfm, you start to reap the benefits of visual ColdFusion development. By simply clicking the mouse a few times, you can bind multiple recordset columns to numerous text boxes. Do the following:

1. Open dynamicAction.cfm.

2. As shown in Figure 6.13, bind a recordset column to the applicable text box by selecting the text box, selecting the recordset column in the Data Bindings panel, and clicking the Bind button. Ensure that input.text is selected in the Bind list box menu.

3. Save your work.

When you bind a recordset column to a text box or text area, the text box turns light blue and the variable name appears.

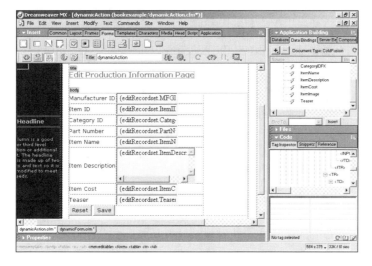

Figure 6.13   When you bind a recordset column to a text box, its color changes to light blue and the variable name appears.

Testing the Page

To test dynamicAction.cfm, you can use Dreamweaver's Live Data view. The Live Data view lets you see, from within Dreamweaver, what the processed page will look like. The Live Data view is especially useful for testing action pages that use URL variables.

The Live Data View button is located on the Document toolbar. After you click the button, give Dreamweaver a minute or two to generate the results. When Dreamweaver has finished, the text boxes in the Document window change color to yellow.

Because dynamicForm.cfm passes the itemSelection variable in a URL, you can specify URL variables in the Live Data view to further test the page. To create a URL variable, follow these steps:

1. Click the Live Data Settings button. The Live Data toolbar appears. Click the Settings button. The Live Data Settings dialog box appears, as shown in Figure 6.14.

2. Click the plus (+) button. Your cursor appears in the Name column of the URL Request box. Type **itemSelection**. In the Value column, enter a valid item identification number, which can be found in the exampleapps database.

3. Click OK. If a valid item identification number was entered, the Live Data view displays the results of the page processing, as shown in Figure 6.15.

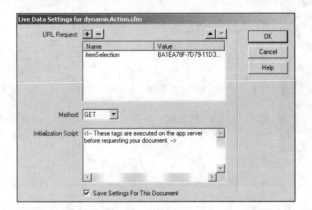

Figure 6.14   The Live Data Settings dialog box lets you create decoy URL variables to test the ColdFusion page.

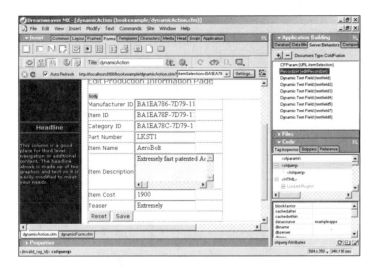

Figure 6.15 The Live Data view populates the text boxes with the query without ever leaving the Dreamweaver environment.

You can use the Live Data view to change query results to test the user interface design. For example, if a text string is too long for a text box, you can adjust the width of the text box to accommodate the results.

Also, notice the textbox displaying the recordset column ItemCost. Currently, it is not specific to any currency. To format the ItemCost into a dollar amount, select the text box with your cursor. In the Data Bindings panel, select the ItemCost column and scroll to the right. In the Format submenu, select Currency, US Dollar.

The Live Data view updates the format automatically.

Summary

In this chapter, you learned how to use recordsets to make dynamic form objects in form and action pages and you used Dreamweaver's dynamic form object features to provide interactive user interface elements, such as list box menus and text boxes. In the next chapter, you will learn how to validate form data with CFML and Dreamweaver.

7

Validating Data and Handling Errors

WHEN YOU ALLOW USERS TO USE FORMS to submit information that will be saved in a database, you must make every effort to ensure that the data being saved conforms to your database table specifications. If the data in your database becomes corrupt or inaccurate, users will quickly find another web site to use.

For example, if you create a form that lets users save personal information, a number of form fields are set up to accept the information, such as name, address, social security number, credit card numbers, telephone numbers, and email addresses.

You use ColdFusion logic to validate dynamically the data passed from form pages. Data validation logic can take many forms, including conditional logic like CFIF and CFELSE tags, built-in ColdFusion functions like isNumber and isDefined, and custom functions known as user-defined functions (UDFs). As their name suggests, UDFs are custom functions that you, or other developers, write to perform granular processing tasks, such as data validation.

When you validate data entered by the user and find an error, you should present the user with a descriptive message explaining the error. This is commonly referred to as *error handling*. Error handling can be as simple as Dreamweaver's Show Region server behaviors or as complex as specifying custom error templates for individual error types.

In this chapter, you will build two ColdFusion pages: a form page and an action page. In addition, you will download a ColdFusion page from www.cflib.org, which will let you import a library of UDFs.

For more information about using databases, see Chapter 4, "Working with Databases."

Validating Form Data

When you pass data, such as text fields, menu values, and hidden form fields, from a form page to an action page, you can evaluate and manipulate the data using ColdFusion tags and functions in the action page. For example, the following CFIF statement evaluates whether a form variable is equal to one. If it is, a message is displayed confirming that fact. If it is not, another message is displayed:

```
<cfif form.var EQ 1>
    You passed one.
    <cfelse>
    You did not pass one.
</cfif>
```

In addition, you can use a ColdFusion function in a CFIF statement to evaluate the data for certain conditions. The following example evaluates a URL variable to check whether it is a number:

```
<cfif isNumeric(form.var)>
    You passed a number.
    <cfelse>
    You did not pass a number.
</cfif>
```

In the example, the IsNumeric function checks the value in form.var to see whether it is numeric. The function returns a Boolean to indicate true or false.

Additional CFML constructs exist for dynamic evaluation of data, including CFSWITCH and CFCASE. For more information, see Chapter 14, "Conditional Logic Problems and Solutions."

Using UDFs for Data Validation

Although ColdFusion provides a wide array of built-in functions, you might discover situations for which you need custom functions, or UDFs. You can create UDFs yourself or you can download UDF libraries to use in your ColdFusion applications.

One UDF library web site is the Common Function Library (CFLIB) Project (www.cflib.org). CFLIB contains a variety of open-source, freely available UDF libraries for ColdFusion. The UDF libraries take the form of

ColdFusion pages. To use the UDFs contained in the libraries, you use the CFINCLUDE tag to import the UDFs into the current page, as the following example shows:

```
<cfinclude template="StrLib.cfm">
<cfif IsCreditCard(form.CCvar, VISA)>
    Your credit card number is valid.
    <cfelse>
    Your credit card number is not valid.
</cfif>
```

In the example, the CFINCLUDE tag imports the UDFs contained in the StrLib.cfm page. The IsCreditCard function, a UDF, evaluates the CCvar form variable for proper format for a Visa credit card. You could create the UDF yourself, but why reinvent the wheel?

User Beware

Keep in mind that the CFLIB UDFs are open source. Although every effort is made to ensure that UDFs on CFLIB work as advertised, no guarantees are made. Make sure that you read any comments listed for a UDF on the web site, and test it for yourself.

When you use the CFINCLUDE tag, you are importing the code in the ColdFusion page referenced by the tag into the ColdFusion page that contains the tag. For example, imagine two ColdFusion pages. The first ColdFusion page, named includeExample.cfm, serves as the included page and contains the following code:

```
<cfset var1 = "Hello from CFINCLUDE!">
```

As you can see in the code, the includeExample.cfm page simply creates a variable. The second ColdFusion page, which includes includeExample.cfm, contains the following code:

```
<cfinclude template = "includeExample.cfm">
<cfloop from=1 to=5>
    <cfoutput>#var1#</cfoutput><br>
</cfloop>
```

In the code, the CFINCLUDE tag references includeExample.cfm, which contains the var1 variable. The CFLOOP tag loops over the CFOUTPUT statement, which displays the var1 variable. Notice that var1 is imported from includeExample.cfm.

In addition to importing variables from one ColdFusion page into another, you can also create UDFs using CFScript or the CFFUNCTION tag in a ColdFusion page. You can then import those functions into other ColdFusion pages.

For example, the isAlphaNumeric UDF from the StrLib UDF library checks a value to make sure it consists of letters or numbers, as the following example shows:

```
/**
 * Checks if a string is alphanumeric
 *
 * @param str  String you want to check.
 * @return Returns a Boolean value.
 * @author Marcus Raphelt (cflib@raphelt.de)
 * @version 1, November 2, 2001
 */
function IsAlphanumeric(str)
{
    if (REFindNoCase("[^a-z0-9]", str) eq 0)
        return true;
    else
        return false;
}
```

The code, which was contributed to CFLIB.org by Marcus Raphelt, uses an
if/else statement and the REFindNoCase function to evaluate a passed value. The
REFindNoCase function uses a regular expression, [^a-z0-9], to search for the letters A to Z and the numbers 0 to 9. Notice that, depending on the result of
the regular expression results, a Boolean value is returned to the calling page.

Giving Credit

When you use UDFs that you did not create in your code , you should give the creator his or her due
by including the commented text, including the developer's name and email address.

To download the StrLib UDF library, follow these steps:

1. In the bookexample directory in your web root, create a folder named
   UDFlib. You will save the StrLib.cfm file to this directory.

2. Open your web browser and go to www.cflib.org.

3. In the CFLIB home page, select Libraries.

4. In the libraries page, select StrLib. As you can read in its description,
   StrLib stands for String Library. In other words, the StrLib.cfm page contains a collection of string evaluation and manipulation functions.

5. In the StrLib page, select the Download this Library link. Your web
   browser's download dialog box should appear. Save the StrLib.cfm page
   in the UDFlib directory in your web root.

The StrLib page is now ready to use in your ColdFusion pages.

You can also make UDFs part of the Dreamweaver workspace by creating
snippets that contain the CFScript for the UDF. For more information, see
Chapter 22, "Customizing Dreamweaver for ColdFusion Development."

Building formValidation.cfm

In formValidation.cfm, you will build a simple form page that contains six text fields and a submit button. You need to create a text field for the following information: name, email, web site URL, social security number, credit card number, and zip code. No database queries or dynamic elements are required on this page.

To build formValidation.cfm, follow these steps:

1. Create a new ColdFusion page from the bookexample template, and save it as formValidation.cfm in the chap7 folder in the bookexample directory.

2. Insert a FORM tag into the Body section. In the FORM tag's Property Inspector, enter **formValidationResults.cfm**. (You will create this page in the next section.) Select POST in the Method menu.

3. Place your cursor in the Body section, and create a table with seven rows, two columns, and no border.

4. In the right-hand column, insert a text field in each of the first six rows. For each text field, give it a descriptive name, such as "name" or "email."

5. In the left-hand column, enter a text description for the text field in each row, such as "Name" or "Email Address," as shown in Figure 7.1.

6. Insert a Submit button in the last table row.

7. Save your work.

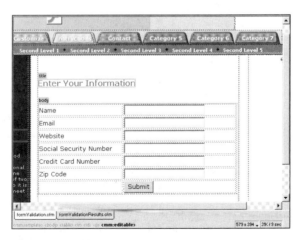

Figure 7.1 When finished, the formValidation.cfm page is a simple form page that lets users enter personal information.

Building formValidationResults.cfm

To build formValidationResults.cfm, you are going to work with the CFML and HTML code to change the background colors dynamically based on the results of the UDFs used for data validation. In addition, you will use the Bindings panel to create form variables to insert into the page.

1. Create a new ColdFusion page from the bookexample template, and name it **formValidationResults.cfm**.

2. Place your cursor in the Body region of the page, and insert a table with two rows, two columns, and no border. In the left-hand column, enter **Passed** in one row and **Failed** in the other row. In the right-hand column, change the Passed cell background color to #00FF00, which is green. For the Failed cell, change the background color to #FF0000, which is red.

3. Below the table created in the previous step, insert another table with six rows, two columns, and no border.

4. In the left-hand column, mirror the descriptions that you entered in formValidation.cfm, such as "Email Address" and "Zip Code."

5. Using the Bindings panel, create six form variables. Each form variable's name should correspond to a text field name in formValidation.cfm, as shown in Figure 7.2.

Figure 7.2   Using the Bindings panel, you create local variables to change background colors dynamically.

6. Using your mouse, select the right-hand column. In the Property Inspecto make the background color white. This ensures that each table row contains the bgcolor attribute, which you will make dynamic later.

7. In the Document toolbar, click the Show Code and Design Views button. In the Code View, scroll up to the top of the document.

8. In the CFML Basic toolbar of the Insert panel, click the CFINCLUDE button. The Tag Editor dialog box for CFINCLUDE appears.

9. In the Tag Editor dialog box, click the Browse button and select the StrLib.cfm file in the UDFlib directory. When you click the OK button, the following code appears:

```
<cfinclude template="UDFlib/StrLib.cfm">
```

Figure 7.3 shows the Code and Design View of the formValidationResults.cfm page.

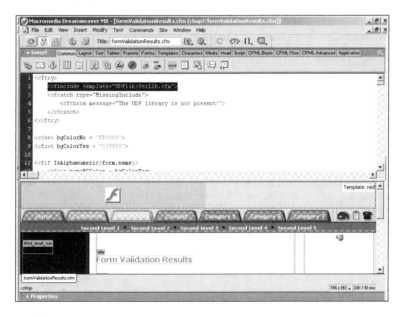

Figure 7.3 As shown in Code View portion of the document window, the CFINCLUDE tag references the StrLib.cfm UDF library.

10. Create two local variables, bgColorYes and bgColorNo, to contain the color values for the background colors. Set their values as shown here:

```
<cfset bgColorNo = "FF0000">
<cfset bgColorYes = "33FF33">
```

Notice that the leading hash sign (#) is not present. You will supply the hash sign outside the CFOUTPUT statement so that ColdFusion will not try to evaluate the value as a ColdFusion variable.

11. Create a CFIF statement that uses the IsAlphanumeric UDF to evaluate the name form variable. If the UDF returns true, set the nameBGColor variable equal to bgColorYes. If the UDF returns false, set the nameBGColor variable to bgColorNo, as shown in the following example:

```
<cfif IsAlphanumeric(form.name)>
<cfset nameBGColor = bgColorYes>
<cfelse>
<cfset nameBGColor = bgColorNo>
</cfif>
```

The nameBGColor variable will be created and used later in the HTML to change the background color dynamically.

12. Repeat Step 11 for each form variable passed from formValidation.cfm, substituting the appropriate StrLib UDF for the validation. You should use the following UDFs in the page: IsAlphanumeric, IsEmail, IsURL, IsZipUS, IsCreditCard, and IsSSN.

13. Using the Bindings panel, create six local variables with the following names: nameBGColor, emailBGColor, websiteBGColor, ccnBGColor, ssnBGColor, and zipBGColor.

14. In the Design View portion of the document window, place your cursor in the table cell with form.name. The Code View portion of the document window changes to show the table row HTML. Remember, you should be using Code and Design View.

15. Highlight the entire value in the bgcolor attribute of the TD tag except the leading hash sign (#). In the Bindings panel, select the nameBGColor variable and click the Insert button. The code should look like the following example:

```
<tr>
    <td>
        <p>Name</p>
    </td>
    <td bgcolor="#<cfoutput>#Variables.nameBGColor#</cfoutput>">
        <strong><cfoutput>#Form.name#</cfoutput></strong>
    </td>
</tr>
```

In the example, Variables.nameBGColor, which was set by the results of the IsAlphanumeric UDF, supplies the color value.

16. Repeat Step 15 for each form variable table row. Only change the background color for the table row cells containing a form variable.

17. Save your work.

Congratulations—you just created a ColdFusion page that evaluates the form variables passed from formValidation.cfm with UDFs and dynamically changes the background color of form field cells. The colors change to indicate whether the data passed was valid.

To check your code, the following example shows the completed data validation code:

```
<cftry>
    <cfinclude template="UDFlib/StrLib.cfm">
    <cfcatch type="MissingInclude">
        <cfthrow message="The UDF library is not present!">
    </cfcatch>
</cftry>

<cfset bgColorNo = "FF0000">
<cfset bgColorYes = "33FF33">

<cfif IsAlphanumeric(form.name)>
    <cfset nameBGColor = bgColorYes>
    <cfelse>
    <cfset nameBGColor = bgColorNo>
</cfif>

<cfif IsEmail(form.email)>
    <cfset emailBGColor = bgColorYes>
    <cfelse>
    <cfset emailBGColor = bgColorNo>
</cfif>

<cfif IsURL(form.website)>
    <cfset websiteBGColor = bgColorYes>
    <cfelse>
    <cfset websiteBGColor = bgColorNo>
</cfif>

<cfif IsSSN(form.ssn)>
    <cfset ssnBGColor = bgColorYes>
    <cfelse>
    <cfset ssnBGColor = bgColorNo>
</cfif>

<cfif IsCreditCard(form.ccn)>
    <cfset ccnBGColor = bgColorYes>
    <cfelse>
    <cfset ccnBGColor = bgColorNo>
</cfif>

<cfif IsZipUS(form.zip)>
    <cfset zipBGColor = bgColorYes>
    <cfelse>
    <cfset zipBGColor = bgColorNo>
</cfif>
```

Notice that CFTRY, CFCATCH, and CFTHROW tags are used to catch errors and display error messages. For more information about handling errors, see "Handling Errors" later in this chapter.

Testing the Application

To test this application, it's best just to use a web browser. Enter the URL to the formValidation.cfm page, such as `http://localhost:8100/bookexample/chap7/formValidation.cfm`. Your web browser should look like the one shown in Figure 7.4.

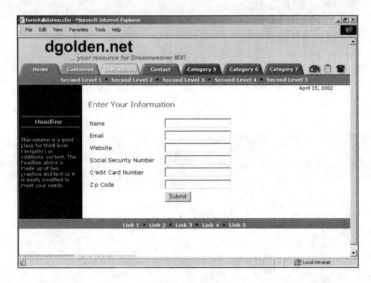

Figure 7.4   The formValidation.cfm page shows a simple form page when displayed in a Web browser.

In the text fields, enter information into the blanks. Try different combinations to see the results of the data validation, as shown in Figure 7.5.

If you receive unexpected results, such as data being validated that should throw an error, check the following areas:

- Make sure the text boxes in formValidation.cfm match the variables used in formValidationResults.cfm.

- Make sure that the proper UDF evaluates the proper form variable.

- If you are receiving page processing errors, make sure that all CFIF statements have closing CFIF tags.

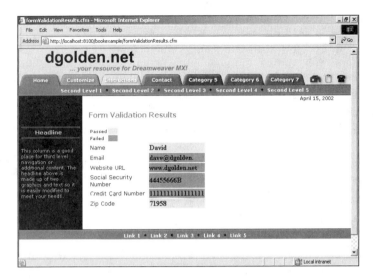

Figure 7.5 The formValidationResults.cfm page indicates whether the data passed from formValidation.cfm is valid.

Handling Errors

ColdFusion offers numerous features for handling any errors that occur when processing a page request, including the CFERROR tag, the CFTRY tag, the CFCATCH tag, and the CFTHROW tag. You actually used a simple form of error handling in the last section. Because error handling is simply evaluating a condition and executing code based on the evaluation, changing colors based on the outcome of data validation is one way of handling user input errors.

Dreamweaver provides Show Region server behaviors that, as the name implies, show a region based on a condition. Dreamweaver includes Show Region server behaviors that evaluate recordsets returned by database queries. For example, the Show Region If Recordset Is Not Empty server behavior shows whatever it is applied to only if the designated recordset contains records.

If you want to write a little CFML, you can use the CFTRY and CFCATCH tags to perform more sophisticated error handling.

1. Open formValidationResults.cfm, and click the Show Code and Design Views button on the document toolbar.

2. Using the Code View, highlight the CFINCLUDE tag that you created in the previous section, and using the CFML Flow toolbar of the Insert panel, click the CFTRY button. Opening and closing CFTRY tags appear around the highlighted code, as the following example shows:

```
<cftry><cfinclude template="UDFlib/StrLib.cfm"></cftry>
```

3. Before the closing CFTRY tag, insert a CFCATCH statement using the CFCATCH button in the CFML Flow toolbar of the Insert panel. The CFCATCH dialog box appears.

4. In the CFCATCH dialog box, select MissingInclude in the Exception Type menu, as shown in Figure 7.6. Click the OK button. The following code appears:

```
<cfcatch type="MissingInclude"></cfcatch>
```

MissingInclude exceptions check for missing files imported by a CFINCLUDE tag.

5. After placing your cursor between the opening and closing CFCATCH tags, insert a CFTHROW tag using the CFTHROW button in the CFML Flow toolbar of the Insert panel. The CFTHROW dialog box appears.

6. In the CFTHROW dialog box, enter **The UDF library is missing!** in the Message text field. Click the OK button. The CFTHROW tag appears:

```
<cfthrow message="The UDF library is missing!">
```

When the StrLib.cfm page is not present, the CFTHROW tag displays the message.

7. Save your work.

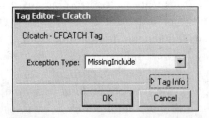

Figure 7.6   In the CFCATCH dialog box, you
specify the type of exception to catch. In this case,
you want to catch MissingInclude exceptions.

Testing the Application

Like the previous section, the easiest way to test this application is to use your web browser. Keep in mind that you want to throw a template exception.

1. Go to the UDFlib directory in your web root at CFusionMX/ wwwroot/bookexample/.

2. Move the StrLib.cfm page out of the UDFLib directory so that ColdFusion will not find it when it when it processes the CFINCLUDE tag in the formValidationResults.cfm page. You can replace it after you finish testing.

3. Open your web browser and go to the formValidation page at `http://localhost:8100/bookexample/chap7/formValidation.cfm`.

4. Enter values in the text fields, and click the Submit button.

As shown in Figure 7.7, the formValidationResults.cfm page throws an error that contains the message that you specified in the CFTHROW tag.

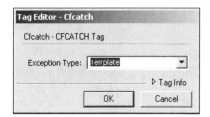

Figure 7.7 The formValidationResults.cfm page throws an error that contains the message that you specified in the CFTHROW tag.

Note
You can create custom error templates for your ColdFusion applications by using the Settings page in the ColdFusion Administrator.

Summary

In this chapter, you learned how to use UDFs to validate form data. In addition, you learned how to catch validation errors and display descriptive error messages. In the next chapter, you will learn how to display database records in a dynamic table.

Displaying Results with ColdFusion

8

Displaying Records in a Dynamic Table

IN THIS CHAPTER, YOU LEARN HOW TO display database records in a dynamic table. Using the Dreamweaver server behaviors and dialog boxes, you can quickly build a sophisticated HTML table for displaying database results.

Understanding the CFML behind Dynamic Tables

To structure records for display to the user, you can bind a recordset to an HTML table. In Dreamweaver, *binding* means associating a page element with a recordset or variable. When ColdFusion processes the page, it creates a table row for each record in the recordset. In Dreamweaver, you can accomplish this in one dialog box, or you can customize the display of the table by applying Show Region server behaviors.

You can further customize the table by taking advantage of recordset filtering to give the user the capability to sort on column names. In addition, by writing a little CFML, you can alternate the table rows' colors.

In CFML, the CFOUTPUT tag encloses the code to repeat. For each record in the recordset, the code enclosed by the CFOUTPUT tag executes. So, if a recordset contains 10 records, the code with the CFOUTPUT tags repeats 10 times.

(The `Queary=""` attribute of the `CFOUTPUT` tag causes the repeat of 10 times for each record.) For example:

```
<table cellspacing="2" cellpadding="2" border="0">
<tr>
    <th>First Name</th>
    <th>Last Name</th>
</tr>
<cfoutput query="exampleQuery">
<tr>
    <td>#parkQueryF.firstName#</td>
    <td>#parkQueryF.lastName#</td>
</tr>
</cfoutput>
</table>
```

In the example, for each record in the `exampleQuery` recordset, the `CFOUTPUT` tag executes the HTML table rows. After ColdFusion processes the page, the HTML might look like this:

```
<table cellspacing="2" cellpadding="2" border="0">
<tr>
    <th>First Name</th>
    <th>Last Name</th>
</tr>
<tr>
    <td>Jane</td>
    <td>Doe</td>
</tr>
<tr>
    <td>John</td>
    <td>Doe</td>
</tr>
<tr>
    <td>Yahoo</td>
    <td>Doe</td>
</tr>
</table>
```

For more information about recordsets and querying databases, see Chapter 4, "Working with Databases."

In this chapter, you will build a ColdFusion application that lets users filter and customize the display of the records in the `tblParks` table. You can find the `tblParks` table in the exampleapps database. The `tblParks` table contains records for various parks throughout the United States. This application requires four pages:

- filterParks.cfm—This page uses three dynamic menus that let users filter what records are shown. It also uses Show Region server behaviors to hide a list box if no records are present.

- displayParksState.cfm, displayParksRegion.cfm, and displayParksType.cfm—These pages dynamically generate tables based on the values passed from the filterParks.cfm page.

Figure 8.1 shows the files and their interactions with the database.

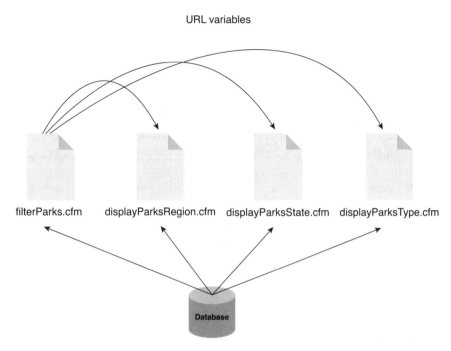

Figure 8.1   This ColdFusion application contains four pages. Each page interacts with the database. The display pages must receive a URL variable to execute.

Building filterParks.cfm

The filterParks.cfm page displays three menus that contain the states, regions, and park types. Each menu is bound to a separate recordset. Each recordset queries the database for all unique names in the STATE column, REGION column, or PARKTYPE column.

The page also contains three Show Region server behaviors, which ensure that a menu displays only if the corresponding recordset contains records. If no records exist, the drop-down menu is not displayed and a message appears that states no records were found. To build the filterParks.cfm page, execute the following steps:

1. Create a new ColdFusion page from the bookexample template, and name it **filterParks.cfm**.

2. In the Bindings panel, create a recordset by clicking the plus (+) button, and in the submenu that appears, select RecordSet (Query). The Recordset dialog appears.

3. You are going to write a little SQL from scratch. In the Recordset dialog, click the Advanced button. The Recordset dialog offers more options, as shown in Figure 8.2. Name the recordset **stateFilterQ**. Select exampleapps from the Data Source menu. In the SQL text panel, enter the following SQL:

```
SELECT DISTINCT STATE
FROM tblParks
WHERE STATE NOT LIKE ' '
ORDER BY STATE ASC
```

   In the SQL, the SELECT statement specifies which table column should be included in the recordset. Notice that the DISTINCT command is used. This returns a list of only the unique states, which eliminates duplicates. The FROM statement specifies the database table to use. The WHERE statement uses the NOT LIKE command to ensure that each record actually contains information. The ORDER BY statement specifies the database column to sort the recordset by. In this case, ASC denotes ascending sorting. Click the OK button.

4. After placing your cursor in the Body section, insert a FORM tag. A red broken-line box appears.

5. In the FORM tag's Property Inspector, enter **displayParksState.cfm** in the Action text box. (This page will be created in the next section.) Select GET in the Method menu.

6. After making sure your cursor is inside the FORM box, insert a table with two rows, three columns, and no border.

7. In the top row, enter **Select a State:** in the left-hand cell. In the right-hand cell, insert a Submit button. In the middle cell, insert a menu.

8. In the menu's Property Inspector, name the menu **STATE** and click the Dynamic button. In the Dynamic List/Menu dialog box, shown in Figure 8.3, select stateFilterQ from the Options From RecordSet menu. Select STATE from both the Labels and Values menus. Click the OK button.

9. In the next table row, enter **No records found!**

10. Using your cursor, select the top row of the table. In the Server Behaviors panel, click the plus {+} button. In the submenu that appears, select Show Region, Show Region if Recordset Is Not Empty.

11. In the Show Region dialog box, select stateFilterQ from the Recordset menu. Click the OK button. A CFIF tab surrounds the first row. (This row will only appear if the stateFilterQ recordset contains records.)

12. Select the second row with your cursor, and insert a Show Region if Recordset Is Empty server behavior for the stateFilterQ recordset. This row will appear only if the stateFilterQ recordset contains no records.

13. Repeat Steps 2 through 11 to create tables and dynamic menus for each recordset, naming each `REGION` or `PARKTYPE`. In addition, set each `FORM` tag's `ACTION` attribute to the appropriate ColdFusion page, which will be created in the next section.

14. Save your work.

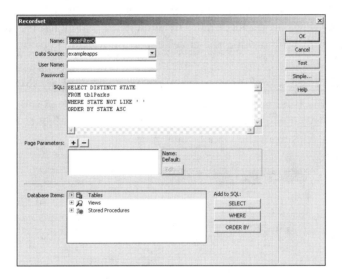

Figure 8.2   In the Recordset dialog box, you create a recordset that selects only unique state names from the `STATE` column of the `tblParks` table. Using a `WHERE` statement ensures that no blank entries show up in the menu.

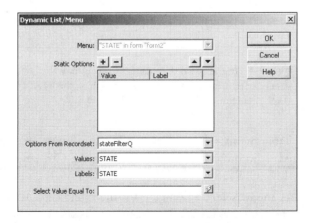

Figure 8.3   In the Dynamic List/Menu dialog box, you display and return only the `STATE` column.

Building the Display Pages

To display the parks according to the selection made in the filterParks.cfm page, you need to create three display pages: displayParksState.cfm, displayParksRegion.cfm, and displayParksType.cfm. All three display pages look identical, but each outputs a different list of parks. Each page contains a dynamic table and Show Region server behaviors. In addition, by inserting a few lines of CFML, you can create a dynamic table that alternates row colors automatically, thereby making the tables easier for your users to read. Follow these steps:

1. Create a new ColdFusion page and name it **displayParksState.cfm**.

2. Using the Bindings panel, create a new recordset named parkQuery. In the simple layout of the RecordSet dialog box, shown in Figure 8.4, select exampleapps from the Data Source menu.

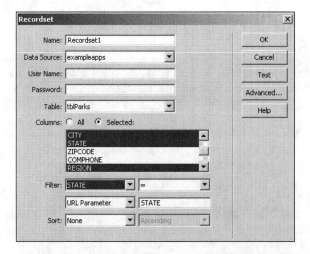

Figure 8.4   In the Recordset dialog box, you filter the query results by returning only the records in which the STATE column equals the STATE URL variable.

3. From the Table menu, select tblParks. In the Columns section, select the Selected radio button, and holding down the Ctrl key, select the PARKNAME, CITY, STATE, REGION, and PARKTYPE columns.

4. In the Filter menu, select STATE, = for the operator, and URL Parameter, and enter **STATE**. This name corresponds to the menus in filterParks.cfm. Click the OK button.

5. Place your cursor in the Body section. In the Application toolbar of the Insert panel set, click the Dynamic Table button. The Dynamic Table dialog box appears.

6. In the Dynamic Table dialog box, shown in Figure 8.5, select parkQuery from the Recordset menu. Select the All Records radio button in the Show section. Enter **0** in the Table Border, Cell Padding, and Cell Spacing text boxes. Click the OK button, and the dynamic table appears in the Body section.

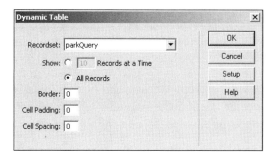

Figure 8.5   In the Dynamic Table dialog box, you select the recordset for Dreamweaver to use to create the table.

Note

If you specify a number of records to display at a time, you must create recordset navigation functionality to display all the records. For more information, see Chapter 9, "Creating Recordset Navigation."

The table consists of two rows and five columns. That's the same number of columns as you selected when you created the recordset. Dreamweaver automatically creates a header row for you and populates the row with the column names. In addition, a Repeat Region server behavior for the parkQuery recordset generates the table row for each record in the recordset.

7. In the Document toolbar, click the Show Code and Design Views button to split the screen to reveal the code.

8. In the Code View pane, find the CFOUTPUT statement for the Repeat Region server behavior. Modify the opening CFOUPUT tag to look like the following:

```
<cfset varTemp = "true">
<cfoutput query="parkQuery">
    <cfif varTemp EQ "true">
        <cfset backColor = "##FFFFFF">
        <cfset varTemp = "false">
    <cfelse>
        <cfset backColor = "##CCCCCC">
        <cfset varTemp = "true">
    </cfif>
    <tr bgcolor = "#backColor#">
        <td> <p>#parkQuery.PARKNAME#</p></td>
        <td> <p>#parkQuery.CITY#</p></td>
        <td> <p>#parkQuery.STATE#</p></td>
        <td> <p>#parkQuery.REGION#</p></td>
        <td> <p>#parkQuery.PARKTYPE#</p></td>
    </tr>
</cfoutput>
```

In the example, the CFSET tag creates the varTemp variable and sets it equal to "true". The CFIF tag evaluates whether it is equal to "true". If it is, the backColor variable is set to white, and the varTemp variable is set to "false".

If the varTemp variable is not equal to "true", the CFELSE tag executes, which sets the backColor variable to gray and sets the varTemp variable to "true".

Finally, in the TR tag that creates the table row, the bgcolor attribute is set to the value of the backColor variable. Therefore, the background color alternates for every record row.

9. Save your work.

Adding Column Sorting

To let users sort the order in which recordsets are displayed, you can make the header row names hyperlinks that contain a URL parameter. The URL parameter supplies the variable value in the ORDER BY statement.

 The hyperlinks actually point back to the display page. When the link is clicked, the page reloads to show the sorted table. To enable recordset sorting, follow these steps:

1. Open displayParksState.cfm.

2. Open the parkQuery Recordset dialog box, and click the Advanced button. In the Recordset dialog box, replace the existing ORDER BY statement with the following:

    ```
    ORDER BY '#URL.SORT#' ASC
    ```

    In the example, the URL.SORT variable supplies the column to sort on, which is passed using the URL specified in the hyperlink.

3. Still in the Recordset dialog box, add URL.SORT to the Page Parameters in the Advanced Recordset dialog box. Set its default value to STATE. This creates a CFPARAM tag, which provides a variable value even if it is not passed from the calling page. By using the CFPARAM tag, you eliminate the need for passing additional parameters from the page. Click the OK button.

4. Select PARKNAME in the top table row with your cursor. In the Common toolbar, click the Hyperlink button. The Hyperlink dialog box appears.

5. In the Hyperlink dialog box, shown in Figure 8.6, enter **Park Name** in the Text text box. Click the Browse button next to the Link menu. The Select File dialog box appears.

6. In the Select File dialog box, select displayParksState.cfm. Click the Parameters button. The Parameters dialog box displays.

7. In the Parameters dialog box shown in Figure 8.7, create two parameters, STATE and SORT. Set the SORT parameter to PARKNAME, which is the name of the database column to sort. Set the STATE parameter to STATE, which is the name of the database column in the SQL WHERE statement. Click the OK button.

8. In the Select File dialog, click the OK button.

9. In the Hyperlink dialog box, select _self in the Target menu and click OK. The _self TARGET attribute tells the web browser to pass the URL parameters back to itself.

10. Repeat Steps 1 through 9 for each database column in the table.

11. Save your work.

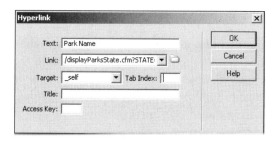

Figure 8.6 In the Hyperlink dialog box, you can quickly set up a hyperlink to link to another page.

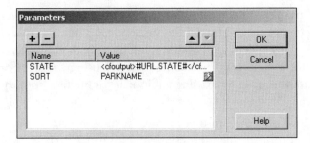

Figure 8.7   In the Parameters dialog box, you create
parameters that will be passed in the URL to
filter the recordset.

Testing the Application

You can use the Live Data view to test your application in real time. You
can also specify different URL variables so that you can test different
combinations.

1. Open the displayParksState.cfm page.

2. In the Live Data Settings dialog box shown in Figure 8.8, create two
   URL Requests, SORT and STATE, by clicking the plus (+) button.
   Enter a state abbreviation, such as "MA", for STATE, and enter a column
   name for the SORT URL request. Click the OK button.

3. In the Document toolbar, click the Live Data View button. In the toolbar
   that appears, click the Settings button. The Live Data Settings dialog
   box appears.

4. Select GET from the Method menu.

5. Click the OK button.

If you don't see graphics files in your ColdFusion page when using the Live
Data View, you must upload the page's support files, such as graphics or multimedia files, to the testing server. By default, Dreamweaver uses the web root
directory specified in the site definition. You can change the directory to an
alternate location using the Testing Server category in the Preferences dialog
box (Edit, Preferences).

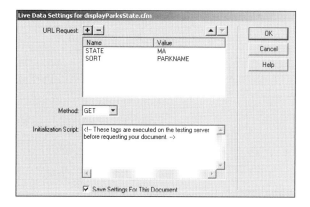

Figure 8.8 The Live Data Settings dialog box lets you create URL and FORM variables to test your ColdFusion pages in real time.

Summary

In this chapter, you learned how to display database records in a dynamic table. You also learned how to use Dreamweaver's Repeat Region server behavior to customize table display. In the next chapter, you learn how to build ColdFusion pages that use recordset navigation to display large recordsets.

9

Creating Recordset Navigation

IN THIS CHAPTER, YOU BUILD A COLDFUSION application that uses recordset navigation to page through large recordsets. Recordset navigation controls let the user display the records as he or she sees fit rather than having to scroll through long pages. The user experience is better than without navigation, and you don't have to worry about constantly changing your ColdFusion pages to accommodate an ever-growing database.

Recordset Navigation

If you have ever been to a web site that lists hundreds of products in one long page, you realize the value of recordset navigation. Although ColdFusion has no problem creating a giant table that contains hundreds of records, your users will quickly become lost and find another web site to visit.

Recordset navigation consists of displaying records in increments, rather than all at once. *Incremental recordsets* allow a specific number of records from a recordset to display at a time. For example, if a recordset contains 20 records, you can build a ColdFusion page that displays 5 records at a time. Of course, you can't anticipate how many pages will be needed to display a recordset. That's where ColdFusion comes in.

When ColdFusion queries a database and returns a recordset, the number of records in that recordset, sometimes called the *recordset length,* is known. Using the length of the recordset with the CFQUERY attributes startrow and endrow, ColdFusion can display a specified number of records at a time and know how many records are remaining in the recordset.

So, using a little CFML logic, you can build automatic navigation controls—such as First, Last, Next, and Back—to let users navigate recordsets as they see fit. In addition, you can create dynamic text that shows how many records were found, how many records are shown, and how many records are remaining.

Dreamweaver provides server behaviors that automate creating recordset navigation. In this chapter, you will use the techniques that you learned in the previous chapters—such as creating a recordset, passing variables, and displaying the records in a dynamic table—to build a recordset navigation system for the tblParks database table using the recordset navigation server behaviors.

This ColdFusion application requires the following pages:

- filterParksSimple.cfm—This page will let the user select records to display. You created this page (filterParks.cfm) in Chapter 8, "Displaying Records in a Dynamic Table." For this application you just need to make a few minor adjustments.

- filterResults.cfm—In this page, you will display the initial set of records and provide recordset navigation controls. Records will be displayed in a dynamic table.

- filterResultsDetail.cfm—In this page, you will display the details of a selected record in the filterResults.cfm page.

Figure 9.1 shows a simplified representation of the ColdFusion application created in this chapter.

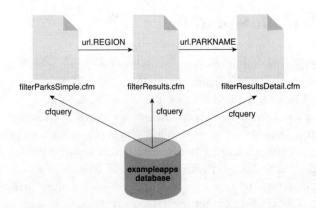

Figure 9.1   This ColdFusion application contains three pages— filterParksSimple.cfm, filterResults.cfm, and filterResultsDetail.cfm.

Building filterParksSimple.cfm

You created the filterPark.cfm page in Chapter 8 to let users filter the records contained in the tblParks database table. In this chapter, you use a simplified version of filterParks.cfm, saved as filterParksSimple.cfm, which lets the user choose to view parks by region. To create this simpler page, follow these steps.

1. Using the Site panel, select filterParks.cfm. Right-click on the file, and in the submenu that appears, select Duplicate. A file named Copy of filterParks.cfm appears.

2. Rename Copy of filterParks.cfm to filterParksSimple.cfm, and open it.

3. In the document window, delete the tables containing the menus for states and park type, so that the page looks like the one shown in Figure 9.2.

4. Select the FORM tag from the Common tab in the Insert Bar, and in its Property Inspector, enter **filterResults.cfm**, which you will create in the next section. Select GET in the Method menu.

5. Save your work.

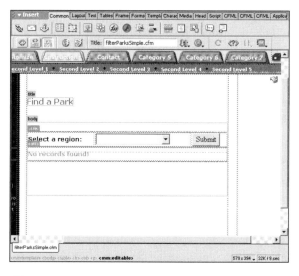

Figure 9.2   The filterParksSimple.cfm page contains only one menu, which allows users to filter the database results according to region

As an alternative to a menu, you could create an image map of the United States and include URL variables in the hyperlinks. In addition, you could create a Flash movie using Flash Remoting. For more information about using Flash Remoting with ColdFusion, see Chapter 20, "Building Flash Remoting Services."

Building filterResult.cfm

The goal of the filterResults.cfm page is to display the parks by region using the URL variable passed from filterParksSimple.cfm. You also want to build recordset navigation controls so users can browse the records.

To accomplish these tasks, you will build the following dynamic page elements:

- A dynamic table to display the records
- A recordset navigation bar
- A recordset navigation status message

Building the Dynamic Table

Building the dynamic table in the filterResults.cfm page consists of defining a recordset, creating a table, and applying a Repeat Region server behavior to a table row. To build the page, follow these steps:

1. Create a new ColdFusion page from the bookexample template, and name it filterResults.cfm.

2. Using the Recordset dialog box, as shown in Figure 9.3, create a recordset named regionalParksQ. The recordset should return the PARKNAME, CITY, STATE, REGION, and PARKTYPE columns. In addition, it must filter the query results using the REGION URL variable, which is passed from filterParksSimple.cfm. The REGION URL should equal (=) the REGION column.

3. Create a table with three rows, four columns, and no border.

4. In the top table row, enter the HTML table column names for the table, including Park Name, City, State, and Park Type.

5. In the middle row, insert a database column into each cell as dynamic text. The database column should match the HTML table column headers.

6. Using your mouse, select the middle table row. Using the Server Behaviors panel, apply a Repeat Region server behavior. In the Repeat Region dialog box, shown in Figure 9.4, select the regionalParkQ recordset, and specify that five records are displayed at a time.

   If you set the number of records displayed, ColdFusion will only repeat the region that number of times or less (depending on how many records are in the recordset).

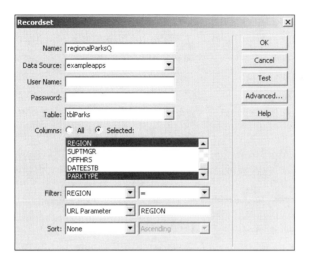

Figure 9.3   The `regionalParksQ` recordset selects four database columns and filters the results by the `REGION` URL variable.

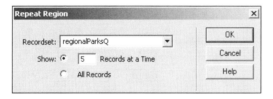

Figure 9.4   Using the Repeat Region server behavior, you can specify the number of records returned at a time. In this case, five records are returned to each page.

7. To alternate the row colors for each record, switch to Code and Design View mode and find the `CFOUTPUT` statement for the middle table row. Insert the following `CFSET` tag before the opening `CFOUTPUT` tag:

```
<cfset varTemp = "true">
```

Directly after the opening `CFOUTPUT` tag, insert the following CFML:

```
<cfif varTemp EQ "true">
    <cfset backColor = "##FFFFFF">
    <cfset varTemp = "false">
<cfelse>
    <cfset backColor = "##CCCCCC">
    <cfset varTemp = "true">
</cfif>
<tr bgcolor="#backColor#">
```

In the code, the CFSET tag creates the varTemp variable and sets it equal to "true". The CFIF tag evaluates whether varTemp is equal to "true". If it is, the backColor variable is set to white, and the varTemp variable is set to "false".

If the varTemp variable is not equal to "true", the CFELSE tag executes, which sets the backColor variable to gray, and sets the varTemp variable to "true".

Finally, in the TR tag that creates the table row, the bgcolor attribute is set to the value of the backColor variable. Therefore, the background color alternates for every record row.

8. In the bottom table row, enter **No records found!**

9. Using your mouse, select the bottom table row. Using the Server Behaviors panel, apply a Show Region if Recordset Is Empty server behavior for the regionalParksQ recordset. This table row, including the "No records found!" message, displays only when no records are returned from the database query.

10. Save your work.

Building the Recordset Navigation Bar

A recordset navigation bar consists of hyperlinks and Show Region server behaviors. The hyperlinks all reference the same page, but also pass URL variables that specify what records should be displayed in that page.

For example, the following hyperlink directs the page to go to the first page of a recordset:

```
<a href="filterResults.cfm?PageNum_regionalParksQ=1">First</a>
```

In the example, the hyperlink passes the PageNum_regionalParksQ variable, which is equal to 1, to the filterResults.cfm page. The variable tells the CFML logic in the page to go to the first page of the recordset. The CFML that Dreamweaver generates to provide recordset navigation is relatively complex, as the following example shows:

```
<cfset MaxRows_regionalParksQ=5>
<cfset StartRow_regionalParksQ=Min((PageNum_regionalParksQ-1)
    *MaxRows_regionalParksQ+1,Max(regionalParksQ.RecordCount,1))>
<cfset EndRow_regionalParksQ=Min(StartRow_regionalParksQ+
    MaxRows_regionalParksQ-1,regionalParksQ.RecordCount)>
<cfset TotalPages_regionalParksQ=Ceiling(regionalParksQ.RecordCount/
    MaxRows_regionalParksQ)>
<cfset QueryString_regionalParksQ=Iif(CGI.QUERY_STRING NEQ "",
    DE("&"&CGI.QUERY_STRING),DE(""))>
```

```
<cfset tempPos=ListContainsNoCase(QueryString_regionalParksQ,
    "PageNum_regionalParksQ=",",","&")>
<cfif tempPos NEQ 0>
    <cfset QueryString_regionalParksQ=ListDeleteAt
        (QueryString_regionalParksQ,tempPos,"&")>
</cfif>
```

As you can see, the CFML consists of a series of CFSET tags and a CFIF statement. The first four variables, StartRow_regionalParksQ, EndRow_regionalParksQ, TotalPages_regionalParksQ, and QueryString_regionalParksQ contain the first row in the recordset, the last row in the recordset, the total number of pages in the recordset, and the number of records to display, respectively. The tempPos variable and the CFIF statement search the URL query string for a specific value, and if present, delete it.

CGI Variables

You might have noticed that the CFML code in the previous example uses CGI variables. In this context, CGI variables access some of the hidden HTTP header properties passed to and from web browsers. For a complete list of CGI variables, see the ColdFusion documentation.

Fortunately, Dreamweaver builds this CFML for you. To build recordset navigation, Dreamweaver gives you the following options, listed from difficult to easy:

- Difficult—Build the navigation bar from scratch in the CFML code.
- Medium—Use the Recordset Navigation and Show Region server behaviors.
- Easy—Use the Recordset Navigation Bar button in the Application tab.
- Very Easy—Use the Master/Detail Pages button in the Application tab, which automatically creates a recordset navigation bar.

In this section, you will use the Recordset Navigation Bar button in the Application tab. With just one dialog box, you can create a dynamic navigation bar. Follow these steps to build the navigation:

1. Open filterResults.cfm, and place your cursor in the Body region, below the dynamic table created in the last section.

2. In the Application tab of the Insert panel group, click the Recordset Navigation Bar button. The Recordset Navigation Bar dialog box appears.

3. In the Recordset Navigation Bar dialog box, select the regionalParksQ recordset. Select the Text radio button in the Display Using section. Click OK. The navigation bar appears, as shown in Figure 9.5.

As you can see, the navigation bar generated by Dreamweaver consists of four hyperlinks and four Show Region server behaviors. The hyperlinks pass URL variables back to the page so that the appropriate records are displayed. The Show Region server behaviors make the navigation controls dynamic—for example, the First and Last controls do not appear when the user is on the first or last record page.

If you select the Images radio button, the recordset navigation bar will look much like the track navigation controls on a CD player, including Forward, Reverse, First, and Last, as shown in Figure 9.6.

4. Save your work.

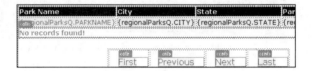

Figure 9.5   Dreamweaver can automatically generate a recordset navigation bar, which saves you a considerable amount of CFML coding.

Figure 9.6   Because a recordset navigation bar is essentially just hyperlinks, you can also use image files to represent the controls. The default Dreamweaver navigation bar images look similar to a CD player's track navigation controls.

Building the Recordset Navigation Status Message

A recordset navigation status message simply shows users how many total records were found and what records are shown on the current page. Like recordset navigation controls, a recordset navigation status message displays three of the variables created in the CFML that Dreamweaver generates when you insert a recordset navigation bar.

As you can see in the following example, a recordset navigation status message consists of normal text with three dynamic text insertions:

```
<cfoutput>Records #StartRow_regionalParksQ# to #EndRow_regionalParksQ# of
#regionalParksQ.RecordCount#</cfoutput>
```

In the example, the CFOUTPUT tags enclose three variables, which are set in CFML logic generated by Dreamweaver when you insert a recordset navigation bar. Just like the recordset navigation controls, Dreamweaver automatically generates the necessary CFML for you.

Also like the recordset navigation bar, Dreamweaver gives you the following choices for building recordset navigation status messages, listed from most difficult to easiest:

- Difficult—Build the navigation status message by hand.
- Medium—Build the navigation status message using the Display Record Count server behaviors.
- Easy—Build the navigation status message using the Recordset Navigation Status button in the Application tab.
- Easiest—Build Master/Detail page sets using the Master/Detail Page Set button in the Application tab.

In this section, you will use the Recordset Navigation Status button in the Application tab. To create the navigation status message, follow these steps:

1. Open filterResults.cfm and place your cursor above the dynamic table in the editable Body region.

2. In the Application tab in the Insert panel group, click the Recordset Navigation Status button. The Recordset Navigation Status dialog box appears.

3. In the Recordset Navigation Status dialog box, shown in Figure 9.7, select the regionalParksQ recordset. Click OK. The recordset navigation status message appears, as shown in Figure 9.8.

4. Save your work.

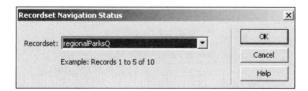

Figure 9.7 In the Recordset Navigation Status dialog box, you select the recordset for the status message.

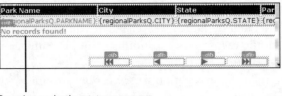

Recordset navigation status message

Figure 9.8   The recordset navigation status message consists
of three dynamic text insertions. You can customize the
display however you like.

Testing the Application

To test the filterResults.cfm page, you can use the Live Data View:

1. Open filterResults.cfm, and open the Live Data Settings dialog by selecting View, Window, Live Data Settings.

2. In the Live Data Settings dialog box, shown in Figure 9.9, click the Plus
   (+) button to create a URL request named REGION, and give it the
   value "Southwest Region." Click OK.

3. Click the Live Data View button in the Document tab.

Notice that the other dynamic page elements, including text areas and the
recordset navigation bar, appear as in a web browser, as shown in Figure 9.10.

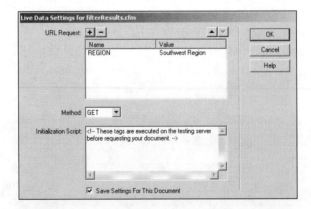

Figure 9.9   In the Live Data Settings dialog box, you create
URL parameters to pass to the ColdFusion page. In this case,
you create one URL variable named REGION. Using this
feature, you can simulate another page, such as
filterParksSimple.cfm, passing a URL variable.

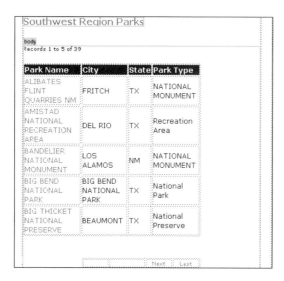

Figure 9.10 The Live Data view shows what the page might look like in a web browser. The Live Data view feature of Dreamweaver lets you test a page without leaving the Dreamweaver environment.

Creating filterResultsDetail.cfm

The filterResultsDetail.cfm page displays the details of a record that users select in filterResults.cfm. To select the record, users will click on the name of a park in filterResults.cfm. The hyperlink will contain the name of the park as a URL variable. In filterResultsDetail.cfm, the URL variable is used to filter the query to the park and display the results.

Dreamweaver provides two ways of creating data drill-down pages:

- More Difficult—Create the hyperlink using the Hyperlink button in the Common tab.
- Easier—Build Master/Detail pages using the Master/Detail Page Set button in the Application tab.

To learn how to build the page yourself, you'll use the more difficult technique of creating the Master/Detail Page Set with hyperlinks. In this section, you will use the Hyperlink button in the Common tab:

1. Open filterResults.cfm and highlight the dynamic text that displays the park name, such as regionalParksQ.PARKNAME.

2. In the Common tab, click the Hyperlink button. The Hyperlink dialog box displays.

3. In the Hyperlink dialog box, click the folder icon. The Select File dialog box displays.

4. In the Select File dialog box, enter **filterResultsDetail.cfm** in the File Name text box. You'll create this page later in this procedure.

5. Still in the Select File dialog box, click the Parameters button. The Parameters dialog box displays.

6. In the Parameters dialog box, shown in Figure 9.11, create a parameter named PARKNAME. For the value, select the Value column, and click the lightning bolt button that appears. The Dynamic Data dialog box displays.

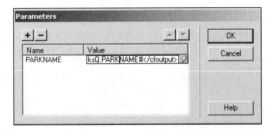

Figure 9.11   In the Parameters dialog box, you create URL variables to pass in the hyperlink.

7. In the Dynamic Data dialog box, shown in Figure 9.12, select the PARKNAME column of the regionalParksQ recordset. Click OK in the Dynamic Data, Parameters, and Select File dialog boxes.

In the Hyperlink dialog box, you don't need to enter anything in the Text text box because ColdFusion will supply the information dynamically.

Now, every time ColdFusion processes the CFOUTPUT statement for the dynamic table, a hyperlink is automatically created for each park name. Each hyperlink passes the name of the park as a URL variable.

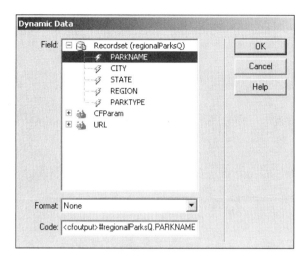

Figure 9.12   In the Dynamic Data dialog box, you bind the value of the PARKNAME column to the value of the PARKNAME URL variable.

8. Create a new ColdFusion page from the bookexample template, and name it **filterResultsDetail.cfm**.

9. Create a recordset named **parkDetailQ** that returns all columns for the tblParks table and filters the results using the PARKNAME URL variable.

10. Place your cursor in the Body section of the document window and insert a table with 12 rows, 2 columns, and no border.

11. In the left-hand column, enter a brief description for each database column, such as Address1, Region, and Manager.

12. In the right-hand column, insert each database column into the corresponding table cell as dynamic text, as shown in Figure 9.13.

13. In the Title section of the document window, insert the PARKNAME URL variable as dynamic text. After the dynamic text, enter **Details**. This creates a dynamic title for the detail page.

14. Save your work.

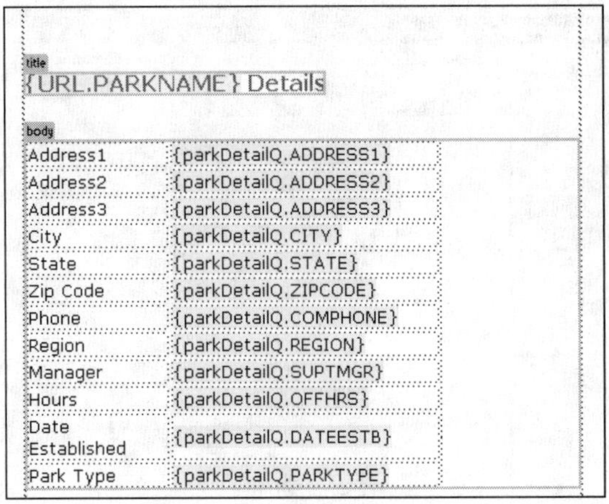

Figure 9.13   The filterResultsDetail.cfm page is a simple
table that contains only the dynamic text needed.

When filterResultsDetail.cfm displays in a user's browser, the database column variables display as the corresponding record columns, which were filtered by the PARKNAME URL variable. If you want to create a hyperlink back to filterResults.cfm, you can use two variables—the REGION recordset variable and the CGI.HTTP_REFERER variable—to create a dynamic hyperlink.

To create a button that dynamically links back to the previous page, follow these steps:

1. In filterResultsDetail.cfm, create an additional table row at the end of the table in the editable Body region, and merge the cells in the new row.

2. Keeping your cursor in the new table row, click the Hyperlink button on the Common tab of the Insert Bar.

3. In the Hyperlink dialog box, enter **Back** in the Text text box. In the Link text box, enter any word. (In the following steps, you will make the link dynamic.) Click the OK button.

4. Click the Code and Design View button in the document window.

5. In the Design View pane of the document window, select the Back hyperlink.

6. In the Code View pane of the document window, select the word that you entered in the Hyperlink dialog box and delete it.

7. Using the CFML Basic tab in the Insert Bar, click the CFOUTPUT button, and in the CFOUTPUT dialog box that appears, click the OK button. In this case, you don't need to specify any CFOUTPUT attributes.

8. After clicking the Surround with # button in the CFML basic tab, type **CGI**. When you type the period, a code hint menu appears that lists the available CGI variables. In the code hint menu, select HTTP_REFERER. The `CGI.HTTP_REFERER` variable displays the URL of the page that linked to the current page. In this case, it's filterResults.cfm.

9. Remember that filterResults.cfm depends on the `REGION` parameter, passed as a URL variable, for its `CFQUERY` statement. So, you need to include a `REGION` variable in the hyperlink. To do so, enter a question mark (**?**) after the closing `CFOUTPUT` tag.

10. In the Bindings panel of the Application panel group, drag the `REGION` column of the `parkDetailQ` recordset directly after the question mark. A `CFOUTPUT` statement appears, which contains the `parkDetailQ.REGION` variable.

Your final code should look like the following example:

```
<cfoutput>#CGI.HTTP_REFERER#</cfoutput>?<cfoutput>#parkDetailQ.REGION#
    </cfoutput>
```

To further develop the pages in this application, think about recordset navigation controls that you've seen on other web sites. Sometimes, a menu is provided to select each page in the recordset directly rather than having to page back and forth. Also, you could use session handling to create a list of previously viewed pages. For more information about session handling, see Chapter 16, "Sessions and the Application Variable Scope."

Summary

In this chapter, you learned how to build dynamic recordset navigation with ColdFusion and Dreamweaver. In addition, you used URL variables to filter recordsets and display detail pages. In the next chapter, you'll learn how to use ColdFusion's built-in charting and graphing engine to display records dynamically as interactive charts and graphs.

10

Charting Dynamic Data

AS THE OLD SAYING GOES, A PICTURE is worth a thousand words. For ColdFusion, you could say that a dynamic chart is worth a thousand dynamic tables. Using the CFCHART, CFCHARTSERIES, and CFCHARTDATA tags, you can create dynamic charts to display database query results and hard-coded data points.

Using the *CFCHART, CFCHARTSERIES,* and *CFCHARTDATA* Tags

These tags work together to produce one or multiple graphs. The CFCHART and CFCHARTSERIES tags are required to make a graph—the CFCHART tag attributes control general chart characteristics, and the CFCHARTSERIES tag represents the actual chart. For every data set that you want to graph, you insert a CFCHARTSERIES tag between the opening and closing tags of a CFCHART statement, as the following example shows:

```
<cfquery name="chartQuery" datasource="exampleapps">
    SELECT ItemName, ItemCost
    FROM tblItems
</cfquery>
```

```
<cfchart>
    <cfchartseries type="scatter"
    query="chartQuery"
    itemcolumn="ItemName"
    valuecolumn="ItemCost">
</cfchart>
```

In the example, the CFCHART statement encloses the CFCHARTSERIES tag. You reference the recordset to chart in the CFCHARTSERIES query (recordset name), itemcolumn (recordset column that supplies the names of the charted values), and valuecolumn (recordset column that supplies the values to chart) tag attributes. The type attribute specifies the type of chart to use. This example uses a scatter chart, as shown in Figure 10.1.

The CFQUERY statement in the example, which queries the tblItems table of the exampleapps data source, supplies the recordset. When ColdFusion processes the CFCHARTSERIES tag, it processes the chart according to the contents of the recordset referenced in the query attribute. Depending on the chart type used, two recordset columns, referenced in the itemcolumn and valuecolumn attributes, act as the basis for the X and Y axes or for pie slices. For each record in the recordset, ColdFusion creates a data point and places it on the graph.

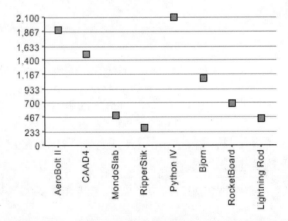

Figure 10.1 In a scatter chart, ColdFusion plots each record as a chart point in relation to the X and Y axes, which are supplied by the recordset.

> **Charting Data**
>
> When you want to chart dynamic data, you must consider what data are best suited for visual display. Large groups of numbers, such as salary averages or the gross domestic product of various countries, always work well in charts. Keep in mind that by charting a data set, you want to let people compare the data visually to other data. If you have only five records, a dynamic table makes more sense than a chart. If you're working with hundreds of records, charting the data looks more attractive.

The CFCHARTDATA tag lets you add a data point to a chart manually. When ColdFusion processes the CFCHARTSERIES tag with a CFCHARTDATA tag, it includes the CFCHARTDATA data point in the chart with the other values from the recordset. If you want to add multiple data points, just add multiple CFCHARTDATA tags. The following CFML adds two data points to the previous example:

```
<cfchart>
    <cfchartseries type="scatter"
        query="chartQuery"
        itemcolumn="ItemName"
        valuecolumn="ItemCost">
        <cfchartdata item="BuggieBoy" value="1200">
        <cfchartdata item="WonderWand" value="2000">
    </cfchartseries>
</cfchart>
```

In the code, two CFCHARTDATA tags are enclosed by the opening and closing CFCHARTSERIES tags. Figure 10.2 shows the extra data points. Although these CFCHARTDATA tags contain static values for the item and value attributes, you could easily make the attribute values dynamic. For example, the following CFML uses FORM variables to supply the values for the item and value columns:

```
<cfchart>
    <cfchartseries type="scatter"
        query="chartQuery"
        itemcolumn="ItemName"
        valuecolumn="ItemCost">
        <cfchartdata item="#form.item1#" value="#form.itemValue1#">
        <cfchartdata item="#form.item2#" value="#form.itemValue2#">
    </cfchartseries>
</cfchart>
```

In the code, the item and value attribute values have been replaced with FORM variables, which would be passed from another ColdFusion or web page. You could also make the whole CFCHARTDATA tag dynamic by enclosing it in a CFLOOP tag and iterating over an array, another recordset, or a struct. For more information, see Chapter 14, "Conditional Logic Problems and Solutions."

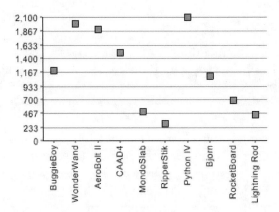

Figure 10.2 You use the `CFCHARTDATA` tag to supply additional data points to a chart, beyond those in the recordset.

In Dreamweaver, your main interface to the `CFCHART`, `CFCHARTSERIES`, and `CFCHARTDATA` tags is the Tag Chooser. You can open the Tag Chooser by selecting Insert menu, Tag. After the Tag Chooser appears, you select CFML tags in its tree structure, and select the CFML tag that you want. When you select a tag, its Tag Editor dialog box displays.

As shown in Figure 10.3, the Tag Editor dialog box for `CFCHART` consists of nine categories: General, Dimensions, 3D Appearance, Multiple Series, Tips, Markers, Labels, Grid Lines, and Font. Using the options provided in the CFCHART Tag Editor dialog box, you can change almost any aspect of the chart's appearance.

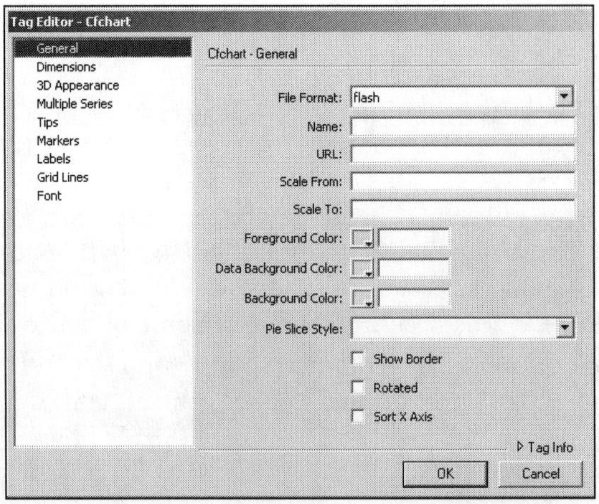

Figure 10.3 In the CFCHART Tag Editor dialog box, you can set numerous display and format options for a chart, including file format, 3D appearance, and font.

ColdFusion offers a wide variety of chart types, including pie, scatter, line, step, area, bar, triangle, cylinder, curve, and cone. You specify the chart type in the CFCHARTSERIES tag's type attribute. Table 10.1 contains the available chart types and descriptions.

Table 10.1 **Chart Types**

Type	Description
Pie	Pie charts show the size of individual data points in comparison to the whole.
Scatter	Scatter charts work best for showing relationships between multiple data sets, which you would supply with multiple CFCHARTSERIES tags.
Line	Line charts show changes in data sets in a linear fashion. Like scatter charts, you can compare data sets by adding multiple CFCHARTSERIES tags.
Step	Much like a line chart, step charts demonstrate changes in data sets in a linear fashion. However, instead of angled lines from one data point to the next, step charts look like a staircase with 90-degree changes in direction.
Area	Area charts work best for showing change in the scale of data sets over time, including the relationship between additional data sets.
Bar	Bar charts compare data points individually. Because each data point represents a bar, bar charts work best for smaller data sets. A chart with a hundred individual bars can quickly become confusing.
Curve	Related to the line and step charts, curve charts use curved lines to connect data points.
Triangle, Cone, and Cylinder	Essentially just different permutations of a bar chart, triangle, cone, and cylinder charts show individual data points using different shapes.

In this chapter, you will build a ColdFusion application consisting of three pages: a form page, an action page that contains the CFCHART and CFCHARTSERIES tags, and a detail page. The ColdFusion application charts the tblParks table by the REGION or PARKTYPE columns. The tblParks table works very well for charts because of the large number of records.

Building the Form Page

The selectParkChart.cfm page serves as a form page in which users select the chart display options, including chart type, whether the chart should be 3D, and what database table to chart. When the user clicks the Submit button, his or her selections are passed to viewParkChart.cfm, which renders the chart.

To build selectParkChart.cfm, follow these steps:

1. Create a new ColdFusion page from the bookexample template, and save it as selectParkChart.cfm in the chap10 directory.

2. Place your cursor in the body section of the document window, and insert a FORM tag. In the Property Inspector for the FORM tag shown in Figure 10.4, enter **viewParkChart.cfm** in the Action text box. You will create this page in the next section. Select POST in the Method menu.

3. After making sure your cursor rests within the broken red line box, insert a table with four rows, two columns, and no border.

4. In the right-hand cell of the first table row, insert a menu using the List Menu button in the Forms toolbar of the Insert panel. A menu appears in the cell.

5. In the menu's Property Inspector, name the menu **groupSelect**, and click the List Values button. The List Values dialog box appears.

6. In the List Values dialog box shown in Figure 10.5, create two values, **By Region** and **By Park Type**. For the By Region entry, assign REGION as its label; for By Park Type, assign PARKTYPE as its label. Click the OK button. These values will be used in the SQL statement in viewParkChart.cfm to filter the database query.

7. In the right-hand cell of the second table row, insert another menu and name it chartType. Click the List Values button.

8. In the List Values dialog box, create four values labeled Bar Chart, Line Chart, Area Chart, and Pie Chart, as shown in Figure 10.6. For the values, enter **BAR**, **PIE**, **AREA**, and **LINE**, respectively. Click the OK button. These values will be used in the CFCHARTSERIES tag in viewParkChart.cfm to specify the chart type to render.

9. In the right-hand cell of the third table row, insert a radio group using the Radio Group button on the Forms toolbar of the Insert panel.

10. In the Radio Group dialog box, name the radio group select3D and create two radio buttons, as shown in Figure 10.7. Label the buttons Yes and No, and provide the same for the values. Click the OK button.

11. In the bottom table row, insert a Submit button.

12. In the left-hand table column, enter descriptions for each form control, as shown in Figure 10.8.

13. Save your work.

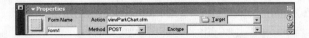

Figure 10.4 In the FORM tag's Property Inspector, you specify viewParkChart.cfm and the POST method. The selections made in the page will affect how the chart renders in the action page.

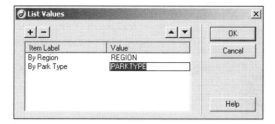

Figure 10.5 In the List Values dialog box, you can populate a menu by hand rather than using a recordset. This variable is passed to the action page, where it is used as a parameter in a CFQUERY statement.

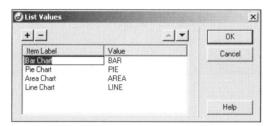

Figure 10.6 In another List Values dialog box, you create the necessary labels and values to let the user choose what type of chart to display.

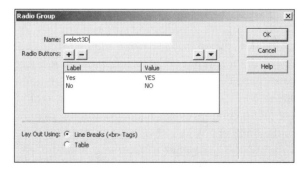

Figure 10.7 In the Radio Group dialog box, you can create multiple radio buttons at one time. All radio buttons created as a radio group share the same name, in this case select3D. The radio buttons let users select whether to display the chart in 3D.

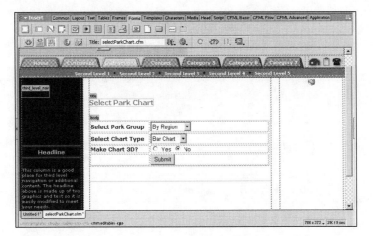

Figure 10.8   When finished, the selectParkChart.cfm page provides users with three controls to adjust what table column to chart, what kind of chart to display, and whether the chart will be three-dimensional.

Building the Dynamic Graph

The viewParkChart.cfm ColdFusion page serves as the action page to the form page selectParkChart.cfm. In viewParkChart.cfm, you create a recordset that contains advanced SQL, which groups the records and counts the number of records in each group.

As described in this chapter's introduction, charts work best for displaying large sets of numbers. However, the tblParks database table does not contain any columns in which all the records share common numeric identifiers. However, many of the records share common values in the PARKTYPE and REGION columns. That's because the majority of the parks are categorized by region and park type.

Many database tables contain words, such as names, addresses, and descriptions, in addition to numbers. When charting nonnumeric data sets, you must use the SQL in the CFQUERY statement to represent nonnumeric records, such as park names, as numbers. Usually, this is accomplished by using SQL commands to count the frequency of phrases in a recordset and then using that count as data points in the chart.

In SQL, you can group records by a column and count the number of records in each group. The records in the recordset consist of the group name and the numbers in that group, as shown in Figure 10.9.

Now that you have the recordset, you just need to create the chart itself. Using the CFCHART and CFCHARTSERIES tags, you build dynamic charts. The CFCHART tag sets the general display attributes for the individual graphs, each of which are created by a CFCHARTSERIES tag.

In the `CFCHARTSERIES` tag, you specify the recordset and recordset columns to use for the graph values and labels. You also specify the type of chart to create.

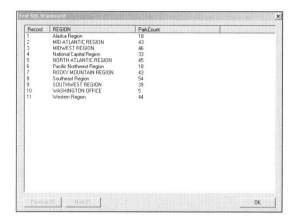

Figure 10.9 In the Test SQL Statement dialog box, which appears when you click the Test button in the Recordset dialog box, you see parks grouped by region and the number of parks in each region.

To build viewParkChart.cfm, follow these steps:

1. Create a new ColdFusion page from the bookexample template, and save it as viewParkChart.cfm in the chap10 directory.

2. Using the Bindings panel, create three form variables with the same names as the menus and radio buttons in selectParkChart.cfm: `groupSelect`, `chartType`, and `Select3d`.

3. Again using the Bindings panel, create a recordset named parkQuery. Select exampleapps in the Data Source menu, and select tblParks in the Table menu. Click the Advanced button.

4. In the Advanced layout mode of the Recordset dialog box, shown in Figure 10.10, modify the SQL in the SQL text area to appear as follows:

```
SELECT #form.groupSelect#, count(PARKNAME) as ParkCount
FROM tblParks
WHERE #form.groupSelect# <> NULL
GROUP BY #form.groupSelect#
HAVING count(PARKNAME) > 1
```

In the SQL, the `SELECT` statement uses the form variable `groupSelect`, which is passed from selectParkChart.cfm, to designate one of the table columns to return. The other column returned, `PARKNAME`, is not actually returned as a list of park names. The `count` SQL command counts the number of records using PARKNAME as the key. Keep in mind that the GROUP BY statement categorizes the records by either the PARKTYPE or REGION table columns.

The WHERE and HAVING statements further filter the recordset. The WHERE statement excludes any record in which the REGION/PARKTYPE column is blank. The HAVING statement excludes any group that contains less than one record, which makes the chart appearance cleaner. However, this filtering does remove some valid records.

If you want to keep all the records, just leave out the WHERE and HAVING statements.

Click the OK button.

5. In the Body section of the document window, insert a table with one column, two rows, and no border.

6. Place your cursor in the top table row, and click the View Code and Design Views button in the Document toolbar. The view splits between the Design View and the Code View.

7. Using your mouse, place your cursor after the first TD tag in the table HTML. In the CFML basic toolbar of the Insert panel, click the CFOUTPUT button. In the CFOUTPUT dialog box that appears, click the OK button. The opening and closing CFOUTPUT tags appear. You use the CFOUTPUT tags because you will make some of the tag attributes dynamic. Place your cursor between the opening and closing CFOUTPUT tags.

8. Right-click your mouse, and in the submenu that appears, select Insert Tag. The Tag Chooser dialog box displays.

9. In the Tag Chooser dialog box shown in Figure 10.11, select CFML Tags, cfchart. Click the Insert button. The CFCHART Tag Editor dialog box displays.

10. In the CFCHART Tag Editor dialog box shown in Figure 10.12, select flash in the File Format menu on the General page. Selecting flash as the file format lets you add URLs to a detail page, which you will create in the next section. For the purposes of this tutorial, you don't need to specify any other attributes on this page. If you don't need interactivity in your charts or if you know that users will not have the Flash Player installed, you can choose to generate the chart images as JPEG or PNG files.

11. In the Dimensions page, enter **"800"** for Chart Height and **"600"** for Chart Width. These values are in pixels, so this chart will dominate the page.

12. In the 3D Appearance page, click the Show 3D button. Even though you will make this value dynamic, this instructs the CFCHART tag dialog to include the attribute when it generates the code.

13. In the Labels page, enter **#Form.groupSelect#** for the X Axis Title. The form value will supply the label for the X axis. Enter **Number of Parks** for the Y Axis Title.

14. Click the OK button, and the opening and closing CFCHART tags, including the attributes that you set in the CFCHART dialog box, appear. In the show3D attribute, highlight Yes. Using the Bindings panel, select the select3D form variable, and click the OK button.

15. After making sure your cursor is between the opening and closing tags of the CFCHART statement, right-click again, and select Insert Tag. In the Tag Chooser dialog, select CFML, CFCHARTSERIES. Click the Insert button, and the CFCHARTSERIES Tag Editor dialog box appears.

16. In the CFCHARTSERIES Tag Editor dialog box shown in Figure 10.13, select any chart type in the Type menu. You'll make it dynamic later. Enter **parkQuery** for Query, and **#Form.groupSelect#** for Item Column. Enter **ParkCount** for Value Column. (You created the ParkCount column in the SQL.) Click the OK button. The CFCHARTSERIES tag with the attributes that you specified appears.

17. In the type attribute, highlight the value that you selected in the CFCHARTSERIES Tag Editor dialog box, and using the Bindings panel, insert the chartType form variable. Enter **#Form.groupSelect#** in the Series Label text box.

18. In the Design View, select the top table row with your mouse. In the Server Behaviors panel, click the plus (**+**) button, and in the submenu that displays, select Show Region, Show Region if Recordset is Not Empty. In the dialog box that appears, select the parkQuery recordset and click the OK button. A CFIF tab appears around the top table row. Using this server behavior, this table row, which contains the CFCHART and CFCHARTSERIES tags, will execute only when the parkQuery recordset contains records.

19. Place your cursor in the bottom table row and enter **No Records Found**. Using your mouse, select the bottom table row. Using the Server Behaviors panel again, apply a Show Region if Recordset Is Empty for the parkQuery recordset. If the parkQuery recordset does not contain any records, the table row will be displayed along with the message.

20. Save your work.

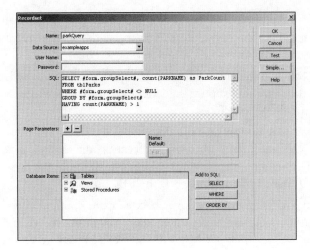

Figure 10.10 In the advanced layout of the Recordset dialog box, you create a relatively sophisticated SQL statement that groups the records and counts the number of records in each group.

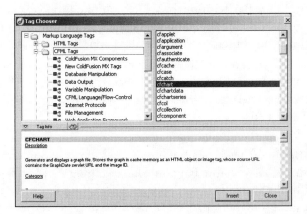

Figure 10.11 In the Tag Chooser dialog box, you can insert every tag in the CMFL language. The Tag Chooser also categorizes the CMFL tags by function, so you can easily find the tag that you need.

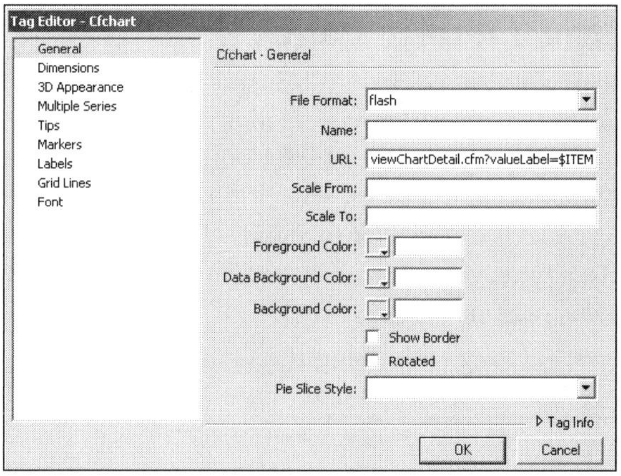

Figure 10.12 In the CFCHART Tag Editor dialog box, a number of pages exist to categorize the numerous CFCHART tag attributes.

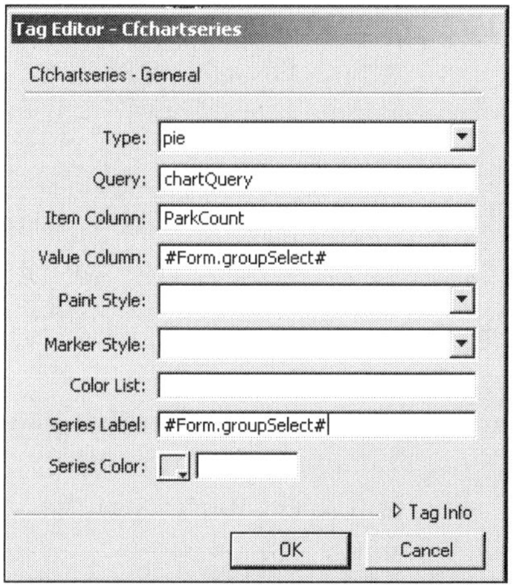

Figure 10.13 In the CFCHARTSERIES Tag Editor dialog box, you configure which query will be charted, what chart type will be displayed, and which recordset columns will supply the value and item chart columns.

Building the Details Page

In the CFCHART tag, you can specify a URL and special URL variables that, when the chart is rendered as a Flash movie, include a dynamic URL. When the user clicks on an individual chart entry, which translates to the itemColumn attribute of the CFCHARTSERIES tag, the web browser is directed to a details page.

You can use special URL variables to supply dynamic values to the details page. In the details page, you use the URL variables to filter a database query that displays the record's details.

1. Open viewParkChart.cfm. Using the Code View, add the following URL attribute to the CFCHARTSERIES tag:

   ```
   url="viewChartDetail.cfm?valueLabel=$ITEMLABEL$&type=$SERIESLABEL$"
   ```

   In the example, the URL references the viewChartDetail page, which you will create next. The URL variables valueLabel and type contain the ITEMLABEL and SERIESLABEL CFCHART variables, respectively.

   Notice that CFCHART variables use dollar signs ($) rather than hash signs (#), like normal ColdFusion variables. The ITEMLABEL variable translates to the label of the chart item clicked. The SERIESLABEL variable translates to the selectGroup form variable, which you supplied in the CFCHARTSERIES tag.

2. Click the OK button.

3. Create a new ColdFusion page from the bookexample template, and save it as viewChartDetail.cfm in the chap10 directory.

4. Using the Bindings panel, create two URL variables named valueLabel and type.

5. Again in the Bindings panel, create a recordset named chartQuery. In the Recordset dialog box, as shown in Figure 10.14, select exampleapps in the Data Source menu, and select tblParks in the Table menu. In the SQL text area, build the following SQL:

   ```
   SELECT PARKNAME, CITY, STATE, REGION, PARKTYPE
   FROM tblParks
   WHERE #URL.type#
   LIKE '%#URL.valueLabel#%'
   ORDER BY PARKNAME ASC
   ```

   In the SQL, notice the URL variable references. Because the LIKE constructor is used, you must enclose the valueLabel URL variable in single quotes (') and percent signs (%). The single quotes signify that the contents are text, and the percent signs indicate that any part of the contents can be considered a match.

6. Place your cursor in the Body section of the document. In the Application toolbar of the Insert menu, click the Dynamic Table button. The Dynamic Table dialog box appears.

7. In the Dynamic Table dialog box, select chartQuery in the Recordset menu, as shown in Figure 10.15. Select the All Records radio button in the Show section. Enter zero (0) for the border. Click the OK button. The dynamic table appears in the Body section.

8. Save your work.

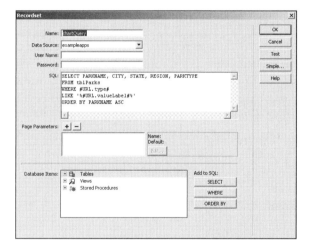

Figure 10.14 In the SQL in the Advanced Recordset dialog box, you reference the URL variables passed from the chart in viewParkChart.cfm.

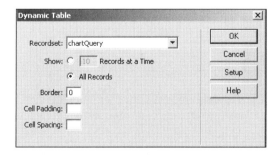

Figure 10.15 In the Dynamic Table dialog box, you can create a recordset-powered table that displays the results of a database query in just a couple of clicks.

Testing the Application

To test this application, use a web browser—Dreamweaver's Live Data View does not support Flash movies, thereby hamstringing your debugging efforts.

1. Open your web browser, and go to
   `http://localhost:8500/bookexample/chap10/selectParkChart.cfm`. The web browser displays the form page, as shown in Figure 10.16. The URL assumes that you are using the ColdFusion internal web server. If you are using IIS, the port number (8500) is not needed.

2. In selectParkChart.cfm, make your selections and click the Submit button. The viewParkChart.cfm page displays.

3. In viewParkChart.cfm you see the graph, as shown in Figure 10.17. Notice that a chart legend is automatically generated. Using your mouse, hover your cursor over the chart. As you see, pop-up messages provide details on charted elements. Click on a charted element. The viewChartDetail.cfm page displays.

4. In the viewChartDetail.cfm page, as shown in Figure 10.18, you see the dynamic table that was filtered based on which charted element you clicked in viewParkChart.cfm.

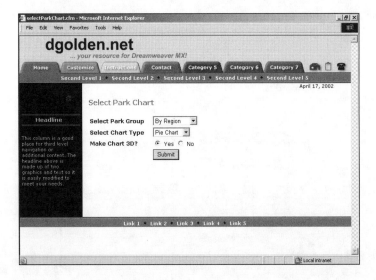

Figure 10.16   The selectParkChart.cfm page lets users configure the chart to their personal preferences.

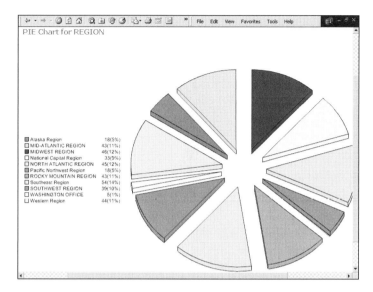

Figure 10.17 The viewParkChart.cfm page displays the chart. You can interact with the chart by hovering your cursor over and clicking on a charted element.

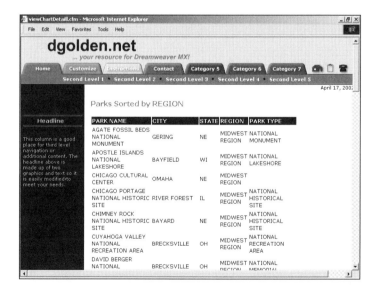

Figure 10.18 The viewChartDetail.cfm page displays a dynamic table, which is filtered on URL variables passed from the chart in viewParkChart.cfm, that shows detail park listings.

Summary

In this chapter, you learned how to use ColdFusion's charting feature to generate dynamic graphs from database records. In addition, you learned how to build dynamic links that connect data points in the chart to detail pages. In the next chapter, you will learn how to insert new records into the database.

IV

Processing ColdFusion Forms

11

Inserting a Record into the Database

WITHOUT THE CAPABILITY TO SAVE USER INFORMATION to a database, the web would be a very different place. Online shopping, user registration, secure authentication, and web-based email—the majority of interactivity expected in today's web sites—would simply not exist.

Despite the widespread opinion of the uninitiated that inserting records into databases is difficult, Dreamweaver MX and ColdFusion MX make the process quite simple. In fact, to insert a record into a database, ColdFusion requires only one tag, `CFINSERT`.

To learn more about databases, see Chapter 4, "Working with Databases."

Inserting Records

In this chapter, you will insert new employee information into the `tblEmployees` table. Using the Databases panel, look at the columns in the `tblEmployees` table. As shown in Figure 11.1, you can see which columns are available and what types of data they accept. For example, `DeptIDFK` accepts a character string no greater than 35 characters long.

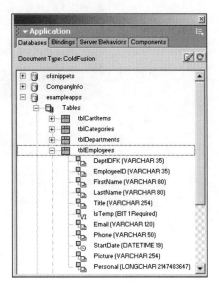

Figure 11.1 The Databases panel displays all data sources registered in the ColdFusion Administrator. Notice that each table column displays what kind and how large the saved data can be, such as [VARCHAR35].

Keeping that in mind, you can plan what information you want to gather and save to the database. To gather the user information you will build a wizard, which consists of a series of pages linked together. The first two pages in the wizard gather user information and forward the information to the confirmation page. In the confirmation page, the data entered by the user will be displayed side-by-side with the database record. The last page of the wizard inserts the information into a database. The following pages make up the wizard:

- insertWizardStart.cfm—Contains a dynamic text box in which the departments are displayed.
- insertWizardNext.cfm—Contains text boxes for first and last name, employee identification number, title, and permanent/temporary status.
- insertWizardConfirm.cfm—Displays the information that the user entered for confirmation, and inserts the record into the database.
- insertWizardFinal.cfm—Displays the results.

Figure 11.2 depicts the application structure for the employee registration wizard.

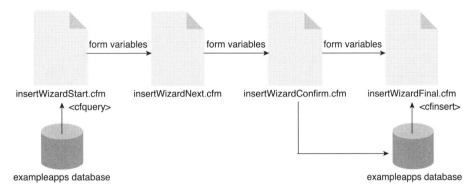

form variables   form variables   form variables

insertWizardStart.cfm   insertWizardNext.cfm   insertWizardConfirm.cfm   insertWizardFinal.cfm
▲ <cfquery>   ▲ <cfinsert>

exampleapps database   exampleapps database

Figure 11.2   A wizard consists of multiple linked pages. Only the third page actually inserts the record into the database.

Creating the First Wizard Page

Wizards gather user information across multiple pages and insert the combined set of information into the database. Therefore, you must transport user selections from page to page. To accomplish that, you use hidden form fields.

To start, you will create a page with a dynamic text box and pass its value to the next page. In this first page, the user will select the department for the new employee.

1. Create a new ColdFusion page from the book template, and name it **insertWizardStart.cfm**.

2. In the Server Behaviors panel, click the plus (+) button. In the submenu that appears, select Recordset. If the Recordset dialog appears in advanced mode, click the Simple button to display the simple layout.

3. In the Recordset dialog box, name the recordset **deptQuery**, as shown in Figure 11.3. In the Data Source menu, select exampleapps. In the Table menu, select tblDepartments. The tblDepartments database table contains only two columns, DepartmentName and DepartmentID, so keep the All radio button selected in the Columns section of the dialog box. Click the OK button. Recordset (deptQuery) appears in the Server Behaviors panel.

4. Place your cursor in the body section. Click the Form button in the Form tab of the Insert toolbar. The form box, made of a broken red line, appears. In the form Property Inspector, select POST in the Method menu. In the Action text box, type **insertWizardNext.cfm.** You'll create this page in the following section.

5. Make sure your cursor rests within the Form box. In the Common toolbar, click the Table button. The Table dialog box appears.

6. In the Table dialog, create a table with three columns and one row with no border. Click the OK button.

7. Back in the document window, place your cursor in the far left table cell, and enter **Select a department:**.

8. Using the Forms toolbar, insert a menu into the middle table cell. In the menu's Property inspector, name it **deptID**. The name will identify the value when it is passed to insertWizardNext.cfm.

9. Select the menu with your cursor. In the Server Behaviors panel, click the plus (+) button. In the submenu that appears, select Dynamic Form Elements, List Box/Menu.

10. In the Dynamic/List Menu dialog box, select deptQuery in the Options From Recordset menu, as shown in Figure 11.4. In the Values menu, select DepartmentID. You will pass this value to the next page. In the Labels menu, select DepartmentName. This value will be displayed in the list/menu box by ColdFusion. Click the OK button. The menu changes color to light blue and grows wider.

11. Place your cursor in the far right cell of the table. Using the Forms toolbar, insert a button. In the button's Property Inspector, change its label to Next.

12. Save your work.

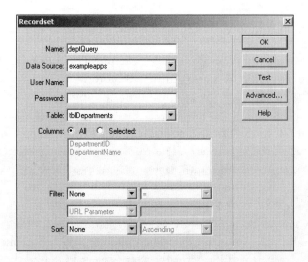

Figure 11.3   In the Recordset dialog box, you build the
deptQuery recordset. You want all columns in the table, so the
All radio button is selected in the Columns section.

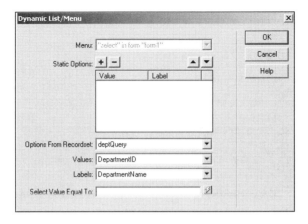

Figure 11.4 In the Dynamic List/Menu dialog box, you bind the deptQuery recordset columns to the Values and Labels menus. The form's value attribute will be passed to the next page in the wizard.

Creating the Second Wizard Page

In the second wizard page, you will create a number of text boxes with which the user will enter data. In addition, you will use a hidden form field to hold the form variable passed from insertWizardStart.cfm. You will also set up the page to insert the data collected in it into the database.

Before building the page, you should familiarize yourself with the database columns in the tblEmployees table of the exampleapps database. Table 11.1 contains the available columns and a brief description.

Table 11.1 *tblEmployees* Columns

Column Name	Description
DeptIDFK	Department ID, this value is passed from InsertWizardStart.cfm
EmployeeID	Employee ID, the user will enter this value
FirstName	Employee first name, the user will enter this value
LastName	Employee last name, the user will enter this value
Title	Employee tile, the user will enter this value
IsTemp	Yes (0) or no value (-1), the user will select a checkbox to indicate employment status
Email	Employee email address, the user will enter this value
Phone	Employee telephone number, the user will enter this value
StartDate	Employee hire date, the user will enter this value
Picture	Employee digital photograph file, not used in this wizard
Personal	Employee personal statement, not used in this wizard

Figure 11.5 shows the contents of the `tblEmployees` table before any records are added.

Building insertWizardNext.cfm consists of two parts:

1. Creating the user interface
2. Inserting the record into the database

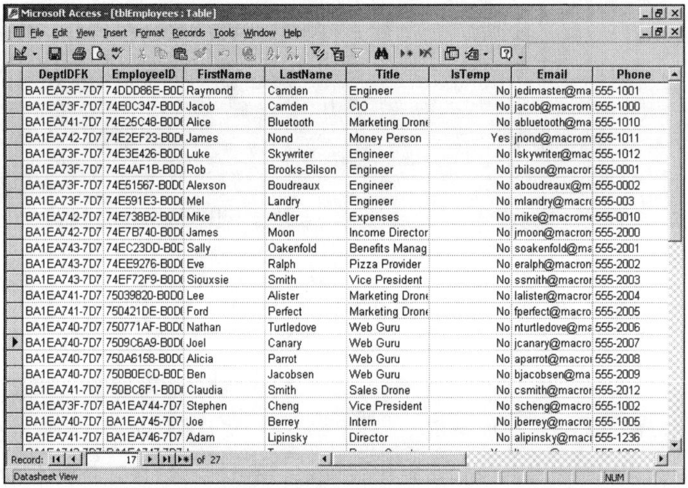

DeptIDFK	EmployeeID	FirstName	LastName	Title	IsTemp	Email	Phone
BA1EA73F-7D7	74DDD86E-B0D	Raymond	Camden	Engineer	No	jedimaster@ma	555-1001
BA1EA73F-7D7	74E0C347-B0D(	Jacob	Camden	CIO	No	jacob@macrom	555-1000
BA1EA741-7D7	74E25C48-B0D(	Alice	Bluetooth	Marketing Drone	No	abluetooth@ma	555-1010
BA1EA742-7D7	74E2EF23-B0D(	James	Nond	Money Person	Yes	jnond@macrom	555-1011
BA1EA73F-7D7	74E3E426-B0D(	Luke	Skywriter	Engineer	No	lskywriter@mac	555-1012
BA1EA73F-7D7	74E4AF1B-B0D	Rob	Brooks-Bilson	Engineer	No	rbilson@macror	555-0001
BA1EA73F-7D7	74E51567-B0D(	Alexson	Boudreaux	Engineer	No	aboudreaux@m	555-0002
BA1EA73F-7D7	74E591E3-B0D(	Mel	Landry	Engineer	No	mlandry@macr	555-003
BA1EA742-7D7	74E738B2-B0D(	Mike	Andler	Expenses	No	mike@macrom	555-0010
BA1EA742-7D7	74E7B740-B0D(	James	Moon	Income Director	No	jmoon@macron	555-2000
BA1EA743-7D7	74EC23DD-B0D	Sally	Oakenfold	Benefits Manag	No	soakenfold@ma	555-2001
BA1EA743-7D7	74EE9276-B0D(	Eve	Ralph	Pizza Provider	No	eralph@macron	555-2002
BA1EA743-7D7	74EF72F9-B0D(	Siouxsie	Smith	Vice President	No	ssmith@macror	555-2003
BA1EA741-7D7	75039820-B0D0	Lee	Alister	Marketing Drone	No	lalister@macror	555-2004
BA1EA741-7D7	750421DE-B0D(	Ford	Perfect	Marketing Drone	No	fperfect@macro	555-2005
BA1EA740-7D7	750771AF-B0D(	Nathan	Turtledove	Web Guru	No	nturtledove@ma	555-2006
BA1EA740-7D7	7509C6A9-B0D(	Joel	Canary	Web Guru	No	jcanary@macro	555-2007
BA1EA740-7D7	750A6158-B0D(	Alicia	Parrot	Web Guru	No	aparrot@macro	555-2008
BA1EA740-7D7	750B0ECD-B0D	Ben	Jacobsen	Web Guru	No	bjacobsen@ma	555-2009
BA1EA741-7D7	750BC6F1-B0D(	Claudia	Smith	Sales Drone	No	csmith@macror	555-2012
BA1EA73F-7D7	BA1EA744-7D7	Stephen	Cheng	Vice President	No	scheng@macro	555-1002
BA1EA740-7D7	BA1EA745-7D7	Joe	Berrey	Intern	No	jberrey@macror	555-1005
BA1EA741-7D7	BA1EA746-7D7	Adam	Lipinsky	Director	No	alipinsky@macr	555-1236

Figure 11.5 As seen in Microsoft Access, the `tblEmployees` table contains a variety of rows, not all of which are used in this wizard.

Creating the User Interface

For the most part, creating the user interface for a form that inserts a record into a database does not differ from any other web page. As you follow the steps to create the user interface, keep in mind that the contents of each text box will be inserted into the database:

1. Create a new ColdFusion page from the bookexample template, and save it as insertWizardNext.cfm.
2. Place your cursor in the body section of the document window and insert a `FORM` tag. In the `FORM` tag's `ACTION` attribute, type **insertWizardConfirm.cfm**, the last wizard page that inserts the record into the database.

3. Making sure your cursor rests inside the FORM tag box, insert a table with nine rows, three columns, and no border.

4. Insert a text field in each of the first eight cells of the middle column. Give each text field a name that corresponds to each database column, such as FirstName, LastName, and so on. To see the completed page, refer to Figure 11.6.

5. In one of the middle column cells, insert a menu and name it isTemp. Create two list items, Permanent with a value of 0 and Temporary with a value of a 1. The isTemp column asks the question, "Is this employee temporary?" So, if the employee is permanent, you want to store 0 for no. The isTemp database column contains Yes or No values, which also can be represented as 0 for yes and −1 for no.

6. In the left-hand column, enter the description for each text field. For examples, look at Figure 11.6.

7. In the right-hand column, enter a description for what the user should enter in each text field as you see fit.

8. In the bottom row, insert two buttons into the middle column cell. Make one button a Next button and the other button a Reset button.

9. Place your cursor in the left-hand column cell of the bottom table row. In the Forms toolbar of the Insert panel, click the Hidden Field button. The Hidden Field icon appears in the cell.

10. In the Bindings panel, click the plus (+) button. In the submenu that appears, select Form Variable. The Form Variable dialog box appears.

11. In the Form Variable dialog box, name the variable deptIDFK—the same name as the database column. This hidden field stores the department ID that the user selects in insertWizardStart.cfm.

12. In the hidden form field's Property Inspector, click the Lightning Bolt button, which displays the Dynamic Data dialog box. In the Dynamic Data dialog box, select the deptIDFK form variable, and click the OK button.

13. Save your work.

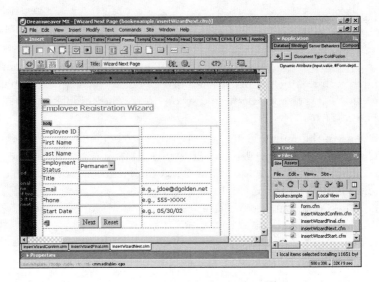

Figure 11.6   When complete, the insertWizardNext.cfm user interface contains a number of text fields, plus a hidden form field.

Creating the Confirmation Page

The confirmation lets users see the information that they entered in insertWizardNext.cfm. This page is intended to increase the accuracy of the data contained in your database. Although outside the scope of this chapter, you would also want to validate the data on the server, including verifying that the user entered the correct data format and querying the database for identical records. For more information about data validation techniques, see Chapter 7, "Validating Data and Handling Errors."

This confirmation page displays the form values passed from insertWizardNext.cfm and inserts the record into the database. If the user accepts the confirmation and clicks the Save button, the information is inserted into the exampleapps database, again using form variables.

Building the confirmation page requires three steps:

1. Create the confirmation page user interface.

2. Test the application.

3. Insert the record into the database.

Creating the User Interface

To create the confirmation page user interface, follow these steps:

1. Create a new ColdFusion page, and save it as insertWizardConfirm.cfm.

2. Place your cursor in the body section of the document window, and insert a FORM tag. You don't need to configure the ACTION or METHOD attributes in the Property inspector at this time. The Insert Record dialog will automatically populate attributes in the following steps.

3. Making sure your cursor rests within the form box, insert a table with 10 rows, 2 columns, and no border.

4. In the left-hand table column, insert descriptions of the form fields, just like you did in insertWizardNext.cfm. In the right-hand column, insert a text box for each form field and give each box a name that mirrors the corresponding database column, as shown in Figure 11.7.

5. For the isTemp variable, use a menu with a little CFML logic. If 1 is passed in the isTemp variable, you want to show Yes in the menu; if 0 is passed, you want to show No. Remember, the user will also be able to change the values in this page. Here is the code:

   ```
   <select name="isTemp" id="isTemp">

   <cfif form.isTemp EQ 1>
       <option value=1 selected>Yes</option>
       <option value=0>No</option>
   <cfelse>
       <option value=1>Yes</option>
       <option value=0 selected>No</option>
   </cfif>
   ```

   In the example, the SELECT tag contains a CFIF statement. The CFIF tag checks the isTemp variable to see whether it contains 1. If it does, two OPTION tags are executed with Yes selected. If the isTemp variable is not equal to 1, it must be equal to 0. The CFELSE tag executes the OPTION tags with No selected.

> **NOTE**
> You can use the Code and Design View to work directly with the code and see the page design at the same time.

6. Somewhere within the table, insert a hidden form field and name it deptIDFK. This field will contain the deptID variable passed from insertWizardNext.cfm.

7. In the Bindings panel, create nine form variables. Each form variable name should match the text box names in the insertWizardNext.cfm page.

8. In the right-hand table column, bind the form variables to the corresponding text boxes and hidden form field.

9. In the bottom table row, insert a button. In its Property Inspector, change the label to Save.

10. Save your work.

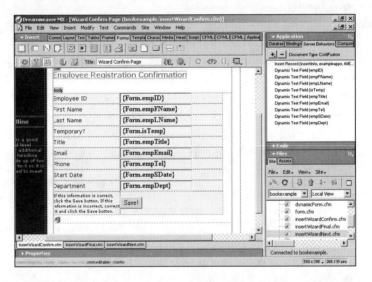

Figure 11.7 When complete, the insertWizardConfirm.cfm page contains a number of text fields, similar to insertWizardNext.cfm, to display the information entered in insertWizardNext.cfm.

Testing the Application

Before you build the page that inserts the record into the database, test the pages that you've built so far. To test applications that consist of more than two pages, it's usually easiest to use a web browser, just like your users will:

1. Open insertWizardStart.cfm in Dreamweaver, and in the Document toolbar, click the Preview/Debug in Browser button. As shown in Figure 11.8, the first wizard page displays.

2. In the menu, select Development and click the Next button. The insertWizardNext.cfm page displays.

3. In the second wizard page, enter information in the text fields, as shown in Figure 11.9. Click the Next button. The insertWizardConfirm.cfm page displays.

4. As you can see in Figure 11.10, the information that you entered in the insertWizardNext.cfm page displays.

Figure 11.8 In a web browser, you choose a department from the ColdFusion-powered menu.

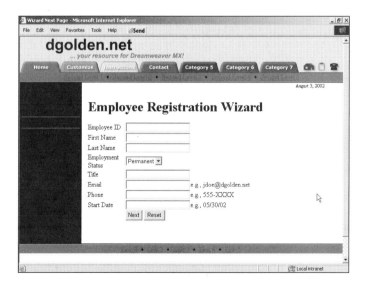

Figure 11.9 In a web browser, the user enters employee information in insertWizardNext.cfm. Notice that the deptID variable does not display because it is a hidden field.

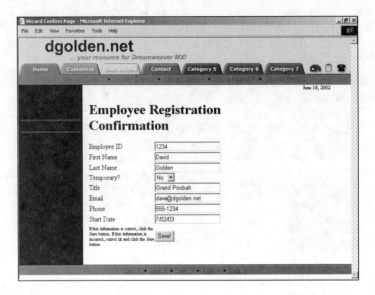

Figure 11.10   In insertWizardConfirm.cfm, the user sees the information
that he or she entered in insertWizardNext.cfm.

Inserting the Record into the Database

Now that you have built the user interface, you're ready to insert the information into the database. Dreamweaver and ColdFusion make inserting records very easy.

In the CFML code, the CFINSERT tag performs the record insertion. The CFINSERT tag offers a variety of optional attributes, but it requires only two attributes: datasource and tableName. The datasource attribute specifies the database to use, and tableName specifies the database table to use.

In Dreamweaver, you specify the datasource and table name in the Insert Record dialog box. To populate the column cells, you must supply the column names as form fields. The value entered in the form fields will be inserted into the database. You actually already did this when you named the form fields in insertWizardNext.cfm.

Working with Records

As described in Chapter 4, you should take care great care when inserting, deleting, and updating records in the database. If your database records contain inaccurate information, users will not use your application, which wastes all of your hard work.

Follow these steps to insert the form values from the insertWizardConfirm.cfm page into the `tblEmployees` table of the `exampleapps` database:

1. In insertWizardConfirm.cfm, place your cursor within the editable Body region of the document window. In the Server Behaviors panel of the Application panel group, click the plus (+) button. In the submenu that appears, select Insert Record.

2. In the Insert Record dialog box shown in Figure 11.11, select the data source and the database table, and match the form fields to the database table columns. In the Data Source menu, select exampleapps. In the Insert Into Table menu, select tblEmployees.

3. Using the Columns, Value, and Submit As menus, assign a form field to a database column, and designate the data type. If the form field names are the same as the database column names, Dreamweaver automatically matches the appropriate form field to the corresponding database column. If you used different names, select the database column that you want to receive a value, and in the Value menu, select the corresponding form variable.

4. Although most form fields can be submitted as Text, pay special attention to the `isTemp` and `StartDate` columns. In the `tblEmployees` columns in the Database panel of the Application panel group, notice that the `isTemp` column requires a `BIT` data type, and the `StartDate` column requires a `DATETIME` data type. The `BIT` data type translates to a ColdFusion Boolean type, which is 1 or 0. Some databases can also represent a Boolean as Y or N. In the Value menu for `isTemp`, you can select Numeric, Checkbox 1.0, or Checkbox MS Access. The `DATETIME` type translates to the ColdFusion date type. In the Value menu for `StartDate`, select Date or Date MS Access.

5. Click the Browse button next to the After Inserting, Go To text box. In the Select a Redirect File dialog box that appears, enter **insertWizardFinal.cfm** in the File Name text box. You will create this file in the next section.

6. Still in the Redirect File dialog box, click the Parameters button. In the Parameters dialog box, enter **deptIDFK** in the Name column. In the Value column, click the Lightning Bolt button that appears when you click the column. In the Dynamic Data dialog box that appears, select the `deptIDFK` form variable, and click the OK button. Click OK in the Parameters dialog box and the Redirect File dialog box.

Dreamweaver automatically generates a CFLOCATION tag that redirects the page after the database insertion. The URL parameter will filter a recordset in insertWizardFinal.cfm.

7. Click the OK button in the Insert Record dialog box.

8. Save your work.

In the Server Behaviors panel, an Insert Record entry appears, as shown in Figure 11.12.

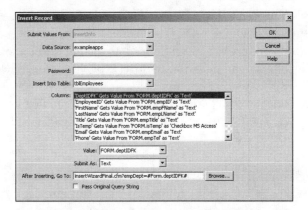

Figure 11.11   Using the Insert Record dialog, you bind database columns to the hidden fields that contain the information originally entered in insertWizardNext.cfm.

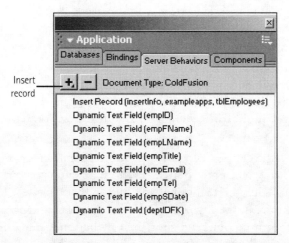

Figure 11.12   When you finish creating the Insert Record server behavior, an Insert Record entry appears in the Server Behaviors panel.

Creating the Final Wizard Page

The insertWizardFinal.cfm page lets a user see the record that he or she just inserted in the context of other departmental employees. To show the user the results of the record insertion, you will create a recordset that uses the empDept form variable to filter the query results. You will then build a table in insertWizardFinal.cfm that displays the query results.

You will need to create two recordsets: one to get the department name from the tblDepartments table and another to query the database for all employees working in the department in which the new employee was just added:

1. Place your cursor in the editable Body region of the document window, and insert a table with one row, two columns, and no borders.

2. In the Bindings panel, create a new recordset, named deptQuery, that queries the tblDepartments table and filters the results with the deptIDFK variable.

3. Place your cursor in the left table cell, and insert the FirstName column of the deptQuery recordset. In the right table cell, insert the LastName column.

4. Create another recordset, named resultQuery, that queries the tblEmployees table and filters the results using the form.empDept variable.

5. Using your mouse, select the whole table. Using the Server Behaviors panel, select Repeat Region. The Repeat Region dialog box displays. The Repeat Region Server Behavior dynamically creates a table row for each record contained in the resultQuery recordset.

6. In the Repeat Region dialog, select resultQuery in the Recordset menu. Select the All Records radio button in the Show section, as shown in Figure 11.13.

7. Save your work.

Figure 11.13 Using the Repeat Region dialog, you create a table row that is repeated for every record returned from a database query.

To learn more about the Repeat Region Server Behavior, see Chapter 8, "Displaying Records in a Dynamic Table."

When insertWizardFinal.cfm executes, it will use the form variables passed from insertWizardConfirm.cfm to insert the record into the database, and it will query the `tblEmployees` table to display current employees in the selected department, which should contain the new employee.

Summary

Congratulations, you have just built a ColdFusion application that saves new employee information into a database. In this chapter, you learned how to use form variables to pass information from one ColdFusion page to another. In addition, you learned how to use the Dreamweaver Insert Record behavior. To further develop this application, you could validate the data before submitting it to the database and handle database errors by displaying descriptive error messages. For more information about validation, see Chapter 7.

In the next chapter, you will learn how to update existing records in the database.

12

Updating a Record in the Database

I N THIS CHAPTER, YOU LEARN HOW TO update existing records in a database. Using the Update Record server behavior in Dreamweaver, which generates a CFQUERY statement, you can build a ColdFusion application that updates database records in a matter of minutes.

About Updating Records

Giving users the ability to update information stored on the server is critical to building an interactive web site. If you have ever changed your address online, you've updated records in a database.

In Dreamweaver, building a ColdFusion application that updates a database is very similar to building record insertion or deletion functionality. You use the Update Record server behavior, shown in Figure 12.1, which you access from the Server Behaviors panel in the Application panel group.

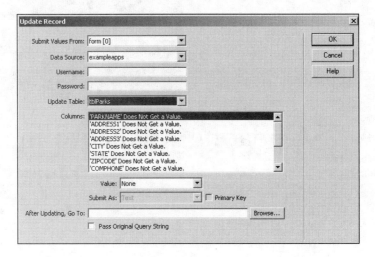

Figure 12.1 The Update Record dialog box gives you all the controls you need to update database records using ColdFusion.

The Update Record server behavior generates a CFQUERY statement that contains the SQL UPDATE command, as the following example shows:

```
<cfquery datasource="exampleapps">
    UPDATE tblParks
    SET ADDRESS1 = '#FORM.address1#'
    WHERE PARKNAME = '#FORM.name#'
</cfquery>
```

In the SQL, the UPDATE command references the tblParks table in the exampleapps database. The SET command names the table column to update and the variable to use in the update. The WHERE command locates the record to be updated.

At the same time, Dreamweaver generates additional code that makes updating records in the database more safe and reliable. For example, instead of just generating the standard SQL as in the previous example, Dreamweaver also provides CFIF statements to ensure that the updated data has been passed to the page, as the following example shows:

```
<cfquery datasource="exampleapps">
    UPDATE tblParks SET ADDRESS1=
    <cfif IsDefined("FORM.address1") AND #FORM.address1# NEQ "">
        '#FORM.address1#'
    <cfelse>
        NULL
    </cfif>
    WHERE PARKNAME = '#FORM.name#'
</cfquery>
```

In the code, a `CFIF` statement evaluates the form variable, which will be used to update the database, to make sure that it is present and contains a value. If it doesn't, a null value is entered in that table column.

> **Note**
> Dreamweaver also generates data validation code for inserting records and deleting records.

Remember, like any operations that modify databases, updating database records requires proper security precautions, such as user authentication. In addition, data type validation ensures that the information entered in the web browser is in the correct format.

For more information about building secure ColdFusion applications, see Chapter 17, "Building User Authentication." For more information about form validation techniques, see Chapter 7, "Validating Data and Handling Errors."

When you're planning to build a ColdFusion application that updates a database, you should put yourself in the role of the user. First, the user will need to see a list of records that can be updated. Once the user has selected the record to update, he or she needs a page in which to modify the record. After the user has modified the record to his or her liking, a confirmation page is always a good idea so that users can see what they entered. Finally, another page lets the user see the updated record. Therefore, this application requires four pages:

- displayParks.cfm—This page displays all records in the database table and lets users select a record to update.

- updateRecord.cfm—This page lets users edit the contents of the record selected in displayParks.cfm. Text boxes are populated automatically from the database.

- confirmUpdate.cfm—This page lets users see the information that they entered in the updateRecord.cfm page by displaying the new data using form variables and the old data using a filtered query.

- displayParksAfter.cfm—This page shows the updated record and provides a dynamic menu to edit another park record.

Figure 12.2 shows the files and their interactions with the database.

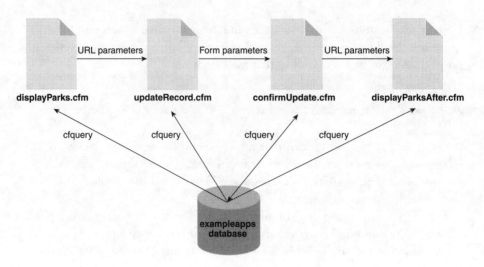

Figure 12.2 This ColdFusion application contains four pages. While each page interacts with the database, the third page actually updates the database.

To learn more about databases, see Chapter 4, "Working with Databases."

Building displayParks.cfm

The displayParks.cfm page lets the user select the park to update. It consists of a menu that contains all park names in the database table. The page will also check if records exist in the tblParks table. If no records exist, the drop-down menu will not be displayed and a message will appear that states that no records were found.

  To build the page, you create a simple form page that uses a dynamic menu to display the customer names from the database.

1. Create a new ColdFusion page from the bookexample template, and name it displayParks.cfm.

2. After placing your cursor in the Body section, insert a FORM tag. A broken-line red box appears.

3. In the FORM tag's Property Inspector, enter **updateRecord.cfm** in the Action text box. This page will be created in the next section. Select GET in the Method menu.

4. After making sure your cursor is inside the FORM box, insert a table with three rows, two columns, and no border. You'll insert the form objects for this page in this table.

5. Because we don't need more than one cell in the middle and bottom rows, merge the two cells in the middle row and then merge the two cells in the bottom row. In the top row, enter **Parks**. In the left-hand cell, and insert a menu into the right-hand cell.

6. In the Data Bindings panel, create a new recordset. As shown in Figure 12.3, name the recordset parkQuery. In the Data Source menu, select exampleapps. In the Table menu, select tblParks. In the Columns section, select PARKNAME. Click the OK button.

7. In the menu's Property Inspector, enter **selectedPark** for the name, and click the Dynamic button. The Dynamic List/Menu dialog box appears.

8. In the Dynamic List/Menu dialog box, select parkQuery in the Options From Recordset menu, as shown in Figure 12.4. In the Values and Labels menus, select PARKNAME. Click the OK button.

9. Insert a Submit button into the second row, and in the third row, enter **No Records Found!**

10. With your cursor, select the first two rows of the table. In the Server Behaviors panel, select Show Region if RecordSet is Not Empty. The Show Region if Recordset is Not Empty dialog box appears. Click the OK button.

11. Select the bottom table row and insert a Show Region if RecordSet Is Empty server behavior. This row will be displayed only if no records are found.

12. Save your work.

When finished, your ColdFusion page should appear similar to Figure 12.5.

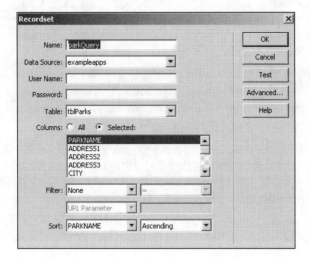

Figure 12.3 In the Recordset dialog box, you create a recordset that selects only the PARKNAME column of the tblParks table.

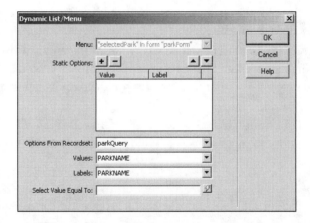

Figure 12.4 In the Dynamic List/Menu dialog box, you display and return the PARKNAME column.

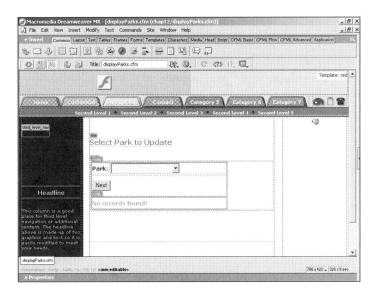

Figure 12.5 When finished, the displayParks.cfm page contains a simple menu, a button, and a Show Region server behavior.

Building updateRecord.cfm

In the updateRecord.cfm page, a ColdFusion query populates the text boxes in the page with the contents of a database record. Each text box maps to a specific column. Using the URL variable passed from displayParks.cfm, the database query is filtered to one record, which is displayed in the text boxes.

The user is free to edit the information in the text boxes. Until the Save button is clicked in confirmUpdate.cfm, the database remains unchanged. When the Next button is clicked on the updateRecord.cfm page, the edited information in the text boxes is sent to the confirmation page.

To build updateRecord.cfm, follow these steps:

1. Create a new ColdFusion page from the bookexample template, and name it **updateRecord.cfm**.

2. Place your cursor in the Body section, and insert a FORM tag. In the Action text box, enter **confirmUpdate.cfm**. You will create this page in the next section. In the Method menu, select POST.

3. Insert a table within the FORM tag box with eight rows, four columns, and no border.

4. In the Bindings panel of the Application panel group, click the plus (+) button, and in the submenu that appears, select Recordset (Query). In the Recordset dialog box shown in Figure 12.6, enter **parkQueryF** in the Name text box. Select exampleapps in the Data Source menu. You want to return all the columns in the table, so keep the All radio button selected. To filter the recordset, select PARKNAME equal to the URL Parameter selectedPark. There's no need to sort the recordset, because it contains only one record. Click the OK button.

5. Insert text boxes and descriptions. To make things easier, each text box name should correspond to the database column name it will update. For example, the PARKNAME column would map to the ParkName text box, the ADDRESS1 column would map to the Address1 text box, and so on. Be sure to leave an empty row at the bottom. Give each text box a descriptive name to identify the corresponding form variable.

6. Using the Bindings panel, bind each column in the parkQueryF recordset to the corresponding text box. The text boxes will turn light blue and the variable name will appear in the box background.

7. Using your cursor, select the first seven rows of the table. Insert a Show Region if Recordset is Not Empty server behavior for the parkQueryF recordset. Now, the text boxes will only appear if a record is returned from the database.

8. Select the bottom table row, and merge the table cells. After making sure that the row is still selected, insert a Show if Recordset Is Empty server behavior. In the row, enter the message **No Records Found!** This row will be displayed only if no records are returned from the database.

9. Insert a button labeled Next.

10. Save your work.

Your page should appear similar to the one shown in Figure 12.7.

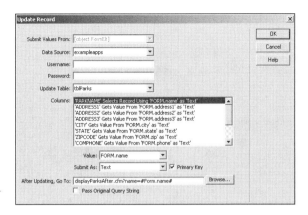

Figure 12.6 When you create the `parkQueryF` recordset, you filter the recordset to a single record using the `selectedPark` URL variable.

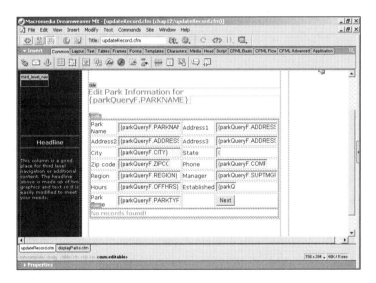

Figure 12.7 The updateRecord.cfm page contains a variety of dynamic elements, including text boxes and Show Region server behaviors.

Testing updateRecord.cfm

To test the updateRecord.cfm page, use the Live Data View, which re-creates what your page will look like in a browser. At the same time, you can still make changes to the page, just like in Design View. To open Live Data View, click the Live Data View button on the Standard toolbar.

For updateRecord.cfm to execute correctly, you must pass a `selectedPark` URL variable that contains a valid park name. You can do this in Live Data View using the Live Data Settings dialog box, as shown in Figure 12.8. The Live Data Settings dialog box lets you create form (`POST`) and URL (`GET`) variables.

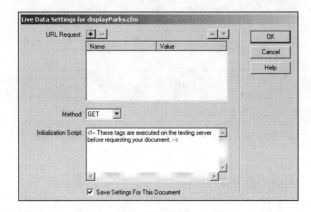

Figure 12.8   The Live Data Settings dialog box lets you create URL and form variables, as well as specify initialization scripts, such as setting application and server scope variables.

To test updateRecord.cfm, follow these steps:

1. After making sure that updateRecord.cfm is open, select the View menu, Live Data Settings.

2. In the Live Data View dialog box shown in Figure 12.9, click the plus (+) button. In the Name column, enter **selectedPark**. In the Value column, enter a name of a park from the `CFEXAMPLES` database, such as **ACADIA NATIONAL PARK**. Because this is a URL variable, make sure that GET is selected in the Method menu. Click the OK button.

3. In the Standard toolbar, click the Live Data View button. Depending on your computer's performance, Dreamweaver might pause for a moment before displaying the Live Data View. When it does display, you should see the text boxes populated with the park details, as shown in Figure 12.10.

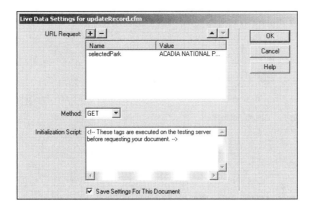

Figure 12.9 In the Live Data Settings dialog box, you re-create the `selectedPark` URL variable and supply a park name as its value. Make sure that you select GET in the Method menu.

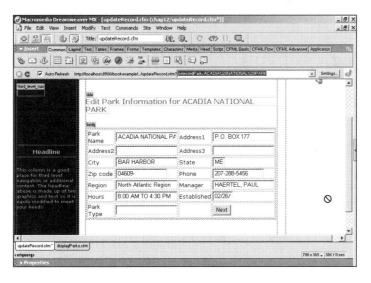

Figure 12.10 When properly configured, the Live Data View of the updateRecord.cfm page shows the page as it would appear in a user's web browser.

If the No Records Found message displays or if you receive an error, check the following areas:

- Make sure that the URL variable contains a valid park name, which you can check in the database.
- Check the parkQuery recordset to ensure that it is filtered by the selectedPark URL variable.
- Make sure you have saved updateRecord.cfm before using Live Data View.

After you get Live Data View working as expected, try different parks in the selectedPark URL variable to see how they display. Notice that some text boxes, such as Address2 and Address3, are not always populated. That's because not every record in the tblParks table contains a value for every column.

Also, if the width of your text boxes is too large or not large enough, you can change the values in the Property Inspector. The page will regenerate to show your changes.

Building confirmUpdate.cfm

The confirmUpdate.cfm page displays the information that the user updated in updateRecord.cfm. In updateRecord.cfm, you created a FORM tag that uses the POST method. In confirmUpdate.cfm, you will display the form variable values in the page. The user can see the information that he or she entered and confirm that the updated information is accurate before saving it to the database.

In addition, the confirmUpdate.cfm page contains the Update Record server behavior, which actually updates the database record. To use the Update Record server behavior, you must create placeholders using hidden form fields to store the updated data in the page. Figure 12.11 shows what the completed page will look like in Dreamweaver.

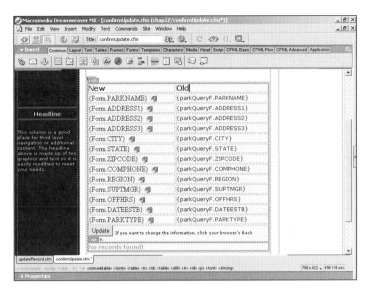

Figure 12.11   In confirmUpdate.cfm, in addition to updating the record in the database, you use form variables and recordset data to provide users with a confirmation page that lets them compare the updated information with the information stored in the database.

If you name the hidden form fields the exact name of the corresponding database columns, the Insert Record server behavior automatically binds the two together.

1. Create a new ColdFusion page from the bookexample template, and name it confirmUpdate.cfm.

2. Place your cursor in the Body section, and insert a FORM tag. Don't bother setting the ACTION and METHOD attributes; the Update Record server behavior does this for you.

3. Insert a table within the FORM tag box with 17 rows, 2 columns, and no border.

4. Create a recordset named parkQueryF. Filter the recordset using the FORM variable name passed from updateRecord.cfm.

5. In the top row, enter **New** in the left-hand column. In the right-hand column, enter **Old**.

6. In the cells below the New column, insert a form variable for each text box in updateRecord.cfm. Figure 12.12 shows the Bindings panel's listing of the form variables. In the cells below the Old column, insert the parkQueryF recordset column as dynamic text.

7. Beside each dynamic text element in the New column, insert a hidden form field, bind it to a form variable passed from updateRecord.cfm, and give it the same name as the corresponding form variable. Although invisible to the user, the hidden form fields store the updated data for the Update Record server behavior to use. The hidden form fields are also used by the Update Record server behavior to generate the necessary CFML.

8. Merge the cells in each of the last two table rows. In the second to last row, insert a Submit button.

9. In the last row, enter **No records found!**

10. Using your cursor, select the rows containing the column labels, dynamic text, and Submit button. Insert a Show Region if Recordset is Not Empty server behavior. If no recordset is present, the page user interface will not be displayed.

11. Select the last row with your cursor, and insert a Show Region if Recordset is Empty server behavior. If no recordset is generated, the error message **No records found!** displays.

12. In the Server Behavior panel, click the plus (+) button. In the submenu that appears, select Update Record. The Update Record dialog box appears.

13. In the Update Record dialog box shown in Figure 12.13, select examplesapps in the Data Source menu and tblParks in the Update Table menu. In the Columns listbox, the tblParks database columns are listed. Select each column, and bind the column to the corresponding form variable using the Value menu.

    Remember, the Update Record dialog box actually uses form elements to update the database. You supplied these in the form of hidden form fields. You must also select a database column to serve as the primary key that identifies the record to update. Choose PARKNAME because it is always unique for each record.

    Finally, click the Browse button next to the After Submitting Go To text box. In the Select a Redirect File dialog box, enter **displayParksAfter.cfm** in the File text box. You will create this file in the next section.

Next to the URL text box, click the Parameters button. In the Parameters dialog box, create a parameter called **name**, and bind the value to the form.name variable. This creates a URL parameter that the page passes to displayParksAfter.cfm to filter the database query.

Click the OK button in the Parameters, Select a Redirect File, and Update Record dialog boxes.

14. Save your work.

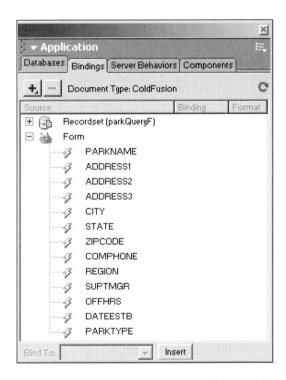

Figure 12.12   The Bindings panel lists the form variables to insert into the page. Notice that the names of the form variables mirror the names of the text boxes in updateRecord.cfm, which are the same as the column names of the tblParks database table. You can drop and drag form variables into the table cells in the page.

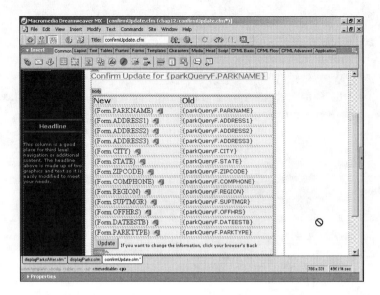

Figure 12.13 In the Update Record dialog box, you bind database columns to hidden form fields that contain the updated information. Notice that another hidden form field is created by the Update Record server behavior.

Building displayParksAfter.cfm

The displayParksAfter.cfm page displays the updated record and contains a dynamic menu to let users edit another record. It also contains four Show Region server behaviors, which provide the user with a descriptive message if no database records are found.

1. Create a new ColdFusion page from the bookexample template, and name it displayParksAfter.cfm.

2. Place your cursor in the Body section of the document window, and insert a FORM tag. In the FORM tag's Property Inspector, enter **updateRecord.cfm** in the Action text box, and select GET in the Method menu. This lets users select another park record to update in the dynamic menu and pass the selection to the updateRecord.cfm page as a URL variable.

3. After making sure that your cursor rests inside the FORM tag box, insert a table with 10 rows, 4 columns, and no border.

4. Create a recordset named parkQueryF. Like the parkQueryF recordset in confirmUpdate.cfm, this parkQueryF recordset selects all columns from the tblPark table and filters the results by the URL parameter passed by the Update Record server behavior in confirmUpdate.cfm.

5. By entering text and creating dynamic text from the parkQueryF record-set, make the page appear similar to the one shown in Figure 12.14.

6. Create another recordset named parkQueryNames from the tblParks table. Select only the PARKNAME column because it is the only column required.

7. Merge the cells in the third-to-last and last table rows. In those rows, enter the message **No records found!**

8. Using your mouse, select the third table row from the bottom. Using the Server Behaviors panel, insert a Show Region if Recordset Is Empty. In the Show Region if Recordset Is Empty dialog box, select the parkQueryF recordset. A cfif tab appears around the row.

9. Repeat the previous step for the bottom table row, except you should select the parkQueryNames recordset.

10. In the second-to-last table row, insert a menu and a Submit button. In the menu's Property Inspector, click the Dynamic button. Bind the Value and Display values to the PARKNAME column of the parkQueryNames recordset. The Value attribute will be passed to updateRecord.cfm as a URL variable.

11. Using your cursor, select the table rows containing dynamic text, and insert a Show Region if Recordset is Not Empty server behavior for the parkQueryF recordset. The cfif tab appears around the rows.

12. Using your cursor, select the row containing the dynamic menu, and insert a Show Region if RecordSet is Not Empty server behavior for the parkQueryNames recordset.

13. Save your work.

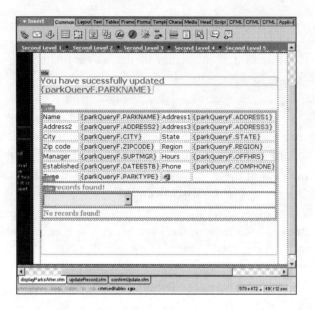

Figure 12.14   The displayParksAfter.cfm page contains dynamic text, a dynamic menu, and Show Region server behaviors.

Testing the Application

Located in the Results panel group, which spans the bottom of the Dreamweaver workspace, the Server Debug panel shows a graphical representation of the debugging information returned by ColdFusion. To open the Server Debug panel, select the Window menu, Results, Server Debug.

The Server Debug panel presents the information in a tree structure separated by debugging information type. For example, as shown in Figure 12.15, the General tree contains a broad range of information, such as the time stamp, the ColdFusion page's location, and the total execution time.

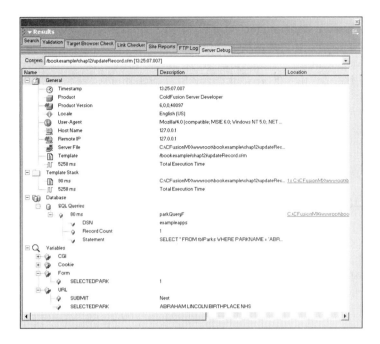

Figure 12.15   The Server Debug panel contains a graphical representation of the debugging information returned from ColdFusion. The General tree structure provides common information about page processing.

The Server Debug panel also works well for testing applications for errors or trying to track down a bug. When an error occurs, the panel shows an exclamation point and an error message. For example, when a form variable is not passed to a page that requires one, the Server Debug panel looks like Figure 12.16.

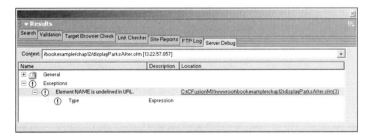

Figure 12.16   The Server Debug panel displays error messages produced by ColdFusion, such as missing parameters.

To use the Server Debug panel, you must turn on debugging in the ColdFusion Administrator and use the Server Debug view. The Server Debug panel is also useful for paging through an application to see what form and URL variables are passed, as well as the SQL statements executed.

Turn Off Debugging

Remember to turn off debugging, or restrict it to certain IP addresses, when you deploy your application. Your users will probably not want to see the details of application server processing.

Summary

In this chapter, you built a ColdFusion application that updates a database table. You also learned about the SQL required to update a database record and pass information between pages using form and URL variables. In the next chapter, you learn how to delete records.

13

Deleting a Record in the Database

Much like building ColdFusion applications that create and update database records, building a ColdFusion application that deletes records consists of building a series of pages. In this chapter, you use the Delete Record server behavior in Dreamweaver to create the necessary CFML.

Deleting Records

The records in the database are the heart of a dynamic web site, so letting users delete records on the server should make you nervous. You must carefully plan what users would want to delete. Proper security measures, such as role-based security, must be applied. For more information about building secure ColdFusion applications, see Chapter 17, "Building User Authentication."

In ColdFusion applications, user information is stored on the server as records in databases, such as username, password, name, email address, and so on. In previous chapters, you learned how to create and update records. The final piece to the database puzzle, deleting records, uses the Delete Record server behavior to generate the necessary CFML.

Although the Delete Record server behavior generates the necessary code automatically, you should be familiar with the details of the CFML. To delete a record in CFML, you use the DELETE FROM command within a SQL CFQUERY statement. When the database receives the SQL instructions, it deletes the record specified with FROM. You can filter the delete by adding WHERE. For example:

```
<cfquery datasource="exampleapps">
    DELETE FROM tblItems
    WHERE ItemID='#FORM.ItemID#'
</cfquery>
```

In this example, the DELETE FROM command references the tblItems table in the exampleapps data source. The SQL filters the recordset by the ItemID form variable.

Like the Insert Record and Update Record server behaviors, Dreamweaver also generates a CFIF statement for Delete Record that only executes the CFQUERY statement if a specific variable is passed. This protects your database records from inadvertent deletion. For example:

```
<cfif IsDefined("FORM.ItemID") AND #FORM.ItemID# NEQ "">
    <cfquery datasource="exampleapps">
        DELETE FROM tblItems
        WHERE ItemID='#FORM.ItemID#'
    </cfquery>
</cfif>
```

In the example, the CFIF statement checks for the existence of the ItemID form variable and determines whether it contains a value. If the variable is present, the CFQUERY statement executes.

In this chapter, you will build a ColdFusion application that lets users delete products from the product information page on the web site and the database. This application requires three pages:

- displayRecords.cfm—For users to delete records, they must first know what records are available for deletion. In this page, you will build a Repeat Region that displays the results of a database query.

- confirmDelete.cfm—This page will show users the records they picked to delete. The page will display the records chosen in the previous page, and it will also contain the code that actually deletes the record.

- displayRecordsAfter.cfm— This page will show the remaining records in the database. This page will also contain show-if regions that display messages according to the results of the delete.

Figure 13.1 shows the files and their interactions with the database. To learn more about databases, see Chapter 4, "Working with Databases."

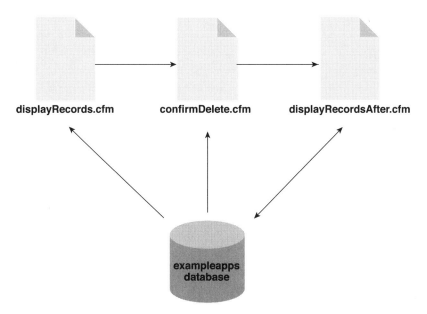

Figure 13.1   Each ColdFusion page interacts with the database, using the CFQUERY tag with different SQL statements.

Building displayRecords.cfm

The displayRecords.cfm page displays the product records available for deletion. To build the page, you create a simple form page that uses a dynamic table to generate the product list from the database. In each table row, you'll create a dynamic hyperlink that links to a detail page, confirmDelete.cfm.

To create displayRecords.cfm, follow these steps:

1. Create a new ColdFusion page from the bookexample template.

2. After placing your cursor in the editable Body region of the document window, insert a table with two rows, three columns, and no border.

3. Select the bottom row of the table, and right-click your mouse. In the submenu that appears, select Table, Merge Cells. In the cell that replaces the three cells, enter a message such as "**No records found!**".

4. In the Data Bindings panel, create a new recordset. In the Recordset dialog box that appears, name the recordset **itemQuery**, as shown in Figure 13.2. In the Data Source menu, select exampleapps. In the Table menu, select tblItems. Make sure the All radio button is selected in the Columns section. Click the OK button.

5. Using your cursor, select the top row of the table. In the Server Behaviors panel, select Repeat Region. In the Repeat Region dialog box that appears, select the itemQuery recordset and the All Records radio button, as shown in Figure 13.3. Click the OK button.

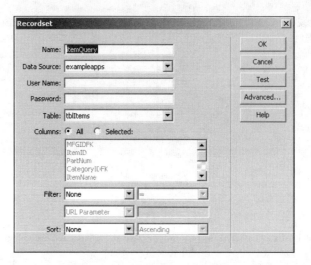

Figure 13.2 In the Recordset dialog box, you create a recordset that contains all of the records in the tblItems table.

Figure 13.3 Using the Repeat Region dialog box, the table that displays the results of the itemQuery recordset is elongated dynamically to accommodate the number of records exactly.

6. Place your cursor in the leftmost table cell. In the Common tab of the Insert bar, click the Hyperlink button. In the Hyperlink dialog box, enter **temp** in the Text text box. You'll supply the name from the itemQuery recordset later. Enter **confirmUpdate.cfm** in the Link text box. (You'll create confirmUpdate.cfm in the next section.)

7. Click the Parameters button. In the Parameters dialog box that appears, enter **itemID** in the Name column. In the Value column, click the Lightning Bolt button. In the Dynamic Data dialog box, select the ItemID column of the `itemQuery` recordset. This creates a URL parameter that passes the `ItemID` of the record selected to the detail page, confirmUpdate.cfm.

8. Click the OK button in the Dynamic Data, Select File, and Hyperlink dialog boxes. In the document window, the hyperlink appears as temp. With your cursor, highlight temp, and in the Bindings panel, select the ItemName column of the `itemQuery` recordset. Finally, click the Insert button, and temp is replaced with the dynamic text identifier `{itemQuery.itemName}`.

9. Place your cursor in the second table cell from the left. In the Bindings panel, select the itemDescription column, and click the Insert button.

10. Place your cursor in the far right table cell. In the Bindings panel, select the itemCost column, and click the Insert button.

11. Using your cursor, select the second table row in the document window. In the Server Behaviors panel, click the plus (+) button. In the submenu that appears, select Show Region, Show Region if Recordset Is Empty. In the Show Region if Recordset Is Empty dialog box, select the `itemQuery` recordset and click the OK button. In the document window, a CFIF tab appears around the table row.

    Now, the `No Records Found` message will display only if the `itemQuery` recordset is empty. You can also apply a Show Region if Server Behavior is Not Empty to the first table row in the document window. When done, the table row will display only if the `itemQuery` recordset contains records.

12. Save your work.

Your page should look similar to the one shown in Figure 13.4. Although simple, displayRecords.cfm generates a large amount of HTML when ColdFusion processes the Repeat Region.

Figure 13.4   The finished page contains a table and a few
form elements.

Testing the Page

Even though you have created only one page, it's always a good idea to test your
application as you build it. To test the page, click the Live Data View button in
the Document toolbar. The page should look like the one shown in Figure 13.5.

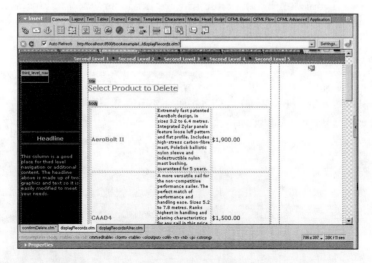

Figure 13.5   In Live Data View, the product list displays.

Building confirmDelete.cfm

The confirmDelete.cfm page serves as a confirmation for users to make absolutely sure that they want to delete this record. It displays the item or items that the user selected in displayRecords.cfm. To accomplish this, you will build a recordset that filters the records by the `itemID` URL variable passed from displayRecords.cfm:

1. Create a new ColdFusion page and name it confirmDelete.cfm.

2. Place your cursor in the Body section, and insert a `FORM` tag. In the Action text box, enter **displayRecordsAfter.cfm**. You will create this page in the next section. In the Method menu, select POST.

3. Insert a table within the FORM tag box with 10 rows, 2 columns, and no border.

4. Create a recordset named "itemQueryFiltered". In the Recordset dialog box, shown in Figure 13.6, select the exampleapps data source and the tblItems table. In the Columns section, click the Selected radio button and the following columns: ItemName, ItemDescription, ItemID, PartNum, CategoryIDFK, ItemCost, and Teaser. (You do not use the ItemImage column.) Filter the recordset using the **itemID URL** variable passed from displayRecords.cfm.

5. In the right table column, insert an itemQueryFiltered recordset column value into each cell.

6. In the left table column, enter descriptions for each column value, such as Manufacturer ID, Item Name, and so on.

7. In the ninth row, insert a Submit button and a warning message, as shown in Figure 13.7. After all, there's no going back once the button is pressed.

8. In the last table row, insert the message **No Records Found**. Next, using the Server Behaviors panel, apply the Show Region if Recordset Is Empty server behavior for the `itemQueryFiltered` recordset. This row will only display if the `itemQueryFiltered` recordset does not contain any records.

   You can also apply a Show Region if Recordset is Not Empty server behavior to the first nine rows of the table. When done, the rows will not appear unless the `itemQueryFiltered` recordset contains records.

9. Save your work.

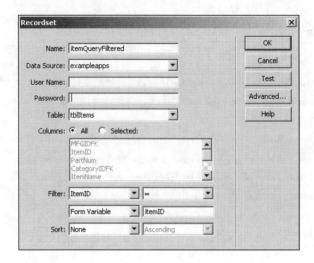

Figure 13.6 In the Recordset dialog box, you create the itemQueryFiltered recordset. You filter the recordset by the form variable passed from displayRecords.cfm.

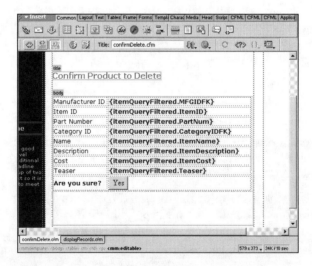

Figure 13.7 The finished deleteConfirm.cfm page contains a simple table with dynamic values of the record items.

Building displayRecordsAfter.cfm

The displayRecordsAfter.cfm page plays dual roles. From a user-interface perspective, it displays the contents of the tblItems table without the deleted record to show that the record is gone. From a database perspective, you include the CFML code that deletes the record selected in confirmUpdate.cfm.

The following two sections will help you build the displayRecordsAfter.cfm page.

Using the Delete Record Server Behavior

To build the code that deletes the record, follow these steps:

1. Create a new ColdFusion page from the bookexample template, and name it displayRecordsAfter.cfm.

2. In the Server Behaviors panel, click the plus (+) button. In the submenu that appears, select Delete Record. The Delete Record dialog box appears.

3. In the Delete Record dialog box, select Primary Key Value in the First Check If Variable Is Defined menu, as shown in Figure 13.8. The Primary Key Value, in this case the itemID form variable, identifies the record to delete. You can also specify the parameter that serves as the primary key. For example, if you select Form Parameter and enter **itemID** for the name, Dreamweaver creates a CFIF statement that executes the CFQUERY statement that evaluates whether the FORM parameter is present. This serves as a basic cautionary measure against accidental deletions.

4. Still in the Delete Record dialog box, select exampleapps in the Data Source menu. In the Table menu, select tblItems. In the Primary Key Column menu, select ItemID. This setting specifies the table column that identifies the record to delete. In the Primary Key Value menu, select Form Parameter and enter **itemID** for the name. This setting identifies the form variable passed from displayRecords.cfm.

   Leave the After Deleting, Go To setting empty. You just want to delete the record and stay on the same page.

5. Save your work.

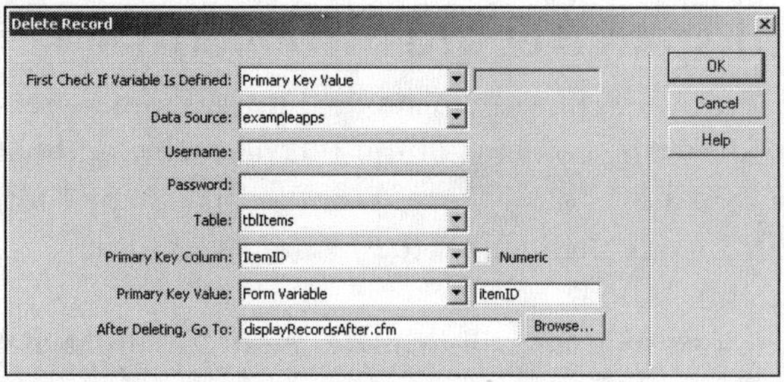

Figure 13.8 In the Delete Record dialog box, you provide the Primary Key column and the variable to specify which record to delete. In this page, you use the form variable passed from displayRecords.cfm.

If you want to build an error-handling feature that will display messages if the record deletion fails, you can use the Code View to insert a CFTRY/CFCATCH statement. You wrap the CFTRY statement around the CFQUERY statement that contains the SQL code to delete the record. For example:

```
<cfif IsDefined("FORM.ItemID") AND #FORM.ItemID# NEQ "">
<cftry>
    <cfquery datasource="exampleapps">
        DELETE FROM tblItems
        WHERE ItemID='#FORM.ItemID#'
    </cfquery>
    <cfcatch type="database">
        <p>A database error occurred. Here is the message:</p>

        <p><cfoutput>#cfcatch.Message</cfoutput></p>

        <p>Please contact the system administrator!</p>
    </cfcatch>
</cftry>
</cfif>
```

In the code, the CFTRY statement encloses the CFQUERY and CFCATCH statements. The CFCATCH tag specifies that database errors will be caught. Inside the CFCATCH statement, you can include HTML or CFML code to display a message. In the example, an error message is displayed that contains the variable cfcatch.Message, which displays the database error produced by ColdFusion. For more information about additional CFCATCH variables, see the ColdFusion documentation.

Building the User Interface

The displayRecordsAfter.cfm page's user interface consists of a dynamic table that displays a recordset containing the records in the tblItems table to show that the deleted record has been removed. The page also uses a Show Region server behavior to display page elements based on whether the recordset is empty. If the recordset is empty, it means that no records exist in the tblItems table. The Show Region server behavior also displays a message that describes the situation. If the recordset is not empty, the records are displayed in a dynamic table row. To create the interface, do the following:

1. Create a new ColdFusion page from the bookexample template, and name it displayRecordsAfter.cfm.

2. Place your cursor in the editable Body region of the document window, and insert a table with five rows, one column, and no border.

3. Create a recordset named itemQuery. Like the itemQuery recordset in displayRecords.cfm, the itemQuery recordset in this page selects all columns from the tblItems table in the exampleapps database, as shown in Figure 13.9.

4. In the top row of the table, enter **Remaining Records**.

5. In the Server Behaviors panel, click the plus (+) button. In the submenu that appears, select Display Record Count, Display Total Records. In the Display Total Records dialog box, select the itemQuery recordset, and click the OK button.

6. In the second table row, enter the message **No Records Found**. Using your mouse, select the second table row from the top. In the Server Behaviors panel, click the plus (+) button. In the submenu that appears, select Show Region, Show if Recordset Is Empty. In the Show Region if Recordset Is Empty dialog box, choose the itemQuery recordset, and click the OK button. A CFIF tab appears on the on the table row.

   Behind the scenes, Dreamweaver inserts a CFIF statement that evaluates the record count of the itemQuery recordset. If the record count is zero, the table row displays. If the record count is not zero, the table row doesn't display.

7. Using your mouse, select the next three table rows. Using the Server Behaviors panel, apply the Show Region if Recordset Is Not Empty server behavior. In the Show Region if Recordset Is Not Empty dialog box, choose the itemQuery recordset, and click the OK button. A CFIF tab appears around the three rows.

8. Select the middle of the three rows in the CFIF statement that you created in the previous step. Split the row into three columns. Also, apply the Repeat Region server behavior for the itemQuery recordset to the row. To see the completed page, refer to Figure 13.10.

9. In the leftmost cell, insert the item name using the Binding panel. In the middle cell, insert the teaser column. In the far right cell, insert the ItemCost column.

   If the itemQuery recordset contains one or more records, when ColdFusion processes the page, all records in the tblItem table are displayed.

10. In the last row, insert a hyperlink to displayRecords.cfm in case the user wants to delete another record.

11. Save your work.

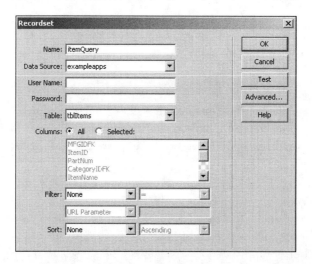

Figure 13.9   In the Recordset dialog box, you select all items in the tblItems table.

Figure 13.10   The finished displayRecordsAfter.cfm page
contains a number of dynamic elements, including a total
record count variable, conditional display logic,
and dynamic table rows.

Testing the Application

If debugging is turned on, ColdFusion returns valuable debugging information
in the HTML output. To enable debugging, follow these steps:

1. Open the ColdFusion Administrator and click on the Debugging
   Settings link.

2. In the Debugging Settings page, select the Enable Debugging check box,
   as shown in Figure 13.11.

3. Click the Submit Settings button.

With debugging enabled, ColdFusion appends processing information, such as
execution time, to the end of the HTML generated by a ColdFusion page. You
can see this information in a web browser or in the Server Debug tab of the
Results panel.

Turn Off Debugging

Remember to turn debugging off, or restrict it to a certain IP address, when you deploy your application.
Your users will probably not want to see the details of application server processing.

Figure 13.12 shows the debugging information ColdFusion returns when it processes displayRecords.cfm.

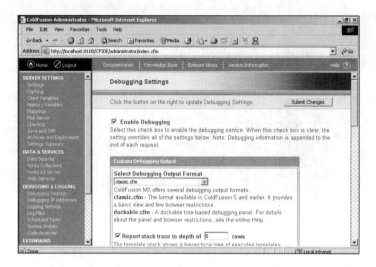

Figure 13.11 The Debugging Settings page of the ColdFusion Administrator lets you configure debugging settings, including enabling and disabling debugging output.

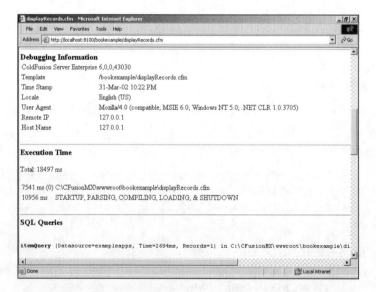

Figure 13.12 With debugging enabled, ColdFusion returns copious amounts of debugging information, including ColdFusion version number and SQL statements.

You can use the Debugging Settings page of the ColdFusion Administrator to customize debugging output and appearance to fit your needs. For example, if you select dockable.cfm in the Debugging Output Format setting, ColdFusion produces a pop-up window that contains the debugging output, as shown in Figure 13.13.

Figure 13.13   With dockable debugging output enabled, ColdFusion produces its debugging information in a separate browser window.

When the dockable debugging output is enabled, two links appear at the bottom of any web page generated by ColdFusion. The Debug Page link refreshes the debugging information for the page. The Docked Debug Pane integrates the pop-up window within the main browser page, as shown in Figure 13.14. When the debugging page is docked, the link in the main browser changes to Floating Debug Pane.

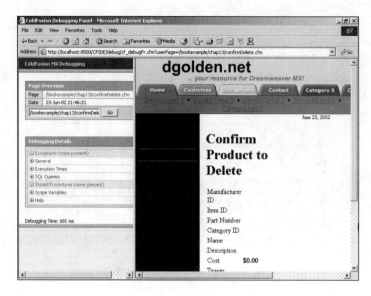

Figure 13.14   When docked, the debugging pane shows the same
information as the floating version.

Summary

In this chapter, you learned how to build a ColdFusion application that deletes
records from the database. Dreamweaver's Delete Record server behavior
handles most of the basic coding for you by automatically generating the
necessary CFML and SQL. You also used the Show Region server behaviors
to selectively display areas of the page. In the next chapter, you learn how to
use CFML to solve common programming problems.

V

Common ColdFusion
Programming Techniques

14

Conditional Logic
Problems and Solutions

O NE OF THE BIGGEST ADVANTAGES TO USING a full-fledged programming language for web application development is the capability to use flow conditional processing to generate dynamically the content of a page. Although it's possible to use only SQL queries to generate dynamic content in a linear fashion directly from a database, the conditional logic capabilities of a programming language can add immeasurably to the flexibility of your application. Most programming languages have conditional logic constructs such as if-then-else and switch statements, and ColdFusion is certainly no exception. CFML has special tags defined that can be used for application flow control.

In this chapter, you will learn how to use the CFML flow control tags to perform conditional processing in an application. CFML provides tags for standard programming logic, including if-elseif-else, switch, and loop logic.

Using conditional logic tags to control execution flow based on an expression gives you great flexibility in generating dynamic content. It is possible to generate very different page content depending on the data you are presenting. For example, an e-commerce application may need to generate an image tag if a picture of a product is available—or not if one isn't. Another possibility is to display an "out of stock" message only if a particular item cannot be found in the inventory. Figure 14.1 shows several common conditional logic structures. This chapter will present an overview of the flow control tags provided by ColdFusion MX. It consists of the following sections:

- Introduction to conditional logic
- Using CFIF, CFIFELSE, and CFELSE
- Using CFSWITCH, CFCASE, and CFDEFAULTCASE
- Using CFLOOP and CFBREAK
- Using conditional logic in your application
- Testing the application

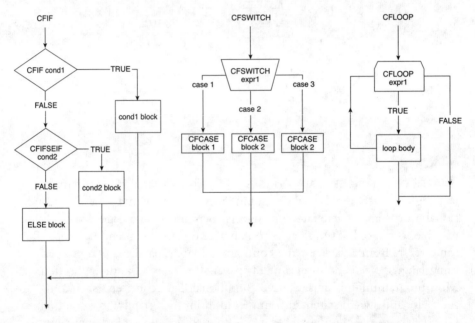

Figure 14.1   The flow control diagrams shown here demonstrate the conditional execution tags covered in this chapter, including CFIF, CFSWITCH, and CFLOOP.

CFML Conditional Logic Overview

CFML provides several different sets of tags that provide conditional logic on a page. Table 14.1 lists them.

Table 14.1   **CFML Flow Control Tags**

Tag Group	Purpose
CFIF/CFELSEIF/CFELSE	Evaluates any expressions and branches based on the result.
CFSWITCH/CFCASE/ CFDEFAULTCASE	Evaluates an expression and branches to the code block representing that value, if any. The default case is chosen if no other case is a match.
CFLOOP/CFBREAK	Repeatedly loops through the same block of code, depending on the result of one of five potential exit criteria.

The next part of this chapter will go into more detail on these tags and how to use them.

Using *CFIF*, *CFELSEIF*, and *CFELSE*

The most commonly used conditional logic element is known as an if-then-else block. It is used to evaluate an expression and execute the code inside its main block if the expression evaluates to a true value.

CFML provides the CFIF tag for this task. The basic format of the CFIF tag is as follows:

```
<cfif expression>
     <!-- Code executed if the expression is true-->.
</cfif>
```

Although this is useful, suppose you want to choose either of two code blocks to execute depending on the value of the expression—one for a true result and one for a false result. Although you could have two CFIF blocks—one comparing the value of expression to true and another comparing it to false—it's not neccesary. CFML has another tag, CFELSE, that not only allows you to write less code, it also saves server CPU processing time because the expression in the CFIF statement needs to be evaluated only once.

```
<cfif expression>
     <!-- Code executed if the expression is true-->.
<cfelse>
     <!-- Code executed if the expression is false-->.
</cfif>
```

That's not the end of what you can do with CFIF because the CFIF statement can also be used to evaluate multiple expressions in a row. The CFELSEIF tag can be inserted after the block of code executed directly by the CFIF statement in order to have another expression evaluated if the initial expression is false.

```
<cfif expression 1>
     <!-- Code executed if expression 1 is true-->.
```

```
<cfelseif expression 2>
       <!-- Code executed if expression 2 is true-->.
<cfelse>
       <!-- Code executed if all prior expressions are false. -->.
</cfif>
```

CFIF/CFELSE Example

The following example shows CFIF being used to evaluate a value returned by a query. The CFIF case is used to display a message if the query doesn't return any entries.

```
<cfif #UserSearch.RecordCount# is 0 >
       <!-- Display message indicating none found -->
       <P>Sorry, no users were found.</P>
<cfelse>
       <!-- Show the list of users -->
       <cfoutput Query="Users">
             #Username#: #LastName#, #FirstName#. Email: #Email# <BR>
       </cfoutput>
</cfif>
```

Using *CFSWITCH, CFCASE,* and *CFDEFAULTCASE*

The CFIF tag is useful for conditional execution when the expression evaluates to a true or false value. But what if the expression could evaluate to several possible values? These are very common—you might want to look at possible values of a form field, or the return value of a function that could return several possible values.

Although you could compare the result of the expression to a particular value in a series of CFIF-CFELSEIF tags, CFML provides another flow control mechanism that makes it cleaner and more efficient to execute code conditionally depending on the result of such an expression.

The CFSWITCH tag evaluates an expression and then executes the code specified by the CFCASE tag that matches the result of the expression. The following list shows the syntax of the CFSWITCH and CFCASE tags.

```
<cfswitch expression="expression">
       <cfcase value="value 1" delimeters="delimeters">
             <!-- Code executed for value 1-->.
       </cfcase>
       <cfcase value="value 2" delimeters="delimeters">
             <!-- Code executed for value 2-->.
       </cfcase>
       <cfdefaultcase>
             <!-- Code executed for default case -->.
       </cfdefaultcase>
</cfswitch>
```

You can see from this code that the CFSWITCH and CFCASE statements have several attributes, which are listed in Table 14.2.

Table 14.2 **CFSWITCH and CFCASE Attributes**

Attribute	Req/Optional	Purpose
expression	Required	A CFSWITCH attribute that results in a scalar value such as a string or numeric value.
value	Required	A CFCASE attribute which provides one (or more) possible values with which to compare the result of the expression. If the value matches, the code contained in the CFCASE block is executed.
delimiters	Optional	The CFCASE attribute can be used to specify one or more characters to use as a separator if the value attribute contains more than one value. Defaults to a comma (,) if not present.

Using the *CFDEFAULTCASE* tag

If none of the CFCASE values match the result of the expression, you may want to do something anyway. You may have noticed the CFDEFAULTCASE tag in the previous syntax listing. It works like the CFCASE tag, but it doesn't have a value attribute. Instead, the code contained in its body is executed whenever no other CFCASE value matches the result of the CFSWITCH expression.

Evaluating an Expression with *CFSWITCH*

This example shows the CFSWITCH tag used in a hypothetical big Internet bookstore, which also happens to sell videos and CDs. The example displays a different output depending on the type of item returned from a query.

```
<cfoutput query = "GetItemType">
<cfswitch expression = #Type#>
     <cfcase value = "Books">
          #Title# is a book<br><br>
     </cfcase>
     <cfcase value = "DVD">
          #Title# is a DVD<br><br>
     </cfcase>
     <cfcase value = "CD">
          #Title# is a CD<br><br>
     </cfcase>
     <cfdefaultcase>
          Warning: #Title# has an undefined type.<br><br>
     </cfdefaultcase>
</cfswitch>
</cfoutput>
```

Using *CFLOOP* and *CFBREAK*

One common task in applications is to be able to execute the same block of code multiple times in a row.

Although this can be done by simply repeating the same block of code several times in a row on the page, this makes the page bigger and less efficient because all that code has to be loaded into memory to interpret it. It also doesn't allow the code to be executed a variable number of times. Code maintenance becomes a problem as well, because the programmer has to remember to change every instance of that block.

Programming languages such as CFML offer looping as a solution. CFML provides the CFLOOP tag, which can be used for no less than five different types of loops: index loops, conditional loops, looping over a query, looping through a list or file, and looping over a COM collection. These five different types of loops allow the CFLOOP tag to serve the same purpose as several different types of loops in other languages, including do–while, for–next, and for each loops. This section describes each of these different loops.

Looping with an Index

The first mode of the CFLOOP tag is to emulate a for-next loop of other programming languages by using an index set to an initial value and counting up or down to a final value. Each time the index is changed, the code contained in the tag is executed. The following is the syntax of the CFLOOP with an index.

```
<cfloop
     index = "parameter_name"
     from = "beginning_value"
     to = "ending_value"
     step = "increment">
     <!-- HTML or CFML code to execute -->
</cfloop>
```

The index mode of the CFLOOP tag has several attributes, as described in Table 14.3.

Table 14.3   **CFLOOP Index Mode Attributes**

Attribute	Req/Optional	Purpose
index	Required	This is set initially to the from value, and represents the current index value.
from	Required	The starting value of the index.
to	Required	The ending value of the index.
step	Optional	A value used to increment (or decrement) the index value. If not provided, the default step is 1.

Conditional Loops

Like a `CFIF` tag, the `CFLOOP` conditional mode evaluates an expression and executes the code in the body of the tag. The difference, of course, is that once the code has been executed, the expression is re-evaluated to see whether it should be executed again. This form of `CFLOOP` is similar to a `while` loop in other programming languages. The following is the syntax of the `CFLOOP` evaluating a conditional statement:

```
<cfloop
     condition = "expression">
     <!-- HTML or CFML code to execute -->
</cfloop>
```

The only attribute used for conditional execution is the `condition` attribute. The value of this attribute should be an expression such as a function call or a comparison involving a variable.

The following example shows a `CFLOOP` used to execute a conditional loop until a function returns a different value:

```
<cfset Result=0>
<cfloop
     condition = "Result NOT EQUAL 0">
     <cfset Result=MyFunctionThatDoesSomthing()>
</cfloop>
```

Looping over a Query

Looping over items in a recordset returned by a query is another useful function of the `CFLOOP` tag. This can be accomplished by using this general syntax:

```
<cfloop
     query="query_name"
     startRow="row_num"
     endRow="row_num">
</cfloop>
```

The following example shows a query defined and a `CFLOOP` used to loop through the rows and output the names of users logged in to a hypothetical application:

```
<cfquery name = "UsersLoggedIn"
     dataSource = "userdatasrc">
     SELECT * FROM UserTable WHERE loggedin='true'
</cfquery>
<cfloop query - "UsersLoggedIn">
     <cfoutput>#UsersLoggedIn.LastName#,
     #UsersLoggedIn.FirstName#</cfoutput><br>
</cfloop>
```

Looping over a List

A somewhat more mundane use of the CFLOOP tag is to loop through the values in a list (returned by an expression) or a file. The following shows the syntax of the CFLOOP tag when it is used to loop over a list or file:

```
<cfloop
      index = "index_name"
      list = "list_items"
      delimiters = "item_delimiter">
      <!-- CFML or HTML code to execute -->
</cfloop>
```

Table 14.4 lists the attributes that CFLOOP supports while when looping over a list.

Table 14.4 **CFLOOP List or File Loop Attributes**

Attribute	eq/Optional	Purpose
index	Required	The variable that holds the list values as they are looped over.
list	Required	The filename or variable that contains the list to loop over.
delimiters	Optional	A list of characters separating items in the list. A comma (,) is used by default.

It's often useful to loop through a file, doing something (such as displaying) each line of the file. To use CFLOOP in this manner, simply use Carriage Returns and Linefeeds as the delimiter characters, as shown in this example:

```
<cfloop index="line"
      list = "logfile"
      delimiters = "#chr(10)##char(13)#"
      <!-- do something with the line here -->
</cfloop>
```

Looping over a COM collection or structure

COM (Component Object Model) and DCOM (Distributed COM) objects are binary objects that usually are written in C++ or Visual Basic. They provide a standard interface that allows these objects to be called from higher-level languages such as CFML and VBScript in server-side applications.

Programming COM/DCOM objects is beyond the scope of this book, but it should be noted that the CFLOOP tag provides a way to loop over the elements of a collection or structure exposed by a COM object.

The following example shows how a COM object with a class id of Scripting.FileSystemObject (a standard object used to work with files) could be used. First, the CFOBJECT tag is used to create an instance of the COM object, with CFSET being used to set values in the COM object. This example lists all the drives on a system using the Drives collection.

```
<cfobject
        class = "Scripting.FileSystemObject"
        name = "myFSO"
        action = "CREATE">
<cfset myDrives = FSO.Drives>
<cfloop collection=#myDrives# item="drive">
        <cfoutput>Drive letter: #drive.DriveLetter#
                volume name: "#drive.VolumeName#<br>
        </cfoutput>
</cfloop>
```

CFBREAK

The CFBREAK tag works in conjunction with the CFLOOP tag. CFBREAK is used to abort the execution of the loop at that point—no further code is executed.

A typical use for CFBREAK would be to loop through the items in a list, looking for a particular one. After that item is found, the list doesn't need to be searched any more. Here is an example using this tag:

```
<!-- loop through query, use CFBREAK to exit when search term is found -->
<cfloop query="Products">
  <cfif Products.product_desc contains form.searchword>
    <cfoutput>
      <h4>Product found:</h4>
      <b>#product_name#: #product_desc#</b>
    </cfoutput>
    <cfbreak>
  </cfif>
</cfloop>
```

Using Conditional Logic in Your Application

Dreamweaver MX makes it easy to add ColdFusion MX conditional logic to your application. When you create a ColdFusion document, the Insert bar adds three categories specifically for adding CFML tags to your page. One of these is the CFML Flow panel, and it includes items for all the conditional logic tags mentioned in this chapter. Figure 14.2 shows the CFML Flow panel of the Insert bar.

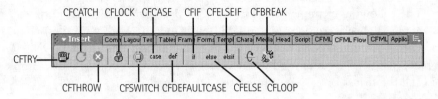

Figure 14.2 The CFML Flow panel of the Insert bar is an easy way to add CFML conditional logic tags to your document.

Adding a *CFIF* tag

Dreamweaver simplifies the task of creating CFIF, CFELSEIF, and CFELSE tags. Follow these steps to add a CFIF tag to a document:

1. Using the Site Panel, create a new ColdFusion page from the bookexample template, and name it Conditionals.cfm.

2. Place your cursor in the Body editable region in Design view or Code view.

3. In the CFML Flow Panel of the Insert Bar, click the CFIF button. The Code View will open if it is not already open, and the CFIF and it's closing tag will be inserted. The cursor will be placed inside the CFIF tag, where you can type in the expression to evaluate. This is shown in Figure 14.3.

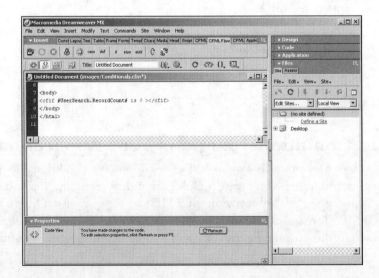

Figure 14.3 When you add a CFIF tag using the CFML Flow panel, the Code view is opened, and the opening and closing tags are entered at the current cursor location.

To add a CFELSEIF or CFELSE tag, you can position the cursor before the closing CFIF tag, and click the appropriate button in the CFML Flow panel. The tag will be inserted at the cursor position. Note that this tag insertion is not smart—the tag is inserted wherever you have the cursor positioned, even if it's in the middle of another tag. Position the cursor carefully.

CFIF Example

This example will use the tblEmployees table from the exampleapps database used in previous chapters. This example shows the CFIF, CFIFELSE, and CFELSE tags to process the output of a CFOUTPUT tag using a query.

To start, define the query and use it with the query attribute of the CFOUTPUT tag:

```
<cfquery name="EmployeeQuery" datasource="exampleapps">
    select * from tblEmployees
</cfquery>
<cfoutput query="EmployeeQuery">
    Last Name: #LastName#, First Name: #FirstName#, Department:
```

Next, the CFIF block is used to display different output depending on the result of the evaluated expressions.

```
        <cfif Title is "Engineer">
            Engineering
        <cfelseif Title is "Web Guru">
            Web Development
        <cfelseif Title contains "Manager">
            Management
        <cfelse>
            Other
        </cfif>
    </cfoutput>
```

Adding a *CFSWITCH* tag

Adding a CFSWITCH tag using Dreamweaver MX is much the same as with the CFIF example. However, Dreamweaver gives you a little more control over the process in this case. Follow these steps to add a CFSWITCH tag:

1. Using the Site Panel, create a new ColdFusion page from the bookexample template and name it SwitchExample.cfm.

2. Place your cursor in the Body editable region in Design view or Code view.

3. In the CFML Flow Panel of the Insert Bar, click the CFSWITCH button. The Tag Editor dialog box opens, prompting you to enter the expression that should be evaluated by the CFSWITCH. This is shown in Figure 14.4.

4. To enter CFCASE and CFDEFAULTCASE values, click the appropriate button on the CFML Flow Panel. In the case of CFCASE, the Tag Editor dialog box opens once again, prompting you to enter the value to be compared, as well as any delimiters you may want to use.

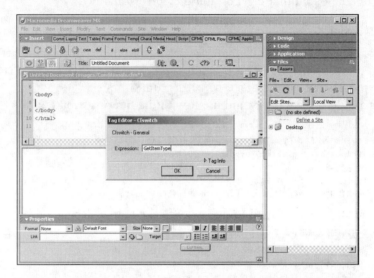

Figure 14.4   The Tag Editor dialog box is activated when you add a CFSWITCH tag to a document. Here, you can enter the expression that the CFSWITCH should evaluate.

CFSWITCH Example

The previous example can also be written using the CFSWITCH tag. This can be more efficient than the CFIF example because the expression is evaluated only once.

```
<cfquery name="EmployeeQuery" datasource="exampleapps">
    select * from tblEmployees
</cfquery>
<cfoutput query="EmployeeQuery">
    Last Name: #LastName#, First Name: #FirstName#, Department:
    <cfswitch expression=#Title#>
        <cfcase value="Engineer">
            Engineering
        </cfcase>
        <cfcase value="Web Guru">
            Web Development
    </cfcase>
    <cfcase value="Manager">
        Management
    </cfcase>
```

```
        <cfdefaultcase>
            Other
        </cfdefaultcase>
        </cfcase>
    </cfoutput>
```

Adding a *CFLOOP* tag

The CFLOOP tag is the most complex of the CFML flow control tags, considering the five different uses. Because of this, using Dreamweaver to set the options is particularly helpful. Follow these steps to add a CFLOOP tag:

1. Using the Site Panel, create a new ColdFusion page from the bookexample template and name it.

2. Place your cursor in the Body editable region in Design view or Code view.

3. In the CFML Flow Panel of the Insert Bar, click the CFLOOP button. The Tag Editor dialog box opens, prompting you to choose the type of CFLOOP you want. This is shown in Figure 14.5.

4. Choose a Loop Type. You can choose from any of the five CFLOOP types: Index, Conditional, Query, List, and Collection. The attributes displayed will be the appropriate ones for the type.

5. Enter values for the attributes.

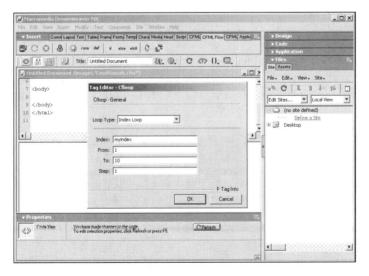

Figure 14.5 The Tag Editor dialog box for the CFLOOP tag shows you the attributes appropriate for the Loop Type you choose.

If you want to add a CFBREAK tag to a loop, you can do so with Dreamweaver as well. Simply put the cursor at the position you wish to add the CFBREAK (using the Code View), and click the CFBREAK button on the CFML Flow Panel.

CFLOOP Query Example

This example, like the previous one, uses the tblEmployees table from the exampleapps database. In this example, you will use two nested CFLOOP tags to display a table containing a list of employees. The output will consist of three columns. So, the outer CFLOOP will generate the columns and the inner CFLOOP will display the data from the query in those columns.

To start, you need to define a query. In this case, for simplicity's sake, get all columns from the tblEmployees table.

```
<cfquery name="EmployeeQuery" datasource="exampleapps">
    select * from tblEmployees
</cfquery>
```

Next, define the outer loop. In this case, we know that we want three columns, so add a CFLOOP tag. Because the data will be displayed in columns, we'll add a table for formatting. In addition, we define two variables for the start and end items in the query for this column.

```
<table><tr>
<cfloop index="colindex" from="1" to="3" step="1">
    <cfset start= colindex*10 - 9>
    <cfset end=start+9>
```

The inner loop is now used to display the items in a column. We'll use another CFLOOP tag, this time the Query type.

The start and end variables defined earlier are used as the startrow and endrow attribute values of the CFLOOP. In addition, after the start variable is used to set startrow, it can be modified. Here we will use it to display the row number.

```
        <td valign="top">
        <cfoutput>
        <center><b>Column #colindex#</b></center>
        <cfloop query="EmployeeQuery" startrow=#start# endrow=#end#>
            #start#.  #LastName#, #FirstName#<br>
            <cfset start=start+1>
        </cfloop>
        </cfoutput>
        </td>
        </cfloop>
    </tr></table>
```

Figure 14.6 shows the example in the Dreamweaver editor in both Code view and Design view. Notice that Dreamweaver shows a placeholder value for all variables that the CFOUTPUT displays, and the CFLOOP tags are shown as invisible elements (if you have the Invisible Element visual aid turned on. (Go to Check View, Visual Aids, Invisible Elements to turn it on.)

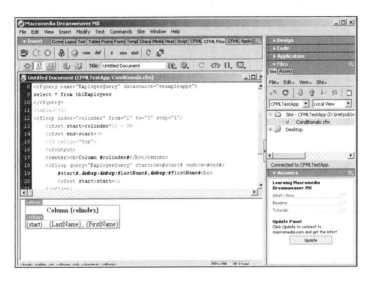

Figure 14.6 Conditional Logic tags are invisible elements. The Dreamweaver Design view can provide helpful representations of the elements so you can see at a glance how they fit into the flow of the page.

Testing the Application

Testing an application with conditional logic is no different from testing files in previous chapters. The Preview in Browser button will launch the web browser.

Any CFML tags are executed by ColdFusion before the resulting page is displayed, allowing you to see the page as a site visitor would see it.

The Preview in Browser button launches your web browser and directs it to the appropriate page. Figure 14.7 shows how the code for this section's example is displayed in the web browser.

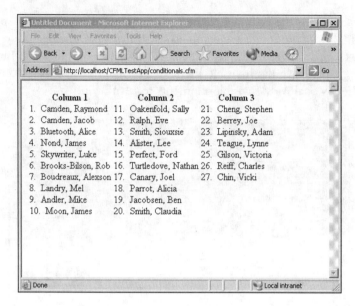

Figure 14.7   Conditional processing is done by ColdFusion before a page
is sent to the web browser. The result in this case is a table displaying a
number of records from a query.

If you completed all the steps in the previous section without receiving an
error, the ColdFusion application should work. However, if you receive
an error or the page doesn't display correctly, check the following areas:

- Make sure that the file has been saved.
- Make sure that ColdFusion is running by opening the ColdFusion
  Administrator. If it displays, ColdFusion is working.
- Check the Server Behaviors Panel for exclamation points next to the list
  of inserted behaviors. If you see an exclamation point, double-click that
  behavior and fix the problem.
- Verify the exampleapps data source in the ColdFusion Administrator's
  Data Sources page. You should receive a verification message.

Summary

In this chapter, you learned how to use the CFML conditional logic tags to
control the processing flow of an application. You learned how to use the
CFIF/CFELSEIF/CFELSE, CFSWITCH/CFCASE/CFDEFAULTCASE, and CFLOOP/CFBREAK tags
to generate dynamic content by evaluating expressions and variables. In the
next chapter, you will learn about debugging and error handling in
ColdFusion MX and Dreamweaver MX.

15

Debugging and Error Handling

IT'S PRETTY EASY TO DEVELOP A ONE- OR TWO-PAGE static web site using an HTML editor. Without the dynamic data-driven capabilities of a server-based application, there isn't a whole lot that can go wrong that is outside of your control.

However, when it comes to using a modern technology such as ColdFusion MX to create a large data-driven application, the debugging and error-handling capabilities of the development environment can be very effective in increasing developer productivity and code quality.

Fortunately, ColdFusion and Dreamweaver MX give you a lot of options when it comes to debugging and error handling in your applications. This chapter will show how you can take advantage of them.

This chapter consists of the following sections:

- Introduction to ColdFusion and Dreamweaver debugging and editing features
- Using ColdFusion MX debugging and error-handling features
- Using Dreamweaver MX debugging and error-handling features

Introduction to Debugging and Error Handling

Debugging an application occurs primarily during development. It's important not only for finding errors in your code and solving problems, but also for just understanding exactly what the code is doing. It's worthwhile to debug every page of an application and look at the debugging output at least once so that you can search for any behavior or inefficiency that you might not have anticipated when writing the code.

Disabling Debugging

Although debugging features are essential during development and can be helpful when you have problems in production, you don't want to leave debugging enabled all the time. Debugging output should usually be disabled on production servers. Disabling debugging output can help secure your site by ensuring that users can't see debugging information that could be misused by malicious lurkers. You will also see increased server performance if debugging is disabled. If you do find it necessary to debug an application on a production server, ColdFusion allows you to enable debugging only for certain IP addresses. This option is described later in this chapter.

Although debugging is primarily a development tool, proper error handling is another story. One of the keys to creating robust web applications is to make the best use of error-handling capabilities possible. Good error handling is an indication of professional site design and can influence how users feel about the site and whether they will return.

The key to this is to make sure that any errors that occur are as invisible to the end user as possible. This is accomplished by recognizing that some errors are out of your control. You need to take into account such things as database connectivity failure, and provide a seamless way to redirect the user somewhere else when errors do occur.

Using ColdFusion MX's Debugging and Error-Handling Features

ColdFusion MX provides extensive debugging and error handling capabilities, so it can be a bit overwhelming to decide where to start. This section will show you how to configure your ColdFusion Application Server to provide exactly the error and status information that you need. You will also see how to use CFML's error-handling tags in your pages.

Using the ColdFusion Administrator Debugging Settings Page

The place to begin when discussing ColdFusion MX's debugging features is the Debugging Settings section of the Administrator. This page is where you enable debugging, select items to monitor, enable performance monitoring, and more. The Debugging Settings page is shown in Figure 15.1.

Hint

Remember, the default location for the ColdFusion Administrator login page is:

`http://servername/cfide/Administrator/index.cfm`

Replace *servername* with the IP address or fully qualified domain name of the web server. If running locally, the server name is commonly localhost or 127.0.0.1. If running locally on Windows, you can also access the Administrator through the Start menu.

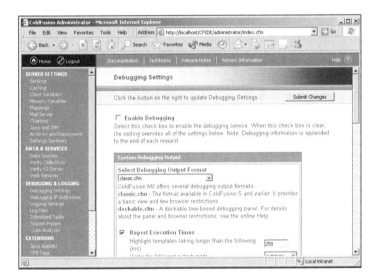

Figure 15.1 The ColdFusion Administrator Debugging Settings page is the starting point for configuring all server debugging options.

Table 15.1 lists the options on the Debugging Settings page:

Table 15.1 **Administrator Debugging Settings Page Options**

Setting	Description
Enable Debugging	This option enables or disables the debugging output. If this option is not checked, no debugging information is collected or displayed. Debugging is off by default.

continues

Table 15.1   **continued**

Setting	Description
Select Debugging Output Format	This option sets how debugging output is displayed. There are two options: classic.cfm provides a format similar to previous versions of ColdFusion. The debugging information is appended to the end of the page being debugged. Dockable.cfm is new to ColdFusion MX and uses DHTML to display debugging information in a separate window using an expandable tree.
Report Execution Times	This option can help you find pages with slow response times. All page execution times will be reported, and you can also set a threshold value so that all execution times that exceed the value will be displayed in red. You can also specify a summary or a more detailed tree-based display. This option is selected by default.
Database Activity	This option can be checked to enable reporting of all SQL database activity. This option is selected by default.
Exception Information	This option causes any exceptions raised in a request to be reported. This option is selected by default.
Tracing Information	This option displays an entry for every CFTRACE tag in an application. CFTRACE can override this setting with the inline attribute. CFTRACE is described in more detail later in this chapter. This option is selected by default.
Variables	Selecting this option allows ColdFusion variables to be displayed. Suboptions allow specific variable scopes to be enabled or disabled, including Application, CGI, Client, Cookie, Form, Request, Server, Session, and URL. All are selected by default, with the exception of Application, Server, and Request. Variables is selected by default.
Enable Robust Exception Information	This option specifies the information that should be displayed on the exception error page. Enabling this option causes the page to display the following when appropriate: the path and URL of the page that caused the error, the line number and the surrounding code, SQL statements and data sources, and a Java stack trace. This option is selected by default.
Enable Performance Monitoring	On Windows NT- and 2000-based servers, this option enables standard NT performance counters that display information about the ColdFusion Application Server. This option is cleared by default.
Enable CFSTAT	This option enables the use of ColdFusion's CFSTAT command-line utility for performance monitoring. CFSTAT displays the same performance information as the NT performance monitoring utility (Perfmon).

Using the Debugging IP Addresses Page

By default, debugging messages are only displayed to local users (those using the local IP address 127.0.0.1). It is possible that you will want to allow debugging messages to be displayed for other users, say the development machine if the ColdFusion server is running remotely. On the Debugging IP Address page of the ColdFusion Administrator, you can specify additional IP addresses. You can also disable debugging for the local user by removing the local IP address. The Debugging IP Address page is shown in Figure 15.2. If all IP addresses are removed from the list, debugging messages are sent to all users.

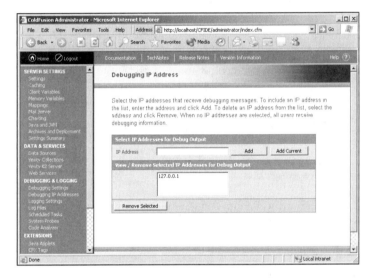

Figure 15.2   The Debugging IP Address page allows you to limit debugging messages to browsers accessing your site from specific IP addresses.

To add a new debugging IP address to the list, launch the ColdFusion Administrator and follow these steps:

1. Select the Debugging IP Addresses link from the menu on the left.

2. Enter an IP address that you want to receive debugging messages.

3. Click Add. As an alternative, you can skip Step 2 and simply click Add Current to add the IP of the current machine.

To remove an IP address from the list, do the following:

1. Select an IP address from the list.

2. Click Remove Selected, and verify that the IP is no longer on the list.

Using and Understanding Debugging Information

Whether you choose the classic ColdFusion debugging window, which is appended to the bottom of the page you are debugging, or the new dockable tree display, which opens in a separate window, the debugging information is the same. This debugging output, a sample of which is shown in Figure 15.3, is displayed every time a page request is completed.

The dockable tree display has some advantages. It allows you to collapse the sections of the debugging information in which you aren't interested. It can also appear in a separate window, which in some cases may be preferable. The classic ColdFusion debugging window is still useful, though, because it can be used on a wider variety of browsers.

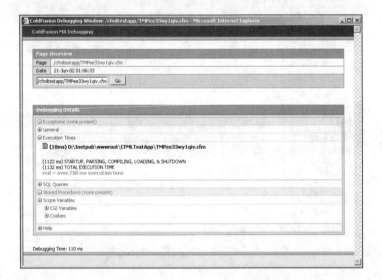

Figure 15.3   ColdFusion MX's dockable debugging window shows up in a separate window from the page you are debugging and has a collapsible tree view to make it easy to use.

The debugging window is divided into several sections. In the dockable display, it is displayed as a tree view with each section collapsed to make it easier to find the section that interests you. Each section shows a different aspect of the server status.

Exceptions

The Exceptions debugging category (shown in Figure 15.4) shows information about any exceptions thrown during page processing. These include application-defined exceptions as well as ColdFusion exceptions caught by the page. Exceptions and how to handle them are covered in more detail in the later section, "CFTRY/CFCATCH Syntax."

Figure 15.4 The Debugging Output's Exceptions section shows information about any exceptions that have occurred.

General

The General debugging category shows information relating to the version of the server and the browser. This section is shown in Figure 15.5. The values displayed in the General section are as follows:

- ColdFusion server version
- The locale and language used for message output
- The user agent (browser) type and version that is making the request
- The IP address of the client making the request
- The host name of the machine running the ColdFusion server

Figure 15.5 The Debugging Output's General section shows information about both the client and server environments.

Execution Times

The Execution Times section, shown in Figure 15.6, gives information about how much time it took to process the request, including times for each of the pages processed during the request. Any request that uses an additional page, including the Application.cfm file, custom tags, and any CFINCLUDE included files, will have those pages listed in the Execution Times section.

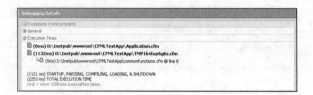

Figure 15.6   The Debugging Output's Execution Times
section shows a tree view with processing times for all files
accessed during a request.

SQL Queries and Stored Procedures

For pages that execute SQL queries or stored procedures, the next two choices in the debugging window give some performance information related to them.

The SQL Queries section displays the following items:

- File name of the page from which the request was made, including the time that the request was made
- Name of the query (from the CFQUERY tag); if the query is cached, that will be displayed next to the name
- The text of the SQL statement
- The datasource name
- The number of records returned
- The query execution time

The stored procedures section displays some of the same data, along with some other information specific to stored procedures:

- Instead of a query name, the stored procedure name is displayed.
- Parameters for the procedure are displayed in a table, specified with CFPROCPARAM tags.
- A table containing procedure result sets returned, as specified in the CFPROCRESULT tag.

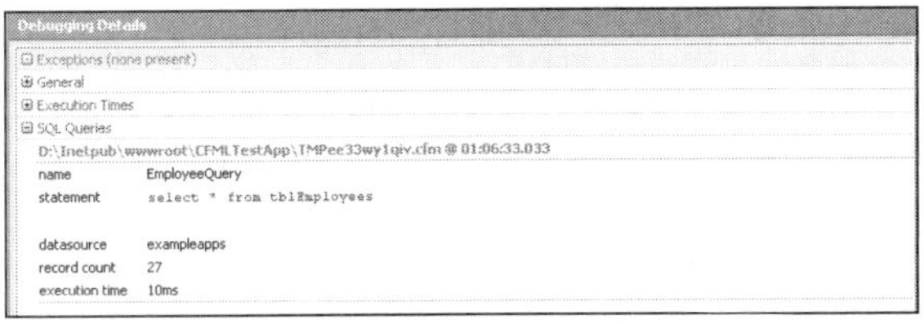

Figure 15.7   The SQL Queries section shows how long a
SQL request took and how many records it returned.

Scope Variables

As was shown earlier, the Administrator Debugging Settings include options
for several variable scopes to be debugged. When variable debugging is enabled
and one or more scopes are checked, the debugging output displays the values
for all variables in those scopes.

Some of the most useful variable scopes are described here:

- URL and Request variables—Lists variables from the HTTP request or
  query string
- Form variables—Lists form field values posted to the page with a form
  submission
- CGI variables—Lists the values of all server environment variables
  available to an application
- Session variables—Displays variables local to the current session
- Application variables—Displays variables globally scoped to every
  instance of the application

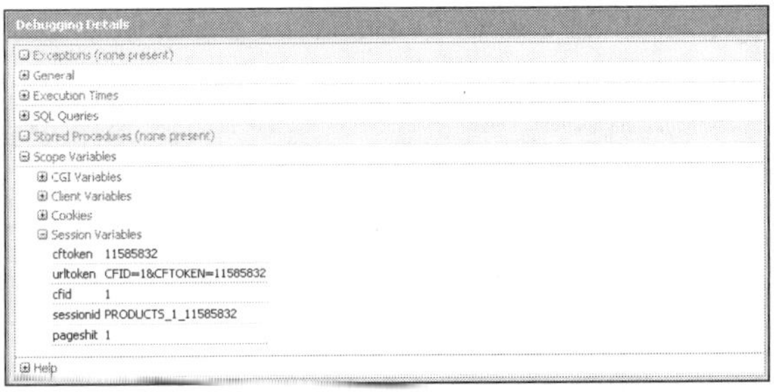

Figure 15.8   The Scope Variables section displays several
categories of variables.

Building Automatic Email Notifications

All of those debugging messages and logs aren't worth anything if nobody is around to see them. Even if you are lucky enough to have an around-the-clock monitoring staff, you probably want to have your application notify someone automatically if there is a problem.

ColdFusion MX makes it easy to add email notification capabilities to your web application with its built-in SMTP connectivity and the CFMAIL tag.

Configuring ColdFusion for SMTP

In order to make use of ColdFusion's email support, you must first configure it to use your SMTP server in the administrator. Fortunately, this is a pretty simple process because the ColdFusion administrator has one page where you can configure all SMTP settings. The Mail Server Settings page is shown in Figure 15.9. If you have access to an SMTP mail server, follow these steps to configure ColdFusion to use it for email notification:

1. Launch the ColdFusion Administrator, and select the Mail Server link from the menu on the left.

2. Specify your SMTP mail server in the Mail Server box. You can use an Internet address (such as mail.mycompany.com) or just an IP address.

3. If your mail server uses something other than the standard SMTP port number (25), enter it in the Server Port box.

4. If your mail server is slow, you can adjust the amount of time ColdFusion waits when trying to connect in the Connection Timeout box. The default value is 60 seconds.

5. If you would like to have ColdFusion spool email at something other than the default of 15 seconds, enter a new value for the Spool Interval.

6. Check the Verify Mail Server Connection if you want ColdFusion to test the connection settings when you submit them. This is recommended. If the connection fails, you may need to contact the system administrator for your web and mail server to assist you.

7. Finally, you can select the detail level for logging SMTP errors (such as inability to connect to the server). You can also choose to log all email that ColdFusion sends.

8. Click Submit Changes to save the changes. If you have chosen to verify the connection, the Mail Server Settings page will reload with the result of the connection attempt at the top.

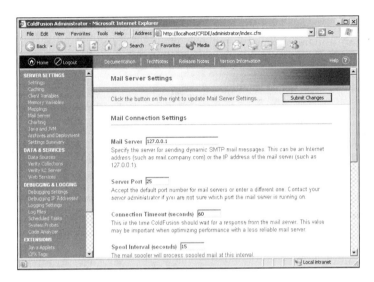

Figure 15.9 Use the Mail Server Settings page to configure ColdFusion
to talk to your SMTP mail server.

The *CFMAIL* Tag

Now that you have ColdFusion configured to send email notifications, you
need to add email support to your web application. You can use the CFMAIL
tag in your application pages to send an SMTP message for just about any
condition that you can think of.

The CFMAIL tag works similarly to the CFOUTPUT tag—the only difference is
the destination of the output. Whereas CFOUTPUT generates text for an HTML
page, CFMAIL generates SMTP mail messages. Because of this similarity, CFMAIL
supports the same attributes that CFOUTPUT does. In addition, it provides
several attributes of its own to set various mail parameters. Table 15.2 lists the
CFMAIL-specific attributes.

Table 15.2 **CFMAIL Tag Attributes**

Attribute	Description
subject	Specifies the subject of the email message.
from	Specifies the email address of the sender.
to	Specifies the email address to send to. This can also be a list of recipients—simply separate additional addresses with a comma.
cc	An optional attribute specifying a carbon copy recipient. This can also be a comma-separated list of recipients.

continues

Table 15.2   **Continued**

Attribute	Description
bcc	Specifies a blind carbon copy address or comma- separated list of addresses. Blind carbon copy addresses are not visible to other recipients, making them useful for mailings in which privacy is important.
SpoolEnable	This attribute can be set to "yes" to make ColdFusion save a copy of the email until the next spool operation.

Sending an Email Message

Using the CFMAIL tag is very much like using the CFOUTPUT tag. Simply put it in a page (using the CFMAIL object on the Dreamweaver MX CFML Advanced tab of the Insert bar if you like). The following example shows how CFMAIL can be used to generate an email message in response to a form submission:

```
<html>
<head>
    <title>Mail Confirmation</title>
</head>
<body>
<h1>Registration Confirmation</h1>
<cfmail
    from="#Form.FromAddress#"
    to="#Form.DestAddress#"
    subject="#Form.Subject# ">
    #Form.Body#
</cfmail>
Thank you for registering.
</body>
</html>
```

In this example, the necessary CFMAIL tag attributes are filled with values from form variables. The body of the message, likewise, is retrieved from a form variable and inserted in the output.

It's easy to see how this page could be changed to make it a generic mailer page. An additional Form or URL variable could provide a page to redirect to after the mailing is complete. The CFLOCATION tag could then perform the redirect:

```
<cflocation url="#Form.RedirectPage#">
```

Then, any form that needs to send email as part of its submission could set this page in the form action and the confirmation page as a hidden form field named RedirectPage.

Exception Handling

Good exception handling is one of the best ways to make sure that errors in your pages won't bring the whole application crashing down. ColdFusion provides several tags for exception handling, including CFTRY and CFCATCH. You will probably find that these are two of the most important tags you will use when it comes to error handling.

CFTRY and CFCATCH are the basic exception-handling tags ColdFusion applications use to trap errors. You can use them to prevent otherwise fatal errors from being reported to the user, which can improve the user's experience on the page. In fact, you can use them any place an error might occur, such as when accessing potentially volatile outside sources, such as databases, files, or servers that may not be available even though the ColdFusion server is running.

CFTRY/CFCATCH Syntax

In order for your code to directly handle an exception, the tags in question must appear within a CFTRY block. You then follow the CFTRY block with CFCATCH blocks, which respond to potential errors. When an exception occurs within the CFTRY block, processing is thrown to the CFCATCH block for that type of exception.

Here is an outline for using CFTRY and CFCATCH to handle errors:

```
<cftry>
    <!-- Potentially volatile application code goes here -->
    <cfcatch type="exception type1">
        <!--Exception handling code for exception type 1 goes here -->
    </cfcatch>
    <cfcatch type="exception type2">
        <!--Exception handling code for exception type 2 goes here -->
    </cfcatch>
    <cfcatch type="Any">
        <!-- Default exception handling code goes here -->
    </cfcatch>
</cftry>
```

You may have noticed that there are multiple CFCATCH tags allowed within each CFTRY. This allows you to handle different exception types differently. For example, when validating a user login, you will want to handle the case of an invalid username or password differently from the case of a failure to connect to the database.

If you just want to ignore a nonfatal error, you can use an empty CFCATCH tag with no body, as follows:

```
<cfcatch Type = any />
```

An exception may be thrown that isn't handled by a CFCATCH tag. This can happen if you don't have a catch that handles the "any" type, or if another exception is thrown or rethrown inside a CFCATCH block. In these cases, the code execution will continue to move up a level in the code until another CFTRY/CFCATCH block is encountered. If no other CFTRY/CFCATCH blocks are found, an error message is displayed showing the exception that occured. Improve your error handling by adding appropriate CFCATCH tags to handle this error in the future.

ColdFusion Logs

As important as debugging information is to developing and diagnosing problems with applications, you shouldn't leave debugging on all the time. It's quite likely, however, that you will want to keep track of important events that occur in your application. ColdFusion's logging capabilities give you a standard, built-in way to generate and manage log files for various circumstances.

Logging Configuration

The Administrator Logging Settings page, shown in Figure 15.10, is where you customize the way that ColdFusion creates log files and some standard logging values.

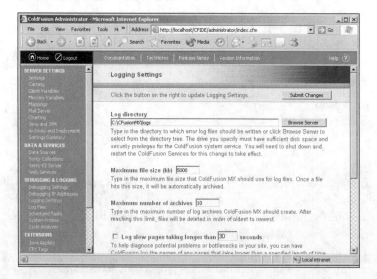

Figure 15.10   The Administrator's Logging Settings page is where you configure logging for your ColdFusion server and application.

Table 15.3 lists the options on the Logging Settings page.

Table 15.3 **Logging Settings Page Options**

Setting	Description
Log Directory	Specifies a location for log files. This directory must have appropriate security allowing the ColdFusion server access. See your web server administrator if you have any questions about setting security for the directory.
Maximum file size	Sets a maximum log file size. ColdFusion will archive a log file when it exceeds this size.
Maximum number of archives	This setting can be used to control how many archive files for a particular log will be kept. When this is exceeded, the oldest archives are deleted to make room for more.
Log slow pages taking longer than [*n*] seconds	This setting can be used to track page requests that take longer than the specified amount of time. This can be useful for tracking pages over time so you can determine when the load on your site is heaviest and when it might be time to add more server horsepower. These pages are logged to the server.log file.
Log all CORBA calls	This setting causes any CORBA calls to be logged to the server.log file.
Enable logging for	If you use ColdFusion scheduled tasks, this setting can be used to log when tasks are run.

The *CFLOG* Tag

Aside from the standard logging items, ColdFusion provides the CFLOG tag for custom logging messages. The CFLOG tag can be inserted anywhere in a CFML page to log information about the application status at that point. It will log any text message that you choose as well as the severity, time of occurance, and other information.

The CFLOG tag is especially useful when used in CFCATCH blocks. Logging a message when an exception occurs ensures that you will be aware of it even if you don't witness the exception personally.

The CFLOG tag has the attributes shown in Table 15.4.

Table 15.4 *CFLOG* **Tag Attributes**

Attribute	Description
file	Specifies the log file to write to. This can be a custom log file or one of the standard ones.
type	The message severity. Possible values are Information, Warning, Fatal, or Error.

continues

Table 15.4 **Continued**

Attribute	Description
text	Specifies the text of the message. This can be any text including variable values or a list of recipients. Simply separate additional addresses with a comma.
application	A yes value for this attribute will log the application name. Yes is the default.
thread	A yes value will log the thread ID for the application. Yes is the default.
Date	A yes value will log the current date.
time	A yes value will log the current time. Yes is the default.

The code for the CFLOG tag that generates an error message looks like the following:

```
<cflog type="Error"
    file="myapplogfile"
    text="Exception error
    Exception type: #Error.type#
    Template: #Error.template#,
    Remote Address: #Error.remoteAddress#,
Diagnostics: #Error.diagnostics#">
```

This example could be used, for instance, as part of an error page defined by a CFERROR tag. The variable Error is used on error pages to determine how the error occurred.

Viewing Logs

You could view logs by loading a particular log file directly into a text editor or viewer, or process the file by another program. ColdFusion provides the Log Files page, shown in Figure 15.11, which gives you a few nice features over and above what you can get from Notepad.

The Log Files page lists all of the standard and custom log files that have been created in the directory specified on the Logging Settings page, along with their size and the date and time they were last modified. You can view a log file by clicking directly on the name, or by selecting multiple log files with the checkboxes on the left and clicking View Log Files. Other options on the Log Files page allow you to download log files, archive them, or delete them.

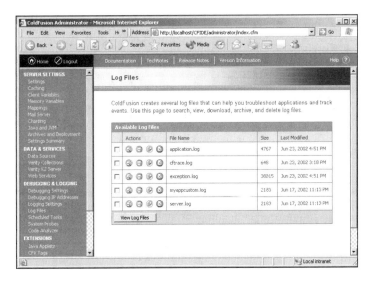

Figure 15.11   The Administrator's Log Files page is a convenient interface
for managing, viewing, and searching standard and custom log files.

The Log Viewer, shown in Figure 15.12, is launched when you select a log
file. This page takes the raw information in the log file and formats it for
easy reading. There are two options on this page for altering how the log is
displayed:

- View Raw Data—Any log messages that contain HTML formatting will
be displayed as plain text.

- Compact View—Checking this option makes the log viewer display 20
items on a page instead of 10, and truncates long message text.

If you are viewing a log created by a `CFLOG` tag and you specified `yes` for any of
the options, including application name, thread id, date, or time, these
will be displayed above the message text. The severity of the event is always
displayed.

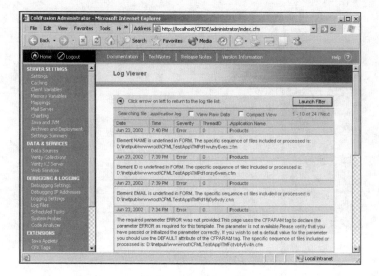

Figure 15.12 The Log Viewer formats a log file for easy viewing.

In the Log Viewer, you can narrow down the values displayed or search for a specific log message using the Launch Filter button. This button opens the filter window, shown in Figure 15.13. In this window, you can specify criteria for any of the log values, including the severity, as well as search terms to use when searching the text.

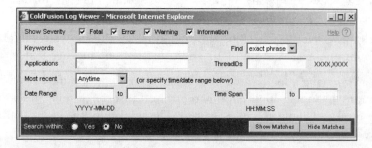

Figure 15.13 You can use filters to show only those log entries that meet the criteria for which you are looking.

Using Dreamweaver MX's Debugging and Error-Handling Features

Up to now, this chapter has focused on the debugging features provided by ColdFusion, and for the most part, debugging and error handling are a function of the ColdFusion server environment. But there are also several features provided by Dreamweaver MX that can help with debugging and error handling.

The *CFPARAM* Tag

The CFPARAM tag is a CFML tag that can test for the existence of a variable. It can also provide a default value if the variable doesn't exist. The syntax for the CFPARAM tag is as follows:

```
<cfparam name="variable_name"
   type="data_type"
   default="default_value">
```

If you use the CFPARAM tag with just the name attribute, ColdFusion will only check for the existance of the variable. If it does not exist, the ColdFusion server displays an error message. This mode is used for error checking.

Another option is to use the default attribute to specify a value. If the variable doesn't exist, it will be created and set to this default value. This ensures that the variable is always created and set to at least the default value.

With the optional type attribute, CFPARAM can validate the type of a variable as well. If the type of the variable doesn't match the value of the type attribute, an error message is generated and processing stops. Table 15.5 lists the possible type values.

Table 15.5   *CFPARAM* Type Attribute Values

Type Value	Required Data Type
any	Any type
array	Any array value
binary	A binary value
boolean	Can be true, false, yes, or no
date	Any valid date or time value
numeric	Any number
query	Must be a Query.object
string	A string or single character value
struct	A structure
UUID	A Universally Unique Identifier
variableName	A valid variable name

Dreamweaver MX provides a server behavior that simplifies the task of adding a CFPARAM tag, as well as a button on the CFML Basic panel of the Insert bar. Although both the server behavior and the button insert the same code, they act a little differently.

The server behavior inserts its tag above the head of the document, which is usually before any variables have been created. Therefore, it's used mainly for creating new variables or for testing variables in a wider scope. The Server Behavior window lists all variables added with the CFPARAM behavior, as shown in Figure 15.14.

The CFPARAM button on the Insert bar, on the other hand, inserts the tag at the current cursor location, which makes it a little more flexible to use.

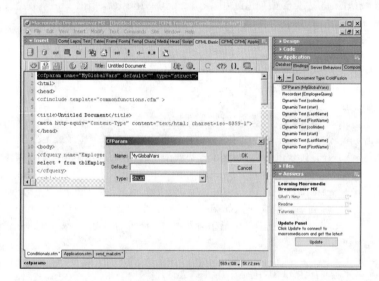

Figure 15.14 Dreamweaver MX CFPARAM server behavior simplifies the task of adding variables to a CFML page.

Show Region Server Behavior

Another Dreamweaver server behavior deals with recordsets and allows you to specify an action to take depending on the result of the query.

As the previous chapter discussed, ColdFusion provides several tags that allow you to do conditional execution on a page. The Show Region server behavior is an automatic way to insert conditional processing to a section of code, either showing or hiding it depending on whether a recordset returned by a query is empty. This is primarily useful for showing a message if the recordset is empty, or if an error occurred when connecting to the database.

The Show Region server behaviors are listed here:

- Show If Recordset Is Empty
- Show If Recordset Is Not Empty
- Show If First Page
- Show If Not First Page
- Show If Last Page
- Show If Not Last Page

The last four options are useful when displaying buttons to page through a list of items. You could use these options to show a Previous button on every page but the first one, and a Next button on every page except the last one.

To use a Show Region server behavior, as shown in Figure 15.15, do the following:

1. Select a section of a page in Design view or in Code view.
2. Click the plus (+) button in the Server Behaviors panel. (If this panel is not visible, choose Window, Server Behaviors to open it.)
3. Choose Show Region from the menu that pops up.
4. From the submenu, choose one of the listed Show Region behaviors.
5. Click OK to add the behavior.

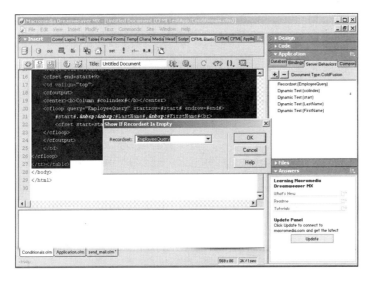

Figure 15.15 The Show Region server behaviors allow you to customize the display of a block of code depending on special recordset results.

Summary

In this chapter, you learned how to use ColdFusion MX's debugging features, including custom error templates, automatic email notification, exception handling, and logs. You also used Dreamweaver MX's debugging features, including the server behaviors, and learned how to use the debugger. In the next chapter, you will learn about session and application variables and how and when you should use them.

16

Sessions and the Application Variable Scope

IN STANDALONE APPLICATION DEVELOPMENT, WHEN YOU CREATE a variable, it is usually available for as long as you need it, safely stored in memory. Web applications, on the other hand, are different. The web is stateless by nature, which means that each request made to a web server isn't necessarily related to or followed by any other request. For this reason, server applications need to be a little smarter when it comes to managing the client state.

ColdFusion MX provides several different levels of persistent variables to help with this, including Session variables (those unique to an individual session) and Application variables (those that are global across all application sessions). Figure 16.1 shows the scope of both of these persistent variable types. Persistent variables are those that are maintained across multiple page requests by some means, and are either returned to the server with each request or live on the server in memory.

In order to understand how ColdFusion handles sessions, we need to address several topics. This chapter consists of the following sections:

- Introduction to ColdFusion persistent variable scopes
- Using the Application.cfm file
- Using ColdFusion Sessions and Session variables
- Using ColdFusion Application variables

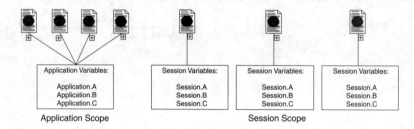

Figure 16.1   Application and Session variable scopes maintain variable persistence between page requests. Application variables are shared by all pages, whereas Session variables are unique for each client.

Introduction to ColdFusion Persistent Variable Scopes

Consider the stateless nature of a web application. A browser makes a request to the server. The server processes the request, generates a page based on the information in the request, and returns the page to the browser. At this point, the server usually forgets about the application, freeing up resources so that it can handle other requests.

There are times, however, when you want to keep track of variables from request to request and from page to page. ColdFusion provides two variable scopes, Session and Client, that can be used to maintain variable values between requests. Although they can be used for similar purposes, there are some differences between the two scopes. Here is a brief summary of the features of Client and Session scopes:

- Client—Client variables are tied to a specific browser and are available across multiple sessions. Client variables are typically stored as cookies or database entries. Client variables can be used for such things as user preferences that you want to maintain over more than one session.

- Session—Session variable values are unique for a single browser during a single session, and are available from request to request. They are kept in memory on the server until the session times out after a period of inactivity.

Another type of variable that you may want to have accessible over multiple requests are application setting variables. These variables are available on every server-side page, and aren't usually changed by an application, although they can be. ColdFusion provides the Application and Server scopes for this purpose:

- Application—Application variable values are the same for and available to every session of an application. Application variables are useful places to hold values that all sessions will need, such as data sources or initialization variables.

- Server—Server variables are available to all applications on a server. They are useful if your server is running more than one application that needs to have the same information available. These could include server or cluster status variables, global data sources, or other shared data.

This chapter focuses primarily on the Application and Session scopes because they are the most commonly used.

Session Variable Limitations

Although Session variables are often used to store values between requests, they do have a drawback. They are stored in memory, so they are available only on the machine on which they are created. Although this is fine in a lot of cases, many of today's high-powered web applications use server clusters with many servers handling requests for a single application. This means that a session that has a request handled by one server might hit a different one on the next request. In these situations, Session variables aren't as useful; however, you could use Client scope variables instead, because their values are usually stored in a database or in browser cookies.

Using the Application.cfm File

This section will explain how to create an Application.cfm file and how to define application options in it. Any discussion of ColdFusion persistent variable scopes should begin with the Application.cfm file. This file can be used to specify settings for the application, not the least of which are those for Client, Application, and Session variable management.

The Application.cfm page is a special ColdFusion page that is automatically loaded once for each CFML file in the same directory in which it is processed. This makes its settings available throughout the application. A single Application.cfm page can be used for an entire application, including files in subdirectories, or you can create a separate Application.cfm page for each subdirectory. This gives you some flexibility in that you can put separate applications in a subdirectory and give them unique Application.cfm settings, or have one big complex application spread out into several subdirectories. The choice is dependent on your particular application needs.

You can create an Application.cfm page with Dreamweaver, although it doesn't provide a way to create one automatically. The easiest way to create one is to create an empty text file and save it as Application.cfm. To do this, follow these steps:

1. In Dreamweaver, choose File, New from the main menu, or use File, New File from the Site panel.

2. Choose Other from the Category list.

3. Choose Text from the Other list.

4. Click Create. This will create an empty text file.

5. Choose File, Save As, and enter **Application.cfm** as the file name. The Application.cfm file belongs in the same directory as your CFML files, so browse to the site root if necessary. Then click Save.

You will now have an empty CFML file without the standard HTML tags that Dreamweaver usually puts in every new CFML page, as shown in Figure 16.2. These tags aren't needed in the Application.cfm file.

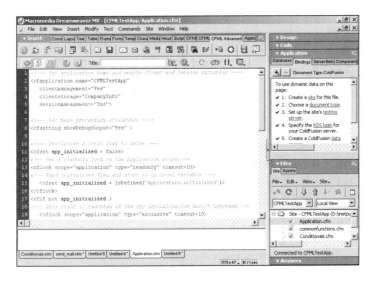

Figure 16.2   Like any other ColdFusion file, the Application.cfm file can be created and edited in Dreamweaver MX.

Application.cfm Options

Several options can be set using the Application.cfm page. These are organized into several categories, which are described in the following sections.

The *CFAPPLICATION* Tag

The CFAPPLICATION tag does what its name implies—it defines the most basic settings of an application. The syntax of the CFAPPLICATION tag is as follows:

```
<cfapplication name="appname"
   clientManagement="yes¦no"
   clientStorage="registry¦cookie¦datasource"
   sessionManagement="yes¦no"
   setClientCookies="yes¦no"
   setDomainCookies="yes¦no"
   sessionTimeout= #CreateTimeSpan(days, hours, minutes, seconds)#
   applicationTimeout= #CreateTimeSpan(days, hours, minutes, seconds)#>
```

The name attribute is what actually defines a page as belonging to a particular ColdFusion application. All pages that implicitly include this specific Application.cfm file will belong to the same application and share application scope information. Name values can be up to 64 characters long, so you can give your applications fairly descriptive names.

The other attributes of the CFAPPLICATION tag are optional, but if specified, they will override the settings in the ColdFusion Administrator.

You can choose whether to use Client scope, Session scope, or both types of variables. To use Client scope variables, set the clientManagement attribute to "yes". To enable Session scope variables, set the sessionManagement attribute to "yes". Setting both to yes will enable both scopes.

If you enable Client scope variables, the clientStorage attribute specifies how you want these stored. You have the following options:

- Registry (default)—Stores the Client variables in the Registry. Although this is the default, it is not available on Unix and is not recommended for anything other than the simplest needs.

- Cookie—Stores the Client variables in a cookie that is saved by the browser on the client. There are browser limitations to this method; for example, the browser must have cookies enabled. Some browsers also limit the number of cookies and the size of cookies, so beware. If you choose to save Client variables as cookies, set the setClientCookies attribute to "yes" to enable them. If your application is spread across multiple clusters, you will need to set the setDomainCookies attribute to true as well, so that cookies are saved at the domain level and not the host level. It should be noted that cookies are not without problems. Some browsers, particularly older ones, don't handle cookies or put size limitations on them. There are also users who distrust cookies and disable them entirely.

- Datasource—If you specify a data source, ColdFusion can store Client variables in a database. Although this method is the most robust and doesn't require that the user enable cookies, it requires a login mechanism in order to identify the user's record in the database. In some cases, if you have a database that supports table creation from SQL, ColdFusion can even create all of the tables necessary. Look on the Client Variables page in the Administrator, shown in Figure 16.3, for details on how to create these tables automatically for databases that support table creation. If your database doesn't support SQL table creation, you must create the tables (named CDATA and CGLOBAL) yourself. The ColdFusion MX online documentation gives detailed instructions on how to do this.

The other attributes of the CFAPPLICATION tag are for specifying the Session and Application timeout values. These are the amount of idle time before Session and Application variables, respectively, expire. These timeout values are set using the CreateTimeSpan function with the appropriate days, hours, minutes, and seconds as parameters, as shown in the previous CFAPPLICATION syntax listing.

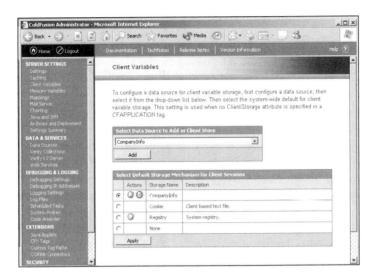

Figure 16.3 The Client Variables Administrator page is where you can select a data source for storing Client scope variables.

The *CFSETTING* Tag

Another important tag that can go on the Application.cfm page is the CFSETTING tag. This tag can be used to specify page settings, including the request timeout, whether the page will generate debug output, and whether to set a page so it will only output text generated by CFOUTPUT tags. The syntax of the CFSETTING tag looks like this:

```
<cfsetting name="appname"
    requestTimeout="yes¦no"
    showDebugOutput="yes¦no"
    enableCFOutputOnly="yes¦no">
```

The following table describes each of the attributes supported by CFSETTING:

Table 16.1 *CFSETTING* Tag Attributes

Attribute	Description
requestTimeout	Specifies a value for the page request timeout. If the page request takes longer than the specified amount of time, an error is generated.
showDebugOutput	Shows debugging output for a page. Note that debugging must be enabled in the Administrator for this to have any effect. See Chapter 15, "Debugging and Error Handling," for more information about debugging output.
enableCFOutputOnly	When set to yes, disables output of all text that isn't inside CFOUTPUT tags.

CFSETTING

Although it is common to use the CFSETTING tag in the Application.cfm file, it can also be used at any time on a CFML page to override these settings. This can be useful if you want to use a different timeout value on one particularly slow page, or if you want to enable debugging of an individual file.

Error Handling

Another tag commonly used application-wide is CFERROR, which can be used to define custom error-handling pages for several types of errors. Although it is possible to add CFERROR tags to an application page, it is also a good tag to use in the Application.cfm file because doing so makes the same error pages available across the application automatically. This gives your application consistent error handling without a lot of effort. CFERROR has the following syntax, which is described in Table 16.2.

```
<cferror type="error type"
    template="templatefile.cfm"
    mailTo="email_address"
    exception="exception_type">
```

Table 16.2   **CFERROR Tag Attributes**

Attribute	Description
type	One of the following values:
	Request: Request error, generated if a requested CFML file cannot be found.
	Validation: Used to handle form validation errors.
	Exception: Error page is loaded for an unhandled exception type specified by the exception attribute.
template	Specifies the name of the ColdFusion page to load in the event of an error.
mailto	Specifies the email address available on the template page for the error handler to send an alert message to. Use the variable Error.mailto to access it.
exception	Specifies a standard or custom exception type handled by this page.

Login Processing

Because the Application.cfm file is automatically loaded with each page request, it's a good place to put user authentication code if your web site requires users to log in. ColdFusion provides several tags for this purpose, including CFLOGIN, CFLOGINUSER, and CFLOGOUT.

Login processing is outside the scope of this chapter, but it is discussed in detail in Chapter 17, "Building User Authentication."

Variables Scope Variables

Another type of variable scope that hasn't been mentioned up to this point is simply called Variables scope. In ColdFusion, Variables scope is another way of saying local variables, which are only available on the page on which they are created.

It is possible to define Variables scope variables in the Application.cfm file using CFSET or CFPARAM tags. Although the same instance of the variable isn't shared among every page, at least a variable with the same name and value will be created on every page. You just have to keep in mind that if you change the value of one of these variables in code, it won't be persistent and instead will be initialized to the default value on the next page request. For this reason, it is better to use these variables for static variables that do not need to be changed.

ColdFusion Sessions and Session Variables

A session refers to the unique interaction of one client with the ColdFusion server during a single use of an application. Any number of pages may be viewed during a session. Because a session is tied to an individual user, ColdFusion can maintain a separate session variable space, which can be used to store variables.

It's pretty easy to tell when a new session starts. When a request comes in from a new client, ColdFusion creates the session space for that user. Because the web is stateless, however, it's not always possible to tell exactly when the client is done using the application, allowing the session to be discarded. Even if you provide a means for a user to log out of your application, it's possible in the volatile world of Internet communications that it'll never happen—the user could close the browser without logging off, the connection could be disconnected, and so on.

Because of this uncertainty, sessions have a timeout value associated with them. After a certain period of inactivity, ColdFusion will automatically clear the session out of memory.

The default timeout for sessions is 20 minutes. ColdFusion allows this value to be set in the ColdFusion Administrator (on the Memory Variables page), or with the CFAPPLICATION tag, as shown earlier in this chapter. If it is set in both places, the CFAPPLICATION value takes precedence. However, the CFAPPLICATION sessionTimeout cannot be set to a value greater than the one on the Memory Variables page.

Even with automatic session timeouts, it's still a good idea to provide a manual method for a user to log out. By doing so, ColdFusion can clear the session right then and there, freeing up the session memory for other uses. It also helps to keep any private information that may be stored in Session variables as secure as possible by forcing the user to log in again.

At this point, you may be wondering how ColdFusion identifies a request as belonging to a particular session. The answer is a combination of two predefined Session variables: the `Session.CFID` (client ID) and the `Session.CFTOKEN` (client security token) are used together to identify a session. These values are usually stored on the client in a cookie so that ColdFusion can match a request up with the appropriate session. In the event that cookies are disabled, another variable, `Session.URLToken`, passes the combined values of the `CFID` and `CFTOKEN` from page to page in the URL.

Proper Session Scope Usage

Session variables are a great place to store information that needs to be carried over from one page to the next, but they should also be used in moderation. Keep in mind that ColdFusion must allocate memory for every session variable, and the larger the variable the more space it will take. When you have a server with hundreds or thousands of simultaneous users, session memory usage can start to add up. So, you might want to think twice before you start keeping huge chunks of text in a Session variable. In many cases, using cached queries can make more sense.

Another good reason to avoid storing huge amounts of complicated data in the Session scope is that the application might eventually need to run in a clustered environment, as is becoming the norm for large web applications. Memory-based Session variables cannot be used in a clustered environment, so you may need to switch to Client scope variables instead, which can be stored in a database or in a client cookie between requests. Client scope variables can only be simple data types, so if you limit your Session variable usage to simple types as well, you'll be well prepared for any future modifications.

A good use for Session variables is to store user-specific information at the beginning of a session so that it can be used throughout the application. For example, you might want to keep the user's name around to personalize the output of a page or load color and layout preferences so that each page can be displayed according to the user's previous settings.

Enabling Session Variables

Before you can take advantage of Session variables in your application, you have to enable them. There are two places where this must be done—in the ColdFusion Administrator and in a CFAPPLICATION tag.

To enable Session variables in the ColdFusion Administrator, do the following:

1. Launch the ColdFusion Administrator and select the Memory Variables link from the left-side menu. This page is shown in Figure 16.4.

2. Make sure Enable Session Variables is checked.

3. If your ColdFusion application works in conjunction with Java 2 Enterprise Edition (J2EE) components, you can check the Use J2EE session variables check box so that you share values between the two environments.

4. Set a Maximum Timeout value for Session Variables. The CFAPPLICATION timeout value cannot exceed this maximum. The default is two days. A real-world value would be closer to 30 minutes.

5. Set a Default Timeout value for Session Variables. This value can be over-ridden by the CFAPPLICATION tag in an application.

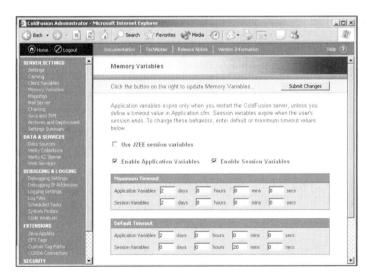

Figure 16.4 Enable Session and Application variable scopes and set timeout values for them on the Administrator Memory Variables page.

To enable Session variables with CFAPPLICATION, do the following:

1. Create an Application.cfm file if you don't already have one.

2. Add a CFAPPLICATION tag, and set its name attribute to identify the application.

3. Set the sessionManagement attribute to "yes".

. 4. If you like, you can override the default Session timeout value set in the Administrator using the sessionTimeout attribute.

This code sample shows a CFAPPLICATION tag enabling Session variables and setting the sessionTimeout value to 1 hour and 30 minutes.

```
<cfapplication name="ImageProcessor"
    sessionManagement="Yes"
    sessionTimeout=#CreateTimeSpan(0,1,30,0)#>
```

Creating and Deleting Session Variables

Session variables are created in the same way as Variable scope variables, with the CFSET tag. There is, however, a little more that has to be done. Because Session variables (and all shared-memory variables) are stored in a shared memory, it is possible that more than one access at a time will be attempted. Given ColdFusion's multithreaded nature, it is possible that two threads could attempt to write to a variable at the same time. This could cause unpredictable results.

The *CFLOCK* Tag

ColdFusion provides the CFLOCK tag to prevent two threads from accessing the same memory variable. This tag allows two kinds of locks to be created: exclusive and read-only. Use the type attribute to set the type of lock you want:

- exclusive—When in effect, only one thread at a time can access a variable.

- readOnly—These are faster than exclusive locks, because multiple readOnly locks can be active at once. This prevents an exclusive lock from being obtained until all readOnly locks are released.

The scope attribute is also important—use it to set the variable scope you are locking: Session, Application, or Server.

Using Session Variables

Using the CFLOCK and CFSET tags, you create new Session variables as in this example:

```
<cflock scope="Session" timeout=20 type="Exclusive">
  <cfset Session.MessageBoardThread = 100>
</cflock>
```

When you need to access a Session variable, you must lock it once again. This needs to be done even if you are just reading it, because another thread might try to write to it at the same time. You can, however, use `type=readOnly` to allow other threads access to the variable at the same time, as in this example:

```
<cflock scope="Session" timeout=20 type="readOnly">
  <cfoutput>
     Your search of #Session.MessageBoardThread# returned #count# values.
  </cfoutput>
</cflock>
```

In order to modify a Session variable, however, you must again use an exclusive lock:

```
<cflock scope="Session" timeout=20 scope="Session" type="Exclusive">
  <cfset Session.MessageBoardThread = GetNextThreadFunction()>
</cflock>
```

When you are done using a Session variable, it's a good idea to delete it to conserve memory. Use the `StructDelete` function to delete a variable. Don't forget the lock!

```
<cflock scope="Session" timeout=20 type="Exclusive">
  <cfset StructDelete(Session, "MessageBoardThread")>
</cflock>
```

Using Client Scope Variables

Although they can be used for similar purposes, the storage methods of Client and Session scope variables are very different, and each has some distinct advantages over the other.

Whereas Session (and Application) variables are stored in a shared memory pool, Client scope variables are in memory only while a page request is being processed. They are then stored either in the Registry, a database, or as a client cookie, depending on the value you set for the `clientStorage` attribute of the `CFAPPLICATION` tag.

Like Session variables, Client scope variables can be used to maintain the value of variables between page requests. Unlike Session and Application scopes, however, Client variables can only be simple data types, including numbers, Booleans, strings, or date and time values. Client variables cannot be used to store more complex data such as arrays, structs, or query objects.

CFWDDX **Tag**

Although Client variables must be simple data types, ColdFusion does have a way to get around this if you need to store more complex data. The CFWDDX tag can be used to convert complex data structures into an XML string, which can then be stored as a Client variable. This method uses Web Distributed Data Exchange (WDDX) encoding, developed originally by Allaire. More information about WDDX and its capabilities at www.openwddx.org.

Creating Client–Scoped Variables

To create a Client variable and set its value, use the CFSET or CFPARAM tag with the Client prefix, as shown in this example:

```
<cfset Client.DefaultTextColor="#FF0000">
```

You could also use the CFPARAM tag to test for the existence of a Client variable and create it if it doesn't exist:

```
<cfparam name="Client.DefaultTextColor" default="#FF0000">
```

Notice that, unlike Session variables, you do not need to lock Client variables because they are not stored in shared memory, so there is no chance of two threads trying to access the same memory space at the same time. Once a Client variable is set, it is available on any page in the application.

Using Application Variables

So far, we've discussed Session and Client variables, both of which are unique to a single client. Application variables work similarly to Session variables. The difference is that they are automatically available to all sessions and from all pages of the application.

The best use for Application variables is to store information that needs to be read often but changed rarely. This could include server file paths, database connection strings, or other constants. For the most part, Application variables are set only once, when the application starts. If you use them to store initialization information for the first client that accesses the application, subsequent clients will benefit from having the variables already in memory.

As with Session variables, Application variables must be locked before they are used, and so should be set or read only inside a CFLOCK tag block.

Enabling ColdFusion Application Variables

You must enable Application variables in the ColdFusion Administrator in order to use them. To enable Application variables, do the following:

1. Launch the ColdFusion Administrator and select the Memory Variables link from the left-side menu.

2. Make sure Enable Application Variables is checked.

3. Set a Maximum Timeout value for Application variables. This value must be less than the CFAPPLICATION timeout value. The default is 2 days. As with the Session timeout, a more realistic value should be entered, perhaps 30 minutes.

4. Set a Default Timeout value for Application variables. This value can be overridden by the CFAPPLICATION tag in an application, using the applicationTimeout attribute.

Initializing Application Variables

There is a bit more overhead involved with creating Application variables compared with those of other scopes. Because Application variables are shared between all sessions, you must take a little more care when creating them to ensure that they are created and initialized only once. The following sample code shows the steps that must be taken to initialize the Application variable scope.

First, create a local variable that we will use later to hold the initialization status.

```
<!--- Initialize a local flag to false --->
<cfset app_initialized = false>
```

Then, use CFLOCK to lock the application scope, and get the value of the Application.initialized variable. It is assigned to a local variable so that the CFLOCK is held for as little time as possible.

```
<!-- Get a readonly lock on the Application scope-->
<cflock scope="application" type="readonly" timeout=10>
<!-- Read initialized flag and store it in local variable --->
   <cfset app_initialized = IsDefined("Application.initialized")>
</cflock>
```

The next block is executed if the application hasn't been initialized. Use it to set any application variables. Finally, set the Application.initialized variable to ensure that this block will be executed only once.

```
<cfif not app_initialized >
<!-- This block is executed if the app initialization hasn't happened -->
   <cflock scope="application" type="exclusive" timeout=10>
      <cfif not IsDefined("Application.initialized") >
         <!-- Set initial application variable values here -->
         <cfset Application.MyGlobalVar1 = "MyVarValue" >
         <!-- Set the Application scope initialization flag
```

```
                    so that future initialization won't take place -->
           <cfset Application.initialized = "yes">
         </cfif>
      </cflock>
   </cfif>
```

This code block should be inserted into the Application.cfm file. When it executes, the existance of an Application variable called `Application.initialized` is checked. If it is not found to exist, the exclusive lock takes place, and all of the Application variable initialization is done.

Summary

In this chapter, you learned how session and application variable scopes function. You learned how to manage sessions with ColdFusion, and how to create and set options for the Application.cfm file. You also saw how to make use of Session scope in your applications. In the next chapter, you will learn about ColdFusion's user authentication features and how to use them in your applications.

Building User Authentication

WHETHER YOU ARE BUILDING AN E-COMMERCE APPLICATION, a web site for a software company that provides software downloads, or even a hobbyist message board, you need user authentication. Many web applications need to keep track of visitors or provide areas that are accessible by registered members only. Authentication can also be valuable in securing vital data from hackers.

When you use ColdFusion MX to build your application, user authentication features are provided automatically. All you have to do is add them to your application.

ColdFusion would be an excellent environment for building user-authenticated applications even without the custom tags it provides for this purpose, simply due to its database-driven nature. However, ColdFusion MX provides a security framework that makes authentication even easier.

This chapter consists of the following sections:

- An introduction to ColdFusion user security
- Using Dreamweaver's User Authentication server behaviors
- Using user authentication in an application

ColdFusion MX Security Changes

ColdFusion MX uses a completely different security model for authentication than previous versions, and older security tags are no longer supported. If you are familiar with the older ColdFusion authentication tags such as CFAUTHENTICATE and CFIMPERSONATE, or are updating an application written for ColdFusion 5 or earlier to ColdFusion MX, you will want to pay special attention to the information in this chapter.

Introduction to ColdFusion User Security

User security consists of two parts: authentication and authorization. The first stage, authentication, takes place when a user logs in with an assigned ID and password. This information is kept in memory by ColdFusion for as long as the user stays logged in or the session is active. ColdFusion supports two types of authentication: Basic HTTP authentication and Application authentication.

The second part of user security is authorization. That is, once the user is logged in to an application, a role is assigned to the user that determines the areas of the application that are available to him or her. All three of these security aspects are discussed in the following sections.

Basic HTTP Authentication

HTTP authentication is a feature provided by web servers for simple security. The user is presented with a dialog box (shown in Figure 17.1) in which a user ID and password are entered. The web server then validates the information using its own security mechanism. Once logged in, the browser will transparently send the authentication information in the background for each subsequent page request.

ColdFusion comes into play at the authorization level. Once a user is logged in, the authentication information provided to the web server is available.

One thing to keep in mind is that HTTP authentication is sent in plain text, making it nonsecure by itself. HTTP authentication should be used with HTTPS if security is a concern.

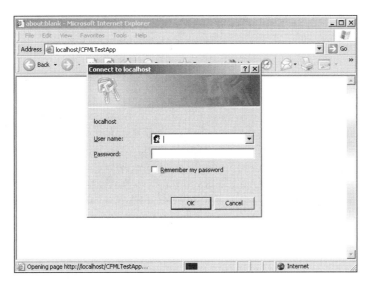

Figure 17.1   With basic HTTP authentication, security is controlled by the web server, and users log on using the familiar security dialog.

Application Authentication

Application authentication doesn't rely on the web server to provide security; instead, all user authentication is provided by the application itself. With this method, the application determines whether a user is logged in, redirecting the user to a login page if necessary. Application authentication is the most common authentication type in ColdFusion.

Authorization

The second part of user security is authorization. Once the user is logged in to an application, a role is assigned to the user that determines which areas of the application are available. For example, a message board might have *users* who can read and post messages, *moderators* who have control over a portion of the board and are able to access some administrative functions, and *administrators* who can assign and revoke moderator privileges, create new board sections, and so on. Each user has an assigned role.

ColdFusion User Security Tags

ColdFusion provides several tags solely for user security purposes. They are described in this section.

The *CFLOGIN* Tag

The heart of ColdFusion user authentication is the CFLOGIN tag. The code in the body of the CFLOGIN tag is executed only if the user is not already logged in. This means that all of the authentication code can be placed in the CFLOGIN block and shared across an entire application automatically.

The body of a CFLOGIN block will contain a CFLOGINUSER tag that is used to present the authentication information to ColdFusion. The CFLOGIN tag has three optional attributes, which are presented in Table 17.1.

Table 17.1 *CFLOGIN* **Tag Attributes**

Attribute	Description
idleTimeout	ColdFusion will automatically log a user out if there have been no page requests during the idle timeout period, set in seconds. There is a default value of 1800 seconds, or 30 minutes.
applicationToken	You can specify an identifier that is used to identify which ColdFusion applications can be accessed using the login information. By default, the login is limited to the application name specified in the CFAPPLICATION tag.
cookieDomain	This specifies the Internet domain for which the ColdFusion security cookie is valid. By default, there are no domain limitations.

When inside the CFLOGIN block, the tag provides a structure, also named cflogin, which contains the user's ID and password. In the case of Web server (HTTP) authentication, the cflogin structure is filled when the user logs in using a basic login page. When application authentication is used, the structure is filled from an applicatin login form page submission that contains fields named j_username and j_password.

The *CFLOGINUSER* Tag

The CFLOGINUSER tag is also important for user authentication. This tag is used to supply authentication information to ColdFusion, including the user's ID, password, and any roles they might have. CFLOGINUSER has no body.

The CFLOGINUSER tag has the following syntax:

```
<cfloginuser
    name = "name"
    password = "password"
    roles = "role1[,role2]">
```

The CFLOGINUSER tag's three attributes are all required. They are described in Table 17.2.

Table 17.2 *CFLOGINUSER* **Tag Attributes**

Attribute	Description
name	The username of the current user. This attribute is required.
password	The current user's password. This attribute is required.
roles	A single role, or a comma-separated list of roles for this user. If multiple roles are supplied in a comma-separated list, there should be no spaces between the roles and the commas because ColdFusion will process the spaces as part of the role name.

The CFLOGIN and CFLOGINUSER tags are usually used together in the Application.cfm file as the core of ColdFusion's user authentication features. An example using both of these tags along with the cflogin structure for basic Web server authentication is shown here:

```
<cfapplication name="MessageBoard">
<cflogin>
   <cfif IsDefined( "cflogin" )>
      <cfif cflogin.name eq "admin">
         <cfset roles = "user,admin">
      <cfelse>
         <cfset roles = "user">
      </cfif>
      <cfloginuser name="#cflogin.name#" password="#cflogin.password#"
         roles="#roles#" />
   <cfelse>
      <!--- this block should never happen with basic authentication --->
      <h1>Authentication data is missing.</h1>
      Try to reload the page or contact the site administrator.
      <cfabort>
   </cfif>
</cflogin>
```

A step-by-step walk-through of this example will be helpful in understanding it:

1. The CFLOGIN tag indicates the beginning of an authentication block. This code is executed only if the current user is not logged in.

2. If the user is logging in, the body of the tag is executed. First the code checks for the existence of the cflogin structure. Authentication in this case is done by the web server, so this structure should always exist. If this were an application authentication example, not finding a cflogin structure could be used to direct the user to a login form page.

3. In this simple example, the determination of the user's role is done by looking at the username. In this case, if this username is "admin," the role is set to both user and admin so code for all roles is accessible.

4. Finally, the CFLOGINUSER tag is used to actually log the user in and set his or her role. At this point, the CFLOGIN block is usually finished and does not need to be called again unless the user logs out (using the CFLOGOUT tag) or is automatically logged out after a timeout.

An example that uses application authentication is a little more complicated because more responsibility is placed on the application:

```
<cfapplication name="MessageBoard">
<cflogin>
    <cfif IsDefined( "cflogin" )>
        <cfif cflogin.name IS "" OR cflogin.password IS "">
            <cfoutput>
                <H2>You must enter a User Name and Password</H2>
            </cfoutput>
            <cfinclude template="mbloginform.cfm">
            <cfabort>
        <cfelse>
            <cfquery name="loginQuery" dataSource="MessageBoard">
            SELECT username, roles
            FROM Members
            WHERE
                username='#cflogin.name#'
                AND password='#cflogin.password#'
            </cfquery>
            <cfif loginQuery.username EQ cflogin.name AND loginQuery.Roles NEQ "">
                <cfloginuser name="#cflogin.name#"
                     password="#cflogin.password#"
                    roles="#loginQuery.roles#">
            <cfelse>
                <cfoutput>
                    <H2>The supplied username or password is invalid.<br>
                    Please try again</H2>
                </cfoutput>
                <cfinclude template="mbloginform.cfm">
                <cfabort>
            </cfif>
        </cfif>
    <cfelse>
        <cfinclude template="mbloginform.cfm">
        <cfabort>
    </cfif>
</cflogin>
```

1. Like the previous example, the CFLOGIN tag indicates the beginning of an authentication block.

2. The first thing done in the CFLOGIN body is a check for the existence of the cflogin structure. If it is not found, the login form page, named mbloginform.cfm in this example, is displayed. This form must provide

two form fields named j_username and j_password. When the form is submitted, the cflogin structure is created with their values. In this example, if the structure has been created but either of the values is empty, a validation message and the the mbloginform.cfm page are displayed to reprompt for the username and password.

3. If the username and password field are provided and are not empty, they can be used to query a database to validate the user and obtain any roles. If the query fails, the mbloginform.cfm page is displayed.

4. If a recordset is returned from the query, the username and roles are checked against the appropriate database columns, in this case loginQuery.username and loginQuery.roles. If these contain the valid username, the user's information is valid and the CFLOGINUSER can then be called to log the user in and set role(s).

The *CFLOGOUT* Tag

The CFLOGOUT tag can be used to log the user out. It can be called in response to a form submission from a login button, for example.

CFLOGOUT is a standalone tag that has no attributes or body.

The *GetAuthUser* Function

The GetAuthUser function is one of two new functions in ColdFusion MX that can be used to enhance user authentication. This function can be called to get the name of the currently logged-in user. This can be used for the display of personalized information:

```
<P>Authenticated User: <cfoutput>GetAuthUser()</cfoutput></P>
```

The *IsUserInRole* Function

The IsUserInRole function can be used to determine whether the current logged-in user belongs to a specific role. The role is passed in as a parameter to the function. It returns True if the user belongs to the specified role, False if not. This function is typically used with a CFIF block to conditionally execute a block of code depending on whether the user belongs to a particular role:

```
<cfif IsUserInRole("Admin") >
   <!--Administrator-specific code -->
<cfelse>
   <!-- Non-administrator-specific code -->
</cfif>
```

Using Dreamweaver's User Authentication Server Behaviors

ColdFusion MX's authentication features make the addition of user authentication a snap. However, if you are using Dreamweaver MX to generate your ColdFusion code, you have other options.

Dreamweaver MX includes several server behaviors just for adding ColdFusion user authentication tags. These are the Log In User, Restrict Access To Page, Check New Username, and Log Out User behaviors. Like many server behaviors, they insert the necessary ColdFusion tags and automatically add any conditional logic that is required.

The following sections will describe each of these server behaviors and give an example of how they can be used. The examples in this chapter use the CompanyInfo example database supplied with ColdFusion MX.

User Authentication

Although Dreamweaver MX and ColdFusion MX provide similar capabilities for user authentication, the methods each uses are different and not directly compatible. You will have to choose to use either ColdFusion MX's CFLOGIN and CFLOGINUSER tags for authentication or Dreamweaver MX's User Authentication server behaviors in your application.

The Log In User Server Behavior

The Log In User server behavior is used to validate a username and password for the user. This behavior is used in conjunction with a login form. The user enters a username and password on the form and submits it, and the server behavior validates the information using a data source.

Unlike the ColdFusion CFLOGIN tag, the Dreamweaver Log In User Server behavior doesn't go in the Application.cfm file; instead, it goes on the login form page.

To create this form, an example of which is shown in Figure 17.2, follow these steps:

1. Create a ColdFusion login form page, using File, New from the main menu. Create the page layout with Dreamweaver's design tools, and save it in the chap17 folder.

2. Add a form by choosing the Form button on the Forms category of the Insert bar, or choose the Insert, Form menu item. Note that you will be able to see the form boundaries in the Design view if you have the Invisible Elements Visual Aid enabled. Choose View, Visual Aids, Invisible Elements. Give the form a descriptive name.

3. Leave the action and method properties of the form blank. The Log In User server behavior will add these for you.

4. Add form text input elements for the username and password, using the Text Field button on the Insert bar, or the Insert, Form Objects, Text Field menu. Give them descriptive names as well. For the password field, set the input type to password in the Property Inspector.

5. Add a submit button using the Button object on the Insert bar, or use the Insert, Form Objects, Button menu. Make sure that the type is Submit in the Properties window. You should also set the label for the button to "Log In" or something similar so that its purpose is clear.

6. Do other desired HTML formatting on the page. It is common to put form fields in a table, with labels in one column and the form elements in another, so that they will line up nicely.

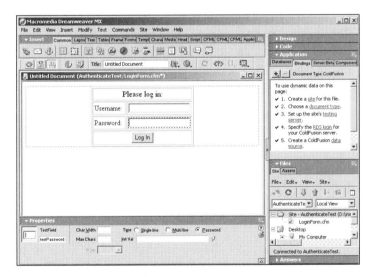

Figure 17.2   A login form page should have two text fields, one for the username and one for the password. Remember to set the password field type as "password" so the password is hidden when the user enters it.

Now that you have a login form created, you can attach the Log In User server behavior to it. This behavior will insert ColdFusion script that executes when the Submit button is clicked to send the form information back to the server. The username and password from the form are then checked with a database query. To add the Log In User server behavior, follow these steps:

1. Click the plus (+) button on the Server Behaviors window, and select User Authentication, Log In User. This will bring up the Log In User dialog box, shown in Figure 17.3.

2. Select the login form that you created in the Get Input From Form dropdown list.

3. Choose the form field you created for the username in the Username Field dropdown list.

4. Choose the form field you created for the password in the Password Field dropdown list.

5. Choose a data source to use for validation. Enter your data source username and password if necessary.

6. Select the table and the columns to use for the username and password validation.

7. Enter a page to redirect to when the login is successful. You can use the Browse button to select a page in your site, if you like.

8. If you want users to go back to the page they attempted to navigate to after logging in, check the Go To Previous URL (if it exists) checkbox. Otherwise, the user will always redirect to the Login Succeeds page.

9. Enter a page to navigate to if the login fails. This will usually be a page that explains that the login failed and gives the user a chance to try again.

10. Choose whether to restrict access based on just username and password, or by access level as well. This will allow you to choose a column to retrieve the user's access level (similar to `Roles` in the ColdFusion tags).

11. Click OK.

Now that you have the login mechanism in place, you are ready to protect application pages to which you want to restrict access. This is done with the User Authentication server behaviors, which include Restrict Access to Page, Log In User, Log Out User, and Check New Username.

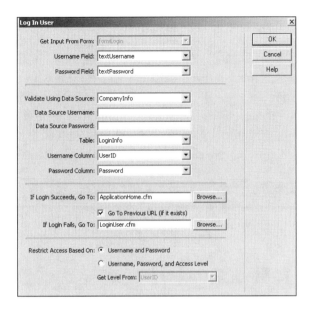

Figure 17.3   The Login User server behavior presents a
dialog box in which you enter all of the relevant login
information including the form name and the database
to run the query against.

The Restrict Access To Page Server Behavior

To protect pages in your application, you can use the Restrict Access To Page
server behavior. Unlike the CFLOGIN and CFLOGINUSER tags, which go in the
Application.cfm file and work across an entire application, this behavior must
be added to each page of the application that you want to protect.

This requires a little more work than the native ColdFusion tags, but adds
a little flexibility because you can leave some pages of your application
unprotected if they don't need it.

To add a Restrict Access To Page server behavior, follow these steps:

1. Click the plus (+) button on the Server Behaviors window, and select
   User Authentication, Restrict Access To Page. This will bring up the
   Restrict Access To Page dialog box shown in Figure 17.4.

2. Choose whether to restrict only to the username and password, or by
   access level as well. Note: If you choose to restrict by access level, you
   must have chosen the corresponding option in the Log In User behavior.

You can edit the Log In User behavior to add the access level restriction by double-clicking on it in the Server Behaviors panel. (Access levels are similar to Roles used by the native ColdFusion authentication tags. You can choose the column from the data source to use as an authentication level as well.)

3. If you chose to restrict by access level, choose the desired level from the list, or create new ones by clicking the Define button.

4. Enter your login form page in the If Access Denied, Go To field.

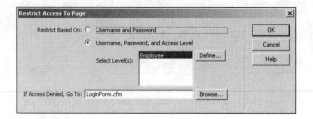

Figure 17.4   The Restrict Access To Page server behavior dialog lets you enter values to redirect users to your login form page if they haven't yet logged in.

The Check New Username Server Behavior

One advantage the Dreamweaver MX authentication server behaviors have over ColdFusion's native tags is the built-in capability to add new user registration to an application. Using only ColdFusion, you would have to write a registration form that allows the user to enter their information along with all of the logic of validating the information to see if the information is already in the database, and other tasks.

The Check New Username server behavior does all of this for you. All you have to do is create the form and add the appropriate server behaviors. If you use access levels for your registration, however, you will still need to have a page accessible only by an administrator who can assign access levels to a user.

To create a registration page form, do the following steps:

1. Create a ColdFusion page using File, New from the main menu. Choose the Dynamic Page category, and ColdFusion as the Dynamic Page type. Save the page in your site folder.

2. Design the page layout with Dreamweaver. Add a form by choosing the Insert, Form menu item. Note: You will be able to see the form boundaries in the Design view if you have the Invisible Elements Visual Aid enabled. Choose View, Visual Aids, Invisible Elements. Give the form a descriptive name.

3. Leave the action and method properties of the form blank. The server behavior will add these for you.

4. Add text input elements for the username and password, using Insert, Form Objects, Text Field. Give them descriptive names as well. For the password field, set the input type to password in the Property Inspector. You can add other information for the user to enter on this form as well, such as a full name and email address.

5. Add a submit button using Insert, Form Objects, Button, and making sure that the type is Submit in the Properties window. You can also set the label for the button to "Sign Up" or something similar so that its purpose is clear.

Now you need to add an Insert Record server behavior, so that the registration behavior can add new user records to the database.

1. Click the plus (+) button on the Server Behaviors window, and select Insert Record. This will bring up the Insert Record dialog box shown in Figure 17.5.

2. Choose a data source (and a username and password, if necessary).

3. Choose a table to insert the record into.

4. For each column in the database that you want to update, select it in the list and choose a form field from the Value list. You can choose a data type as well.

5. Enter the page to navigate to after the record insertion is complete.

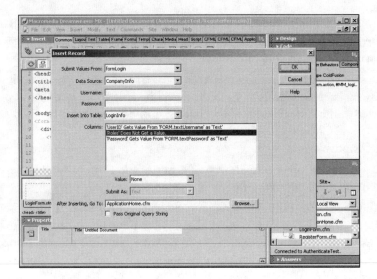

Figure 17.5 Before you can add the Check New Username server behavior, you must have an Insert Record server behavior that it can use to add a record to the database.

The final step is to add the Check New Username server behavior. To do that, follow these steps:

1. Click the plus (+) button on the Server Behaviors window, and select User Authentication, Check New Username. This will bring up the Check New Username dialog box shown in Figure 17.6.

2. Choose the form field used for the username. This will be used to verify that the chosen username isn't already in use before creating a new record.

3. Enter a page to go to if the username already exists.

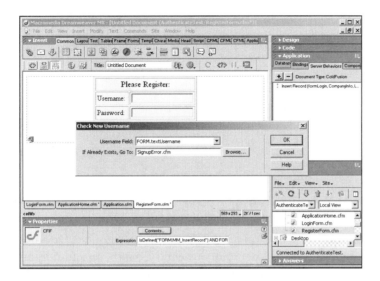

Figure 17.6   The Check New Username server behavior dialog box adds the validation logic for your registration page.

The Log Out User Server Behavior

The final user authentication server behavior is the Log Out User behavior, which simply adds a link to your page that can be clicked on to log out of the application. Alternatively, you can specify that the logout occurs when the page it is on loads. Make sure that the link is in a location that won't be clicked on accidentally and that its purpose is clear.

If you don't provide a means for logging out, or if the user neglects to log out when leaving your application, he or she will be automatically logged out when the session times out.

To add a Log Out User server behavior, do the following:

1. Click the plus (+) button on the Server Behaviors window, and select User Authentication, Log Out User. This will bring up the Log Out User dialog box, shown in Figure 17.7.

2. Choose a log-out method. You can choose to log out when a Log Out link is clicked, or when the page loads.

3. Enter a page to go to when the log out is complete.

4. Click OK.

Figure 17.7 The Log Out User server behavior is used to provide a convenient way to exit your application without having to wait for a session timeout.

Summary

In this chapter, you learned about user security and how to use the ColdFusion user authentication tags and functions. You used Dreamweaver's User Authentication server behaviors to build an authentication framework for an application. In the next chapter, you will learn how to add a search interface for your application.

18

Building a Search Interface

$\mathbf{A}$S A WEB SITE GROWS, IT BECOMES more and more important for users to be able to find the information that they are looking for. It also becomes more difficult. This chapter will show you how to build a search interface for a web site using ColdFusion.

When you create a search page to find information on a web site, you first have to index the site to make it more efficient to search. It would be far too time consuming and use too much of the server processing resources to go through each page. The usual solution is to create a *collection* containing all of the information that you want to search, and to build an index of the values in the collection. This speeds up the search a great deal because the search engine now only needs to look through the index and present the user links to the pages containing the information.

ColdFusion has several features that make building search pages easier. This chapter will teach you how to build search page collections both programmatically and by using the ColdFusion Administrator, as well as how to build a search interface programmatically using CFML. This chapter consists of the following sections:

- Creating a collection
- Indexing a collection
- Building a search interface
- Building a search results page

Introduction to Building a Search Interface

ColdFusion's search capabilities are provided by the Verity search engine. This engine is capable of doing full-text indexing and searching of a wide variety of file types, from text files to common application data formats, such as Microsoft Word or Adobe PDF.

The Verity search engine performs its searches on collections instead of on original documents. A Verity collection is a database that contains *metadata* that describes the information in the document, which allows for very fast and powerful indexed searches.

With the Verity search engine, you can index plain text files in ASCII and Unicode, various application binary data formats including Microsoft Office formats, PDF files, Corel WordPerfect, and many older data formats. You can also index record sets returned from CFQUERY, CFLDAP, or CFPOP tags. This makes the search engine a powerful feature for web sites that provide for document retrieval in many different formats.

In order to add a search interface to your ColdFusion application, it is first necessary to build and index one or more collections. After that, an interface can be constructed to perform a search.

Creating Collections

ColdFusion allows you to create Verity collections either programmatically or using the ColdFusion Administrator. The Administrator method is the quickest and easiest way to create a collection, but it must be done by hand by an administrator.

The programmatic method is more powerful. It allows the application itself to update and maintain the collection, which means that the collection can be reindexed if new documents are added or removed.

Creating and Indexing Collections with the Administrator

The ColdFusion Administrator is the quick and easy way to create a collection. Use this method if you have a fairly static collection of pages.

To create a collection using the Administrator, follow these steps:

1. Open the ColdFusion Administrator, and choose Data & Services, Verity Collections to go to the Verity Collections page shown in Figure 18.1.

2. Enter a name for your collection in the Name field. This name can be descriptive, with multiple words.

3. In the Path field, change the provided path if you want to place the collection somewhere other than the default location. This could be on a different server or on a different drive. The default path is in the verity\collections directory off of the ColdFusion root. Note that this location is where the collection files themselves will be located. This is not the directory that you want to search.

4. If you want to use a language other than English for the collection, choose it from the list.

5. Click Create Collection. The table at the bottom will be updated to show the new collection. The collection is now ready to be indexed.

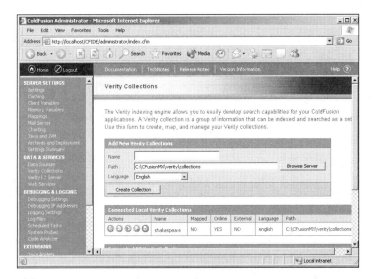

Figure 18.1 The ColdFusion Administrator provides the fastest way to create collections for indexing your site.

Indexing a Collection with the Administrator

Adding documents and indexing Verity collections in the ColdFusion Administrator is just as easy as creating the collection. To index a collection, do the following:

1. On the Verity Collections page, choose the collection you want to index from the Connected Local Verity Collections table. Click on the Index button on the right, or click on the collection name in the table. This will send you to the Index Verity Collections page, shown in Figure 18.2.

2. Make sure the File Extensions field contains a comma-separated list of file extensions for the files you want to index. You may add or remove extensions as necessary.

3. Enter the path of the directory to search for files in the Directory Path field. You may also use the Browse Server button to locate the path.

4. Check the Recursively Index Sub Directories box if you want subdirectories to be searched for files as well.

5. Enter a Return URL. This is a URL corresponding to the document directory so that documents can be retrieved. If you are indexing your web directory, this will be the URL of your web site.

6. Click the Submit button to index the documents.

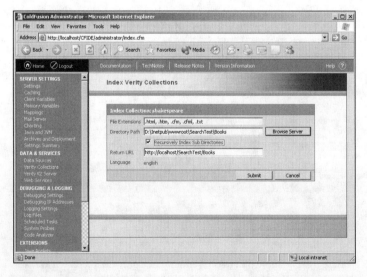

Figure 18.2   You can quickly index a document directory or your web site directory structure using the Index Verity Collections page in the Administrator.

Creating and Indexing Collections Programmatically

Working with collections programmatically is a little more involved than using the Administrator, but it's also more powerful. You should use the programmatic method in these situations:

- When you're indexing query results instead of files. The Administrator only allows collections to be indexed using files.

- When the collection is updated frequently. It's easier to add an update function to code that allows new documents to be added to the collection than it is to require updates through the Administrator.

- When users are able to update the collection. You obviously don't want to allow users access to the Administrator, so you should provide a custom interface.

This section will show how to create and index collections programmatically using CFML tags.

Creating a Collection with the *CFCOLLECTION* Tag

You can create and maintain a collection using the CFCOLLECTION tag. This allows you to either create your own custom interface for managing collections or have the tag work in the background to automatically update a collection. CFCOLLECTION has the following syntax:

```
<cfcollection action = "create"
    collection="Collection Name"
    path="c:\cfusionmx\verity\collections\"
    language="English">
```

The attributes shown in Table 18.1 are available for use with CFCOLLECTION.

Table 18.1 *CFCOLLECTION* **Tag Attributes**

Attribute	Description
action	The desired action to perform on the collection. Possible values are as follows:
	create: Registers a new collection with ColdFusion.
	repair: Fixes a corrupted database.
	delete: Removes a collection. If the collection was created with CFCOLLECTION, its directories are deleted as well.
	optimize: Optimizes the collection for faster searching and recovers empty space.
	list: Returns a query result set using the name attribute value containing all registered collections and their attributes. This is the default value.

continues

Table 18.1   **Continued**

Attribute	Description
collection	This specifies the name of the collection. This can be either a new collection for a `create` or an existing collection for other operations.
path	The path to the collection.
language	This specifies the language used when creating the list. The default is English.
name	This attribute is used only if the `action` attribute is set to `"list"`, in which case it is required. It provides the name of the query results to return.

The CFCOLLECTION tag can be used as the basis for a custom interface for managing collections. You could have a form page that prompts the user to choose a collection and an operation to perform on it. The server application then performs the operation using the CFCOLLECTION tag.

When you are working with the CFCOLLECTION tag, it is recommended that you enclose it in a CFLOCK tag with name="verity" to prevent multiple simultaneous writes to the same collection. The following example shows a list action being used to create a query result set and dump the results:

```
<cflock name="verity">
    <cfcollection action="list" name="rsCollections" >
</cflock>
<cfquery name="queryCollections" dbtype="query">
    SELECT * from rsCollections
</cfquery>
<cfdump var=#queryCollections#>
```

Indexing a Collection with the *CFINDEX* Tag

To add documents to a collection programmatically, use the CFINDEX tag. This tag can be used to populate a collection with metadata from document files or from query result sets. CFINDEX has the following syntax:

```
<cfindex
    collection="collection_name"
    action="action"
    type="type"
    title="title"
    key="ID"
    body="body"
    custom1="custom_value"
    custom2="custom_value"
    URLpath="URL"
    extensions="file_extensions"
    query="query_name"
    recurse="Yes|No"
    language="language">
```

The attributes shown in Table 18.2 are supported by the CFINDEX tag.

Table 18.2   **CFINDEX Tag Attributes**

Attribute	Description
collection	This can be either the name of a collection registered by ColdFusion or the path to a nonregistered collection.
action	The action to perform on the collection. Possible values are:
	update: Updates a collection and adds the value of the key attribute to the index.
	delete: Deletes data specified by the type attribute.
	purge: Deletes all keys from a collection.
	refresh: Re-creates a collection's keys. This tag is required.
type	This attribute specifies the type of collection on which the action will be performed. These are either files or entries from a database query. Possible values for type are:
	file: Performs the action on files.
	path: Performs the action on files matching the extension tag.
	custom: Applies action to query results (if action is "update" or "delete")
title	A title for the collection (for searching).
key	If type="file", this specifies an absolute path to a file. If type="path", it specifies an absolute path. If type="custom" or any other value, key specifies a query column name.
body	If type="custom", body provides ASCII text to search. For queries, it specifies a delimited list of columns.
custom1 and custom2	These attributes can be used to store data during an indexing operation.
URLPath	Specifies a URL path to a file or path if the type is equal to "file" or "path".
extensions	Comma-delimited list of file extensions. "*." can be used to return files with no extension. An example would be ".html, .htm, .cfm, *.".
query	A query used to generate a collection.
recurse	If type="path", all subdirectories are also searched for files to index if recurse="yes".
language	Specifies the language to use. The default is English.

A common use for the CFINDEX tag is to update a collection by adding a new document. This can be done with the action="update" and type="file" values, as shown in this example:

```
<cfindex
    collection="snippets"
    action="update"
    type="file"
    key="c:\inetpub\wwwroot\cfdocs\snippets\abs.cfm"
    urlpath="http://localhost/cfdocs/snippets">
```

Building a Search Interface Page

Once you have an indexed collection, it's possible to perform searches against it. ColdFusion uses the CFSEARCH tag to search a Verity collection.

CFSEARCH behaves much like a CFQUERY tag, except that its results come from a collection instead of a database table, and its search criteria are based on Verity search criteria instead of SQL queries. Both are created and referenced with a name attribute.

The syntax of the CFSEARCH tag is shown here:

```
<cfsearch
    name="search_name"
    collection="collection_name"
    type="criteria"
    criteria="search_expression"
    maxRows="number"
    startRow="row_number"
    language="language">
```

The attributes of CFSEARCH are shown in Table 18.3.

Table 18.3   *CFSEARCH* **Tag Attributes**

Attribute	Description
name	This is the name of the search query.
collection	A collection to search. This can also be a comma-delimited list with multiple collections.
type	The type of search. Possible values are "simple" and "explicit". Explicit searches require operators to be invoked explicitly.
criteria	This is the search criteria, which follows the Verity search rules described in the next section.
maxRows	The maximum number of rows to return. The default is to return all rows.
startRow	The first row number to get. The default is 1.
language	A language used for the query. The default is English. This option requires the ColdFusion International Search Pack.

About Verity Search Criteria

The Verity search engine allows a lot of flexibility in search terms. Whether you take advantage of this flexibility depends on your audience and the type of material you want to search. There are two types of searches that can be done with the CFSEARCH tag: simple and explicit.

Simple Searches

Simple search queries are the most basic type and should be supported by all search pages as the default. A simple search is done by entering a word or a set of comma-separated words into a text field on a form. Wild card characters also are usually allowed. If the search criteria contains commas, Verity treats the comma as a logical OR operator. Without commas, the search treats a list of words as a phrase. Simple searches allow basic operators including AND, OR, and NOT.

An important operator to know about for use with simple queries is the STEM operator. CFSEARCH uses the STEM operator by default to widen possible search terms by looking for alternate forms of the word. For example, if the search is made on the word "box", the results would return documents containing "box", "boxed", "boxing", and "boxes". This behavior can be disabled by using the WORD operator in the query.

> **Verity**
>
> The Verity search engine has a lot of operators and options for search criteria. Because of this, a search interface should have the most common operators listed, as well as a link to another page listing all options. All Verity search engine operators and options are described in detail in the ColdFusion MX documentation.

Explicit Searches

Explicit searches can be done by specifying type="explicit" in the CFSEARCH tag, or they can be specified by the user putting the search terms in quotes.

Building a Search Form

A typical search form will present the user with an input text field where search criteria can be entered, radio buttons indicating whether the search should be simple or explicit, and possibly a list of collections that can be searched.

To create a search form, do the following:

1. Create a ColdFusion page using File, New from the main menu. Create the page layout with Dreamweaver, and save the file into the chap18 folder.

2. Add a form by choosing the Insert, Form menu item. Note: You will be able to see the form boundaries in the Design view if you have the Invisible Elements Visual Aid enabled. Choose View, Visual Aids, Invisible Elements. Give the form a descriptive name.

3. In the form Property Inspector, set the action property of the form to go to dosearch.cfm, or whatever you will want to name the search results page. (This page will be created in the next section.)

4. Set the form Method property in the Property Inspector. You should use the POST method to hide all of the submitted form values in the HTTP request.

5. Add a text field for the search criteria.

6. Add a submit button using Insert, Form Objects, Button, making sure that the type is Submit in the Properties window. You can also set the label for the button to "Do Search" or something similar so that its purpose is clear. Figure 18.3 shows a complete simple search form in Dreamweaver.

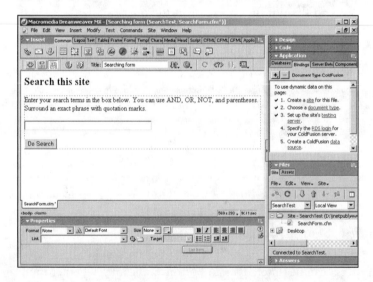

Figure 18.3 Create a search page in Dreamweaver using the form creation tools.

A listing of the simple search page is as follows:

```
<html>
<head>
  <title>Searching form</title>
</head>
<body>
<h2>Search this site</h2>
<form method="post" action="dosearch.cfm">
  Enter your search terms in the box below. You can use AND, OR, NOT, and
  parentheses. Surround an exact phrase with quotation marks.<br><br>
```

```
  <input name="textCriteria" type="text" id="textCriteria" size="50"
  maxLength="50">
  <br><br>
  <input type="submit" value="Do Search">
</form>
</body>
</html>
```

Building a Search Results Page

A Search Results page is the page that contains the CFSEARCH tag and actually performs the search and displays the results. This is the page that the search form page submits to in the action attribute of the form. Figure 18.4 shows our results page.

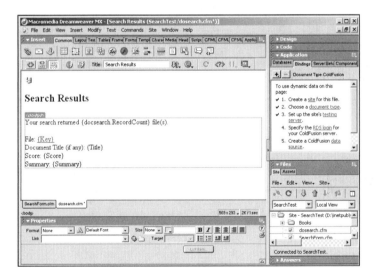

Figure 18.4   The search results page uses the query mode of the CFOUTPUT tag to display the results of the search.

A listing of the results page is as follows:

```
<html>
<head>
  <title>Search Results</title>
</head>
<body>
<!-- Do the search -->
<cfsearch
   name = "docsearch"
   collection = "shakespeare"
   criteria = "#Form.textCriteria#">
```

```
<h2>Search Results</h2>
<cfoutput>
Your search returned #docsearch.RecordCount# file(s).
</cfoutput>

<cfoutput query="docsearch">
  <p>
  File: <a href="#URL#">#Key#</a><br>
  Document Title (if any): #Title#<br>
  Score: #Score#<br>
  Summary: #Summary#</p>
</cfoutput>
</body>
</html>
```

Testing the Search Page

Now that you have created the search form page and the search results page, as well as created and indexed a collection, you are ready to test the search function. Navigate to the search form page and enter some search terms, as Figure 18.5 shows. Then click the Search button.

Figure 18.5 The search criteria can be entered using comma-separated values, phrases, or Verity operators.

The search results page should be displayed next, with the results of the search including a short summary from the document. In addition, a score is displayed showing the relevancy the search terms have with this document. An example of the search results are shown in Figure 18.6.

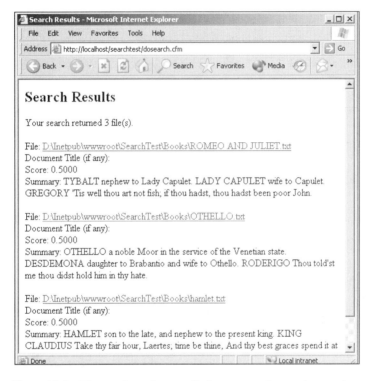

Figure 18.6   The search results page displays a score, the search term that matched, a summary of the document, and a link to the original document.

Summary

In this chapter, you learned how to build a search interface using the CFINDEX and CFSEARCH tags. You also learned how to build a search results page. In the next chapter, you will learn how to use ColdFusion components.

VI

Advanced ColdFusion
Development

19

Using ColdFusion Components

IN THIS CHAPTER, YOU WILL LEARN THE basics of using ColdFusion components. You will use the Create Component dialog box in Dreamweaver to build components quickly and easily. You will then use the component functions to query a directory structure, rename directories, and create new directories.

About Using ColdFusion Components

Introduced in ColdFusion MX, ColdFusion components offer a number of advantages over traditional ColdFusion pages. In particular, ColdFusion components promote code reuse, which greatly simplifies application development and increases the maintainability of your code.

If you're just starting out with ColdFusion development, the immediate benefits of ColdFusion components might not be clear. However, as you gain programming experience, you'll quickly discover two things:

- You'll find yourself re-creating similar code over and over again. For example, each dynamic page must contain a CFQUERY statement. ColdFusion components let you write the code once and use it in all your ColdFusion applications.

- As the size of your ColdFusion applications grows into dozens of ColdFusion pages, maintaining code becomes an ever more challenging proposition. ColdFusion components let you consolidate code into one location, thereby making it very easy to maintain.

ColdFusion components also provide advanced features, such as interacting with the Flash Remoting service and producing web services. For more information on these subjects, see Chapter 20, "Building Flash Remoting Services" and Chapter 21, "Using and Creating Web Services."

Although the basics are the same, you use ColdFusion components differently than ColdFusion pages. ColdFusion components are saved as .cfc files, unlike the .cfm extension of ColdFusion pages. In the component code, you use a special set of CFML tags to construct the component, including CFCOMPONENT, CFFUNCTION, CFARGUMENT, and CFRETURN.

Using these tags, you define component functions, which contain CFML code that performs the processing, such as querying databases, performing conditional logic, and so on. You can use any CFML tag or function in function definitions, just as with ColdFusion pages. Components can contain multiple functions.

You invoke the component functions from other ColdFusion components pages using the CFINVOKE tag, the GET and POST HTTP methods, the Flash Remoting service, and web services. As you can see from the list, ColdFusion components interact natively with many types of callers, which is another advantage over ColdFusion pages.

When executed, the component function returns its results using the CFRETURN tag. It's up to the caller as to how to handle the returned results. If you're invoking the component function from a ColdFusion page and the result is a recordset, you can create a dynamic table, menu, and so on, just like using a CFQUERY object on the same page.

In this chapter, you will build a ColdFusion application that displays the directory structure for the bookexample directory in the web root and lets users upload files and create new directories. This application requires two pages:

- directoryExplorer.cfc—This ColdFusion component queries the file structure and provides additional functions to rename directories and create new directories.
- directoryClient.cfm—This ColdFusion page lets users interact with the directoryExplorer.cfc component functions.

Figure 19.1 shows the files for this application and their interactions with each other.

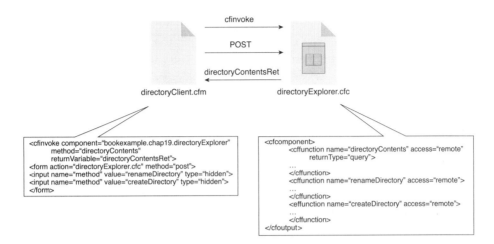

Figure 19.1　This ColdFusion application contains two pages, a ColdFusion component and a ColdFusion page. The ColdFusion page invokes the functions of directoryExplorer.cfc.

Building directoryExplorer.cfc

To build ColdFusion components (see Figure 19.2) in Dreamweaver MX, you use the Components panel. The Components panel, shown in Figure 19.2, lets you create ColdFusion components, see the available components in your web root, insert automatically generated code to invoke component functions, and see the details for components and component functions.

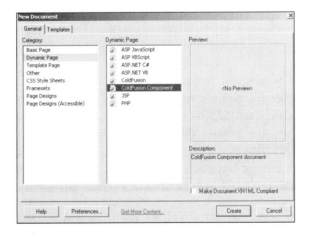

Figure 19.2　The New Document dialog box lets you choose various prebuilt templates, including ColdFusion components.

Dreamweaver's Create Component dialog box, which can be opened by click-ing the plus (+) button in the Components panel, is the main interface for creating ColdFusion components. Keep in mind, you can only generate the necessary tags, also know as constructors, of a ColdFusion component. Using the framework tags as a starting point, you build the ColdFusion application functionality.

The following example, taken from the Dreamweaver ColdFusion component template, shows the basic code required to make a component:

```
<cfcomponent>
    <cffunction name="myFunction" access="public" returntype="string">
        <cfargument name="myArgument" type="string" required="true">
        <cfset myResult = "foo">
        <cfreturn myResult>
    </cffunction>
</cfcomponent>
```

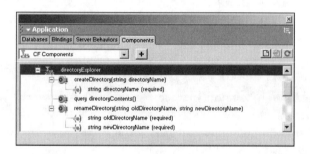

Figure 19.3   The Components panel gives you control over the ColdFusion components in your web root. Using the Components panel, you can create ColdFusion components, view the available components, and insert automatically generated component invocation code.

In the code, the CFCOMPONENT statement, which defines the component, encloses the CFFUNCTION statement. The CFFUNCTION statement defines a component func-tion. When you use ColdFusion components, you call a component function. Therefore, the majority of your CFML code in components resides within the confines of a CFFUNCTION statement. Although you can use only one CFCOMPONENT tag within a component file, you can define multiple component methods by adding additional CFFUNCTION statements:

```
<cfcomponent>
    <cffunction name="myFunction" access="public" returntype="string">
        <cfargument name="myArgument" type="string" required="true">
        <cfset myResult = "foo">
        <cfreturn myResult>
    </cffunction>
    <cffunction name="myFunction2" access="public" returntype="string">
```

```
            <cfargument name="myArgument2" type="string" required="true">
            <cfset myResult2 = "foo">
            <cfreturn myResult2>
        </cffunction>
    </cfcomponent>
```

Although no attributes are required, you can specify additional attributes for the CFCOMPONENT tag, including displayname, extends, and hint. The displayname and hint attributes let you describe the component. The extends attribute lets you specify another ColdFusion component. The current component will inherit the methods of the specified ColdFusion component.

The CFFUNCTION tag typically contains three attributes, including name, access, and returntype. The name attribute specifies the function name, which you use when you invoke a component method. The access attribute specifies what kind of client can call the component methods:

- If you specify remote, the component method is accessible by FORM and GET methods like web pages or ColdFusion pages as a web service and by the Flash Remoting service.
- The private setting restricts invocation to the component itself.
- The package setting restricts invocation to ColdFusion files in the same web root directory.
- The public setting opens up the methods to invocation by HTTP methods, the CFINVOKE tag in ColdFusion pages or components, and so on.

The returntype attribute lets you specify the data type that the component method returns, such as query (recordset), array, struct, string, numeric, and so on. Also, you can use the roles attribute to assign a component method to a security role. Like the CFCOMPONENT tag, the hint and displayname attributes let you describe the component.

Component methods can also accept parameters that are defined with a CFARGUMENT tag within the CFFUNCTION statement. You can specify multiple parameters with multiple CFARGUMENT tags. The CFARGUMENT tag contains more attributes, such as hint and displayname. The required attribute lets you set an argument as required. If a client does not include the parameters when invoking the component method, ColdFusion produces an error. Finally, the CFRETURN tag returns the results of whatever CFML processing occurs within the CFFUNCTION statement. You can use only one CFRETURN tag per CFFUNCTION statement.

When deciding what a component should actually do, think about the repetitive tasks that you perform every day, such as building recordsets. If you find that you build a similar database query over and over again, or other developers are requesting access to your database, you can build a ColdFusion component that queries a database and returns a recordset. Also, you can set the CFFUNCTION tag's access attribute to remote, which makes it available as a web service.

> **Code View**
>
> You must use Code View when building ColdFusion components; Dreamweaver does not support Design View for components.

To generate the necessary CFML for ColdFusion components in directoryExplorer.cfc, follow these steps:

1. Select the Components panel of the Application panel group, and click the plus (+) button. The Create Component dialog box appears.

2. In the Create Component dialog box's Components section, enter **directoryExplorer** in the Name text box, as shown in Figure 19.4. Click the Browse button next to the Component Directory text box. In the Component File Output Directory dialog box, select the chap19 directory. The component file will be saved to this directory.

3. In the Functions section of the Create Component dialog box, as shown in Figure 19.5, click the plus (+) button to create a function. In the Name text box, enter **directoryContents**. In the Access menu, select remote. In the Return Type menu, select query. The returnType CFFUNCTION tag attribute provides data type validation for returning results to the caller.

4. Repeat Step 3 twice to create two more functions, createDirectory and renameDirectory. These component functions do not return anything to the caller, so you do not need to specify a return type.

5. In the Arguments section of the Create Component dialog box, select renameDirectory in the Available Functions menu, as shown in Figure 19.6. Click the plus (+) button to create an argument. In the Name text box, enter **oldDirectoryName**. In the Type menu, select string. Finally, select the Required checkbox. When Required is checked, the component function will throw an error if the parameter is not passed from the caller. This argument passes the parameter passed from directoryClient.cfm to the component function.

   Click the plus (+) button again, and create an argument named newDirectoryName. It is a string and is required.

6. Repeat Step 5 for the createDirectory function to create an argument named directoryName, which is a string and is required.

7. In the Create Component dialog box, click the OK button. The component constructor code is automatically generated, as shown in Figure 19.7.

8. Save your work.

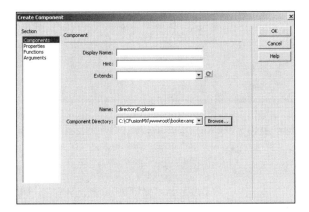

Figure 19.4   The Components section of the Create Component dialog box lets you set general options for a ColdFusion component, including the name and the component directory.

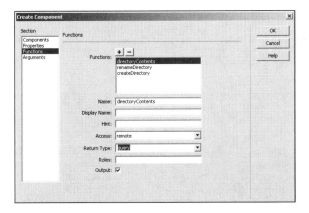

Figure 19.5   The Functions section of the Create Component dialog box lets you create component functions and specify function attributes, including name, access mode, and return data type.

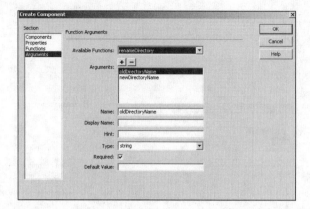

Figure 19.6   The Arguments section of the Create Component dialog box lets you create function arguments, including name and data type.

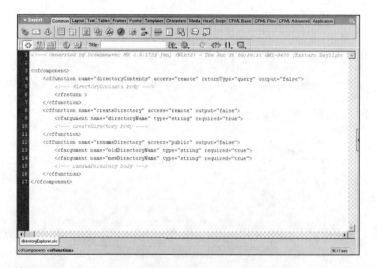

Figure 19.7   In Code View, you can see the component constructor code generated by the Create Component dialog box. Notice that you still need to create the CFML that performs the actual processing.

Although Dreamweaver automatically generates the component constructor code, you must still supply the CFML code for component function processing. You will use the CFDIRECTORY tag in the directoryExplorer component to build the CFML that actually provides the functionality. Follow these steps:

1. Open directoryExplorer.cfc.

2. Using your mouse, place your cursor between the opening and closing tags of the directoryContents CFFUNCTION tags.

3. In the CFML Advanced panel of the Insert bar, click the
   CFDIRECTORY button. The CFDIRECTORY dialog box appears.
   The CFDIRECTORY tag lets you list the contents of directories, create new
   directories, rename directories, and delete directories.

4. In the CFDIRECTORY Tag Editor dialog box, select List in the Action
   menu, as shown in Figure 19.8. The List action queries the specified
   directory and returns the directory structure in a recordset. Click the
   Browse button next to the Directory text box. In the Choose Folder
   dialog box that appears, select the bookexample directory in your web
   root. In the Query Name text box, enter **directoryContents**. This name
   lets you reference the recordset created by the CFDIRECTORY tag. Click the
   OK button. The following code appears:

   ```
   <cfdirectory directory="C:\CFusionMX\wwwroot\bookexample\"
   action="list" name="directoryContents">
   ```

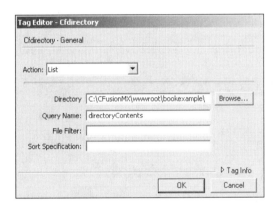

Figure 19.8   Using the CFDIRECTORY dialog box,
you can create a CFDIRECTORY tag that queries a
directory structure and returns the results as a
recordset, which can then be displayed to the user.

5. In the directoryContents function's CFRETURN tag, insert
   directoryContentsQ, as the following example shows:

   ```
   <cfreturn directoryContentsQ>
   ```

   The CFRETURN tag is required to return results to the caller.

6. Using your mouse, place your cursor after the two CFARGUMENTS tags in the renameDirectory function. Click the CFDIRECTORY button again. In the CFDIRECTORY Tag Editor dialog box, select Rename in the Action menu, as shown in Figure 19.9. Click the Browse button next to the Directory text box, and in the Choose Directory dialog box that appears, select the bookexample directory. Copy the contents of the Directory text box into the New Directory text box. Click the OK button. The following code appears:

```
<cfdirectory directory="C:\CFusionMX\wwwroot\bookexample\"
action="rename" newdirectory="C:\CFusionMX\wwwroot\bookexample\">
```

To supply the name of the directory to change and the new directory name, you must append the CFARGUMENT values to the end of each file path in the directory and newdirectory attributes of the CFDIRECTORY tag. Your code should look similar to the following example:

```
<cfdirectory directory=
"C:\CFusionMX\wwwroot\bookexample\#arguments.oldDirectoryName#"
action="rename" newdirectory=
"C:\CFusionMX\wwwroot\bookexample\#arguments.newDirectoryName#">
```

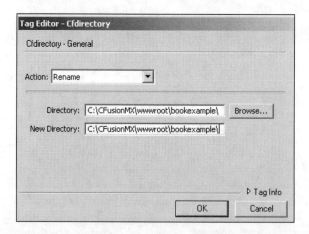

Figure 19.9 You can also use the CFDIRECTORY dialog box to create a CFDIRECTORY tag that renames directories. You need to supply only the old directory path and the new directory path.

7. Place your cursor below the CFDIRECTORY tag in the renameDirectory function. In the CFML Basic panel of the Insert bar, click the CFLOCATION button. The CFLOCATION Tag Editor dialog box appears.

8. In the CFLOCATION Tag Editor dialog box, enter **directoryClient.cfm** in the URL text box, as shown in Figure 19.10. Uncheck the Append Client Variables to the URL check box. Click the OK button. The following code appears:

   ```
   <cflocation url="directoryClient.cfm" addtoken="no">
   ```

   After the CFDIRECTORY tag is processed, the CFLOCATION tag directs the web browser back to the calling page, which will display the results. You will create the directoryClient.cfm page in the next section.

9. Place your cursor after the CFARGUMENT tag in the createDirectory function. Click the CFDIRECTORY button in the CFML Advanced panel. In the CFDIRECTORY Tag Editor dialog box that appears, select Create in the Action menu, as shown in Figure 19.11. Click the Browse button next to the Directory text box, and in the Select File dialog box that appears, select the bookexample directory. Click the OK button, and the following code appears:

   ```
   <cfdirectory directory="C:\CFusionMX\wwwroot\bookexample\" action="create">
   ```

   To supply the new directory name passed from the caller page, you must append the CFARGUMENT value to the directory attribute, as the following example shows:

   ```
   <cfdirectory directory="C:\CFusionMX\wwwroot\bookexample\
   #arguments.directoryName#" action="create">
   ```

10. Place your cursor directly after the CFDIRECTORY tag in the createDirectory function, and click the CFLOCATION button in the CFML Basic panel again. In the CFLOCATION dialog box, enter **directoryClient.cfm**, uncheck the Append Client Variables to the URL check box, and click the OK button.

    After the CFDIRECTORY tag creates the directory, the CFLOCATION tag directs the user's browser back to the calling page, which displays the results.

11. Save your work

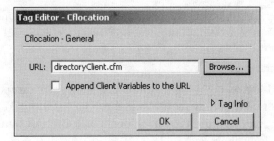

Figure 19.10   Using the CFLOCATION dialog box,
you can create a CFLOCATION tag that directs the
user's web browser back to the calling page.

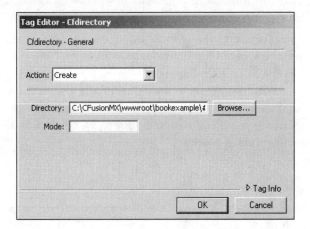

Figure 19.11   Once again using the CFDIRECTORY dialog
box, you can create a CFDIRECTORY tag that creates a new
directory. You need to supply only the new directory path.

Building directoryClient.cfm

The directoryClient.cfm page acts as a form page to invoke component functions of the directoryExplorer ColdFusion component. As described in this
chapter's introduction, you have a wide variety of choices when invoking
component methods. For the purposes of this chapter, you will invoke
functions using the CFINVOKE tag and the POST HTTP method.

In directoryClient.cfm, you will create a dynamic table and menu using the
recordset returned by the directoryContents component. You will also create
two utilities for users to create new directories and rename existing directories.

In ColdFusion pages, you can invoke ColdFusion components using the CFINVOKE tag. The CFINVOKE tag, which can also be used to call web services, acts like any other ColdFusion tag. For example, you can enclose a CFINVOKE tag within a CFIF statement and invoke a component method only when certain parameters are met. You can also call multiple ColdFusion components by using multiple CFINVOKE tags. If you want to invoke a component in the context of a form page, whether ColdFusion or regular HTML, you can specify form or URL variables. Here is an example:

```
<cfinvoke component="bookexample.chap19.directoryExplorer"
    method="directoryContents"
    returnvariable="directoryContentsRet">
```

In the example, bookexample.chap19.directoryExplorer refers to the web root directory structure of the directoryExplorer component, also known as the component package name. A component package is simply the directory in which a component sits. Using the package name, you can have more than one component with the same file name, but because the package name is used, there are no conflicts. Of course, two components with the same name cannot exist in the same directory.

The method attribute specifies the function name to call, which maps the name attribute in the CFFUNCTION statement. In the returnvariable attribute, you give the results a name, or scope, that you use to reference the results returned from the component.

When you need to pass parameters to a component, you use the CFINVOKEPARAM tag. You insert one or more CFINVOKEPARAM tags inside the opening and closing CFINVOKE tags, which are only necessary when using the CFINVOKEPARAM tag. For example:

```
<cfinvoke component="bookexample.chap19.directoryExplorer"
    method="createDirectory">
    <cfinvokeargument name="directoryName"
    value="<cfoutput>#url.directoryName#</cfoutput>"/>
</cfinvoke>
```

In the example, the CFINVOKE statement encloses the CFINVOKEARGUMENT tag, which includes the name attribute that specifies the parameter name and the value attribute that specifies the value to send to the component method. As you can see, you can make the value dynamic, such as using a URL variable passed from another page. In fact, because the CFINVOKE and CFINVOKEPARAM tags are just like any other CFML tags, you can make any of the attributes dynamic.

To build directoryClient.cfm, follow these steps:

1. Create a new ColdFusion page from the bookexample template, and save it as directoryClient.cfm.

2. Click the Show Code View button in the Document toolbar. In the Application panel set, click the Components tab. In the Components panel, click the Refresh button. The Components panel refreshes to show the available components in your web root.

3. Click the plus (+) next to the bookexample.chap19 entry to expand the tree and reveal the component functions for the directoryExplorer component. Notice that each function description lists the data type returned by the component (if any), the function name, and the function arguments (if any).

   Find the directoryContents function, and drag it to the top of the document window. The following code appears:

   ```
   <cfinvoke component="bookexample.chap19.directoryExplorer"
       method="directoryContents"
       returnvariable="directoryContentsRet">
   ```

   As you can see, a CFINVOKE tag is created. In the component attribute, notice that the directory structure is separated by periods, also known as dot syntax. In the example, bookexample.chap19.directoryExplorer refers to the web root directory structure of the directoryExplorer component, also known as the component package name. A component package is simply the directory in which a component sits. Using the package name, you can have more than one component with the same filename, but because the package name is used, there are no conflicts. Of course, two components with the same name cannot exist in the same directory. The method attribute names the component function, and the returnvariable attribute establishes the variable scope to access the component method results.

   You can now use the directoryContentsRet variable scope to build a dynamic table, which you will create in the next step.

4. Click the Show Code and Design Views button. In the Design View, place your cursor in the editable Body region of the document window, and insert a table with three columns, two rows, and no border. In the top row of the table, enter File Name, File Type, and Date Last Modified. These names will serve as the table column headers.

5. In the Design View, using your mouse, select the bottom table row. Open Code View. The TR and TD tags of the bottom table row are highlighted. Using the CFML Basic panel of the Insert bar, click the CFOUTPUT button. The CFOUTPUT dialog box appears.

6. In the CFOUTPUT Tag Editor dialog box, enter **directoryContentsRet** in the Query Name text box, as shown in Figure 19.12. Click the OK button. The following code appears:

```
<cfoutput query="directoryContentsRet">
    <tr>
        <td> </td>
        <td> </td>
        <td> </td>
    </tr>
</cfoutput>
```

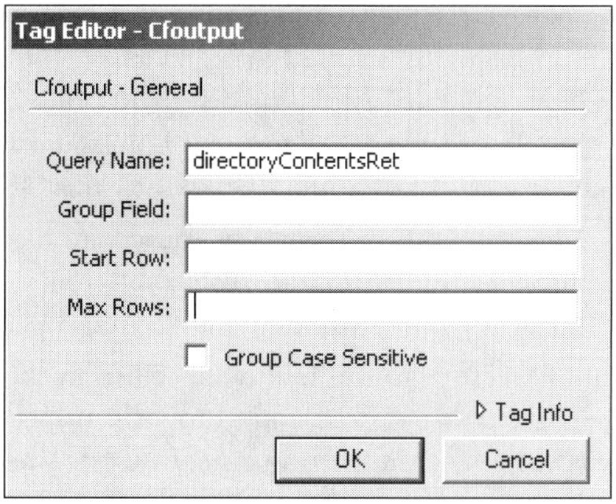

Figure 19.12 Using the CFOUTPUT dialog box, you reference the recordset returned by the directoryContents function of the directoryExplorer component.

7. For each TD tag set contained in the directoryContentsRet CFOUTPUT statement, you must insert the appropriate directoryContentsRet recordset column. The recordset created by the CFDIRECTORY tag contains various columns that describe the files found in the directory, including file name, file type, date last modified, and file size. You reference the columns in a CFDIRECTORY recordset just like a recordset created by a database query, as the following example shows:

```
<cfoutput query="directoryContentsRet">
    <tr>
        <td><p>#directoryContentsRet.NAME#</p></td>
        <td><p>#directoryContentsRet.TYPE#</p></td>
        <td><p>#directoryContentsRet.DATELASTMODIFIED#</p></td>
    </tr>
</cfoutput>
```

As the example shows, insert the `directoryContensRet` recordset columns between the TD tags. You just created a ColdFusion component-powered dynamic table. Because Dreamweaver does not recognize a component-generated recordset in the Bindings panel, you must use Code View to create the necessary CFML by hand.

8. In the Design View, insert a table below the dynamic table that you just created. The table should have three rows, four columns, and a border of one (1). In the top row, merge the cells into one, and enter Directory Utilities as the table header.

9. Using your cursor, select the middle table row. In the Code View, the TR and TD tags are highlighted. In the Forms panel of the Insert bar, click the Form button. In the Form Tag Editor dialog box that displays, enter **directoryExplorer.cfc** in the Action text box, and select post in the Method menu, as shown in Figure 19.13. Click the OK button.

10. Repeat Step 9 for the bottom table row. You create individual FORM tag statements because each table row invokes a different component function.

11. Enter Rename Directory in the first table cell from the left. In the next table cell, insert a menu. In the menu's Property Inspector, enter **oldDirectoryName** for the menu name. In Code View, place your cursor between the opening and closing SELECT tags, and insert a CFOUTPUT statement that references the `directoryContentsRet` recordset. Place your cursor between the opening and closing SELECT tags, and right-click your mouse. In the submenu that appears, select Insert Tag. The Tag Chooser dialog box appears.

12. In the Tag Chooser dialog box, select HTML tags and option. When you click the Insert button, the Option Tag Editor dialog box appears.

13. In the Option Tag Editor dialog box, enter **#directoryContentsRet.NAME#** in the Value and Text dialog boxes, as shown in Figure 19.14. Click the OK button and the following code appears:

    ```
    <option
    value="#directoryContentsRet.NAME#">#directoryContentsRet.NAME#
    </option>
    ```

    You just created a ColdFusion component-powered dynamic menu. This menu lets users select an existing directory to rename in a foolproof way.

14. In the third table cell from the left, insert a text box. In its Property Inspector, name the text box newDirectoryName. This text box lets users enter the new name for the directory.

15. In the far right table cell, insert a Submit button.

16. Also in the far right table cell, insert a hidden form field. Name the hidden form field **method**, and enter **renameDirectory** for the value. When the user clicks the Submit button, the hidden form field will be passed to the directoryExplorer component to supply the component function name. The hidden form field can exist in any table cell, so long as it exists within the FORM tag you inserted in Step 9.

17. In the bottom table row, enter **Create Directory** in the far left cell. In the next table cell, insert a text box named directoryName. This text box supplies the name for the new directory.

18. Merge the third and fourth table cells from the left, and insert a Submit button.

19. In one of the bottom table cells, insert a hidden form field named "method". For its value, enter **createDirectory**. When the user clicks the Submit button on the bottom row, the hidden form field is passed to the directoryExplorer component and supplies the name of the component function to be executed. Figure 19.15 shows the completed table.

20. Save your work.

Congratulations, you just created a ColdFusion component application.

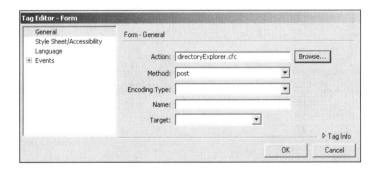

Figure 19.13   In the Form dialog box, you create a FORM tag that targets directoryExplorer.cfc. You will invoke the renameDirectory component function using the POST HTTP method.

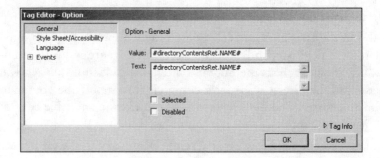

Figure 19.14 In the Option dialog box, you reference the `directoryContentsRet` recordset returned by the directoryContents component function.

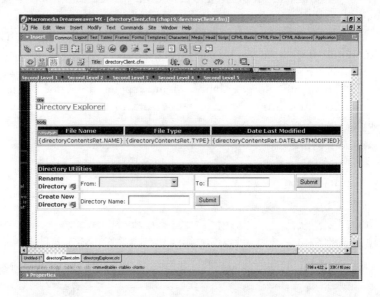

Figure 19.15 In Design View, the completed table contains a dynamic menu and two list boxes.

Testing Your Application

Because Dreamweaver MX does not support Live Data View for ColdFusion components, your best bet for testing is to use your web browser. To test the application, follow these steps:

1. Open your web browser, and go to `http://localhost:8500/bookexample/chap19/directoryClient.cfm`. The page displays as shown in Figure 19.16.

2. As you can see, the dynamic table renders as expected. It shows all the directories in the bookexample directory, the file types, and when they were last modified.

3. Scroll down the page to find the Component Utilities table. Try to rename one of the files the same name as another existing directory, such as trying to rename chap10 to chap11. When you click the Submit button, an error page should display, such as the one shown in Figure 19.17.

4. Using the directory creation utility, enter **CFCsRule** for the name, and click the Submit button. The directoryClient.cfm page should display again with the CFCsRule directory present in the table, as shown in Figure 19.18.

Figure 19.16 The finished directoryClient.cfm page displays in a web browser. Notice the dynamic table that is powered by a `CFDIRECTORY` tag in the directoryExplorer component.

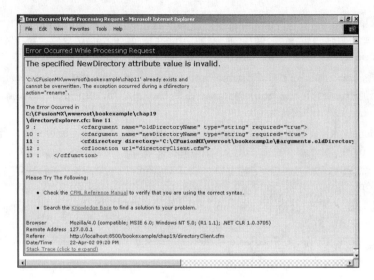

Figure 19.17 An error page displays when you try to do something that is not allowed, such as trying to rename a directory to an already existing directory name.

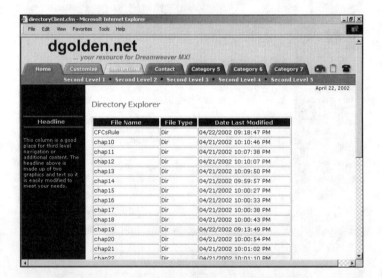

Figure 19.18 After creating a new directory, the directoryClient.cfm page displays again with the new directory listed.

Troubleshooting ColdFusion Components

ColdFusion components are a new technology in ColdFusion and are just now starting to be used in development. If you have problems with component development, you're likely not alone. Before you begin a ColdFusion development project based on a component architecture, thoroughly test the concepts used in your application to make sure components are the right choice for your project.

In addition, because component development differs greatly from traditional ColdFusion page development, you'll likely encounter new problems. To avoid common component pitfalls, remember the following points:

- Think about what you want to accomplish in a component application, and break down what tasks you need ColdFusion to perform. After you have isolated the functionality that you need to use, consider how the code would best fit into the component architecture.

- The data type validation in the CFFUNCTION and CFARGUMENT tags can prove tedious if you have a component with a large number of component methods. The Dreamweaver Components panel can offer some help because it lists the data types for return values and parameters.

- If you plan to access components from Flash Remoting or web services, make sure you set the applicable CFFUNCTION statements' access attributes to remote. It's a small detail that might cause frustration.

- You can only return one value from a component method. If you need to return multiple values, use a complex data type, such as an array or struct.

Summary

In this chapter, you learned how to build and use ColdFusion components. Using the Create Component dialog box of Dreamweaver, you used CFCOMPONENT, CFFUNCTION, CFARGUMENT, and CFRETURN tags to construct a component that lets users manage some of the directories in your web root, including viewing, renaming, and creating new directories.

In the next chapter, you will use ColdFusion components again to build Flash Remoting services, which power dynamic Flash MX applications.

Building Flash Remoting Services

IN THIS CHAPTER, YOU WILL LEARN THE basics of building Flash Remoting services in Dreamweaver MX. Flash Remoting services let you create custom ActionScript functions that return dynamic data to Flash movies. You will build ColdFusion pages and ColdFusion components to power dynamic Flash movies. You will also learn more about the ActionScript required to call Flash Remoting service functions.

About Building Flash Remoting Services

Let's face it: HTML is starting to show some gray hairs. Restrictive formatting options, lack of client-side programming runtime, and constant page refreshes make HTML a less-than-perfect interface for web applications that require sophisticated user interactivity. Still, HTML's tag-based coding model and simplicity make it easily accessible to a wide audience of aspiring developers. Even more important, web browsers are a standard component of any operating system, making HTML the lingua franca of the web.

Technologies do exist to extend web browser functionality, including JavaScript, Java applets, DHTML, and ActiveX. Yet, there is another option. If you look at the installed applications on your computer, you'll likely find the

Flash Player. In fact, industry figures have cited that the Flash Player installation base runs well above 90 percent of PC users. Although best known for animated intro movies for web sites, Flash offers an attractive alternative to HTML and other technologies by providing vector-based animation tools and a client-side programming model, all in one small package.

Flash contains a powerful scripting language, ActionScript, that makes display of dynamic information from a database easy. After you become familiar with ActionScript, you can use its power to create Flash MX interfaces that connect with ColdFusion applications to provide sophisticated user interfaces that are impossible in the traditional HTML and web browser environment.

ColdFusion MX includes the Flash Remoting service, which acts as a gateway for communication between Flash movies and ColdFusion. To interact with Flash movies in ColdFusion, you use the FLASH variable scope in ColdFusion pages. ColdFusion components natively support interaction with Flash movies. Although you should know that Flash Remoting provides the connection between Flash and ColdFusion, you don't need to do any configuration. It just works.

At the same time, you need to have the Flash MX authoring environment installed, as well as the Flash Remoting Components. The Flash Remoting Components add-on provides the necessary Flash Remoting features, such as additional ActionScript classes and the NetConnection Debugger. You can download an evaluation copy of the Flash MX authoring environment from the Macromedia web site (www.macromedia.com). The Flash Remoting Components are free to use and can be downloaded from the Macromedia web site.

In this chapter, you will build a ColdFusion application that displays a menu with employee names and lets you send an email to that employee, all from a Flash movie. The application consists of a ColdFusion page, a ColdFusion component, and a Flash movie:

- coldfusionMovie.swf—This Flash movie interacts with flashPage.cfm and flashComponent.cfc.

- flashPage.cfm—This ColdFusion page will query the database and return the recordset to Flash.

- flashComponent.cfc—This ColdFusion component will accept parameters from Flash, process the results, and return the result to the Flash movie.

Figure 20.1 shows the files for this application and their interactions with each other.

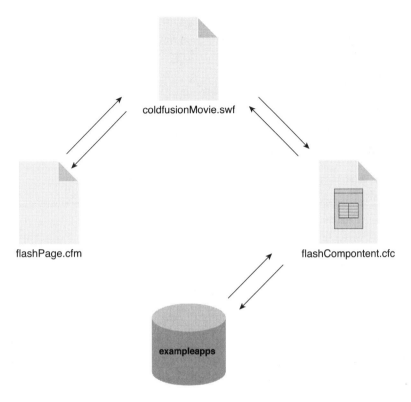

Figure 20.1 This ColdFusion application contains three files: a ColdFusion page, a ColdFusion component, and a Flash movie. Notice that one Flash file communicates with both ColdFusion files.

Building the Flash Movie

Once you have installed the Flash MX authoring environment and the Flash Remoting Components, start the Flash MX authoring environment. When you open the Flash Remoting workspace, you are greeted with an interface similar to the Dreamweaver workspace, as shown in Figure 20.2. However, that sense of familiarity will quickly disappear when you start to explore the workspace.

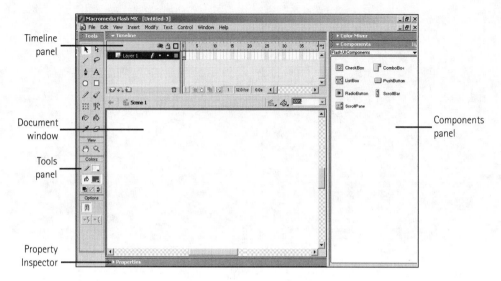

Figure 20.2 Similar to the Dreamweaver workspace, the Flash workspace
contains toolbars, panels, and panel groups.

One of the first differences that you'll notice is the Timeline panel, shown in
Figure 20.3. Because it controls which frames are displayed, the timeline is
central to Flash development. The timeline consists of layers that you can use
to organize the content of the frames. For example, you can create one layer
that contains the ActionScript for the frame and one layer to contain the user
interface elements. You can add layers by clicking the Insert Layer button in
the Timeline panel.

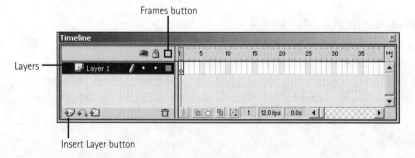

Figure 20.3 The Timeline panel lets you create layers to organize your
frame content, as well as the timeline itself.

Like its counterpart in Dreamweaver, the Property Inspector, shown in Figure 20.4, displays the details of a selected element. Depending on what is selected, the display might contain a number of editable properties and parameters.

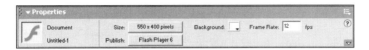

Figure 20.4 The Property Inspector provides access to frame contents, such as text boxes or UI components. The figure shows a ComboBox UI component's parameters.

Also, the Component panel lets you drag and drop prebuilt user interface components into the document window. As shown in Figure 20.5, the Flash UI components consist of common form objects, such as a ComboBox (menu), ListBox (List/Menu), and PushButton (Submit and Reset). Components are actually very complex Flash movie clips, a term used to refer to Flash mini-movies. Movie clips, and components, can be imported into a playing Flash movie seamlessly.

Figure 20.5 The Component panel contains, among other things, user interface components, such as ListBox, ComboBox, and PushButton.

To create elements such as text boxes, rectangles, or circles in the document window, you use the Tools panel. As shown in Figure 20.6, the Tools panel contains a variety of tools, such as color fill, line, eyedropper, and eraser.

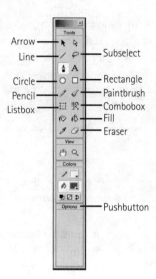

Figure 20.6   The Tools panel contains a variety of features, including line tools, fill tools, rectangle, circle, eraser, and so on. You can also change views and select colors.

In a nutshell, Flash development is very different from traditional HTML development. This chapter does not attempt to teach you Flash design and development. For more information on Flash MX, see *Inside Flash MX* by Jody Keating, New Riders Publishing, 2002. Learning the basics of Flash is strongly recommended; in the meantime, keep the following points in mind when considering Flash:

- Flash movies, as their name implies, consist of a series of frames on a timeline. When the movie loads into the Flash Player, it plays from the first frame to the last frame unless you stop the movie with ActionScript.

- ActionScript is the programming language for Flash. It is a scripting language, much like CFScript and JavaScript, and not a tag-based language like CFML. Many people that first learned programming with HTML find scripting languages unintuitive. For more information on ActionScript, see *ActionScripting in Flash MX* by Philip Kerman, New Riders Publishing, 2002.

- When you create a Flash interface, you'll quickly realize how much more design control you have. Although it can seem a little disorienting, quickly scanning the online Flash MX Help (Help menu, Using Flash) will get you on your way.

▪ If you know anything about Flash, you probably know about its animation abilities. Just like motion pictures, Flash movies can simulate movement by playing through a series of frames in which an object moves a small distance in each frame. When the frames are played, the human eye sees a smooth movement. Flash provides a feature called *tweening*, which automates this process.

Building the Flash Movie Interface

In this section, you will build a simple Flash movie that acts as an HTML form page to send an email to an employee. As shown in Figure 20.7, the employee list is displayed in a menu, and the user enters his or her name and message in a text box. This movie will be just one frame. The Flash movie is essentially just acting as a form page, and doesn't need additional frames for animation.

The movie will also contain two UI components that display employee names from the `exampleapps` data source using recordsets returned from ColdFusion. You'll write the ActionScript to connect to ColdFusion and display the results in the next section. To build the Flash movie interface, follow these steps:

1. In the Flash MX authoring environment, click the File menu, New. Save the file as coldFusionMovie.fla in the chap20 folder of the bookexample directory in the web root.

2. Using the Component panel, insert a ListBox UI component. In its Property Inspector, name the component simply "to", without the quotation marks. Also in the Property Inspector, you should change the width of the component to around 200 pixels so that first and last names can be accommodated. In the next section, you'll populate the component in ActionScript with the recordset returned from ColdFusion.

3. Using the Tools panel, select the Text tool. Text fields come in three flavors: static, dynamic, and input. Static text is used for words and places that stay the same. Dynamic text fields can be changed using ActionScript. Input text fields accept user input. Once you draw a text field with the Text tool, the text field's properties and parameters can be modified in its Property Inspector.

   As shown in Figure 20.7, below the ListBox component, you insert an input text field that will accept the user's name. In its Property Inspector, name the field "from".

4. Below the text box, insert a ComboBox UI component, and name it "cc". To accommodate both first and last names, increase the component's width to around 150 pixels. In the next section, you'll populate the component in ActionScript with the recordset returned from ColdFusion.

5. Below the component, insert two more input text fields named "subject" and "message," respectively. The user will input the body of his or her email in the message text field, so you want to make the field larger than the others, such as 250 pixels wide and 175 pixels high.

6. Insert a PushButton UI component beside the message text field. In its Property Inspector, change the Label parameter to "Send Email", which serves as the button's label. In the Click Handler parameter, enter **buttonClicked**. This is the name of an ActionScript function, which you will create in the next section, that executes when the user clicks the button.

7. You can insert static text fields to give the movie a title and describe the UI components and text fields. Because the movie essentially serves as a form for an email, write your descriptions accordingly.

8. Save your work.

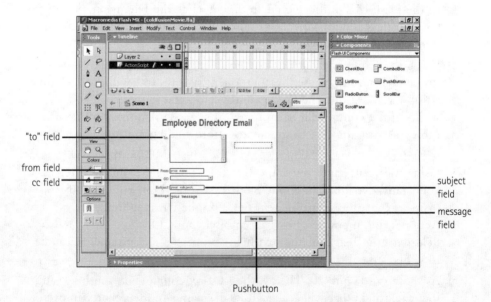

Figure 20.7 When completed, the Flash movie serves as an email form with a collection of text fields and UI components.

Building the Flash Movie ActionScript

Although this book does not attempt to teach you the intricacies of programming ActionScript, you should be familiar with general concepts of scripting languages and ActionScript. For example, to set a variable in CFML, you would use the CFSET tag, as the following example shows:

```
<cfset helloVar = "Hello!">
```

To set a variable in ActionScript, you use the keyword var and end the statement with a semicolon (;), as the following example shows:

```
var helloVar = "Hello!";
```

Another common ActionScript construct is a function definition. Like a ColdFusion user-defined function (UDF) created in CFScript, you create an ActionScript function using the function keyword followed by an associated object, if any, in parentheses, as the following example shows:

```
function setVariables()
{
    var helloVar = "Hello!";
    var byeVar = "Bye!";
}
```

In the code, between the curly braces ({}), two variables are set, helloVar and byeVar. The setVariables function will only execute when it is called. To call the variable, you simply enter its name, as the following example shows:

```
function setVariables()
{
    var helloVar = "Hello!";
    var byeVar = "Bye!";
}
setVariables();
```

In the code, notice that you insert a set of parentheses after the function name. In those parentheses, you can supply a parameter if the function being called requires one. If you use a parameter in a function, you must specify it in the parentheses after the function name, as the following example shows:

```
function setVariables(helloParam, byeParam)
{
    var helloVar = helloParam;
    var byeVar = byeParam;
}
setVariables("hello", "bye");
```

In the code, the setVariables function now requires two parameters, helloParam and byeParam. The parameters are referenced when setting the variables in the function body. Finally, the setVariables function call passes the parameters in the same order as defined in the function definition.

Using ActionScript, you can also manipulate UI components, text fields, buttons, and almost anything else in a movie interface. You use the name that you entered in the movie element's Property Inspector. For example, to populate the `statusMessage` dynamic text field, you use the `text` property, as the following example shows:

```
statusMessage.text = "Hello!";
```

You can also get the value from a movie element, such as a ListBox UI component, using the `getValue` method, as the following example shows:

```
statusMessage.text = to.getValue();
```

In the code, the `statusMessage` text field is populated by the selected value in the ListBox component.

In Flash, you write all ActionScript in the Actions panel, which you can open by selecting Window menu, Actions. You can use the Actions panel in either Normal or Advanced mode. For this book, use the Advanced mode, as shown in Figure 20.8. You can change the mode by clicking the View Options button and selecting Advanced.

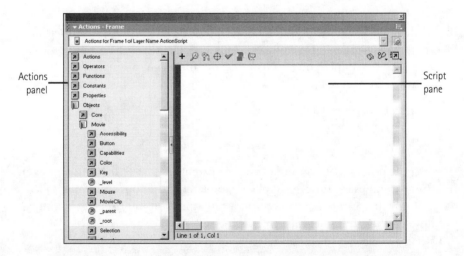

Figure 20.8 The Actions panel lets you write ActionScript in the Flash MX authoring environment. The Advanced mode is shown, which provides direct access to the ActionScript code.

To use the Actions panel in Advanced mode, you simply type in the Script pane. The ActionScript for this movie consists of importing the necessary ActionScript classes, connecting to the ColdFusion page and components, and handling the results returned from ColdFusion, which usually consists of displaying the results in the movie.

Keep in mind that you must apply the ActionScript at the frame level. In the Actions panel, you can use the menu to switch between movie elements. Make sure that Frame 1 is selected, and click the Pin Current Script button. That locks the Actions panel to Frame 1. To build the ActionScript, follow these steps:

1. Import the `NetServices`, `DataGlue`, and `NetDebug` ActionScript classes into the movie, as the following example shows:

```
#include "NetServices.as"
#include "NetDebug.as"
#include "DataGlue.as"
```

The `NetServices` class provides prebuilt functions that automate much of the connection code. The `NetDebug` class enables support for the NetConnection Debugger, which is explained in the "Testing Your Application" section later in this chapter. The `DataGlue` class provides an easy way to populate UI components with recordsets.

2. To connect a Flash movie to a ColdFusion page or component, you must first create a connection object by calling three functions, as the following example shows:

```
NetServices.setDefaultGatewayUrl
    ("http://localhost:8500/flashservices/gateway");
gatewayConnnection = NetServices.createGatewayConnection();
componentService = gatewayConnnection.getService
    ("bookexample.chap20.flashComponent", this);
pageService = gatewayConnnection.getService
    ("bookexample.chap20", this);
```

In the code, the `setDefaultGatewayURL` function specifies the gateway URL of the Flash Remoting service in ColdFusion. The URL is just an address. There is no flashservices/gateway directory in the web root. Next, the `createGatewayConnection` function creates the `gatewayConnection` object, which is an object that represents the connection to Flash Remoting.

To create a service object for a ColdFusion page or component, you use the `getService` function, and in its parameters, you specify the web root directory structure to the ColdFusion page or component. As you can see in the code, the service name syntax differs for ColdFusion components and pages. For ColdFusion components, you enter the web root directory structure and the name of the component, such as bookexample.chap20.flashComponent, using the dot syntax. For ColdFusion pages, you just specify the directory structure, such as bookexample.chap20. The `this` parameter indicates the results will be returned to this timeline.

3. To actually connect to ColdFusion, you must call the service function, which is really calling a method on the service object created in the last step. Before you do that, consider what you want to happen when the Flash movie first loads. First, the to ListBox and cc ComboBox UI components need to be populated. The ColdFusion page, which you will create in the next section, will return a recordset containing the employees. So, you need to call the ColdFusion page, as the following example shows:

```
pageService.flashPage();
```

Notice that `flashPage`, which is actually the filename for the ColdFusion name, is called on the `pageService` object.

4. When a ColdFusion page or component is called from Flash, it automatically returns the results or an error. To handle the results in ActionScript, which usually includes displaying the results, you create a function named the same as the service function and appended by `_Result`. For example:

```
function flashPage_Result(result)
{
    DataGlue.bindFormatStrings(to, result, "#firstname# #lastname#", "#email#");
    DataGlue.bindFormatStrings(cc, result, "#firstname# #lastname#", "#email#");
    statusMessage.text = result.getLength() + " Employees Found";
}
```

In the code, the `flashPage_Result` function references the `result` object, which is created automatically when the results return from ColdFusion. In the function body, two `DataGlue` functions exist, and the `statusMessage` text field is set.

The `BindFormatStrings` function lets you easily bind a recordset to a UI component. In the parameters, you specify the UI component, the recordset to use, and which recordset columns to display and, separated by a comma, return. Notice that both the cc and to UI components are bound to the `result` object, which is a recordset. The `statusMessage` text field's text is changed to reflect the number of records returned by using the `getLength` function.

5. Now you'll create the handler function for the PushButton component. When you inserted the PushButton UI component into the movie, you specified that the Click Handler parameter was `buttonClicked`. The name `buttonClicked` corresponds to the name of a function, as the following example shows:

```
function buttonClicked()
{
    componentService.sendEmail(to.getValue(), from.text, cc.getValue(),
subject.text, message.text);
}
```

In the code, you simply create a function with the same name as the one entered in the Click Handler parameter. In the function body, notice that the `sendEmail` function, called through the `componentService` service object, is used. The `sendEmail` function maps to the ColdFusion function in the flashComponent component of the same name. You'll create that ColdFusion component in the "Building flashComponent.cfc" section.

Five parameters are passed to the `sendEmail` function, each representing a text field or UI component in the movie. You use the `getValue` function to get the user's selection in the UI components to and cc. For the input text fields, you use the `text` property. All of these parameters supply parameters to the `CFMAIL` statement in the ColdFusion component.

6. Because you made a call to ColdFusion, you must handle the results. In addition to `_Result`, you can also handle any errors produced by ColdFusion by using `_Status`. The following example creates two handler functions, `sendEmail_Result` and `sendEmail_Status`:

```
function sendEmail_Result(result)
{
    statusMessage.textColor = "0x00FF00";
    statusMessage.text = "Email Sent!";
}

    function sendEmail_Status(result)
{
    statusMessage.textColor = "0xFF0000";
    statusMessage.text = "Error!";
}
```

In the code, the two functions change the contents of the `statusMessage` text field. The functions execute depending on whether ColdFusion produces an error. If ColdFusion does not produce an error, the `sendEmail_Result` function executes, which displays the message "Email Sent!" and changes the text color to green. If ColdFusion does produce an error, the `sendEmail_Status` function executes, which displays the message "Error!" and changes the text color to red.

7. Save your work.

Publishing the Flash Movie

After you've built the Flash movie, you must publish the movie to create the SWF file. The SWF file is what actually plays in the Flash Player and is what is referenced from the HTML in the web page.

Before you publish a movie, you should remove the `include` reference to NetDebug.as and the `setDefaultGatewayURL` function from the ActionScript.

The NetDebug class and the setDefaultGatewayURL function are needed only during development.

To publish the Flash movie, with the coldfusionMovie.fla file open in the Flash MX authoring environment, select File menu, Publish. If you look in the chap20 folder of the bookexample directory in your web root, you'll see a coldfusionMovie.swf file.

Now, you need to insert the SWF file into a web page. SWF files can be embedded in a regular HTML page or in a ColdFusion page using the Flash button in the Common tab of the Insert bar in the Dreamweaver workspace.

Building flashPage.cfm

When you build ColdFusion pages that interact with Flash movies, you use the FLASH variable scope to access parameters sent by Flash movies and return values back to Flash movies. To access parameters passed from Flash, you have two options:

- Access named parameters from Flash using flash.*paramName*, where *paramName* is the name of the parameter passed from Flash.

- Access ordered parameters, such as parameters passed in an array, using flash.params[1], where [1] specifies the parameter index location of the params object passed from Flash.

To return results to Flash, you use the flash.result variable. Anything that you assign to this variable, including strings, numbers, recordsets, lists, arrays, and structs, is returned to Flash.

In addition, you can use the flash.pagesize variable to return the recordsets in increments to Flash. For example, if you set flash.pagesize to 10, 10 records at a time are returned to Flash. Using these features, you can build recordset navigation in the Flash movie.

In flashPage.cfm, you will build a ColdFusion page that queries the exampleapps database and returns the recordset to Flash. This ColdFusion page exists to interact with a Flash movie, so it doesn't even need to contain any HTML. To build flashPage.cfm, follow these steps:

1. Create a new ColdFusion page by selecting File menu, New. In the New Document dialog box that appears, select the Dynamic category and ColdFusion. Click the Create button. Save the file as flashPage.cfm in the chap20 directory in the bookexample directory of your web root.

2. In the document window, switch to Code View. Delete any HTML present.

3. Using the Bindings panel, create a new recordset named `empQuery`. In the Recordset dialog box, select exampleapps in the Data Source menu. In the Tables menu, select tblEmployees. In the Columns section, select FirstName, LastName, and Email. You don't need to filter the recordset, so click the OK button. The following CFML appears:

```
<cfquery name="empQuery" datasource="exampleapps">
    SELECT FirstName, LastName, Email
    FROM tblEmployees
</cfquery>
```

4. All that's left to do is return the recordset to Flash by assigning it into the `flash.result` variable. For example:

```
<cfset flash.result = empQuery>
```

5. Save your work.

Building flashComponent.cfc

Components make Flash development even easier than ColdFusion pages. First, you don't need to use the FLASH variable scope because ColdFusion components natively support interacting with Flash movies. Also, you can define any number of component functions for Flash movies to call without making additional connections to ColdFusion.

You are going to build a ColdFusion component that contains only one component function, sendEmail. The sendEmail function contains the CFMAIL tag, which lets you send email from ColdFusion applications. The CFMAIL tag is a relatively simple tag with attributes similar to emails that you send every day, such as from, to, cc, subject, and so on. For example:

```
<cfmail to="dave@dgolden.net"
    subject="Got my eye on you"
    from="Secret Admirer">

    Your mail message . . .

</cfmail>
```

In the code, the opening and closing CFMAIL tags enclose the message. Like any CFML tag, you can make the attributes and the mail message dynamic, as the following example shows:

```
<cfmail to="#form.to#"
    subject="#form.subject#"
    from="#form.from#">

    #form.text#

</cfmail>
```

In the component function definition, you'll make the attributes and text dynamic, so that the parameters passed from the Flash movie are used.

> ### SMTP
>
> To use ColdFusion for sending email, you first must connect to a mail server that supports Simple Mail Transfer Protocol (SMTP). Most popular email servers support SMTP; contact your system administrator or read your SMTP server's documentation. In the ColdFusion Administrator, you use the Mail Server page to specify the IP address or the domain for the SMTP server, mail port, connection timeout, and so on.

To build flashComponent.cfc, follow these steps:

1. In the Components panel of the Application panel group, click the plus (+) button to open the Create Component dialog box.

2. In the Create Component dialog box shown in Figure 20.9, name the component flashComponent and select the chap20 folder in the book-example directory of your web root.

3. Create one function named sendEmail, and select Remote in the Access menu.

4. Create five arguments. Name them to, from, cc, subject, and message. Each parameter is of type string and is required.

5. Click the OK button, and Dreamweaver generates the following code:

```
<cfcomponent hint="Send Mail Component">
    <cffunction name="sendEmail" access="remote">
        <cfargument name="to" required="true" type="string">
        <cfargument name="from" required="true" type="string">
        <cfargument name="cc" required="true" type="string">
        <cfargument name="subject" required="true" type="string">
        <cfargument name="message" required="true" type="string">
    </cffunction>
</cfcomponent>
```

   If a CFRETURN tag was generated, delete it. The component does not return anything to Flash.

6. After placing your cursor between the opening and closing tags of the CFFUNCTION statement, click the CFMAIL button on the CFML Advanced tab of the Insert bar. As shown in Figure 20.10, the CFMAIL Tag Editor dialog box appears.

7. In the CFMAIL dialog box's General category, enter **"#arguments.to#"** in the To text box, **"#arguments.subject#"** in the Subject text box, **"#arguments.cc#"** in the CC text box, and **"#arguments.from#"** in the From text box. Click the OK button. If you remember, these are the same names as the parameters passed to the sendEmail function in the Flash movie's ActionScript.

Dreamweaver generates the following code:

```
<cfmail to="#arguments.to#"
    subject="#arguments.subject#"
    from="#arguments.from#"
    cc="#arguments.cc#">
</cfmail>
```

8. Between the opening and closing CFMAIL tags, insert #arguments.message#. This will supply the email text.

9. Save your work.

Your ColdFusion and Flash application is now complete.

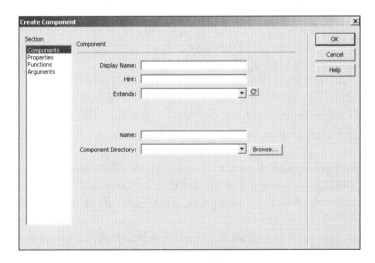

Figure 20.9 The Create Component dialog box provides a structured interface for building a ColdFusion component. Just click a category, such as General, Arguments, or Functions, and the applicable controls appear.

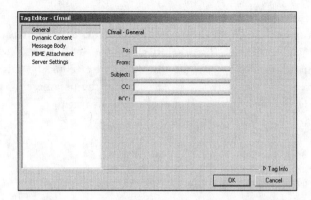

Figure 20.10   The CFMAIL Tag Editor dialog box lets you specify the attribute values, such as From, To, Subject, and CC.

Testing Your Application

Like any ColdFusion application, you could test the Flash application by publishing the Flash movie, embedding the SWF file in a web page, and opening the web page in a browser. In Dreamweaver, you could also use the Server Debug view to try out the application.

You can also test the Flash movie from inside the Flash MX authoring environment. After making sure that you have the ActionScript in place that imports the NetDebug class and sets the default gateway URL, select the Control menu, Test Movie. As shown in Figure 20.11, the Flash movie fills the entire screen.

To see debugging information, you can also use the NetConnection Debugger (NCD) to debug Flash movies that connect to ColdFusion. To open the NCD, select the Window menu, NetConnection Debugger. As shown in Figure 20.12, the NCD displays a copious amount of debugging output, including the contents of recordsets passed to Flash from ColdFusion. The NCD becomes active when you select Test Movie from the Control menu.

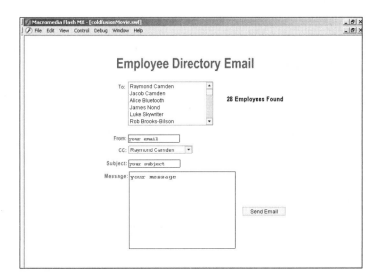

Figure 20.11 When you select Test Movie in the Control menu, the Flash movie plays in the Flash MX authoring environment. The Flash movie behaves just as if it were playing in a web page.

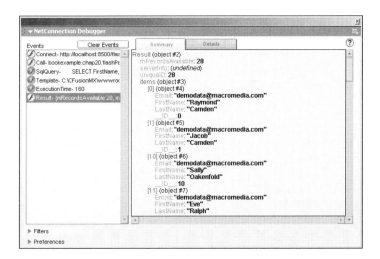

Figure 20.12 The NetConnection Debugger displays lots of debugging information, including recordsets passed from ColdFusion.

Summary

In this chapter, you learned how to build ColdFusion pages and components that serve as Flash Remoting services, which power dynamic Flash MX movies. In addition, you were introduced to the basics of ActionScript development with Flash Remoting, including connecting to ColdFusion, calling service functions, and handling the results.

In the next chapter, you will learn about even more emerging technologies supported by Dreamweaver and ColdFusion: the promising technology called web services.

Using and Creating
Web Services

IN THIS CHAPTER, YOU WILL LEARN HOW to use remote web services in your ColdFusion applications with Dreamweaver. Together, Dreamweaver and ColdFusion remove the complexity of web services to make the process easy, quick, and powerful. In addition, you will learn how to create web services for public consumption by other developers.

About Using and Creating Web Services

Unless you don't follow the web development industry, you've probably already heard about web services. At the same time, you might be confused by the hype swirling around the industry movement toward software as a service. At its core, a web service is application functionality that makes itself available over the Internet using XML-based messaging.

The Extensible Markup Language (XML) describes the functionality provided by a web service, including the available functions, accepted parameters, and results returned. Indeed, one of the greatest advantages of web services lies in their ability to describe themselves to other applications. In addition, XML is used to format the function calls to a web service and return results so that both sides of the interaction understand each other.

Because web services are still in their infancy, you might be a little disappointed in what is available today. At the time of this writing, the majority of web services offered at popular web services registries, such as `www.xmethods.net`, are intended as proof of concept or are in the beta stage of development. However, you can use these web services to perform small tasks in your existing ColdFusion applications, such as validating credit cards, validating addresses, and performing searches on remote databases.

Web services should be used as building blocks in application development. In fact, in ColdFusion, there is little difference between invoking a function on a local component and invoking a function on a remote web service. However, as you read this chapter, keep the following points in mind:

- You cannot control remote web services, so use them with care in your applications. In particular, test the web services thoroughly before using them.

- Although most web services are available for free today, web services are intended to be subscription-based services, much like cable television or your local newspaper. So, web services that you use for free today might charge a fee in the future.

Making Sense of the Web Services Alphabet Soup

If you have investigated web services at all, you might have become confused by all the acronyms floating around, including SOAP, WSDL, and UDDI. Most standards related to web services are XML-based technologies that perform a specific task. When you use or publish a web service in ColdFusion and Dreamweaver, a number of these technologies are at work. Table 21.1 describes the web service technologies used by ColdFusion and Dreamweaver.

Table 21.1 **Web Service Technologies**

Technology Acronym	Meaning	Description
SOAP	Simple Object Access Protocol	An XML-based messaging protocol that formats function calls and responses
WSDL	Web Services Description Language	An XML-based description protocol that lets the caller discover the available functions, parameters, and results.
UDDI	Universal Description, Discovery, and Integration	An XML-based description protocol that lets users of web services find web service providers.

Although ColdFusion and Dreamweaver effectively hide the underlying complexity of web services, you use all of these web service technologies when using or creating a web service. For example, when you register a web service in Dreamweaver, a web service's WSDL description is used to generate the tree structure that appears in the Components panel. Also, ColdFusion automatically produces SOAP-formatted messages using the built-in ColdFusion proxy to communicate with web services.

AXIS

When ColdFusion throws a web service-related error message, it might contain the term *AXIS*. AXIS, the name for SOAP 3.0, serves as the ColdFusion proxy for web services. So, if you see AXIS in an error message, know that it's referring to a SOAP-related error. For more information on AXIS, see the Apache web site at www.apache.org.

Figure 21.1 shows a simplified representation of ColdFusion working with web services.

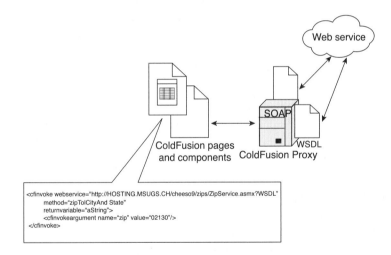

Figure 21.1 ColdFusion automates many of the technologies required for using and creating web services, including SOAP-formatted function calls and WSDL-formatted web service descriptions.

Using Web Services

To use web services in your ColdFusion application, you register the web service in Dreamweaver's Components panel, insert the CFML code into your ColdFusion page or component, and then modify the code so that the proper argument values are specified for the web service.

In the CFML code, you use the CFINVOKE and CFINVOKEARGUMENT tags to call web service functions and return the response. You can actually think of calling web services as invoking a ColdFusion component function. Only the component attribute is changed to a web service URL for a remote WSDL file, as the following example shows:

```
<cfinvoke
    webservice="http://HOSTING.MSUGS.CH/cheeso9/zips/ZipService.asmx?WSDL"
    method="zipTo1CityAndState"
    returnvariable="aString">
        <cfinvokeargument name="zip" value="02130"/>
</cfinvoke>
```

In the example, the webservice attribute references a remote WSDL file hosted on the service provider's server. The method name is defined in the WSDL file as is the zip argument created by the CFINVOKEARGUMENT tag. If you direct your browser to the same URL, you will see the various methods and parameters available from the web service.

WSDL is an XML-based language. In a nutshell, XML provides a markup language to describe structured information. You can think of XML as the equivalent of HTML for data. Instead of writing code to display information on a page, you're writing code that describes the information that is presented on a web page, or just about anything else.

Unlike HTML, XML is not limited to a predefined tag and function set. In fact, you can create a language that describes data for a specific format and purpose. So, WSDL is an XML-based language to describe web services. For more information on XML and WSDL, including official specifications and documentation, see the World Wide Web Consortium web site (www.w3c.org).

Using Web Services in ColdFusion Applications

In this section, you will build a master page and a detail page that lets users select a park from the tblParks database table and, using a web service, display the distance between the user's ZIP code and the park's ZIP code, as shown in Figure 21.2. Although this section uses ColdFusion pages, the same rules apply for ColdFusion components, except that all service invocations reside with component function definitions.

For more information about ColdFusion components, see Chapter 19, "Using ColdFusion Components."

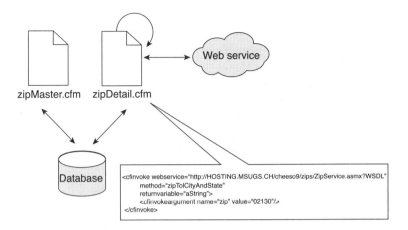

Figure 21.2 This application uses two ColdFusion pages, both of which query the example apps database. In addition, zipDetail.cfm calls two web services that translate the entered ZIP code to the corresponding city and state and get the distance between the entered ZIP code and the selected park's ZIP code.

To create zipMaster.cfm, follow these steps:

1. Create a new ColdFusion page from the bookexample template, and save it as zipMaster.cfm in the chap21 folder in the bookexample directory of your web root. In this ColdFusion page, you will create a dynamic table to display a recordset.

2. As shown in Figure 21.3, create a recordset named `parkQuery` from the tblParks database table that contains the PARKNAME, CITY, ZIPCODE, and STATE table columns. Although no filtering is required, you can order the recordset by a column, such as PARKNAME.

3. Place your cursor in the editable Body region in the document window. Click the Dynamic Table button on the Application panel in the Insert bar. In the Dynamic Table dialog box, shown in Figure 21.4, select `parkQuery` in the Recordset menu, and select 10 records to be shown at a time. Click the OK button, and the dynamic table appears.

4. In the dynamic table, insert another column on the far right. In this column, insert a hyperlink that passes parameters to the zipDetail.cfm page, which you will create in the next section. In the table heading row, enter **"Distance Calculator"**.

5. In the table cell below the header column, insert a hyperlink using the Hyperlink button in the Common panel of the Insert bar. In the Hyperlink dialog box, enter **Calculate!** in the Text text box, and click the folder icon next to the Link text box. The Select File dialog appears.

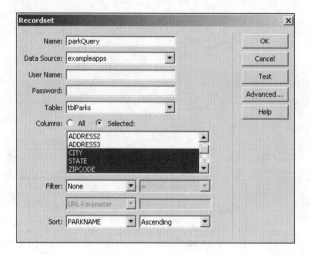

Figure 21.3 In the Recordset dialog box, you create the parkQuery recordset, which contains the PARKNAME, CITY, STATE, and ZIPCODE columns.

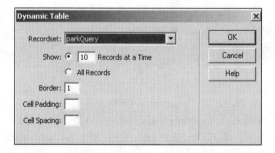

Figure 21.4 In the Dynamic Table dialog box, select the parkQuery recordset and specify that ColdFusion return 10 records at a time.

6. In the Select File dialog box, enter **"zipAction.cfm"** in the File Name text box. You will create this page later in the chapter. Click the Parameters button. In the Parameters dialog box, shown in Figure 21.5, create a parameter named zip. In the Value column, click the Lightning Bolt button. In the Dynamic Data dialog box that appears, select the PARKNAME column of the parkQuery recordset. Click the OK button in the Dynamic Data, Parameters, and Select File dialog boxes.

This creates a CFOUTPUT statement at the end the hyperlink URL. Inside the CFOUTPUT statement, the parkQuery.PARKNAME variable references the PARKNAME value for each record. Whenever a user clicks on a hyperlink, that park record's ZIP code is passed using a URL to the zipAction.cfm page.

7. Below the dynamic table, insert a recordset navigation bar using the Recordset Navigation Bar button on the Application panel in the Insert bar. Also, use the Recordset Navigation Status button in the Application panel to insert a navigation status message.

8. Save your work.

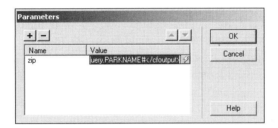

Figure 21.5 To pass dynamic parameters to another ColdFusion page using a URL, you use the Parameter dialog box to set the dynamic parameters' values.

The zipDetail.cfm page, which you will create in this section, must be accessible from zipMaster.cfm via the GET HTTP method (URL) and self-accessible via the POST HTTP method (Form). That's because zipDetail.cfm serves dual purposes: as a detail page for zipMaster.cfm and as an action page for itself to invoke the web services.

To accomplish this task, you use CFIF statements and the IsDefined function to evaluate what parameters are passed to the page. If a URL parameter is passed, you know that zipMaster.cfm is accessing the page. If a URL parameter is not passed, you know that zipDetail.cfm is accessing itself.

In zipDetail.cfm, you create a table that displays the park details filtered to an individual park with either the PARKNAME URL parameter or the PARKNAME parameter. You create a text box that lets users enter their ZIP codes to calculate the distance to the park.

However, most of your work will take place behind the scenes in the CFML. Using the web services registered in Dreamweaver's Components panel, you will drag and drop web service calls into the ColdFusion page and create CFIF statements that execute code based on the presence of different parameters.

To create zipDetail.cfm, follow these steps:

1. Create a new ColdFusion page from the bookexample template, and save it as zipDetail.cfm in the chap21 folder in the bookexample directory of your web root.

2. Create a recordset named `parkQueryF` that selects the PARKNAME, CITY, STATE, and ZIPCODE columns of the tblParks database table, as shown Figure 21.6. It should be filtered by the PARKNAME parameter passed from zipMaster.cfm.

3. Once you create the `parkQueryF` recordset, click the Show Code and Design Views button in the Document toolbar. In the code, scroll up to the top of the page until you find the `CFQUERY` statement.

4. Insert a `CFIF` statement around the `CFQUERY` statement that checks for the existence of the `URL.PARKNAME` variable using the `IsDefined` function. If it is not present, the `CFELSE` tag executes the same `CFQUERY` statement filtered by the `form.Parkname` variable. Here is an example:

```
<cfif isDefined("URL.PARKNAME")>
    <cfquery name="parkQueryF" datasource="exampleapps">
        SELECT PARKNAME, CITY, "STATE", ZIPCODE
        FROM tblParks
        WHERE PARKNAME = '#URL.PARKNAME#'
    </cfquery>
<cfelse>
    <cfquery name="parkQueryF" datasource="exampleapps">
        SELECT PARKNAME, CITY, "STATE", ZIPCODE
        FROM tblParks
        WHERE PARKNAME = '#form.PARKNAME#'
    </cfquery>
</cfif>
```

5. Returning to Design View in the editable Body region, insert a `FORM` tag. In the `FORM` tag's Property Inspector, click the folder icon to open the Select File dialog box. In the Select File dialog box, enter **"zipDetail.cfm"** in the File Name text box. Make sure post is selected in the Method menu. Inside the `FORM` tag, insert a table with three rows, one column, and no border.

6. In the top table row, using the Bindings panel, insert the `parkQueryF` recordset columns as dynamic text, as shown in Figure 21.7. In the middle table row, insert a text field named `zipField` and some descriptive text. Also insert a Submit button. When the user clicks the Submit button, the value entered in the `zipField` text field is passed back to the page as a form parameter, which supplies the user's ZIP code to the web service calls.

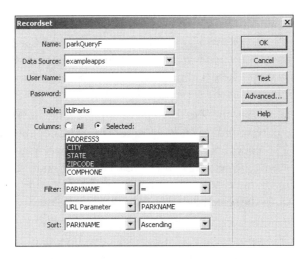

Figure 21.6 In the Recordset dialog box, you create the `parkQueryF` recordset that contains the `PARKNAME`, `CITY`, `STATE`, and `ZIPCODE` columns, just like the `parkQuery` recordset in MasterPage.cfm.

Figure 21.7 Using the Bindings panel, you can drag and drop recordset columns into the page.

7. Insert a hidden form field named PARKNAME. In its Property Inspector, click the Lightning Bolt button next to the Value text box. In the Dynamic Data dialog box, select the PARKNAME column in the `parkQueryF` recordset. This hidden form field, when passed back to zipDetail.cfm, triggers the web service calls.

8. Before you actually create the code to call the web service, you must find the web service. For this application, go to www.xmethods.net, a popular web services registry. Find the web services named ZipToCityState and ZipCodeLookup. The detail page for each web service contains the URL to the WSDL file on the service provider's server.

   As its name implies, the ZipToCityState service takes a ZIP code and returns the corresponding city and state. The ZipCodeLookup service takes two ZIP codes and returns the distances between them. You will use these services to let users enter their local ZIP code. Using the web services, display the city and state name for the ZIP code and find out the distance to the selected park.

9. Back in Dreamweaver, select the Components panel in the Application bar. In the Components panel menu, select web services, and click the plus (+) button. The Add Using WSDL dialog box appears.

10. In the Add Using WSDL dialog box, shown in Figure 21.8, paste the ZipToCityState service's WSDL URL from xmethods.net. In the Proxy Generator menu, select ColdFusion MX. A proxy automatically handles the SOAP messages sent to and from the web service. Click the OK button. The web service appears in the Components panel, as shown in Figure 21.9. You can browse the available functions, parameters, and return values by expanding and collapsing the navigation tree.

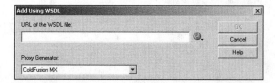

Figure 21.8   In the Add Using WSDL dialog box, you enter the URL to the WSDL file of the web service that you want to use. You can also choose a SOAP proxy or add your own.

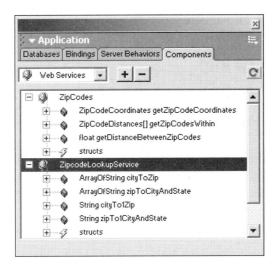

Figure 21.9   When you register a web service in the
Components panel, it appears as a tree structure.
You can expand the tree to see the available functions,
required parameters, and result types returned.

11. Repeat Step 10 for the ZipCodeLookup service.

12. In the Code View, scroll up to the CFIF and CFQUERY statements at the
    top of the page. Under the CFQUERY statement in the CFELSE tag, drag
    the zipToCityAndState function to the Code View, and a CFINVOKE tag is
    generated, as the following example shows:

```
<cfinvoke
webservice="http://HOSTING.MSUGS.CH/cheeso9/zips/ZipService.asmx?WSDL"
    method="zipTo1CityAndState"
    returnvariable="aString">
<cfinvokeargument name="zip" value="enter_value_here"/>
</cfinvoke>
```

Notice that a CFINVOKEARGUMENT tag is automatically generated for the web
service parameters. In this case, only the zip parameter is required. To
make the value attribute of the CFINVOKEARGUMENT tag dynamic, in the
Bindings panel, create a form variable named zipField, the same name as
the text box. Drag the zipField form variable over from the Bindings
panel, and replace the value attribute's default text.

13. Back in the Components panel, drag the `getDistanceBetweenZipCodes` service below the first `CFINVOKE` tag. The following code is generated:

```
<cfinvoke
    webservice="http://www.codebump.com/services/zipcodelookup.asmx?wsdl"
    method="getDistanceBetweenZipCodes"
    returnvariable="aDistanceBetweenZipCodes">
    <cfinvokeargument name="zip1" value="enter_value_here"/>
    <cfinvokeargument name="zip2" value="enter_value_here"/>
</cfinvoke>
```

The `CFINVOKEARGUMENT` tags indicate that two parameters are required, `zip1` and `zip2`. The `getDistanceBetweenZipCodes` function takes the two ZIP codes as parameters and returns the distance between the two locations in miles.

The `zipFile` form parameter and the `ZIPCODE` column in the `parkQueryF` recordset supply the two ZIP codes. It contains the ZIP code for the park that was selected in zipMaster.cfm. It doesn't really matter which ZIP code goes in which `CFINVOKEARGUMENT` tag, but they should look like the following example:

```
<cfinvokeargument name="zip1" value=#form.zipField#/>
<cfinvokeargument name="zip2" value=#parkQueryF.ZIPCODE#/>
```

14. Back in the Design View, in the bottom table row, enter a sentence like the following, "You live in TOWNNAME, which is MILESVAR miles from PARKNAME." In the sentence, `TOWNNAME`, `MILESVAR`, and `PARKNAME` represent placeholders for web service and database variables. In the `zipToCityAndState` `CFINVOKE` tag, the `returnVariable` value is used to access the results of the web service call.

15. In Code View, replace the `TOWNNAME` and `MILESVAR` placeholders with `#aString#` and `#roundedDistance#`, respectively. For the `PARKNAME` placeholder, you simply want to display the selected park's name from the `parkQueryF` recordset. The finished sentence should look like the following example:

```
You live in <cfoutput>#aString#</cfoutput>, which is
<cfoutput>#roundedDistance#</cfoutput> miles from
<cfoutput>#parkQueryF.PARKNAME#</cfoutput>.
```

Keeping Track of Data Types

When working with results returned by the web service, keep in mind the ColdFusion data types corresponding to the web service data types. When a web service returns a double data type, ColdFusion interprets it as a numeric data type. The array, Boolean, string, and binary web service data types translate to the ColdFusion data types of the same name. The web service data type dateTime is translated into the ColdFusion data type date. Finally, the web service complex data type is interpreted as a ColdFusion structure.

16. In Design View, using your mouse, select the bottom table row. In Code View, enclose the TR and TD tags with a CFIF output statement that checks for the existence of the form.zipField parameter, as the following example shows:

```
<cfif isDefined("form.zipField")>
<tr>
<td colspan="3">
<p><strong>You live in <cfoutput>#aString#</cfoutput>, which is
<cfoutput>#roundedDistance#</cfoutput> miles from
<cfoutput>#parkQueryF.PARKNAME#</cfoutput>.</strong></p>
</td>
</tr>
</cfif>
```

You only want to display this sentence if the web service has been invoked. When saved, a CFIF tab appears around the table row in Design View, as shown in Figure 21.10.

17. Save your work.

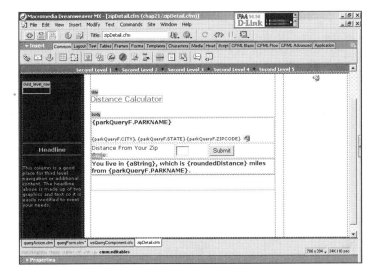

Figure 21.10 In the finished page, the dynamic text elements are shown. Notice that a *CFIF* tab, which indicates that the table row is dynamic, borders the bottom table row.

Testing the Application

To test the application, you want to try all the options as a user would and make sure that the web services are working as you intended.

1. Open your web browser, and direct it to the zipMaster.cfm file. As shown in Figure 21.11, the page should display with no problems.

2. Try the navigation bar and page through park records. When you find Adams National Historic Site, click its Calculate! link. The zipDetail.cfm page displays.

3. As shown in Figure 21.12, the zipDetail.cfm page displays the information for the Adams park. In the ZIP code text box, enter your local ZIP code and click the Submit button. An error page should display.

4. The zipDetail.cfm error page, shown in Figure 21.13, indicates an error with the web service. Remember, whenever you see Axis appear in an error message, a web service error is involved. As you can see in the error message, the zipToCityAndState web service requires the zip parameter to be only five characters. If you look at the Adams ZIP code, it is the extended version with a dash and another four digits.

   Because you can't predict if a park ZIP code will contain five characters or nine, you must use the Left ColdFusion function to disregard any characters after the first five. To make the necessary change, open zipDetail.cfm. In the Code View, find the CFINVOKE tag for the zipToCityAndState web service, and modify the #parkQueryF.ZIPCODE# variable to the following:

   ```
   <cfinvokeargument name="zip2" value=#Left(parkQueryF.ZIPCODE, 5)#/>
   ```

   In the example, notice that the Left function takes two parameters: the name of the string to be modified and the number of characters to save.

5. Save your work, refresh the zipDetail.cfm page in your web browser, and try again.

6. In your web browser, enter your ZIP code again, and click the Submit button. When the page reappears, the sentence and the web service results should appear, as shown in Figure 21.14.

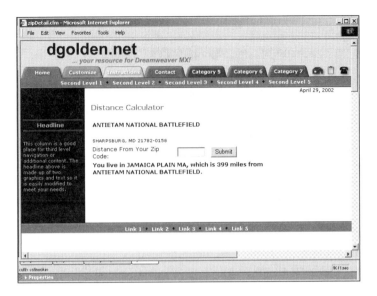

Figure 21.11 When it displays in a web browser, the zipMaster.cfm page presents a dynamic table containing the first 10 records from the `tblParks` database table.

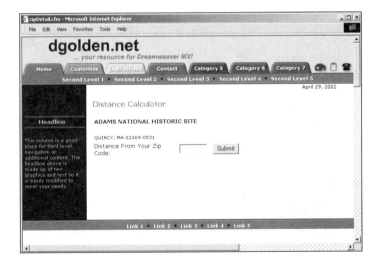

Figure 21.12 When it displays in a web browser, the zipDetail.cfm page displays the details for the selected park and contains the `zipField` text box, which lets users enter their local ZIP codes to find out the distance to the selected park.

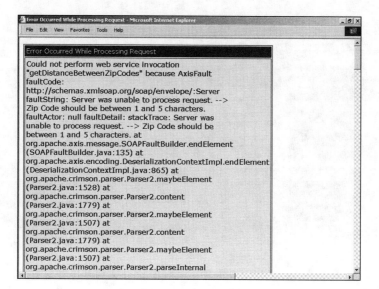

Figure 21.13 When a web service throws an error, study the error message closely for the culprit. In this case, the error lies in an extended ZIP code that contains more than five characters. The web service accepts only five-character zip codes.

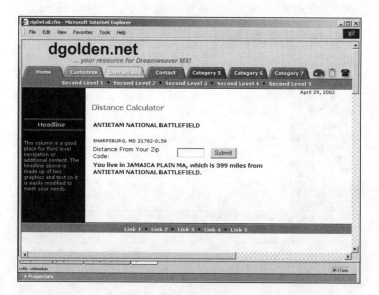

Figure 21.14 After you have worked out all the kinks, the zipDetail.cfm page displays the web service call results in the form of a sentence.

Creating Web Services with ColdFusion Components

To create web services in ColdFusion, you build ColdFusion components. To make component functions available for web service invocation, simply set the `access` attribute of the `CFFUNCTION` tag to `remote`. Also, using the `CFFUNCTION` tag's `returnType` attribute, you must specify the data type returned by the component function, such as `query`, `number`, `string`, `array`, and so on.

ColdFusion components automatically generate the necessary WSDL for remote invocation. In fact, you can see the WSDL file for any component, as long as the `CFFUNCTION` tag's `access` attribute is set to `remote` and a value for the `returnType` attribute is specified. To do this, direct your browser to the components location in your web root, and include WSDL at the end of URL. For example:

```
http://localhost:8500/bookexample/chap21/wsquerycomponent.cfc?wsdl
```

You might be prompted for your ColdFusion Administrator password. Your web browser should display the WSDL file, as shown in Figure 21.15.

Figure 21.15   When you access a component directly with a web browser and specify WSDL at the end of the URL, the ColdFusion component automatically generates the WSDL file.

Displaying WSDL

When accessing a component using a web browser to display the WSDL file, you must make the full URL all lowercase, despite what the actual filename case may be.

In this section, you build a ColdFusion application consisting of a component and two ColdFusion pages. The ColdFusion component contains multiple functions, each of which returns a recordset for a particular exampleapps database table. One ColdFusion page serves as the form page, and the other ColdFusion page serves as the action page. The action page uses the parameters passed from the form page to supply the web service argument values for wsQueryComponent.cfc, and displays the results using dynamic HTML tables.

Figure 21.16 depicts a simplified representation of this application.

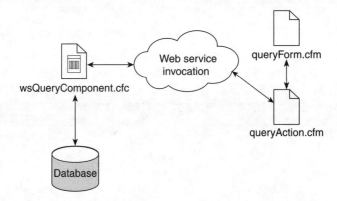

Figure 21.16   This ColdFusion application uses three files: two ColdFusion pages and a component page. The ColdFusion pages invoke web service functions on the component and return recordsets. Notice that only the ColdFusion component interacts with the database.

Building wsQueryComponent.cfc

To build the ColdFusion component, you will use the Create Component dialog box, which generates the file and the framework CFML tags for you. As an alternative, you could create a component by hand using the ColdFusion component template and modifying the code in Code View.

To build wsQueryComponent.cfc with the Create Component dialog box, follow these steps:

1. In Dreamweaver, in the Components panel, select CF Components in the menu.

2. Click the plus (+) button to open the Create Component dialog box.

3. In the Create Component dialog box's Components section, shown in Figure 21.17, enter **"wsQueryComponent"** in the Name text box. Next to the Component Directory text box, click the Browse button. In the Component File Output Directory dialog box that appears, select the chap21 folder in the bookexample directory.

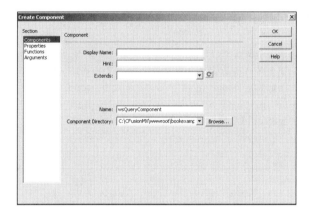

Figure 21.17 In the Create Component dialog box's Components section, you specify the name of the component and where the component file will be saved.

4. In the Functions section of the Create Component dialog box shown in Figure 21.18, create six functions. Name the functions empQueryFunction, deptQueryFunction, catQueryFunction, itemQueryFunction, manQueryFunction, and parkQueryFunction. For each function, select remote in the Access menu. In the Return Type menu, select query.

5. In the Arguments section of the dialog box shown in Figure 21.19, create an argument for each function that returns a string data type. The argument names should correspond to the function names, such as empQueryArgument, catQueryArgument, and so on. Analogous names are not required, but make the code easier to work with.

6. Click the OK button in the Create Component dialog box, and Dreamweaver generates the component file.

7. Using the Bindings panel in the Application bar, create a recordset for each component function. As an example, open the Recordset dialog box and name the recordset **"deptQuery"**. As shown in Figure 21.20, select exampleapps in the Data Source menu, and select tblDepartments in the Tables menu. Choose all records to be returned. In the Filter menu, select DepartmentName equal to (=) an entered value named DepartmentName. When you click the OK button in the Recordset dialog, the following code is generated at the top of the page in Code View:

```
<cfquery name="empQuery" datasource="exampleapps">
    SELECT *
    FROM tblEmployees
    WHERE LastName = 'lastName'
</cfquery>
```

8. Cut the CFQUERY statement, and paste it between the opening and closing tags of the empQueryFunction CFFUNCTION statement. Also, substitute the parameter in the WHERE SQL statement with the name of the CFARGUMENT tag, as the following example shows:

```
<cffunction name="empQueryFunction" access="remote"
returnType="query" output="true">
<cfargument name="lastNameArgument" type="string"
required="true">
<cfquery name="empQuery" datasource="exampleapps">
    SELECT *
    FROM tblEmployees
    WHERE LastName = '#lastNameArgument#'
</cfquery>
<cfreturn empQuery>
</cffunction>
```

Notice that the lastNameArgument variable is surrounded by hash signs (#). This is necessary for the value of the variable to be used in the SQL statement.

9. Repeat Steps 7 and 8 for each component function. You should have functions that query the following exampleapp database tables: tblCategories, tblDepartments, tblEmployees, tblItems, tblManufacturers, and tblParks.

10. Save your work.

As shown in Figure 21.21, you can view both the component functions and parameters in the Components panel.

Component Description

To see an HTML description of the component functions, parameters, and return values, right-click your mouse (Command+click on Macintosh) on a component name, and in the submenu that appears, select Get Description. A new web browser window opens that displays the component description. When accessing this feature, you might be prompted for your ColdFusion Administrator password.

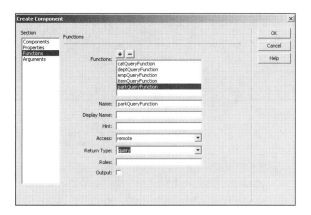

Figure 21.18 In the Create Component dialog box's Functions section, you create the component functions. Make sure you set every component function's access attribute to remote and the return type to query.

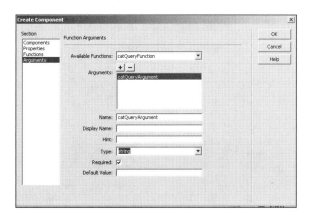

Figure 21.19 In the Create Component dialog box's Arguments section, you create the arguments for the component functions. Make sure to name each argument a distinctive name, and set the type attribute to string. In addition, be sure to set every argument that is required.

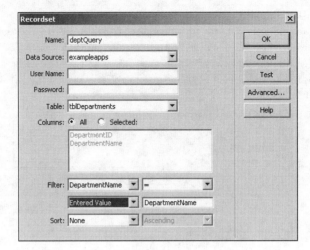

Figure 21.20   You can use the Recordset dialog box to create the recordsets for the web service component. Remember to make each component function's recordset filtered by a parameter.

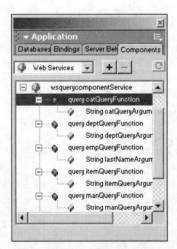

Figure 21.21   The web service component's functions, parameters, and return values are shown in the Components panel on the Application bar.

Building queryForm.cfm

Now turn your attention to queryForm.cfm. In this page, you will create a form page that lets users pass parameters to the queryAction.cfm page, which will invoke the web service functions.

To build queryForm.cfm, follow these steps:

1. Create a new ColdFusion page from the bookexample template, and save it as queryForm.cfm in the chap21 folder in the bookexample directory of your web root.

2. Using Design View, in the editable Body region of the document window, insert a table with 12 rows, 3 columns, and no border.

3. Alternating table rows, insert descriptive text, text boxes, and submit buttons for each component function in wsQueryComponent.cfc, as shown in Figure 21.22. Make sure to name each text box a name that identifies its intended component web service function. For example, name the text box for the empQueryFunction function empQueryArgument.

4. Using Code View, select the TR and TD tags for each table row that contains a text box, and click the FORM button in the Forms panel of the Insert bar. In the Form dialog box that appears, as shown in Figure 21.23, enter **"queryAction.cfm"** in the Action text box. You will create this page in the next section. In the Method menu, select post. When you click the OK button in the Form dialog box, Dreamweaver generates the FORM tag around the table row, as the following example shows:

```
<form action="queryAction.cfm" method="post">
<tr>
<td>
    Find a department:
</td>
<td>
    <input name="deptQueryArgument" type="text"
    id="deptQueryArgument">
</td>
<td>
    <input type="submit" name="Submit6" value="Submit">
</td>
</tr>
</form>
```

You use individual FORM tags because queryAction.cfm uses CFIF tags to execute web service invocations conditionally, based on the presence of passed parameters.

5. Save your work.

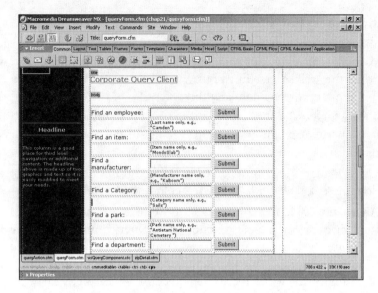

Figure 21.22 In the document window, you see the finished queryForm.cfm page. The page consists of six text fields and submit buttons.

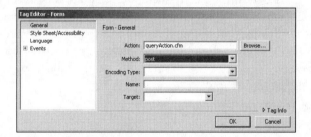

Figure 21.23 Using the Form dialog box, you create six form tags, one for each table row containing a text box and Submit button. You use individual form tags to make it easier to write the conditional logic in queryAction.cfm.

Building queryAction.cfm

In queryAction.cfm, you invoke the web services offered by the wsQueryComponent.cfc file based on which parameter is passed by queryForm.cfm. In addition, you will display the results of the web service function in a dynamic table.

To build queryAction.cfm, follow these steps:

1. Create a new ColdFusion page from the bookexample template, and save it as queryAction.cfm in the chap21 folder of the bookexample directory in your web root.

2. In Code View, insert a `CFIF` statement. Use the `IsDefined` function to test for the presence of the `empQueryArgument` form variable, which is passed from queryForm.cfm, as the following example shows:

   ```
   <cfif IsDefined("form.empQueryArgument")>
   <tr>
       <td> </td>
   </tr>
   ```

3. In the Components panel, select web services in the menu. Click the plus (+) button, and the Add Using WSDL dialog box appears.

4. In the Add Using WSDL dialog box, enter the URL for the wsQueryComponent file and append "WSDL" to the end, as the following example shows:

   ```
   http://localhost:8500/bookexample/chap21/wsquerycomponent.cfc?WSDL
   ```

   Click the OK button, and the wsQueryComponent appears as wsquerycomponentService in the Components panel. As shown in Figure 21.24, you can see the component functions, now web service functions, which you created in the wsQueryComponent.cfc file.

Figure 21.24   Once you add the web service with the Add Using WSDL dialog box, it is available for use in your ColdFusion applications from the Components panel.

5. In the Components panel, drag `empQueryFunction` below the `CFIF` tag. When you do, Dreamweaver automatically generates the `CFINVOKE` tag, as

shown in the following example:

```
<cfif IsDefined("form.empQueryArgument")>
 <cfinvoke
  webservice="http://localhost:8500/bookexample/chap21/wsquerycomponent.cfc?WSDL"
  method="empQueryFunction"
  returnvariable="aQuery">
   <cfinvokeargument name="lastNameArgument"
   value="#form.empQueryArgument#"/>
 </cfinvoke>
</cfif>
```

You place the web service call below the `CFIF` tag because you want it to execute only if the `empQueryArgument` form variable is passed from queryForm.cfm. Notice that the `returnvariable` is set to the default name generated by Dreamweaver. You should change the name to be more descriptive, such as `empQuery`.

6. Below the `CFINVOKE` tag, insert a table with two rows, eight columns, and a border of one. In the code for the top table row, enter the names of the eight columns that you want to return, using the Database panel in the Application bar to see the available columns. In the second row, enclose the HTML table tags in a `CFOUTPUT` statement that references the `empQuery` variable created by the web service call. In each of the table cells, insert a recordset column reference, such as `#empQuery.FIRSTNAME#`. For example:

```
<cfoutput query="empQuery">
<tr>
    <td><p>#empQuery.FIRSTNAME#</p></td>
    <td><p>#empQuery.LASTNAME#</p></td>
    <td><p>#empQuery.PHONE#</p></td>
    <td><p>#empQuery.EMAIL#</p></td>
    <td><p>#empQuery.TITLE#</p></td>
    <td><p>#empQuery.DEPTIDFK#</p></td>
    <td><p>#empQuery.EmployeeID#</p></td>
    <td><p>#empQuery.STARTDATE#</p></td>
</tr>
</cfoutput>
```

If the `empQueryArgument` form variable is present, the web service call to `empQueryFunction` executes, and the recordset is returned. It is available using the variable name specified in the `returnVariable` attribute. Finally, the `CFOUTPUT` statement executes to display the records contained in the `empQuery` recordset.

If the variable is not present, the web service method will not be invoked, and the table will not be displayed.

7. Repeat Steps 5 and 6 for each function of the wsquerycomponentService web service. Create additional CFIF statements that check for the existence of variables.

8. Save your work.

Data Type Translations

The SOAP proxy to web service-friendly data types translate ColdFusion data types. The ColdFusion numeric data type translates to the web service double data type. The ColdFusion data types Boolean, string, and array are translated to the web service data types of the same names. The ColdFusion binary data type is translated to the web service data type base64Binary. The ColdFusion date data type is translated to the web service data type dateTime. The ColdFusion GUID and UUID data types are translated to web service string data types. The ColdFusion component data type is translated to the web service complex data type. The ColdFusion struct data type translates to map, and the ColdFusion query data type translates to QueryBean.

As the previous example shows, if the person calling your ColdFusion web services is also using ColdFusion MX and Dreamweaver MX, he or she can use your databases without needing a connection to the actual data source, a boon to increased security and flexibility across heterogeneous systems.

Although ColdFusion MX does not support UDDI natively, you can manually register your web services on most of the popular web service registries, such as www.xmethods.net or the IBM UDDI registry (www.ibm.com).

Summary

In this chapter, you learned how to use web services in your ColdFusion application, including ColdFusion pages and components. In addition, you learned how to build your own web services using ColdFusion components and use the web services that you build in your own applications. Although the related technologies are still emerging, you should now realize the promise and power of web services.

In the next chapter, you will learn how to customize Dreamweaver MX to speed up your ColdFusion development tasks.

VII

Customizing Dreamweaver

22

Customizing Dreamweaver for ColdFusion Development

IN THIS CHAPTER, YOU WILL LEARN HOW to customize the Dreamweaver MX environment to help you build ColdFusion applications more quickly and easily. Dreamweaver's extensible architecture gives you the capability to customize almost every facet of your development environment, from specifying which panels to display to creating keyboard shortcuts for CFML tags and functions to registering new tag libraries.

This chapter was written using Dreamweaver MX on Microsoft Windows 2000. Dreamweaver on Macintosh offers a different interface and different customization options. For more information on Macintosh customization, please refer to the Dreamweaver documentation (Help menu, Using Dreamweaver).

About Customizing Dreamweaver for ColdFusion Development

The Dreamweaver MX environment helps you build ColdFusion applications effortlessly and efficiently. Customizing the Dreamweaver environment lets you modify the default environment options to fit your specific needs. In fact,

Dreamweaver is built on an extensible architecture with the express intention of letting developers change almost any element within the Dreamweaver environment.

You can customize Dreamweaver in a number of ways. At the most basic level, you can use Dreamweaver's Preferences panel to configure various environment options, including setting different background colors, changing code-hinting tips, and switching default document types.

In addition, using the Keyboard Shortcuts dialog box, you can assign keystroke combinations to specific ColdFusion tags and application objects. You can also automate multiple commands using the Command Recorder feature and the History panel.

Furthermore, you can create and modify tag libraries. Using the Tag Library Editor dialog box, you can customize how the new tags appear in the code and how they relate to the surrounding code or text.

If you find that Dreamweaver's customization options do not provide enough control over the environment, you should investigate building custom server behaviors and Dreamweaver extensions. For more information, see Chapter 23, "Building Custom Server Behaviors" and Chapter 24, "Building Dreamweaver Extensions."

Using the Preferences Panel

You can think of the Preferences panel as your control console for the Dreamweaver MX environment. From changing the color of CFML tags to selecting which version of ColdFusion to validate your CFML against, the Preferences panel should be your first stop when you want to change Dreamweaver's default settings.

To access the Preferences panel, select Preferences from the Edit menu, or you can use the keyboard combination Ctrl+U on Windows or Command+U on Macintosh. When the Preferences panel appears, as shown in Figure 22.1, notice that it contains multiple categories. You can access individual categories by clicking on the desired name in the Category section.

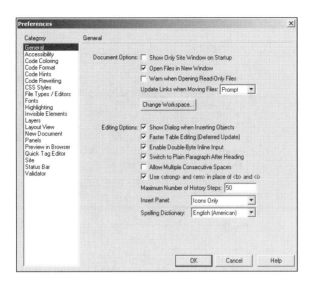

Figure 22.1 Think of Dreamweaver's Preferences panel as
your control console for the Dreamweaver environment. The
Preferences panel is organized according to category of control.

Table 22.1 contains the ColdFusion-related categories and a description of the
controls they contain.

Table 22.1 **Preferences Panel Categories**

Category	Description
General	As shown in Figure 22.1, the General category is split into two subcategories: Document Options and Editing Options. Document Options consist of controls for handling how Dreamweaver opens and moves files. Editing Options include controls for object dialogs, double-byte character support, History panel memory settings, and so on.
	If you click on the Change Workspace button, the Workspace Setup dialog appears, and you can choose from among three types of pre-configured interfaces: the Dreamweaver MX workspace, Homesite/Coder style, and the Dreamweaver 4 interface. This book uses the Dreamweaver MX workspace for its examples.
Accessibility	As shown in Figure 22.2, the Accessibility category lets you choose whether to show Accessibility dialogs when inserting objects into a page. Accessibility options let you include additional information, usually in the form of the HTML ALT tag, for users with vision disabilities. Usually, screen reader programs provide the accessibility vocally to users who cannot see the web page. In addition, you can choose to display large text in the Dreamweaver environment.

continues

Table 22.1   **Continued**

Category	Description
Code Coloring	As shown in Figure 22.3, the Code Coloring category lets you change code color options by document type, including ColdFusion and ColdFusion component. After you select a document type in the Document Type text box, click on the Edit Coloring Scheme button, and the Edit Coloring Scheme for ColdFusion dialog appears.
	In the Edit Coloring Scheme for ColdFusion dialog box, shown in Figure 22.4, you can change every code type that appears in the Code View, including CFML tags, CFScript, and so on. You select a code type in the Styles text box and then select the text and background colors in the menus next to it. By changing the background color of ColdFusion component files, you can easily differentiate between file types when switching between ColdFusion pages and components in Code View.
	If you will be mixing HTML and CFML together in the same ColdFusion page, you might find it useful to change the background of CFML tags and CFScript to make them stand out on the page. In addition, you can make the ColdFusion Query Text code (SQL) bold to emphasize its difference from HTML and CFML tags.
Code Format	As shown in Figure 22.5, the Code Format category lets you choose detailed formatting options for code. In particular, if you're working on a remote Unix server running ColdFusion, you want to choose Unix in the Line Break Type menu. In addition, the Default Tag Case menu lets you specify the default case for tags and tag attributes. You can also set whether to enforce tag case, which might not be a good idea if you like to mix the lower- and uppercase letters.
Code Hints	As shown in Figure 22.6, the Code Hints category lets you configure the automatic code completion feature of Dreamweaver. When working in Code View, by default, Dreamweaver automatically completes tags and code when you type in the document window. Although the majority of developers appreciate the assistance, you might like to write your code unhindered. If so, you can uncheck the Enable Auto Tag Completion and Enable Code Hints check boxes to turn the feature off. In addition, you can set a delay for the code completion Feature and turn code completion on and off for each code type.
Code Rewriting	As shown in Figure 22.7, the Code Rewriting category lets you configure Dreamweaver's automatic code rewriting features. Dreamweaver rewrites files to match the validation scheme for a particular programming language. Although this feature can work very well with HTML files, by default, code rewriting is disabled for ColdFusion pages and components. That's because Dreamweaver might make changes that affect the proper execution of your CFML. The Code Rewriting category also provides automatic encoding of invalid characters in URLs and parameters. This feature offers an extra level of protection against common coding mistakes.

Category	Description
File Types/Editors	As shown in Figure 22.8, the File Types/Editors category lets you specify file types to open automatically in Code View, choose external text and image editors, and so on. If you work with many types of digital media, such as Flash movies and MP3 files, you can designate external programs to open those files from within the Dreamweaver environment.
Fonts	As shown in Figure 22.9, the Fonts category lets you set fonts for the principle code-editing interfaces in Dreamweaver, including Code View and the Tag Inspector. If you've grown tired of looking at the Courier font for code, you can change it here.
Highlighting	As shown in Figure 22.10, the Highlighting category provides highlighting options for the Design View. Of particular interest for ColdFusion development, you can change the background color for dynamic data.
Invisible Elements	As shown in Figure 22.11, the Invisible Elements category lets you select whether to show code elements in Design View using icons. If you find yourself working in Design View most of the time, you should enable the Nonvisual Server Markup Tags option. You can also change the format of how dynamic text is displayed in Design View using the Show Dynamic Text As menu.
New Document	As shown in Figure 22.12, the New Document category allows you to change default document types for Dreamweaver. If desired, you can change the default setting of HTM to a ColdFusion page or component.
Panels	As shown in Figure 22.13, the Panels category lets you select which panels should be on top at all times and which should not. In addition, you can choose panels to include on Dreamweaver's Launch bar.
Preview in Browser	As shown in Figure 22.14, the Preview in Browser category lets you choose which web browser you want to use to preview application pages. You are not restricted to the dominant browsers, such as Microsoft Internet Explorer and Netscape Navigator. As long as you can locate your desired web browser's EXE file, you can use it with Dreamweaver.
Quick Tag Editor	As shown in Figure 22.15, the Quick Tag Editor category lets you configure the Quick Tag Editor to apply changes immediately and set the code hint delay.
Site	As shown in Figure 22.16, the Site category provides numerous controls for the Site panel, including source control, FTP, and Site panel display options. If you work with both local files and files on remote servers, you might want to differentiate their display in the Site panel using the Always Show menus.

continues

Table 22.1 **Continued**

Category	Description
Validator	As shown in Figure 22.17, the Validator category lets you choose whether to validate your code and what validation schema should be used. Code validation is intended to decrease coding errors before the code is deployed, so that additional debugging is not required to fix simple errors. For ColdFusion, you have the option of using validation for every previous version of ColdFusion. This book uses the ColdFusion MX validation scheme.

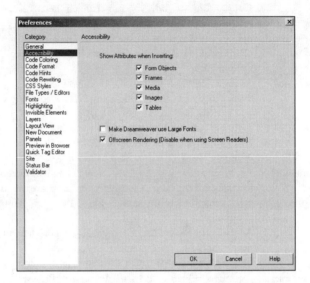

Figure 22.2 In the Accessibility category of the Preferences panel, you can adjust basic document and editing settings.

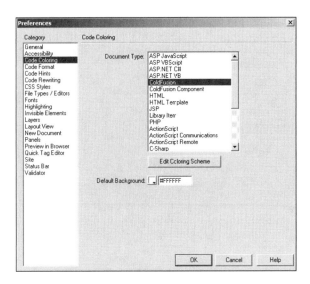

Figure 22.3 The Code Coloring category lets you configure various code coloring options, including default background colors for file types.

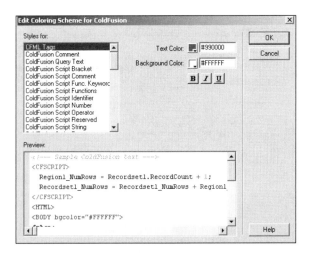

Figure 22.4 The Edit Coloring Scheme for ColdFusion dialog box lets you change code-coloring options for specific code elements of ColdFusion pages, such as CFML tags and SQL statements.

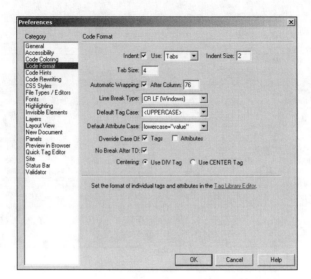

Figure 22.5   The Code Format category of the Preferences panel provides controls for Dreamweaver's automatic code format features, such as line break types and upper- and lowercase tags.

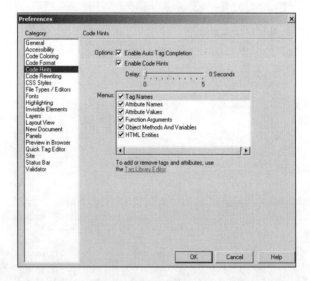

Figure 22.6   The Code Hints category of the Preferences panel lets you toggle Auto Tag Completion and Code Hints features on and off.

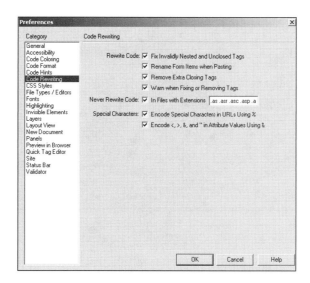

Figure 22.7 The Code Rewriting category lets you configure Dreamweaver's code rewriting features, such as automatically removing extra closing tags and encoding special characters in URL strings.

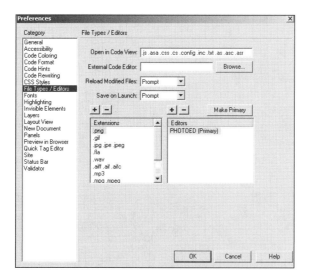

Figure 22.8 The File Types/Editors category of the Preferences panel contains controls for opening files in external editors other than the Dreamweaver environment, specifying whether to reload open files opened outside of Dreamweaver, and so on.

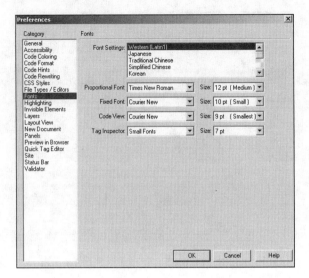

Figure 22.9 The Fonts category provides the ability to alter the fonts used in Code View, the Code Inspector, and so on.

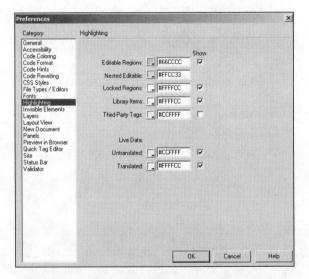

Figure 22.10 The Highlighting category of the Preferences panel provides controls for automatic highlighting of page elements in Design View, such as dynamic data.

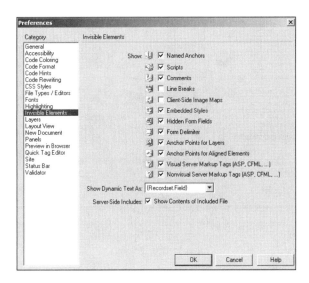

Figure 22.11 The Invisible Elements category of the Preferences panel lets you select what code elements are displayed in Design View using icons, including CFML tags.

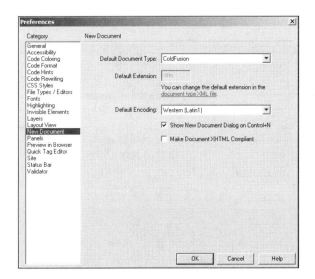

Figure 22.12 The New Document category of the Preferences panel lets you choose the default new document type for Dreamweaver and the default encoding scheme. If you use Dreamweaver mainly for ColdFusion development, you can set the default new document type to ColdFusion page or component.

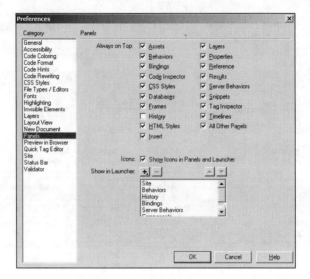

Figure 22.13 The Panels category of the Preferences panel lets you select which panels stay on top. If you uncheck a panel, that panel will disappear when you select another document in the Dreamweaver environment. In addition, you can add or remove panels from the Launcher bar.

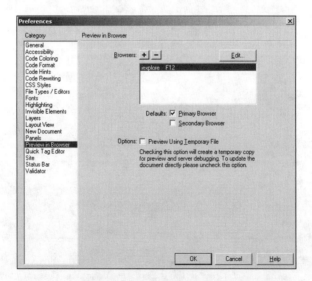

Figure 22.14 The Preview in Browser category provides controls for previewing pages in web browsers, including registering new browsers and choosing whether to create a copy of the page to display in the browser.

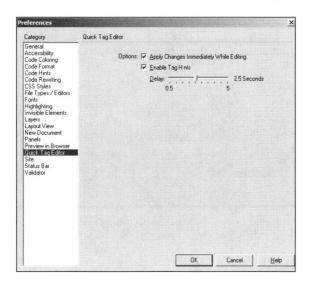

Figure 22.15 The Quick Tag Editor category of the Preferences panel lets you set two options for the Quick Tag Editor, applying changes immediately and code hint display.

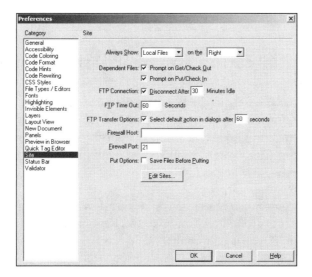

Figure 22.16 The Site category of the Preferences panel lets you set preferences for the Site panel, including source control, FTP, and Site panel display options.

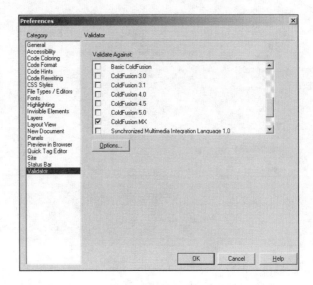

Figure 22.17 The Validator category of the Preferences panel lets you select a version of CFML to validate your code against. You can choose from every version of ColdFusion, including ColdFusion MX.

Using and Creating Keyboard Shortcuts

Although Dreamweaver is a visual development environment designed for use with both the mouse and the keyboard, you can use the keyboard for many tasks that normally require the mouse. For example, you can press the keyboard combination Ctrl+R (Command+R on Macintosh) and the Live Data View appears. If you press the keyboard combination Ctrl+F12 (Command+F12 on Macintosh), the current page is displayed in a web browser for debugging purposes.

You can also customize Dreaweaver's keyboard shortcuts using the Keyboard Shortcuts dialog box. You open the Keyboard Shortcuts dialog box by selecting Edit, Keyboard Shortcuts. When the Keyboard Shortcuts dialog box appears, as shown in Figure 22.18, you see a collection of menus, display windows, text boxes, and buttons.

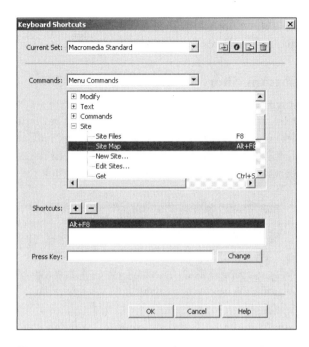

Figure 22.18 The Keyboard Shortcuts dialog box lets you
see existing keyboard shortcut sets and create custom keyboard
sets according to your personal preferences.

Keyboard Shortcuts

You can download a PDF of the Dreamweaver keyboard shortcuts from the Macromedia web site
(`www.macromedia.com/support/dreamweaver/documentation/dwmx_shortcuts/`). You can
also use Appendix C of this book, "Dreamweaver MX Keyboard Shortcuts," which contains a list of
keyboard shortcuts.

Using the Current Set menu, you can select from different keyboard shortcut
sets, including Dreamweaver 3, BBEdit (a popular text editor for the
Macintosh), and Homesite (a popular text editor for the PC). If you recently
migrated to Dreamweaver from one of these programs, you can still use the
same keyboard shortcuts. By default, Dreamweaver MX uses the Macromedia
Default shortcut set.

You can explore the shortcut sets by selecting a command set in the
Commands menu. When you select a command set, such as Menu
Commands, Site Panel, Code Editing, Document Editing, or Site Window, the
keyboard shortcuts contained in that command set display a tree structure in

the window below the Commands menu. You can explore the keyboard shortcuts by expanding and collapsing the tree structure.

Creating a Custom Shortcut Set

To create your own shortcut set, you must first duplicate a set. You duplicate shortcut sets by selecting a shortcut set in the Current Set menu and clicking the Duplicate Set button. When you click the Duplicate Set button, the Duplicate Set dialog appears, as shown in Figure 22.19. In the Duplicate Set dialog box, enter a name for the new shortcut set, and click the OK button.

Figure 22.19 You use the Duplicate Set dialog box to name the new keyboard shortcut set that you create.

After you have duplicated a keyboard shortcut set, you can change keyboard shortcuts and create new shortcuts. To create keyboard shortcuts for common CFML tags, follow these steps:

1. In the Keyboard Shortcuts dialog box, select the new shortcut set in the Current Set menu.

2. Select Menu Commands in the Commands menu. In the tree structure, expand Insert, ColdFusion Basic Objects. Select a CFML tag, such as CFQUERY.

3. After placing your cursor in the Press Key text box, enter a keyboard combination, such as CTRL+ALT+Q. If you enter a keyboard combination that is already used by another command, you will receive an error message indicating what command is currently associated with your desired shortcut.

4. Click the Change button, and the keyboard combination appears in the Shortcuts box.

You can use the Plus (+) button to add a new keyboard combination and the Minus (-) button to remove a keyboard combination. Once you create a keyboard shortcut to a CFML tag, you use the Preferences panel to choose whether to display the corresponding Tag Editor dialog box or just insert the code.

Recording and Using Commands

If you need to record multiple commands from both the mouse and keyboard, you can use Dreamweaver's command recorder to store combinations of keyboard input and mouse clicks. You can record commands in two ways: recording your keyboard and mouse input in the background, or using the History panel and selecting previous commands to store as a set.

Some Dreamweaver commands cannot be stored, such as modifying code directly in Code View or the Quick Tag Editor. In addition, you cannot store some kinds of server behaviors, such as dynamic text and dynamic form elements. When you perform an action that cannot be recorded, you will receive an error message. If you are recording commands in the background, an error message appears that states the command cannot be recorded. If you are using the History panel, a red X will appear on the command icon, as shown in Figure 22.20.

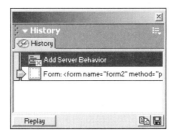

Figure 22.20 The History panel lists the commands that you perform in the Dreamweaver environment. If a red X appears in a command icon, it cannot be saved as a command.

Recording Commands Using the Commands Menu

The Commands menu lets you record commands in the background as you work in Dreamweaver. When you record commands using the Commands menu, you can store only one command set at a time. When you record another command using the Commands menu, the previous command is erased.

When recording is turned on, a tape recorder icon appears next to your mouse cursor. While recording is turned on, perform the commands that you want recorded as the following steps indicate:

1. Start the Command Recorder by selecting Command, Start Recording, or by hitting the keyboard shortcut Ctrl+Shift+X (Command+Shift+X in Macintosh).

2. Using the Bindings panel, create a new recordset from the example apps data source.

3. Using the Application panel in the Insert bar, insert a dynamic table that uses the recordset you created in Step 2.

4. Using the Server Behaviors panel, insert a recordset navigation menu.

5. In the Commands menu, select Stop Recording.

You can use the recorded command by selecting Play Recorded Command from the Commands menu.

Recording Commands Using the History Panel

The History panel serves a dual purpose. You can use it both to roll back changes you've made in a document and to redo changes. In addition, the History panel lets you save commands so you can use them over and over again. To save commands using the History panel, follow these steps:

1. Open the History panel by selecting the Window menu, Others, History or by hitting the keyboard shortcut Shift+F10 on the PC or Macintosh. To clear any items currently in the History panel, right-click (Command+Click on Macintosh) on the History panel and select Clear History.

2. Using the Server Behaviors panel, create a recordset and a dynamic table that displays the recordset.

3. Using your mouse, select the commands that you want to save and click the Save Selected Steps as Command button. In the Save As Command dialog box that appears, as shown in Figure 22.21, enter a name for the command, and click the OK button.

4. To access the recorded command, open the Commands menu. You will see the command listed at the bottom of the menu, as shown in Figure 22.22.

You can edit and delete custom commands using the Edit Command List. For more information about the Dreamweaver keyboard shortcut set, see Appendix C.

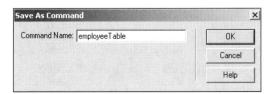

Figure 22.21 The Save As Command dialog box lets you name a custom command set.

Figure 22.22 Once saved, the custom command set appears at the bottom of the Commands menu.

Modifying and Creating Tag Libraries

Dreamweaver organizes its supported programming languages into tag libraries. Each library contains the individual tags and their attributes. For example, the CFML tag library contains all tags in ColdFusion MX and their attributes. Macromedia uses tag libraries in other features, such as Auto Tag Completion, the Tag Editor dialog boxes, and so on.

Behind the scenes, Dreamweaver stores tag libraries as a collection of XML and Visual Tools Markup Language (VTML) files. Dreamweaver's Tag Library Editor provides a visual interface to those files, thereby removing the need for you to understand the underlying technologies in detail.

You use the Tag Library Editor to modify existing libraries, create new libraries, and import external tag libraries. You access the Tag Library Editor by selecting the Edit menu, Tag Library Editor.

The Tag Library Editor provides controls for the following tasks:

- Creating new tag libraries

- Inserting new tags into existing libraries

- Importing tag libraries from various sources, including XML schemas and JSP tag library files

- Modifying the appearance of existing tags

As shown in Figure 22.23, you select the CFML tag library from a tree structure. When you expand the CFML Tags node, a folder appears for each CFML tag. Inside the folder, the tag attributes, if any, are listed. The Used In display panel lets you select the document type in which the tag library is available. Of course, CFML can be used only in ColdFusion pages and components.

If you select an individual tag, the Tag Library Editor display changes to show different controls, such as selecting line breaks and tag case. If you select a tag's attribute, you can change attribute case and data type.

Figure 22.23   The Tag Library Editor provides access to Dreamweaver's tag libraries. Using the Tag Library Editor, you can modify existing tag libraries, create new ones, or insert new tags into existing libraries.

Creating a New Tag Library

Although you can insert new tags into existing libraries, you might want to create a new tag library for additional tags so that you can keep the two tag libraries separate. Creating a new tag library is very useful for integrating ColdFusion custom tags into the Dreamweaver environment.

ColdFusion custom tags let you create or download ColdFusion pages that you save into the ColdFusion custom tag root or web root. To use the functionality in the ColdFusion pages, you simply insert a CFML-like tag, such as `<cf_customTag>`, into your ColdFusion pages or components. ColdFusion automatically finds and executes the custom tag files. In short, custom tags provide an easy way to extend CFML without deviating from standard ColdFusion syntax.

A great source for prebuilt custom tags is the Macromedia ColdFusion Exchange (`http://devex.macromedia.com/developer/gallery/`). Enterprising ColdFusion developers upload custom tags to the ColdFusion Exchange for other ColdFusion developers to use. When you use the ColdFusion Exchange, keep the following points in mind:

- Many ColdFusion custom tags are not free. To use the custom tags in a production environment, you must pay the custom tag developer.
- Like any third-party software, Macromedia does not guarantee that the custom tags work as advertised. Before using custom tags in production, thoroughly test the custom tag.

In the following procedure, you will use the intelliCalendar 1.5 custom tag to create a pop-up calendar that lets users select a date and auto-populate a form text box. At the time of this writing, intelliCalendar is available at no cost on the ColdFusion Exchange. However, the ColdFusion pages for the custom tag are encrypted, meaning that you cannot modify the CFML source code.

To create a new tag library for custom tags, follow these steps:

1. Create a new folder in the bookexample directory of your web root named customTags.
2. Download intelliCalendar 1.5, and unpack the Zip archive into the CustomTags folder.
3. In Dreamweaver, open the Tag Library Editor, and click the Plus (+) button. In the submenu that appears, select New Tag Library. The New Tag Library dialog box appears.
4. In the New Tag Library dialog box, shown in Figure 22.24, enter a name for the tag library, such as CustomTags. Click the OK button.

5. Back in the Tag Library Editor, select ColdFusion and ColdFusion Component in the Used In display box. In the Tag Prefix text box, enter **"cf_"**. All ColdFusion custom tags use this prefix. Click the OK button.

6. Click the plus button again, and select New Tags. The New Tags dialog box appears.

7. In the New Tags dialog box shown in Figure 22.25, select the CustomTags library in Tag Library menu. In the Tag Names text box, enter the name for the new tag, `intelliCalendar`. Click the OK button. An intelliCalendar directory appears beneath the CustomTags library.

   You can set a number of formatting options after you create the new tag, such as case, contents, and line breaks.

8. After making sure the intelliCalendar directory is selected, click the plus button, and select New Attributes. The New Attributes dialog box appears. To find the available attributes for the intelliCalendar custom tag, read the documentation included in the download from the ColdFusion Exchange.

9. In the New Attributes dialog box, shown in Figure 22.26, enter two attribute names, formname and fieldname. Click the OK button in the New Attributes dialog box and the attribute appears beneath the intelliCalendar folder.

   After you have created the new attributes, you can select the data type for the attribute. In this case, both attributes will be text.

To use the custom tag in your ColdFusion applications, simply insert the tag using the Tag Chooser (Insert menu, Tag). As shown in Figure 22.27, the CustomTags tag library contains the `cf_intelliCalendar` custom tag. You must restart Dreamweaver after you create a new tag library for the tag to appear in the Tag Chooser.

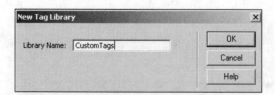

Figure 22.24   The New Tag Library dialog box lets you name and create a new tag library.

Figure 22.25 The New Tags dialog box lets you create new tags for tag libraries. You select the tag library and give the tag a name.

Figure 22.26 The New Attributes dialog box lets you create attributes for tags. You select the tag library, tag, and attribute name.

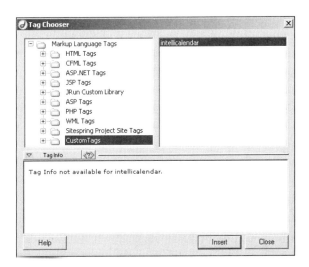

Figure 22.27 After you restart Dreamweaver, the CustomTags tag library appears with the `cf_intelliCalendar` tag listed in the Tag Chooser.

Summary

In this chapter, you learned about the customization features in Dreamweaver that let you tailor the environment to your development needs. In the next chapter, you'll learn how to use Dreamweaver's Server Behavior Builder to create custom server behaviors.

23

Building Custom Server Behaviors

I N THIS CHAPTER, YOU WILL LEARN THE basics of building custom Dreamweaver server behaviors. Custom server behaviors are intended to provide a way to extend Dreamweaver's prebuilt set of server behaviors with creations of your own. When you find yourself performing the same coding tasks over and over again, you might be able to automate some of the work by creating a server behavior designed for a specific task.

You can build custom server behaviors to serve a wide variety of purposes, such as a CFML code block that sends email or returns the names of files in a directory. You can also let other people use the server behaviors that you build by just packaging up a few files.

About Building Custom Server Behaviors

As you gain experience developing ColdFusion applications with Dreamweaver, you might find yourself repeating the same tasks again and again. As you learned in Chapter 19, "Using ColdFusion Components," and Chapter 7, "Validating Data and Handling Errors," ColdFusion provides a number of ways to reuse code, including ColdFusion components and user-defined functions (UDFs).

Dreamweaver also includes features for building new tags and tag libraries, creating custom commands, and creating code snippets for simple blocks of code. Also, you can leverage the Dreamweaver architecture to build custom behaviors that insert multiple code blocks with interactive dialogs for entering parameters.

With all the code-reuse features that ColdFusion and Dreamweaver offer, you should consider which feature best suits the task that you want to accomplish:

- If you need to insert a small code block or UDF, use the Snippets panel.
- If you need to insert a custom CFML tag or a modified version of a standard CFML tag, use the Tag Library Editor to create a new tag library and tags.
- If you need to insert multiple code blocks that require multiple parameters or depend on other CFML tags, create a custom server behavior.
- If you need to build complex behaviors with custom user interfaces, you should build a Dreamweaver extension. For more information, see Chapter 24, "Building Dreamweaver Extensions."

In this chapter, you will build two custom server behaviors that output queries to formats other than HTML. One behavior returns the results to Flash Remoting, which in turn returns the query to a Flash movie. The other behavior inserts two custom tags, downloaded from the ColdFusion Exchange on www.macromedia.com, that create Microsoft Word and Excel files from database queries.

Building Simple Custom Server Behaviors

Accessible from the Server Behaviors panel, Dreamweaver's Server Behavior Builder provides a wizard-like interface that lets you create the code and user interface for custom server behaviors. As shown in Figure 23.1, the Server Behavior Builder lets you build the code block by block. In each code block, you can insert parameters by clicking the Insert Parameter in Code Block button. You can also specify where the server behavior code will be inserted within the page with the Insert Code menu.

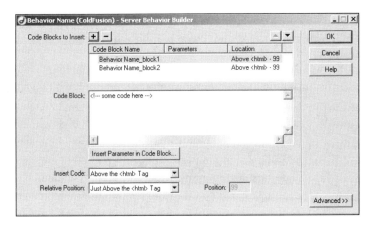

Figure 23.1   Using the Server Behavior Builder, you can insert code blocks and define parameters for those code blocks. In addition, you can configure where the server behavior code will be inserted into the page, such as relative to another tag.

The Server Behavior Builder also offers additional options, such as displaying an icon in the document window using Design View. In the Advanced options, which you can reveal by clicking the Advanced button, you can change the custom server behavior's title in the Server Behaviors panel or choose a code block that is selected when the server behavior is used.

When you click the Next button in the Server Behavior Builder, the Generate Behavior Dialog Box appears. As shown in Figure 23.2, you select user-interface controls for the parameters specified in the Server Behavior Builder. Table 23.1 lists the available controls and a brief description of them.

Table 23.1   **Server Behavior User Interface Controls**

Control	Description
Recordset Menu/Editable	Displays the current recordsets in the page
Recordset Field Menu/Editable	Displays the recordset fields for a selected recordset
CF Data Source Menu	Displays a list of data sources registered in ColdFusion
Connection/Table/ Column Menu	Displays the tables, connections, and columns for a selected ColdFusion data source
Text/Dynamic/Numeric/ URL Field	Displays a text box in which users can enter text, numbers, or URLs
List Menu, Checkbox, Radio Group	Standard user input controls that provide a menu, box, or radio buttons

After you create a custom server behavior, it becomes available in the Server Behavior menu that appears when you click the plus (+) button in the Server Behaviors panel.

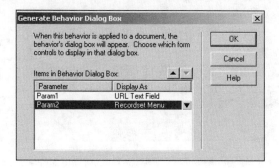

Figure 23.2 The Generate Behavior Dialog Box lets you assign parameters to a variety of menus, text boxes, and radio buttons.

Custom server behaviors need not be complicated. In fact, a custom server behavior can consist of simply one step. As you might recall from Chapter 20, "Building Flash Remoting Services," you return results of ColdFusion page processing to Flash using the `flash.result` variable. For example:

```
<cfset flash.result = empQuery>
```

In this example, `empQuery` represents a recordset that gets returned to Flash. In fact, the recordset is the only part of this code that will ever need to change. A server behavior of this code would need to accept only one parameter, the recordset name.

When you think about how the server behavior user interface should work, think of how you would build a form page for the web. What information needs to be gathered? Would it be easier to provide the user with a menu with a pregenerated list or just to provide a text box?

You must also consider how the code that the server behavior produces interacts with other code already on the page. For example, the sample code relies on a recordset already being defined on the page in a `CFQUERY` statement. Therefore, the server behavior must check for the existence of a `CFQUERY` statement.

To build a custom server behavior that inserts the `flash.result` variable, follow these steps:

1. In the Server Behaviors panel, click the plus (+) button, and in the submenu that appears, select New Server Behaviors. The New Server Behavior dialog box appears.

Building the ReportInWord Custom Server Behavior

Although similar in function, the custom tags have different setup options because of their required attributes. To create the ReportInWord custom server behavior, follow these steps:

1. In the Server Behaviors panel, click the plus (+) button. In the submenu that appears, select New Server Behavior to launch the New Server Behavior dialog box.

2. In the New Server Behavior Dialog Box shown in Figure 23.12, enter a name for the server behavior, such as **ReportInWord**. Click the OK button to launch the Server Behavior Builder.

3. In the Server Behavior Builder shown in Figure 23.13, you are going to create one code block that contains multiple tags: the CFIF and custom tags that actually generate the documents and a small HTML table that inserts the necessary hyperlinks into the page.

   To get started, create the CFIF statement that tests for the existence of the type URL variable. If it is not present, the page executes normally. If the variable is present, another CFIF tag evaluates whether the type variable is set to "word". If it is, the CF_REPORTINWORD custom tag executes. If it is not, the custom tag will not execute. Here is what the code should look like:

```
<cfif isDefined("URL.type")>
<cfif #URL.type# EQ "word">
<cf_reportinword
    PathSaved="C:\CFUSIONMX\WWWROOT\bookexample\chap23\temp.doc"
    reportType="list"
    dsn="value_here"
    reportTitle="value_here"
    tableName="value_here"
    fieldList="value_here "
    orderBy="value_here"
    headerFontColor="9"
  cellFontColor="6"
    listFontSize="12">
<cflocation url="/bookexample/chap23/temp.doc">
</cfif>
</cfif>
```

   In the example, you see the custom tag used. Notice that many of the custom tag attributes need a value specified, for which you will create behavior controls. You will create five parameters for the custom tag: DSN, Report Title, Table Name, Field List, and Order By.

   Also, the PathSaved attribute specifies where the Word document will be saved on the server. The CFLOCATION tag will direct the web browser to open the Word document.

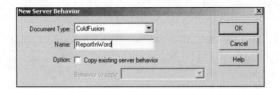

Figure 23.12 In the New Server Behavior dialog box,
enter a descriptive name for the server behavior.
This name will appear in the Server Behaviors menu.

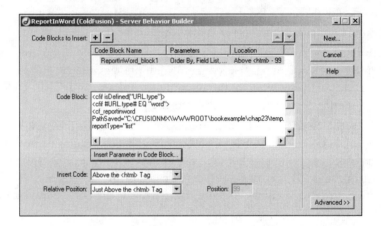

Figure 23.13 In the Server Behavior Builder, you create one code block
with multiple tags, including the CF_REPORTINWORD custom tag, and parameters.

4. Back in the Server Behavior Builder, select Above the <html> Tag in the
Insert Code menu. Click the Advanced button to expand the dialog box.
For Dreamweaver to list the custom server behavior in the Server
Behaviors Panel when inserted into a ColdFusion page, select the If code
block found in document, display behavior in Server Behaviors panel
check box.

5. After you click the Next button in the Server Behavior Builder, the
Generate Behavior Dialog Box appears, as shown in Figure 23.14. In it,
you set the display options for the parameters that you inserted in the
Server Behavior Builder. Because the CF_REPORTINWORD custom tag requires
the data source name, table, and columns, you must use the Connection
form controls.

For the DSN attribute, select Connection Menu, which will display a menu of the data sources currently registered in ColdFusion. For the Report Title attribute, select Text Field. For the Table Name attribute, select Connection Table Menu, which will display the list of tables contained in the selected data source. For the Field List attribute, select Text Field Comma Separated List, which lets users enter a list of table columns from which the Word document will be created. For the Order By attribute, select Connection Column Menu.

Click the OK button.

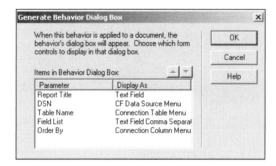

Figure 23.14 In the Generate Behavior Dialog Box, you assign form controls to the parameters created in the Server Behavior Builder.

The ReportInWord custom server behavior is now ready to use. When you select the behavior from the Server Behaviors panel menu, the custom server behavior's dialog pops up, as shown in Figure 23.15.

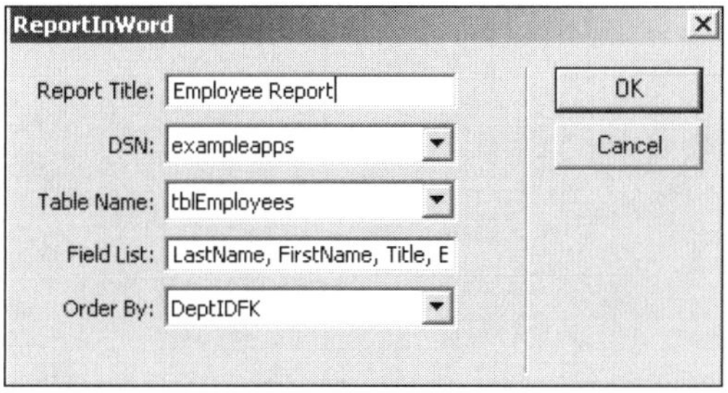

Figure 23.15 The custom server behavior's dialog box, which you just created, appears. Notice that the form controls automatically populate themselves based on what is selected in the DSN menu.

Summary

In this chapter, you learned how to build custom server behaviors in Dreamweaver MX. Using the Server Behavior Builder and its associated dialog boxes, you can build relatively sophisticated server behaviors without touching Dreamweaver's underlying code base.

In the next chapter, you will learn more about Dreamweaver's underlying technologies and how server behaviors, resource panels, and the rest of Dreamweaver work. In fact, with Dreamweaver extensions, you can modify almost any element in the Dreamweaver MX environment.

24

Building Dreamweaver Extensions

IN THIS CHAPTER, YOU WILL LEARN the basics of building Dreamweaver extensions. Dreamweaver extensions let you build custom dialogs, server behaviors, server models, menus, and more. Using the Dreamweaver extension application programming interfaces (APIs), you can build sophisticated user interfaces and dynamic functionality. You can also package your extension and make it available for download by other Dreamweaver users.

Dreamweaver extensions exist as a collection of files that are installed in Dreamweaver. Extensions can change the way Dreamweaver works by modifying the environment or functionality. More often, Dreamweaver extensions add features that are not included "out of the box."

Although this chapter does not teach you how to build an extension step by step, you can learn the general concepts and technologies used in building Dreamweaver extensions. For an in-depth discussion of building Dreamweaver extensions, see the *Dreamweaver MX Extensions* by Laura Gutman (New Riders Publishing, 2002).

About Building Dreamweaver Extensions

If you browse the Dreamweaver Exchange on the Macromedia web site
(www.macromedia.com/exchange/), you'll find dozens of Dreamweaver extensions
that provide functionality not included in Dreamweaver, including new server
behaviors, objects, and panels. The Macromedia Exchange also offers extensions for other Macromedia products, such as Flash and Freehand.

To see a Dreamweaver extension in action, go to Dreamweaver Exchange
on Macromedia.com and download an extension for Dreamweaver MX.
Double-click the MXP file, and the Extension Manager, shown in
Figure 24.1, installs the extension.

If you do not have the Extension Manager installed, go to http://dynamic.
macromedia.com/bin/MM/exchange/em_download.jsp and download the
latest version.

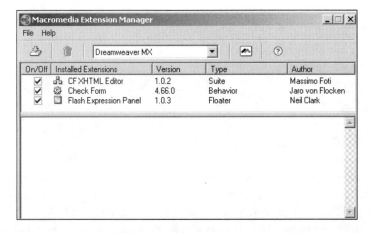

Figure 24.1 The Extension Manager lets you install and uninstall
extensions for Dreamweaver, Flash, Fireworks, and other Macromedia
products. When you install an extension, its name, version number,
and description appear.

To build Dreamweaver extensions, you should be familiar with the following
technologies:

- JavaScript—Dreamweaver uses JavaScript extensively in its extension
  framework. If you are not familiar with JavaScript, you will likely experience a steep learning curve when building Dreamweaver extensions.

- HTML—Dreamweaver includes its own HTML renderer that provides
  the user interface in the Dreamweaver environment for panels, toolbars,
  and so on.

- ColdFusion—If you want to build Dreamweaver extensions for ColdFusion, you obviously need a solid understanding of CFML.
- C++ or Java—You can use dynamic link libraries (DLLs) or JavaBeans to provide advanced functionality, such as integrating Dreamweaver with a custom source control system or legacy databases. Unless you plan to build extensions with C++ or Java, you don't need to worry about learning those programming languages.

If you need more background on these technologies, the following New Riders books will prove very useful:

- *Dreamweaver MX Extensions* by Laura Gutman
- *Inside JavaScript* by Steve Holzner
- *Java for the Web with Servlets, JSP, and EJB: A Developer's Guide to Scalable J2EE Solutions* by Budi Kurniawan

Extensions come in many forms, including server behaviors and floating panels. Dreamweaver extensions for ColdFusion development consist of server behaviors that insert code into the page. As you learned in Chapter 23, "Building Custom Server Behaviors," behaviors are intended to automate code that you find yourself doing repeatedly. In fact, when you create a custom server behavior using the Server Behavior Builder, you are creating a Dreamweaver extension.

This chapter describes the files required to create a server behavior extension in Dreamweaver. Server behavior extensions usually consist of the following files:

- EDML file(s)
- HTM file
- JavaScript file(s)

Understanding the Role of EDML Files

When you create a custom server behavior with the Server Behavior Builder, at least two Extension Data Markup Language (EDML) files and an HTM file that provides the user interface for the behavior are created. The EDML files reside in the Configuration\ServerBehaviors\ColdFusion directory, which you can find under your Dreamweaver installation at Macromedia\Dreamweaver MX\Configuration.

> **Multiple User Logon**
>
> If you use an operating system that lets multiple users log onto it, such as Windows 2000, XP, or NT, or Macintosh OS X, another copy of the Configuration folder exists with user-specific files only.

Used only in Dreamweaver, EDML is a tag-based language that lets you describe how the server behavior should work. When Dreamweaver starts up, it scans the Configuration folder. When it finds an EDML file in a certain folder, such as ServerBehaviors\ColdFusion, it registers the server behavior in the appropriate panel, such as the Server Behaviors panel.

An EDML file consists of tags that describe the extension to Dreamweaver. Dreamweaver generates EDML files when you use the Server Behavior Builder. To write your own from scratch, you can use Dreamweaver or any text editor. The following example defines the Flash Recordset custom server behavior from Chapter 23:

```
<group name="Recordset to Flash"
    version="6.0"
    serverBehavior="Recordset to Flash.htm">
    <TITLE>Recordset to Flash (@@Recordset@@)</TITLE>
    <groupParticipants>
        <groupParticipant name="Recordset to Flash_block1"
        partType="identifier" />
    </groupParticipants>
</group>
```

The GROUP tag declares the server behavior, the version of Dreamweaver, and the HTM file that contains the server behavior's user interface code. The TITLE tag contains the text that will be displayed in Dreamweaver when the behavior has been inserted. The GROUPPARTICIPANTS and the GROUPPARTICIPANT tags reference the other EDML files and their role in the server behavior. For more information on EDML, see the Dreamweaver documentation.

> **@@ Syntax**
>
> Notice that parameters are bracketed by double at signs (@@), such as @@Recordset@@. This is the same syntax used in the Server Behavior Builder.

The participant EDML files represent the code blocks created in the Server Behavior Builder. When you look at the code in the participant EDML files, you will find the EDML tags that actually contain the CFML to be inserted, as the following example shows:

```
<participant version="6.0">
    <insertText location="aboveHTML+99" nodeParamName="__tag">
        <![CDATA[<cfset flash.result = @@Recordset@@>]]>
    </insertText>
    <searchPatterns whereToSearch="tag+CFSET">
        <searchPattern paramNames="Recordset" isOptional="false"
```

```
        limitSearch="all">
            <![CDATA[/<cfset flash\.result = ([^\r\n]*?)>/i]]>
        </searchPattern>
    </searchPatterns>
    <quickSearch>flash.result</quickSearch>
</participant>
```

The PARTICIPANT tag encloses the rest of the tags. The INSERTTEXT tag contains the code to insert into the page, as well as the location at which to insert the code. The CDATA construct lets you specify code or text in EDML files that is not translated by Dreamweaver as an EDML file.

The SEARCHPATTERNS and SEARCHPATTERN tags specify the search parameters for Dreamweaver to find a match in the page. The QUICKSEARCH tag provides a simple text version of the search to provide higher performance for Dreamweaver.

Between the opening and closing SEARCHPATTERN tags, you'll see the CDATA construct and a series of seemingly unrelated characters, such as /<cfset> flash\.result = ([^\r\n]*?)>/i]]. These characters form a regular expression. A regular expression is part of JavaScript and lets you use a special set of characters to specify a search pattern.

The Dreamweaver JavaScript engine uses regular expressions in server behaviors to find matches in the page code. For example, the example regular expression string, [^\r\n]*, finds any character. Also, the forward slash (/} followed by the lowercase letter "i" indicate that case should not be considered in the search.

For Additional EDML Tags

Additional EDML tags and properties exist. For more information, see the Extending Dreamweaver online help. In addition, to learn more about regular expressions, see *Inside JavaScript* by Steve Holzner (New Riders Publishing, 2002).

Understanding the Role of HTM Files

To provide a custom user interface for your server behavior extension, Dreamweaver includes an HTML engine designed for the Dreamweaver environment. Essentially, the Dreamweaver HTML engine lets you design the user interface for your extensions, including server behaviors, using HTML much like a web page.

If you look at the code in an HTM file that accompanies a server behavior, you will see that the DOCTYPE HTML tag differs from web page HTML. In HTML intended for a web browser, the DOCTYPE tag usually looks like the following example:

```
<!DOCTYPE HTML PUBLIC "-//W3C//DTD HTML 4.01 Transitional//EN">
```

In an HTM file for a server behavior, however, the DOCTYPE tag looks like this:

```
<!DOCTYPE HTML SYSTEM "-//Macromedia//DWExtension layout-engine 5.0//dialog">
```

You'll also notice that server behavior HTM files contain a large amount of JavaScript. In fact, the majority of the code in an HTM file is JavaScript. Most server behaviors import multiple JavaScript class files into the HTM page. These classes provide functions that interact with the Dreamweaver environment. For example, the following HTML SCRIPT tags import shared JavaScript classes:

```
<SCRIPT SRC="../../Shared/Common/Scripts/dwscripts.js"></SCRIPT>
<SCRIPT SRC="../../Shared/Common/Scripts/dwscriptsServer.js"></SCRIPT>
<SCRIPT SRC="../../Shared/Common/Scripts/dwscriptsExtData.js"></SCRIPT>
<SCRIPT SRC="../../Shared/Common/Scripts/ServerBehaviorClass.js"></SCRIPT>
<SCRIPT SRC="../../Shared/Common/Scripts/ListControlClass.js"></SCRIPT>
<SCRIPT SRC="../../Shared/Controls/Scripts/RecordsetMenu.js"></SCRIPT>
```

The JavaScript functions that are defined in the HTM page itself enable the dynamic aspects of the server behavior interface, such as recordset menus, menus, and so on. If you scroll past the JavaScript, you'll find the HTML. As shown in the following example, the HTML differs only slightly from the HTML in a web page:

```
<BODY onLoad="initializeUI()">
<FORM NAME="theForm">
  <TABLE BORDER=0>
    <TR>
      <TD ALIGN="right" VALIGN="baseline" NOWRAP>
        Recordset:
      </TD>
      <TD VALIGN="baseline" NOWRAP>
        <SELECT STYLE="width:150px" NAME="Recordset">
          <OPTION SELECTED>*** No %s Found</OPTION>
        </SELECT>
      </TD>
    </TR>
    <TR><TD HEIGHT="1"></TD></TR>
  </TABLE>
</FORM>
</BODY>
```

In the example, notice that the BODY tag specifies the initializeUI JavaScript function to be executed. Like its name implies, the initializeUI function initializes the server behavior user interface by calling the appropriate Dreamweaver API functions, such as populating recordset menus.

Extension Form Objects

The Dreamweaver HTML renderer also recognizes special form objects for server behavior user interfaces. Table 24.1 describes the available objects.

Table 24.1 **Custom Extension Form Objects**

Form Object	Description
Editable Select Lists	Editable select lists let users enter a value in the menu. To enable an editable select list, set the `SELECT` tag's `editable` attribute to `true`.
Database Tree	Database tree controls display the contents of a database. To insert a database tree control, you use the `SELECT` tag. Set the `type` attribute to `DBTree` and specify the other applicable attributes.
Variable Grid	The variable grid control creates a grid with columns. You can use a grid control to create a dynamic table in an extension user interface. To use a variable grid control, you use the `SELECT` tag. Set the `type` attribute to `ParamList` and specify the other applicable attributes.
Tree	A tree control displays data in a file explorer-like interface. Tree nodes can be expanded or hidden. To create a tree control, you use the `MM:TREECONTROL` and `MM:TREECOLUMN` controls.
Color Button	A color button control is a premade color dialog, just like the others used in Dreamweaver, that lets users select colors from a palette. To use a color button control, insert an `INPUT` tag and set its `type` attribute to `mmcolorbutton`.

Understanding the Role of JavaScript

Widely used in web pages, JavaScript provides a run-time scripting language for calling functions and conditional logic. In Dreamweaver, JavaScript provides access to the Dreamweaver APIs, which let you create powerful, sophisticated functionality.

Besides accessing the Dreamweaver APIs, JavaScript also provides access to the Dreamweaver Document Object Model (DOM). The Dreamweaver DOM represents a map of a document, such as HTML in a web page or extension. Using DOM, you can access any HTML tag on the page with a programming language, such as JavaScript.

When building Dreamweaver extensions, you'll find that JavaScript is used in a variety of files, including the HTM file, EDML files, and obviously JavaScript files (*.js). If you look at the Configuration/ServerBehaviors/ColdFusion directory, you'll find that a JavaScript file accompanies some server behaviors, whereas other server behaviors have multiple EDML files.

Although it depends on your personal preference, separate JavaScript files let you move the JavaScript that would otherwise be inserted into the HTM file into a separate file. This lets you maintain the code more easily by separating the majority of the runtime code (JavaScript) from the display code (HTML).

Understanding the Dreamweaver APIs

Dreamweaver offers an API for most elements of the Dreamweaver interface, including menus, dialog boxes, toolbars, and commands. Dreamweaver also provides APIs to access specialized functionality, such as interacting with databases, creating files, and performing HTTP operations. In addition, the Dreamweaver JavaScript API, which includes more than 600 functions, lets you access any Dreamweaver element, including the Dreamweaver DOM.

Table 24.2 describes the extension API categories.

Table 24.2   **Dreamweaver Extension APIs**

Extension API	Description
Behaviors	Behaviors are interactive events that typically take the form of HTML pages in which the user enters parameter values for a form object or other page element.
C-Level Extensibility	If you're familiar with the C programming language, you can define functions in DLL files and call the functions from JavaScript. Using a DLL, you can use the power of C to create sophisticated extension functionality.
Commands	The Commands API lets you perform edits to any part of the current document open in Dreamweaver.
Components	The Components API is used to group functions together for reuse. The Components panel, in which you build and inspect ColdFusion components and web services, uses the Components API.
Data Sources	To add data sources programmatically to Dreamweaver, you use the Data Sources API, which lets you create, delete, inspect, and edit data sources.
Data Translators	The Data Translators API provides functions to convert server-side programming languages, such as CFML, into a form that can be displayed in the Dreamweaver environment.
Floating Panels	True to its name, the Floating Panels API lets you create and manipulate floating panels in Dreamweaver. Floating panels are usually used to expand the capabilities of the Property Inspector for a specific document object.
JavaScript Debugger	Dreamweaver actually includes two JavaScript debuggers, one for Microsoft Internet Explorer and one for Netscape Navigator. When you debug a document in Dreamweaver, the debuggers create the necessary code to make debugging possible, including IF statements and conditional loops.

Extension API	Description
Menu Commands	If you want to create custom menu functionality in Dreamweaver, use the Menu Commands API.
Objects	Objects simply insert blocks of code into pages being edited in Dreamweaver. Once created, the object appears in one of the tabs in the Insert bar or in the Insert menu.
Property Inspectors	Used to extend the venerable Property Inspector, the Property Inspectors API lets you create custom Property panels and override existing ones.
Reports	Dreamweaver can generate a report of all files contained in a site. Using the Reports API, you can generate custom reports or modify the standard Dreamweaver reports.
Server Behaviors	The Server Behaviors API lets you create new server behaviors programmatically. When you use the Server Behavior Builder, you're using the same API. Server behaviors are used to insert or manipulate server-side code, including CFML, into the current Dreamweaver document.
Server Formats	The Server Formats API lets you manipulate how the data returned by the Server Behaviors API function is formatted. You have already used the Server Formats API to format currency values or date/time values. Using the Server Formats API, you can build custom server formats.
Server Models	The Server Models API defines how application servers work in relation to Dreamweaver. The API lets you retrieve various properties of server models, such as file extensions, application server languages, and so on.
Tag Libraries and Editor	Tag libraries contain the tags for a specific programming language, such as CFML. Tag editors let users create and edit tags that they insert into a page. XML files represent Dreamweaver's tag libraries, and tag editors are HTM files that, using JavaScript, retrieve information about a specific tag. Using the Tag Editor API, you can inspect, validate, and apply tags.
Toolbars	The Toolbars API provides the necessary functions to create and manipulate Dreamweaver toolbars. The API includes functions that retrieve current toolbar values, dynamic content, and so on.

The Dreamweaver Utility APIs let you perform specialized functions in Dreamweaver, including interacting with other applications, files, databases, source control systems, and so on. Table 24.3 describes Utility API categories.

Table 24.3   **Dreamweaver Utility APIs**

Utility API	Description
Database	The Database API lets you retrieve information from databases, open database dialog boxes, get database views, and so on. The Bindings and Database panels in the Application bar use the Database API.
Database Connectivity	The Database Connectivity API includes functions to create new database connections and modify existing ones.
Design Notes	The Design Notes API lets you use the Dreamweaver design notes engine to create, open, edit, and interact with design notes programmatically.
File I/O	Using the File I/O API, you can interact with files on the user's local system from Dreamweaver extensions. You can perform a number of functions on files, such as retrieving modification dates, file sizes, file attributes, and so on.
Fireworks Integration	You use the Fireworks Integration API to interact with Macromedia Fireworks, a graphics and web design application. With the API, you can open Fireworks, call JavaScript functions in Fireworks, and so on.
Flash Objects	Using the Flash Objects API, you can create simple Flash movies from Dreamweaver and open existing Flash movies. You can also use the API to read Flash movies and determine file size and object type.
HTTP	The HTTP API lets you interact with remote servers and files using HTTP, much like a web browser. The HTTP API allows you to send and receive text as well as download remote files.
JavaBeans	The JavaBeans API provides a set of functions that let you retrieve information from JavaBeans on your system. A kind of Java object, JavaBeans provides similar functionality to DLL files. The API includes functions for getting JavaBeans methods, classes, properties, events, and error messages.
Source Control	If you need to build an extension that works with a source control system, such as Source Safe or Perforce, you use the Source Control Integration API. The API includes the necessary functions for a source control system, such as saving, opening, modifying, and deleting files. You can also communicate with the source control system to find out what files are checked out, compare file versions, and so on.

Packaging Extension Files

Once you have built and tested your extension file, you're ready to package it as an MXP file. Once packaged, you can upload your extension to the Dreamweaver Exchange on the Macromedia web site or distribute the extension yourself within your organization or personal web site.

To create an MXP file, which contains all of the files for your extension, you must first create an MXI file that describes your extension, where the files should be installed, and so on. MXI files consist of a set of XML-like tags. You can create MXI files in Dreamweaver using the document window in Code View. The following example shows a simple MXI file:

```
<macromedia-extension name="Recordset to Flash" version="1.0"
    type="Server Behavior">
    <products>
        <product name="Dreamweaver" version="6" primary="true" />
    </products>
    <author name="David Golden" />
    <description>
        <![CDATA[ This server behavior returns a recordset to Flash
Remoting.<br><br>]]>
    </description>
    <ui-access>
        <![CDATA[Access Recordset to Flash in the Server Behavior Panel.]]>
    </ui-access>
    <files>
        <file name="Recordset to Flash.edml"
        destination="$dreamweaver/configuration/ServerBehaviors/ColdFusion" />
        <file name="Recordset to Flash_block1.edml"
        destination="$dreamweaver/configuration/ServerBehaviors/ColdFusion" />
        <file name="Recordset to Flash.htm"
        destination="$dreamweaver/configuration/ServerBehaviors/ColdFusion" />
    </files>
    <configuration-changes>
        <server-format-changes servermodelfolder = "ColdFusion">
            <menuitem name="Recordset to Flash"
            file="ServerBehaviors/ColdFusion/Recordset to Flash.htm"
            id="Recordset_To_Flash" />
            <separator id="Recordset_To_Flash_Separator" />
        </server-format-changes>
    </configuration-changes>
</macromedia-extension>
```

As you can see, the MXI syntax is relatively simple, especially if you're already familiar with XML. When you use a code block, with an opening and closing tag, be sure to include the closing tag. For a full listing of the available MXI tags, see the online Help in the Extension Manager. Also, in the Extension Manager directory, you'll find sample MXI files.

To create an MXP file from an MXI file, follow these steps:

1. Open the Extension Manager.

2. Select Package Extension from the Extension Manager File menu, which opens the Select Extension to Package dialog box.

3. In the Select Extension to Package dialog box, select the MXI file that you created. Click the OK button.

4. After the Extension Manager finishes packaging the file, the MXP file is ready for distribution.

Summary

In this chapter, you gained a basic understanding of the technologies and APIs involved in building Dreamweaver extensions. You also learned more about the roles of EDML, HTM, and JavaScript files in the Dreamweaver extension framework.

VIII

Appendixes

Installing ColdFusion MX and Dreamweaver MX

IN THIS APPENDIX, I WILL COVER HOW to install ColdFusion and Dreamweaver. Installing ColdFusion and Dreamweaver is a snap. Macromedia's engineering staff put great emphasis on a seamless installation experience, and it shows. From system detection to configuration options, you will be required to supply only a few pieces of information and select among simple installation options.

Although you do not need to know what files are going where during the installations, you should have a general idea of what is happening. At a high level, here's what happens:

1. When you install any application, another program loads that actually installs the program.

2. The information that you enter into the installation dialogs is used to generate a list of files that should be installed and where they go.

3. The installation program creates the necessary directories and copies the necessary files to your system. During this process, the installation program checks to make sure all files go the correct location.

4. After the necessary files have been copied, the installation program configures the operating system to register the applications and modify system configuration files.

5. The installation is finished and the installation program exits.

So in a nutshell, to install ColdFusion and Dreamweaver, you must prepare your system for the installation, install ColdFusion and Dreamweaver, and perform configuration tasks.

Read the Release Notes

Always read the release notes for ColdFusion and Dreamweaver. They contain valuable, late-breaking information about all aspects of the products, including installation instructions.

Preparing Your System

To prepare your system to install ColdFusion and Dreamweaver, you must check your system requirements and install the necessary components. Although many people install software without reading any documentation, checking the system requirements and release notes should rank high on your installation checklist.

Table A.1 describes the system requirements for Dreamweaver MX.

Table A.1   **System Requirements for Dreamweaver MX**

Requirements	Description
Supported OSes	Windows 98, ME, NT, 2000, and XP. Macintosh OS 9, 9.2.1, and 10.1.
Web browsers	Microsoft Internet Explorer or Netscape Navigator 4 or later.
Hardware requirements	128MB of RAM recommended. 275MB of hard disk space required. Pentium II for Windows and GE3 for Macintosh. Monitor capable of 1024 x 768 pixel resolution recommended.
Java Virtual Machines	Macintosh Java Runtime 2.2 or later.
Microsoft Data Access Components (MDAC)	For database interaction in Windows, you must install MDAC. To download MDAC, visit the Microsoft web site at www.microsoft.com/data. Make sure to download the appropriate MDAC version for your operating system.

Table A.2 describes the system specifications for ColdFusion MX.

Table A.2 **System Specifications for ColdFusion MX**

Specifications	Description
Supported OSes	Windows 98, ME, NT, 2000, and XP. RedHat Linux 6.2 and 7.2. SuSE Linux 7.2 and 7.3. Solaris 7 and 8. HP-UX 11.
Web browsers	Microsoft Internet Explorer or Netscape Navigator 5 or later.
Hardware requirements	512MB of RAM recommended (256MB required). 250MB of hard disk space required. Pentium II for Windows and Linux. SPARC for Solaris. PA-RISC for HP-UX.
Databases	Microsoft Access or SQL Server 7, 2000. Oracle 8.1.7 or 9i. Sybase 11.9.2 or 12. IBM DB2 6.2 or 7.2. Informix 9. MySQL. PostGreSQL. SQLAnywhere.
Web servers	Microsoft IIS 4 or 5. Apache 1.3.12 1.3.22 or 2. iPlanet Enterprise Server 4 or 6. Netscape Enterprise Server 3.6.
JVMs	Sun JRE 1.3 or later. IBM JVM 1.2 or later. (ColdFusion installs a JVM automatically, so there is no need to install one yourself.)
Microsoft Data Access Components (MDAC)	For database interaction in Windows, you must install MDAC. To download MDAC, visit the Microsoft web site at www.microsoft.com/data.

If you plan to install Dreamweaver and ColdFusion on the same system for development, use the greatest system requirement, such as 512MB of RAM. As you can tell from the requirements, you need a powerful system to run ColdFusion and Dreamweaver at the same time.

If you're a Macintosh user, you might be disappointed to find that ColdFusion does not support the Macintosh operating system. However, if you want to run a total non-Windows system, you can develop your ColdFusion applications in Dreamweaver on Macintosh and deploy your application to a Linux or Unix system running ColdFusion.

Install on Separate Systems

Although installing ColdFusion and Dreamweaver on the same system for development purposes is common, it is not recommended. To gauge application server performance properly, you should install and run ColdFusion on a separate system.

Installing ColdFusion and Dreamweaver

After you have checked the system requirements, you're ready to install the software. Although there is no particular order to installing the two products, installing ColdFusion first is recommended. If ColdFusion is already installed, you can immediately begin setting up your site when the Dreamweaver installation completes.

Installing ColdFusion on Windows

If you have a previous version of ColdFusion already installed on your system, the ColdFusion installation program will prompt you either to install ColdFusion MX so that it exists independently of an existing ColdFusion installation or upgrade, which replaces the existing installation.

The following steps and figures come from an installation of ColdFusion on Windows 2000. To install ColdFusion, follow these steps:

1. Depending on whether you're installing ColdFusion from a CD-ROM or from a downloaded file, execute the ColdFusion setup file.

2. Once the ColdFusion program loads, the Welcome dialog box appears, as shown in Figure A.1. Click the Next button.

3. In the License Agreement dialog box shown in Figure A.2, select the I Accept radio button and click the Next button.

4. In the Customer Information dialog box shown in Figure A.3, enter your name, organization, and license keys. If you do not enter a license key, ColdFusion defaults to the Developer Edition, which allows access from only one IP address.

   You'll also notice that you're given the option of installing ColdFusion for all users on the system or just for you. This applies only if your operating system lets different users log in to the same computer, as do Windows 2000 and Windows XP.

   Click the Next button.

5. In the Web Server dialog box shown in Figure A.4, select the web server that you want to use with ColdFusion. ColdFusion MX features a built-in web server named Standalone. Although it works very well, you should not use the Standalone web server for production. You should instead choose IIS, Netscape, iPlanet, or Apache web server. The ColdFusion installation program automatically configures an external web server when you select it. If you want to use a different web server later, see the web server configuration instruction in the ColdFusion installation and configuration documentation. Click the Next button.

6. In the Webroot Folder dialog box shown in Figure A.5, you can select the directories to which the ColdFusion files are copied. Click the Next button.

7. In the Custom Setup dialog box shown in Figure A.6, you can select whether to install various features of ColdFusion, such as documentation and example applications. In the Feature Description section, you can see how much hard drive space is required for an individual feature. If you are installing ColdFusion on a production server, do not install the ColdFusion documentation and example applications. Click the Next button.

8. In the Select Passwords dialog box shown in Figure A.7, you specify passwords for the ColdFusion Administrator and ColdFusion Remote Development Services (RDS). In integrated development environments (IDEs), such as Dreamweaver, RDS is used to connect to data sources and file systems. Click the Next button. (After you finish the installation, you can change your passwords in the ColdFusion Administrator.)

9. In the Ready to Install the Program dialog box shown in Figure A.8, you see a list of your previous choices. After reviewing the list, click the Install button. The ColdFusion installation begins.

10. As the ColdFusion installation proceeds, the Installing ColdFusion MX dialog box, shown in Figure A.9, keeps you abreast of the progress.

11. When the installation finishes, the Success dialog displays, as shown in Figure A.10. Click the Finish button to exit the installation.

ColdFusion Installation
The ColdFusion installation is complex and takes time. Unless you receive an error message, do not stop the ColdFusion installation, even if it appears to have stopped on its own.

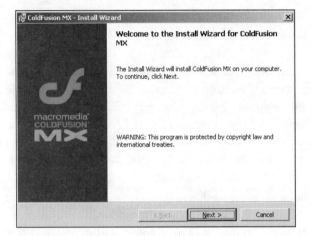

Figure A.1   The Welcome dialog box greets you when you first start the ColdFusion installation.

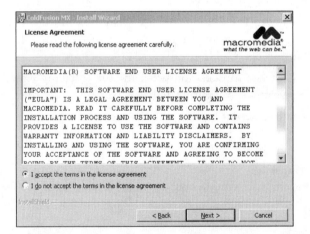

Figure A.2   The License Agreement dialog shows the legal contract that you are agreeing to by installing ColdFusion.

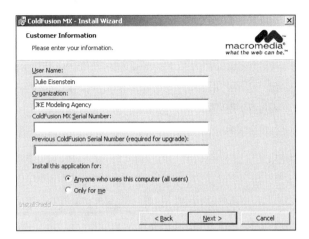

Figure A.3   In the Customer Information dialog box,
you enter your name, organization, and license number.
You can also choose to make ColdFusion available
to all users on the system.

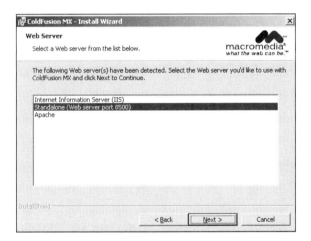

Figure A.4   The Web Server dialog box lets you choose
a web server to use with ColdFusion. The Standalone
option is ColdFusion's built-in server.

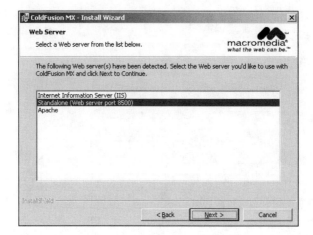

Figure A.5 In the Web Root dialog box, you choose where ColdFusion will be installed.

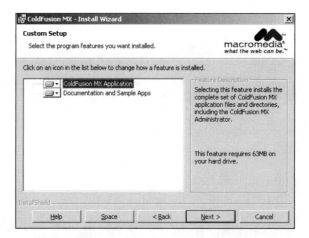

Figure A.6 The Custom Setup dialog box provides controls for choosing individual application features to install. Do not install the ColdFusion documentation and example applications on a production server.

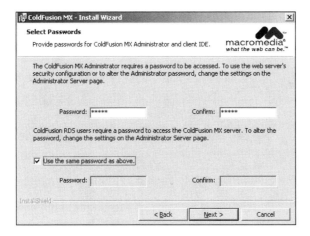

Figure A.7   The Select Passwords dialog lets you specify
passwords for the ColdFusion Administrator and RDS.
If you want to change the passwords at a later date,
use the ColdFusion Administrator.

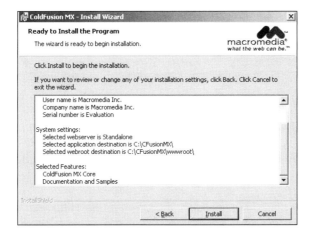

Figure A.8   In the Ready to Install the Program dialog
box, you can review your previous selections. If everything
looks good, click the Install button to start the installation.

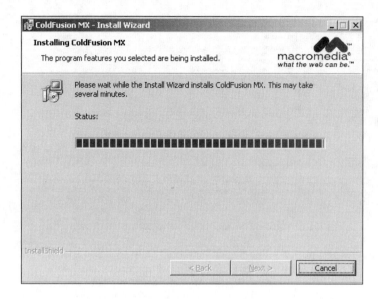

Figure A.9 The Installing ColdFusion dialog box shows the progress of the ColdFusion installation.

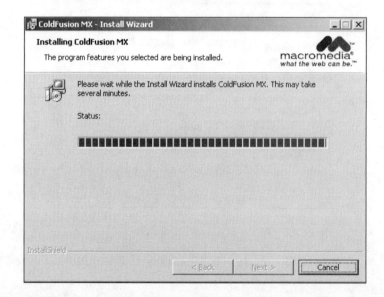

Figure A.10 The Success dialog box displays when the installation completes.

If the ColdFusion Administrator appears after the installation completes, as shown in Figure A.11, the installation was successful. If you installed ColdFusion on Windows NT, 2000, or XP, ColdFusion runs as a service. The ColdFusion service and its related services can be stopped, started, and restarted using the Windows Services panel, as shown in Figure A.12.

If the ColdFusion services do not appear, ColdFusion did not install properly, or you need to restart your computer. For more information about troubleshooting your installation, see the "Installation Troubleshooting" section at the end of this chapter.

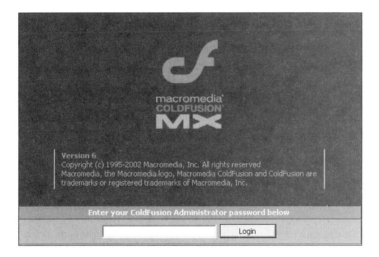

Figure A.11   If the ColdFusion installation is successful, the ColdFusion Administrator login screen displays.

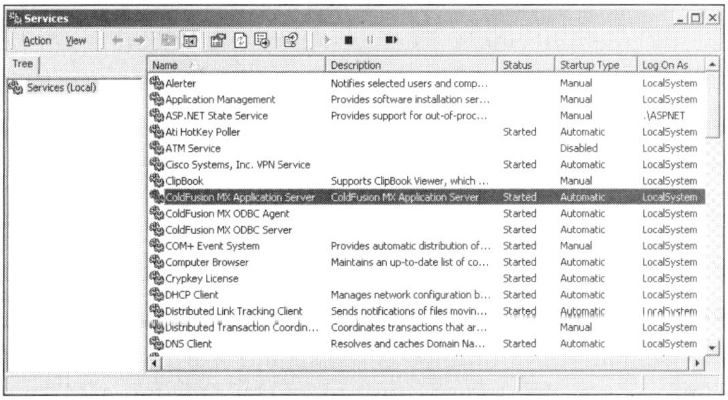

Figure A.12   In the Windows Services panel, you will find three ColdFusion services. You can stop, start, and restart the services using the Services panel options.

Installing ColdFusion on Linux and Unix

If you install ColdFusion on Unix or Linux, you will likely use a telnet client and use command prompts. The ColdFusion command prompt installation is almost exactly the same as the Windows installation dialogs.
To start the installation, follow these steps:

1. In a telnet session, locate the ColdFusion installation file. The file extension is .BIN, such as cfusionmx_linux_us.bin.

2. Prepare the file for installation with the following command:

   ```
   chmod 755 cfusionmx_linux_us.bin
   ```

3. Begin the installation program with the following command:

   ```
   ./cfusionmx_linux_us.bin
   ```

4. After the ColdFusion installation finishes, start ColdFusion using the following command:

   ```
   /cfusionmx/bin/coldfusion start
   ```

   You can use the same command to stop ColdFusion.

Installing Dreamweaver on Windows

Installing Dreamweaver on Windows is even easier than installing ColdFusion. You will be up and running with Dreamweaver before you know it. To install Dreamweaver on Windows, follow these steps:

1. Execute the Dreamweaver installation file. After the installation program loads, the Welcome dialog appears, as shown in A.13. Click the Next button.

2. In the License Agreement dialog box, shown in Figure A.14, the Dreamweaver MX licence agreement appears. If you agree, click the Yes button.

3. In the Customer Information dialog box shown in Figure A.15, enter your name, organization, and license key. Click the Next button.

4. In the Choose Destination Location dialog box shown in Figure A.16, you can select a directory in which to install the Dreamweaver system files or just accept the default. Click the Next button.

5. In the Default Editor dialog box shown in Figure A.17, you can associate Dreamweaver as the default editor for various file types. Make sure that the ColdFusion check box is selected.

6. In the Start Copying Files dialog box, you can review your selections. If everything checks out, click the Next button.

7. After the installation finishes, a Dreamweaver readme HTM file launches in a web browser.

Dreamweaver SSL and SSH FTP Connections

For SSL and SSH FTP connections in Dreamweaver, which might be required by a hosting provider, you must install PUTTY and a third-party SSH client. For more information, visit the Macromedia web site and read the Dreamweaver Technote #16126.

Figure A.13 The Welcome dialog box greets you when you start the Dreamweaver installation.

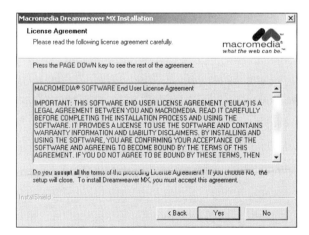

Figure A.14 The License Agreement dialog box contains the license for Dreamweaver.

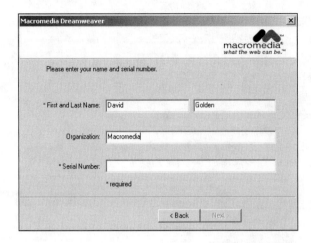

Figure A.15   In the Customer Information dialog box, you enter personal information, including your Dreamweaver license key.

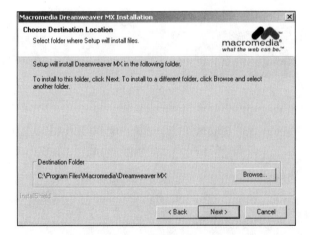

Figure A.16   In the Choose Destination Location dialog box, you can choose where to install the Dreamweaver system files.

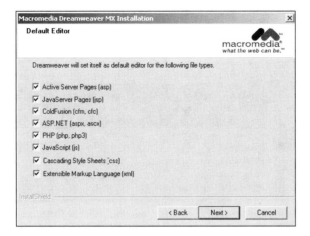

Figure A.17 In the Default Editor dialog box, you choose what document types to associate with Dreamweaver.

Uninstalling ColdFusion and Dreamweaver

In Windows, uninstalling ColdFusion and uninstalling Dreamweaver are essentially the same. To uninstall Dreamweaver or ColdFusion in Windows, follow these steps:

1. In Windows Control Panel, select Add/Remove Programs.

2. In the Add/Remove Programs dialog box shown in Figure A.18, click the Remove button for either Dreamweaver or ColdFusion. The installation program will load and remove the selected program.

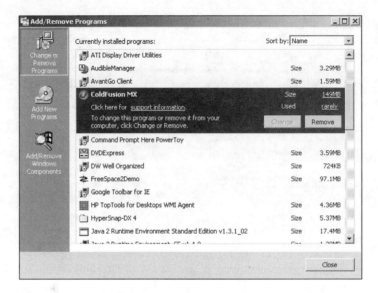

Figure A.18   In the Add/Remove Programs dialog box, you can remove
ColdFusion or Dreamweaver by clicking the Remove button.

To uninstall ColdFusion in Linux or Unix, in a telnet session, navigate to the
uninstall directory, which resides under the cfusionmx installation directory.
Then, enter the following command:

```
./uninstall.sh
```

To uninstall Dreamweaver on Macintosh, drag the Dreamweaver MX
directory to the Trash.

Installation Troubleshooting

If you encounter problems during the installation of Dreamweaver or
ColdFusion, consider the following questions:

- Does your computer meet the minimum system specifications, including
  RAM and CPU speed?
- Did you experience any error dialogs during installation? If so, something
  likely went wrong, even though the installation completed.
- Have you applied custom security policies in your operating system that
  might interfere with ColdFusion or Dreamweaver? If so, contact your
  network administrator or experiment with your system's security policies.

- Did you have an existing installation of Dreamweaver or ColdFusion on your system? If so, did you uninstall the older versions or upgrade? You might try uninstalling the old versions before installing the new versions.

If you still have problems after trying different options, go to the Macromedia Support Center for additional resources (www.macromedia.com/support).

Summary

In this appendix, you learned how to install and uninstall Dreamweaver and ColdFusion. For more information about setting up Dreamweaver, see Chapter 3, "Introducing Dreamweaver MX." For more information about setting up ColdFusion, see Chapter 2, "Introducing ColdFusion MX."

B

ColdFusion MX CFML Tag Reference

THIS CFML TAG REFERENCE APPENDIX CONTAINS a description and attributes of every CFML tag in ColdFusion MX. The tags are organized by tag group. However, you can navigate this reference in two ways:

- By tag group
- Alphabetically

To open the CFML tag reference in the Dreamweaver environment, select Window, Reference. To insert a tag in Dreamweaver, use the Tag Chooser dialog box, which you can open by selecting Insert, Tag. Select Macromedia CFML Reference in the Book menu.

Tag Catagories

CFML tags can be grouped according to the operations that they perform. For example, ColdFusion offers a number of tags that perform database operations, such as CFQUERY, CFINSERT, and CFUPDATE, that would be part of a Database Manipulation category. The following list categorizes the CFML tags by their use:

Deprecated or Obsolete Tags

This reference includes only current CFML tags. A few tags from older versions of ColdFusion have been deprecated (made obsolete) in ColdFusion MX. For more information about deprecated and obsolete CFML tags, see the Macromedia CFML Reference in the Reference panel of the Code Panel group.

ColdFusion Component Tags

CFARGUMENT

```
<cfargument
name="argument name"
type="any"
required="Yes or No"
default="default argument value">
```

Description

Creates a parameter definition within a component definition. Defines a function argument. Used within a CFFUNCTION tag.

This tag must be the first tag in a page.

Attributes

name (Required)

Name for the argument. This is a string.

type (Optional)

This is the data type of the argument, which can be anything, including any, array, binary, Boolean, date, numeric, query, string, struct, uuid, variableName, or a component name.

required (Optional)

Default: No

Determines whether the parameter is required to execute the component method.

default (Optional)

If no argument is passed, this specifies a default argument value. If this attribute is present, the required attribute must be set to "No" or not specified.

Tag Chooser Dialog Box

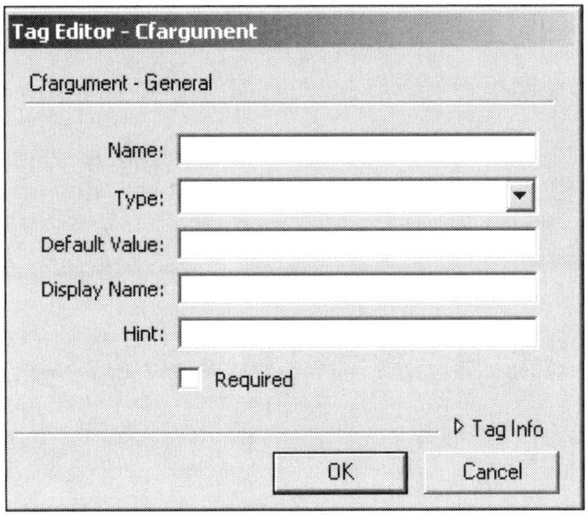

Figure B.1

CFCOMPONENT

```
<cfcomponent>
extends ...
output = "yes" or "no"
    <cffunction ...>
...
    </cffunction>

</cfcomponent>
```

Description

Creates and defines a component object; encloses functionality that you build in CFML within CFFUNCTION tags. This tag contains one or more CFFUNCTION tags that define methods. Code within the body of this tag, other than CFFUNCTION tags, is executed when the component is instantiated.

A component file has the extension .CFC and is stored in any directory of the web application. A component can be invoked in several ways, including from a CFINVOKE tag, from a URL, from within CFSCRIPT, through a web service, and from Flash code.

Attributes

extends (Optional)

Name of parent component from which the component inherits methods and properties. If not specified, the component implicitly inherits the methods and properties of ColdFusion.

output (Optional)

yes: Suppresses component method output.

no: Permits component method output.

Tag Chooser Dialog Box

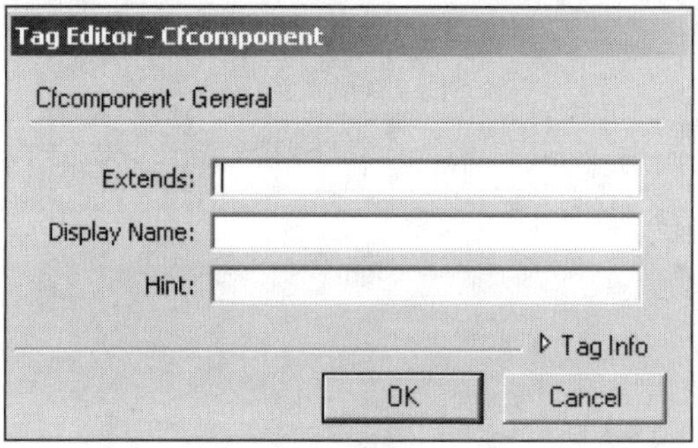

Figure B.2

CFFUNCTION

```
<cffunction
name = "methodName"
returnType = "dataType"
roles = "securityRoles"
access = "methodAccess"
output = "yes" or "no"
exceptions = "exception1, exception2, ...">
```

Description

Defines functionality that you build in CFML. Used within a CFCOMPONENT tag to create a ColdFusion component.

Attributes

name (Required)

A string; a component method that is used within the CFCOMPONENT tag. The valid types are query, string, numeric, boolean, date, struct, array, binary, xml, customFunction, object, any, and the name of a component.

returnType (Optional)

A string; the type of the function return value. If this attribute is omitted, ColdFusion processes this tag as a procedure. If the body contains a CFRETURN tag, ColdFusion throws an error.

roles (Optional)

Default: "" (empty)

A comma-delimited list of ColdFusion security roles that can invoke the method. If this attribute is omitted, all roles can invoke the method.

access (Optional)

Default: public

The client security context from which the method can be invoked:

private: Available only to the component that declares the method.

package: Available only to the component that declares the method or to another component in the same package.

public: Available to a locally executing page or component method.

remote: Available to a locally or remotely executing page or component method, or a remote client through a URL, Flash, or a web service.

output (Optional)

Function is processed as standard CFML.

yes: The function is processed as if it were within a CFOUTPUT tag.

no: The function is processed as if it were within a CFSILENT tag.

exceptions (Optional)

Comma-delimited list of exceptions.

Tag Chooser Dialog Box

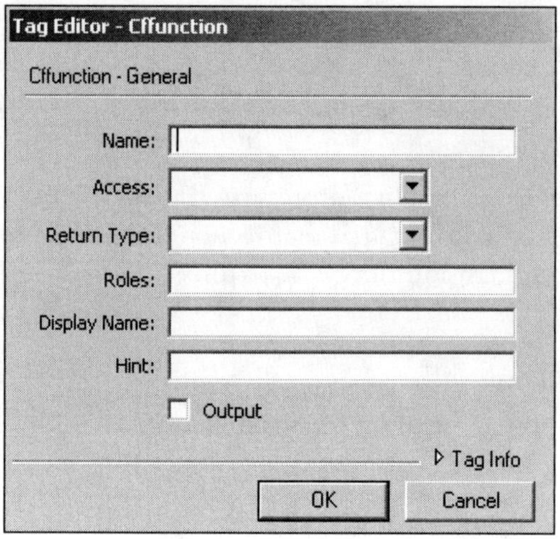

Figure B.3

CFINVOKE

Syntax 1

```
<cfinvoke
component = "component name or reference"
returnVariable = "variable name"
argumentCollection = "argument collection"
...
>
```

Syntax 2

```
<cfinvoke
method = "method name"
returnVariable = "variable name"
argumentCollection = "argument collection"
...
>
```

Syntax 3

```
<cfinvoke
webservice = "taglib-location"
method = "operation_name"
input_params ...
returnVariable = "var_name"
>
```

Description

Invokes component methods from within a ColdFusion page or component.
Operating on components:

- Instantiates a web component and invokes a method on it.
- Invokes a method on an instantiated component.
Operating on web services:

- Invokes a method on a web component.
This tag can pass parameters to a method in the following ways:

- With the CFINVOKEARGUMENT tag.
- As named attribute-value pairs, one attribute per parameter.
- As a structure in the argumentCollection attribute.

Attributes

component (Required if method is not specified)
String or component object; a reference to a component, or a component
to instantiate.

method (Required if component is not specified)
The name of a method; for a web service, the name of an operation.

returnVariable (Optional)
The name of a variable for the invocation result.

argumentCollection (Optional)
The name of a structure; associative array of arguments to pass to the
method.

username (Optional)
Overrides the username specified in data source setup.

password (Optional)
Overrides the password specified in data source setup.

```
Webservice (Optional)
```
The URL of the WSDL file for the web service.

```
input_params
```
Input parameters.

```
argumentCollection="#args#"
```

Tag Chooser Dialog Box

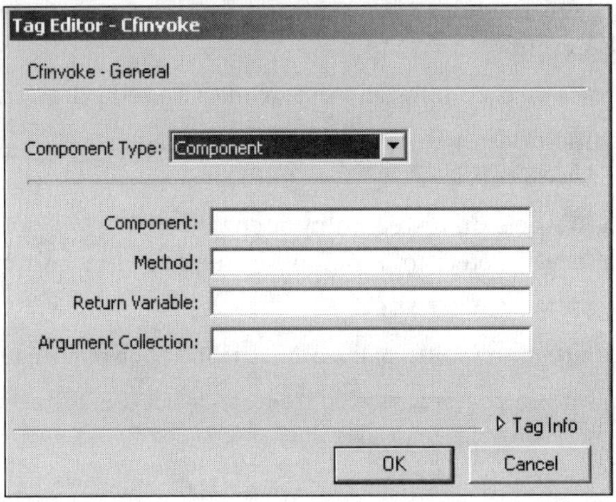

Figure B.4

CFINVOKEARGUMENT

```
<cfinvokeargument
name="argument name"
value="argument value">
```

Description

Passes an argument independently of the CFINVOKE tag.

Attributes

```
name (Required)
```
Argument name.

```
value (Required)
```
Argument value.

Tag Chooser Dialog Box

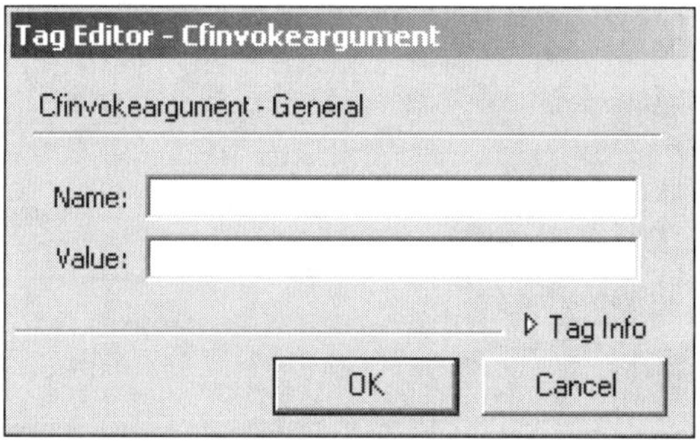

Figure B.5

CFPROPERTY

```
<cfproperty
name="..."
type="..."
...
>
```

Description

Defines components as complex types that are used for web services authoring. The attributes of this tag are exposed as component metadata and are subject to inheritance rules.

Attributes

name (Required)
    A string; a property name. Must be a static value.

type (Optional)
    A string; a property type name. Must be a static value.

Tag Chooser Dialog Box

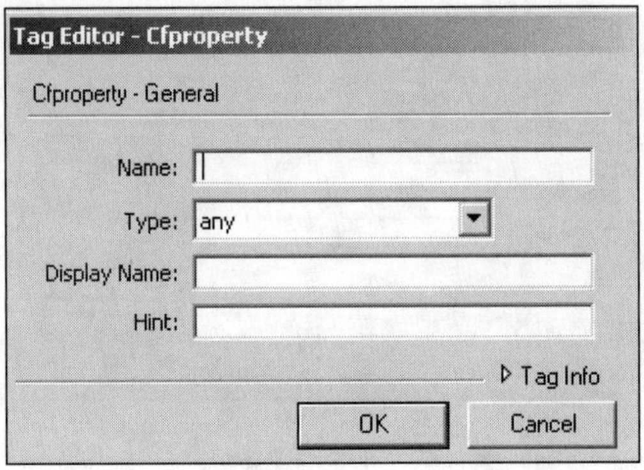

Figure B.6

CFRETURN

```
<cfreturn expr>
```

Description

Returns result values from a component method. Contains an expression returned as a result of the function.

Attributes

expr (Required)
  Function result; value of any type.

Database Manipulation Tags

CFINSERT

```
<cfinsert dataSource = "ds_name"
tableName = "tbl_name"
tableOwner = "owner"
tableQualifier = "tbl_qualifier"
username = "username"
password = "password"
formFields = "formfield1, formfield2, ...">
```

Description

Inserts records in data sources from data in a ColdFusion form or form scope.

Attributes

dataSource (Required)

Data source; contains table.

tableName (Required)

Table in which to insert form fields. Oracle drivers must be uppercase. Sybase drivers are case-sensitive. Must be the same case used when the table was created.

tableOwner (Optional)

For data sources that support table ownership (such as SQL Server, Oracle, and Sybase SQL Anywhere), use this field to specify the owner of the table.

tableQualifier (Optional)

For data sources that support table qualifiers, use this field to specify the qualifier for the table. The purpose of table qualifiers varies among drivers. For SQL Server and Oracle, *qualifier* refers to the name of database that contains the table. For the Intersolv dBASE driver, *qualifier* refers to the directory where DBF files are located.

username (Optional)

Overrides the username specified in ODBC setup.

password (Optional)

Overrides the password specified in ODBC setup.

formFields (Optional)

Default: (all fields on the form, except keys)

Comma-delimited list of form fields to insert. If not specified, all fields in the form are included. If a form field is not matched by a column name in the database, ColdFusion throws an error. The database table key field must be present in the form.

Tag Chooser Dialog Box

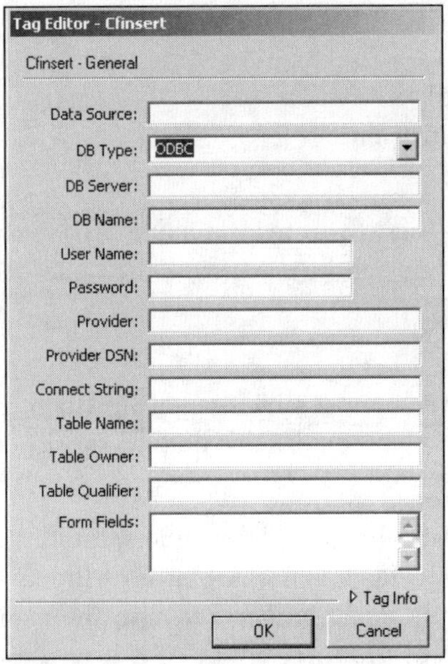

Figure B.7

CFOBJECTCACHE

```
<cfobjectcache action = "clear">
```

Description

Flushes the query cache.

Attributes

action (Required)

  clear: Clears queries from the cache in the Application scope.

Tag Chooser Dialog Box

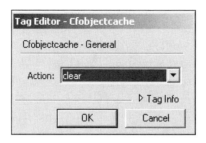

Figure B.8

CFPROCPARAM

```
<cfprocparam type = "in" or "out" or "inout"
variable = "variable name"
dbVarName = "DB variable name"
value = "parameter value"
CFSQLType = "parameter datatype"
maxLength = "length"
scale = "decimal places"
null = "Yes" or "No">
```

Description

Parameter information. This tag is nested within a CFSTOREDPROC tag.

Attributes

type (Optional)

Default: in

in: Passes the parameter by value.

out: Passes the parameter as a bound variable.

inout: Passes the parameter as a bound variable.

Variable (Required if type = "in/inout")

ColdFusion variable name; references the value that the output parameter has after the stored procedure is called.

dbVarName (Required for named notation)

Parameter name that corresponds to the name of the parameter in the stored procedure.

value (Required if type = "in/inout")

Value that corresponds to the value that ColdFusion passes to the stored procedure.

CFSQLType (Required)

SQL type to which the parameter (any type) is bound.

maxLength (Optional)

Default: 0

Maximum length of the parameter.

scale (Optional)

Default: 0

Number of decimal places in the parameter.

null (Optional)

Default: no

Determines whether the parameter is passed as a null value.

yes: Tag ignores the value attribute.

Tag Chooser Dialog Box

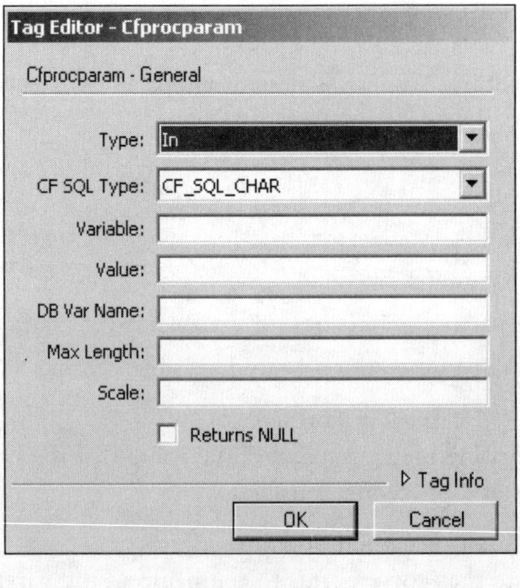

Figure B.9

CFPROCRESULT

```
<cfprocresult name = "query_name"
resultSet = "1 - n"
maxRows = "maxrows">
```

Description

The result set name that other ColdFusion tags, such as CFOUTPUT and CFTABLE, use to access a result set. Identifies which of the stored procedure's result sets to return. This tag is nested within a CFSTOREDPROC tag.

Attributes

name (Required)

Name for the query result set.

resultSet (Optional)

Default: 1

Names one result set, even if the stored procedure returns more than one.

maxRows (Optional)

Default: -1 (All)

Maximum number of rows returned in the result set.

Tag Chooser Dialog Box

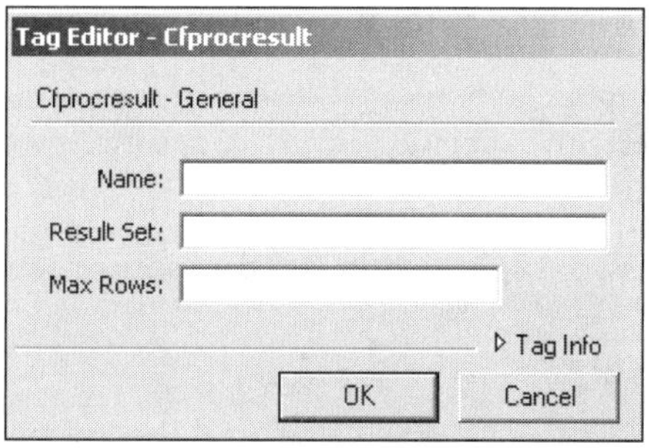

Figure B.10

CFQUERY

```
<cfquery name = "query_name"
dataSource = "ds_name"
username = "username"
password = "password"
maxRows = "number"
blockFactor = "blocksize"
timeout = "seconds"
cachedAfter = "date"
cachedWithin = "timespan"
debug = "Yes" or "No"  or debug>

SQL statement(s)

</cfquery>
```

Description

Passes queries or SQL statements to a data source. It is recommended that you use the CFQUERYPARAM tag within every CFQUERY tag to help secure databases from unauthorized users.

Attributes

name (Required)
> The name of the query. Used in the page to reference the query recordset. Must begin with a letter. Can include letters, numbers, and underscores.

dataSource (Required)
> The name of the data source from which the query retrieves data.

username (Optional)
> Overrides the username specified in the data source setup.

password (Optional)
> Overrides the password specified in the data source setup.

maxRows (Optional)
> Default: –1 (All)
>
> Maximum number of rows to return in the recordset.

blockFactor (Optional)
> Default: 1
>
> Maximum rows to get at a time from the server. Range: 1–100. Applies to Oracle native database drivers and ODBC drivers. Some ODBC drivers dynamically reduce block factor at runtime.

`timeout` (Optional)

Maximum number of seconds that each action of a query is permitted to execute before returning an error. The cumulative time may exceed this value. ColdFusion sets this attribute for JDBC statements. For other drivers, check the driver documentation.

`cachedAfter` (Optional)

Date value (for example, April 16, 1999, 4-16-99). If date of original query is after this date, ColdFusion uses cached query data. This takes effect only if query caching is enabled in ColdFusion Administrator. To use cached data, the current query must use the same SQL statement, data source, query name, username, password, and `dbType`. Year values must be in the range 0–9999:

Values in the range 0–29 are interpreted as 2000–2029.

Values in the range 30–99 are interpreted as 1930–1999.

Values in the range 100–9999 are interpreted as absolute A.D. dates.

When specifying a date value as a string, you must enclose it in quotation marks.

`cachedWithin` (Optional)

Time span, using the `CreateTimeSpan` function. If the original query date falls within the time span, the cached query data is used. `CreateTimeSpan` defines a period from the present back. This takes effect only if query caching is enabled in the Administrator. To use cached data, the current query must use the same SQL statement, data source, query name, username, password, and `dbType`.

`debug` (Optional)

The value and equals sign may be omitted.

`Yes`, or if value is omitted: If debugging is enabled, but the Administrator Database Activity option is not enabled, this displays SQL submitted to the data source and the number of records returned by the query.

`No`: If the Administrator Database Activity option is enabled, this suppresses display.

Tag Chooser Dialog Box

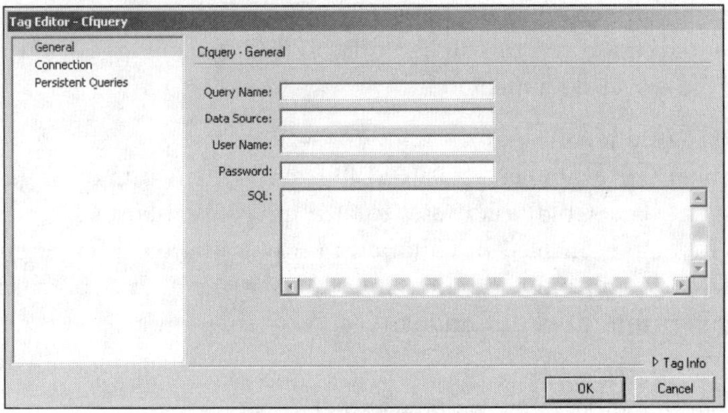

Figure B.11

CFQUERYPARAM

```
<cfquery>
<cfqueryparam value = "parameter value"
CFSQLType = "parameter type"
maxLength = "maximum parameter length"
scale = "number of decimal places"
null = "Yes" or "No"
list = "Yes" or "No"
separator = "separator character">
AND/OR ...additional criteria of the WHERE clause...
</cfquery>
```

Description

Checks the data type of a query parameter. This tag is nested within a CFQUERY tag, embedded in a query SQL statement. If you specify optional parameters, this tag performs data validation.

Attributes

value (Required)

Value that ColdFusion passes to the right of the comparison operator in a WHERE clause.

If CFSQLType is a date or time option:

CFSQLType (Optional)

SQL type that parameter (any type) is bound to.

maxLength (Optional)

The length of the string in the value attribute.

The maximum length of the parameter.

scale (Optional)

Default: 0

The number of decimal places in the parameter. Applies to CF_SQL_NUMERIC and CF_SQL_DECIMAL.

null (Optional)

Default: No

Determines whether the parameter is passed as a null value.

Yes: Tag ignores the value attribute.

list (Optional)

Default: No

Yes: The value attribute is a delimited list.

separator (Required if value = "list")

The character that separates values in the list within the value attribute.

Tag Chooser Dialog Box

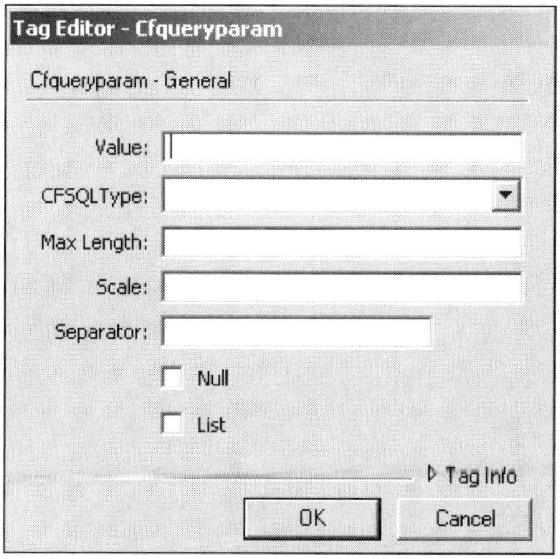

Figure B.12

CFSTOREDPROC

```
<cfstoredproc procedure = "procedure name"
dataSource = "ds_name"
username = "username"
password = "password"
blockFactor = "blocksize"
debug = "Yes" or "No"
returnCode = "Yes" or "No">
```

Description

Executes stored procedures by an ODBC or native connection to a server database. It specifies database connection information and identifies the stored procedure.

Attributes

procedure (Required)

The name of the stored procedure on the database server.

dataSource (Required)

The name of the ODBC or native data source that points to the database that contains the stored procedure.

username (Optional)

Overrides the username in the data source setup.

password (Optional)

Overrides the password in the data source setup.

blockFactor (Optional)

Default: 1

Maximum number of rows to get at a time from the server. Range is 1–100. The ODBC driver may dynamically reduce block factor at runtime.

debug (Optional)

Default: No

Yes: Lists debug information on each statement.

returnCode (Optional)

Default: No

Yes: Tag populates cfstoredproc.statusCode with status code returned by the stored procedure.

Tag Chooser Dialog Box

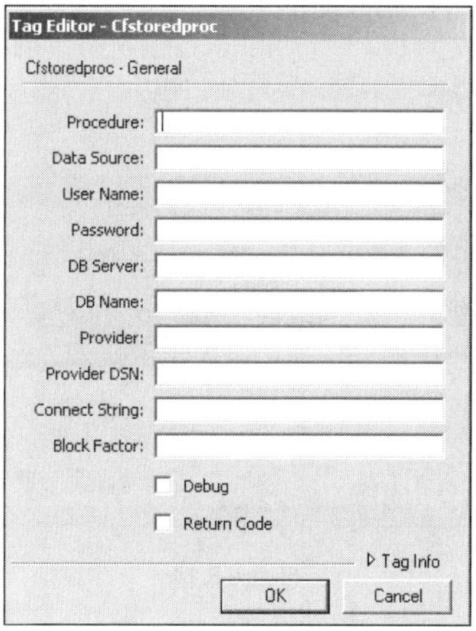

Figure B.13

CFTRANSACTION

```
<cftransaction
action = "begin/commit/rollback"
isolation = "read_uncommitted/read_committed/repeatable_read/serializable " >
queries to execute
</cftransaction>
```

Description

Groups database queries into a unit. Provides database commit and rollback processing.

Attributes

action Optional

Default: begin

begin: The start of the block of code to execute.

commit: Commits a pending transaction.

rollback: Rolls back a pending transaction.

isolation (Optional)

ODBC lock type. Types include read_uncommitted, read_committed, repeatable_read, and serializable.

Tag Chooser Dialog Box

Figure B.14

CFUPDATE

```
<cfupdate dataSource = "ds_name"
tableName = "table_name"
tableOwner = "name"
tableQualifier = "qualifier"
username = "username"
password = "password"
formFields = "field_names">
```

Description

Updates records in a data source from data in a ColdFusion form or form scope.

Attributes

dataSource (Required)

The name of the data source that contains the table.

tableName (Required)

Name of the table to update.

For Oracle drivers: Must be uppercase.

For Sybase drivers: Case-sensitive; must be in same case as was used when the table was created.

`tableOwner` (Optional)

For data sources that support table ownership (for example, SQL Server, Oracle, Sybase SQL Anywhere), this is the table owner.

`tableQualifier` (Optional)

For data sources that support table qualifiers. The purpose of table qualifiers is as follows:

SQL Server and Oracle: Name of database that contains the table.

Intersolv dBASE driver: Directory of DBF files.

`username` (Optional)

Overrides the username value specified in ODBC setup.

`password` (Optional)

Overrides the password value specified in the ODBC setup.

`formFields` (Optional)

Comma-delimited list of form fields to update. If a form field is not matched by a column name in the database, ColdFusion throws an error. The database table `key` field must be present in the form.

Tag Chooser Dialog Box

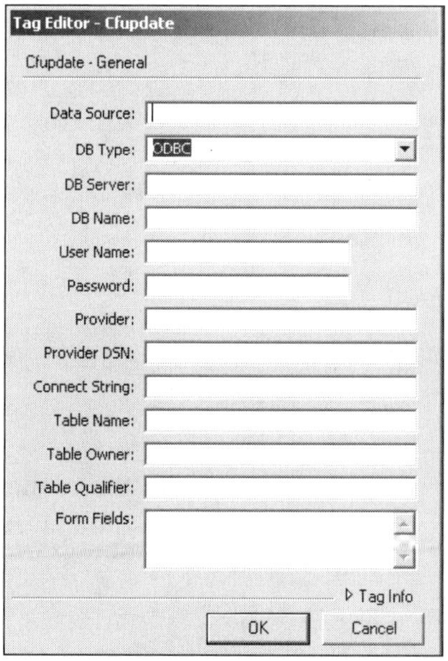

Figure B.15

Data Output Tags

CFCHART

```
<cfchart
format = "flash, jpg, png"
chartHeight = "integer number of pixels"
chartWidth = "integer number of pixels"
scaleFrom = "integer minimum value"
scaleTo = "integer maximum value"
showXGridlines = "yes" or "no"
showYGridlines = "yes" or "no"
gridlines = "integer number of lines"
seriesPlacement = "default, cluster, stacked, percent"
foregroundColor = "Hex value or Web color"
dataBackgroundColor = "Hex value or Web color"
borderBackgroundColor = "Hex value or Web color"
showBorder = "yes" or "no"
font = "font name"
fontSize = "integer font size"
fontBold = "yes" or "no"
fontItalic = "yes" or "no"
labelFormat = "number, currency, percent, date"
xAxisTitle = "title text"
yAxisTitle = "title text"
sortXAxis = "yes" or "no"
show3D = "yes" or "no"
xOffset = "number between -1 and 1"
yOffset = "number between -1 and 1"
rotated = "yes" or "no"
showLegend = "yes""no"
tipStyle = "MouseDown, MouseOver, Off"
tipBGColor = "Hex value or Web color"
showMarkers = "yes" or "no"
markerSize = "integer number of pixels"
pieSliceStyle = "solid, sliced"
url = "onClick destination page"
name = "String"
</cfchart>
```

Description

Generates and displays a horizontal graph file. Stores the graph in cache memory as an HTML object or image tag, whose source URL contains the GraphDate servlet URL and the image ID.

Attributes

format (Required)

> Default: flash
>
> File format in which to save the graph. Format options are flash, jpg, and png.

ChartHeight (Optional)

> Default: 240
>
> Chart height in pixels.

ChartWidth (Optional)

> Default: 320
>
> Chart width in pixels.

scaleFrom (Optional)

> Determined by data. Y-axis minimum value; integer.

scaleTo (Optional)

> Determined by data. Y-axis maximum value; integer.

showXGridlines (Optional)

> Default: no
>
> yes: Display X-axis gridlines.
>
> no: Hide X-axis gridlines.

showYGridlines (Optional)

> Default: yes
>
> yes: Display Y-axis gridlines.
>
> no: Hide Y-axis gridlines.

gridlines (Optional)

> Default: 3 (top, bottom, and zero)
>
> Number of gridlines to display on value axis, including axis; positive integer.
>
> 0: Hide gridlines.

seriesPlacement (Optional)

Default: default

Applies to charts that have more than one data series. Relative positions of series.

default: ColdFusion determines relative positions based on graph types.

Other options include cluster, stacked, and percent.

foregroundColor (Optional)

Default: black

Color of text, gridlines, and labels. Hex value or supported named color.

DataBackgroundColor (Optional)

Default: white

Color of area around chart data. Hex value or supported named color.

borderBackgroundColor (Optional)

Default: white

Color of area between data background and border, around labels, and around legend.

showBorder (Optional)

Default: no

font (Optional)

Default: arial

Name of text font.

fontSize (Optional)

Default: 11

Font size as an integer.

fontBold (Optional)

Default: no

fontItalic (Optional)

Default: no

labelFormat (Optional)

Default: number

This is the format for Y-axis labels. Other options are currency, percent, and date.

xAxisTitle (Optional)
　　Title for the X-axis.

yAxisTitle (Optional)
　　Title for the Y-axis.

sortXAxis (Optional)

　　Default: no

　　yes: Display column labels in alphabetical order along X-axis.

show3D (Optional)

　　Default: no

　　yes: Display chart with three-dimensional appearance.

xOffset (Optional)

　　Default: 0.1

　　Applies if show3D="yes". Number of units by which to display the chart as angled, horizontally. A number in the range −1 to 1, where −1 specifies 90 degrees left and 1 specifies 90 degrees right.

yOffset (Optional)

　　Default: 0.1

　　Applies if show3D="yes". Number of units by which to display the chart as angled, vertically. A number in the range −1 to 1, where −1 specifies 90 degrees down, and 1 specifies 90 degrees up.

rotated (Optional)

　　Default: no

　　yes: Rotate chart 90 degrees. For a horizontal bar chart, use this option.

showLegend (Optional)

　　Default: yes

　　yes: If chart contains more than one data series, display legend.

tipStyle (Optional)

　　Default: mouseOver

　　Determines the action that opens a popup window to display information about the current chart element.

mouseDown: Displays if the user positions the cursor at the element and clicks the mouse. Applies only to Flash format graph files. (For other formats, this option functions the same as mouseOver.)

mouseOver: Displays if the user positions the cursor at the element.

off: Suppresses display.

tipBGColor (Optional)

Default: white

Specifies background color for pop-up tips. Applies only to Flash format graph files. Hex value or supported named color.

showMarkers (Optional)

Default: yes

Sets marker display on and off. Applies to chartseries type attribute values line, curve, and scatter.

yes: Display markers at data points.

markerSize (Automatic)

Size of data point marker in pixels. Integer.

pieSliceStyle (Optional)

Default: sliced

Sets slice style for pie chart. Applies to chartseries type attribute value pie.

solid: Displays pie as if unsliced.

sliced: Displays pie as if sliced.

url (Optional)

URL to open if the user clicks on an item in a data series. You can specify variables within the URL string; ColdFusion passes current values of the variables.

$VALUE$: Value of the selected row; if left blank, the value is an empty string.

$ITEMLABEL$: Label of the selected item. If left blank, the value is an empty string.

$SERIESLABEL$: Label of the selected series. If left blank, the value is an empty string.

Tag Chooser Dialog Box

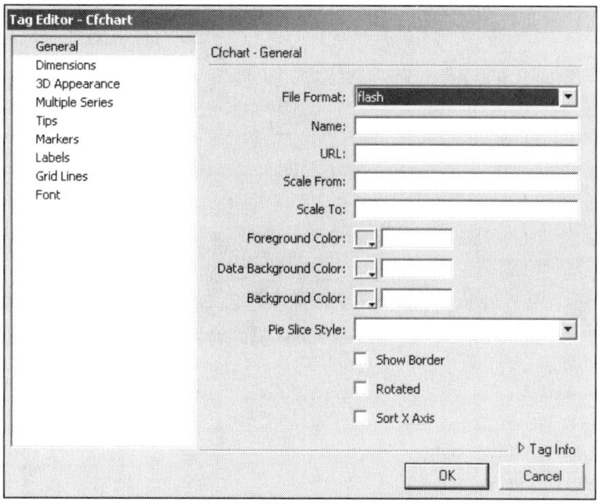

Figure B.16

CFCHARTDATA

```
<cfchartdata
item = "text"
value = "number">
```

Description

Used with the CFCHART and CFCHARTSERIES tags. This tag defines chart data points. Data is submitted to the CFCHARTSERIES tag.

Attributes

item (Required)
  String; data point name.

value (Required)
  Number; data point value.

Tag Chooser Dialog Box

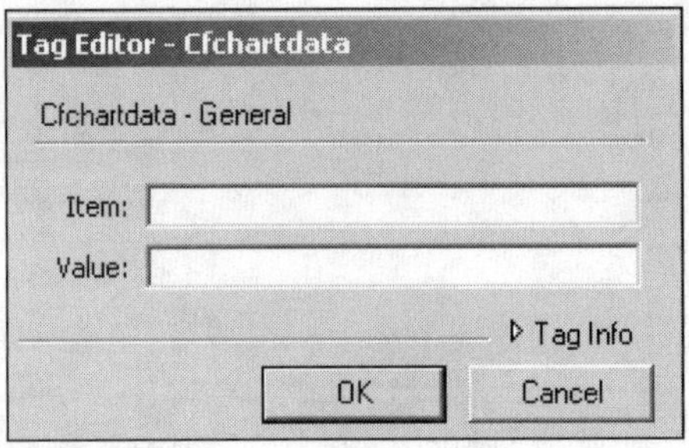

Figure B.17

CFCHARTSERIES

```
<cfchartseries
type="type"
query="queryName"
itemColumn="queryColumn"
valueColumn="queryColumn"
seriesLabel="Label Text"
seriesColor="Hex value or Web color"
paintStyle="plain, raise, shade, light"
markerStyle="style"
colorlist = "list">
</cfchartseries>
```

Description

Used with the CFCHART tag. This tag defines the style in which chart data displays: bar, line, pie, and so on.

Attributes

type (Required)
  Sets the chart display style: bar, line, pyramid, area, cone, curve, cylinder, step, scatter, or pie.

query (Optional)
  Name of the ColdFusion query from which to get data.

`itemColumn` (Required)

Contains the item label for a data point to graph.

`valueColumn` (Required)

Name of a column in the query specified in the `query` attribute; contains data values to graph.

`seriesLabel` (Optional)

Text of data series label.

`seriesColor` (Optional)

Color of the main element (such as the bars) of a chart. For a pie chart, this is the color of the first slice.

`paintStyle` (Optional)

Default: `plain`

Sets the paint display style of the data series.

`plain`: Solid color.

`raise`: The appearance of a button.

`shade`: Gradient fill, darker at the edges.

`light`: A lighter shade of color; gradient fill.

`markerStyle` (Optional)

Default: `rectangle`

Applies to `chartseries` type attribute values line, curve, and scatter. Sets the icon that marks a data point: rectangle, triangle, diamond, circle, letterx, mcross, snow, and rcross.

`colorlist` (Optional)

Applies if `chartseries` = `"pie"`. Sets pie slice colors. Comma-delimited list of hex values or web colors.

Tag Chooser Dialog Box

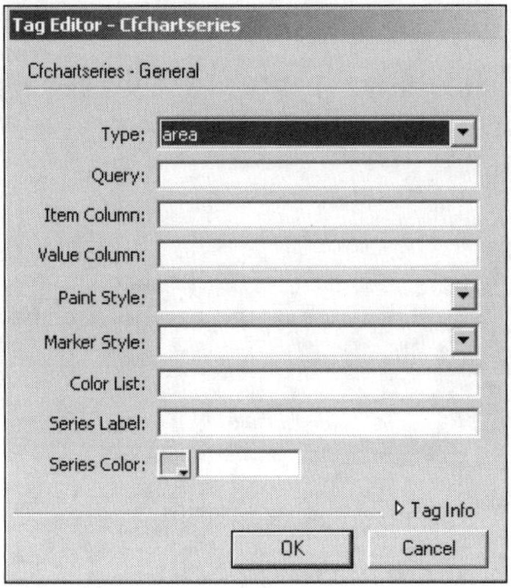

Figure B.18

CFCOL

```
<cfcol
header = "column_header_text"
width = "number_indicating_width_of_column"
align = "Left" or "Right" or "Center"
text = "column_text">
```

Description

Defines table column header, width, alignment, and text. Used within a CFTABLE tag.

Attributes

header (Required)

Column header text. To use this attribute, you must also use the CFTABLE colHeaders attribute.

width (Optional)

Default: 20

Column width. If the length of the data displayed exceeds this value, data is truncated to fit. If the surrounding CFTABLE tag includes the htmltable attribute, width specifies the percent of the table width, and it does not truncate text; otherwise, width specifies the number of characters.

align (Optional)

Default: Left

Column alignment: Left, Right, Center.

text (Required)

Double quotation mark–delimited text; determines what to display. The rules are the same as for CFOUTPUT. You can embed hyperlinks, image references, and input controls.

Tag Chooser Dialog Box

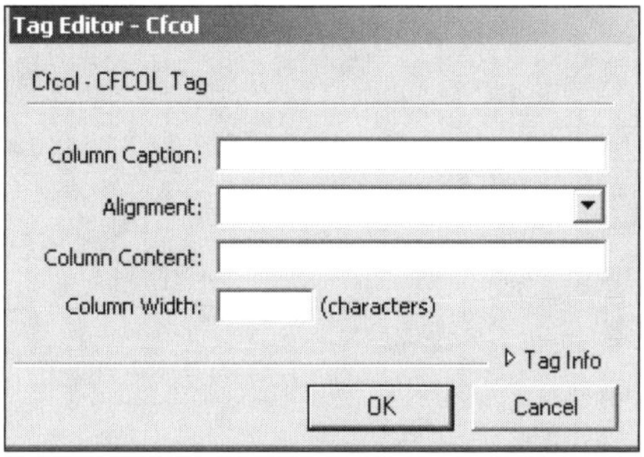

Figure B.19

CFCONTENT

```
<cfcontent
type = "file_type"
deleteFile = "Yes" or "No"
file = "filename"
reset = "Yes" or "No">
```

Description

Sets the file or MIME content type returned by the current page. Optionally, specifies the name of a file to return with the page.

Note: This tag must be enabled in the ColdFusion Administrator.

Attributes

`type` (Required)

File or MIME content type returned by the current page.

`deleteFile` (Optional)

Default: `No`

Applies only if you specify a file with the `file` attribute.

`Yes`: Deletes a file after the download operation.

`file` (Optional)

Name of the file to get. When using ColdFusion in a distributed configuration, the `file` attribute must refer to a path on the system on which the web server runs.

`reset` (Optional)

Default: `Yes`

The `reset` and `file` attributes are mutually exclusive. If you specify a file, this attribute has no effect.

`Yes`: Discards output that precedes call to `CFCONTENT`.

`No`: Preserves output that precedes call to `CFCONTENT`.

`encoding` (Optional)

Default: `ISO-8859-1`

The character encoding of generated output: `text/html` or any valid character encoding.

Tag Chooser Dialog Box

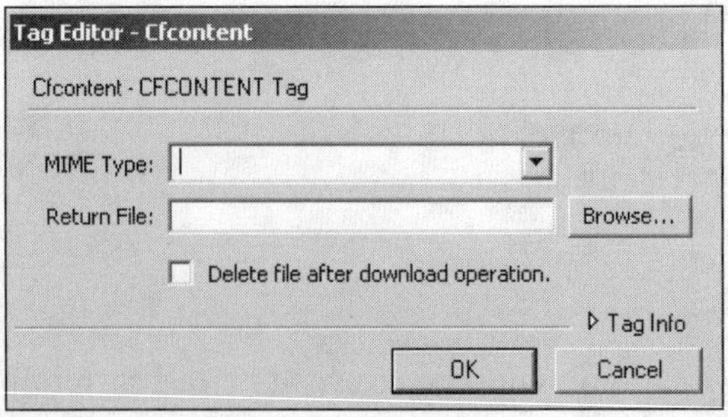

Figure B.20

CFHEADER

```
<cfheader
name = "header_name"
value = "header_value">
```

or

```
<cfheader
statusCode = "status_code"
statusText = "status_text">
```

Description
Generates custom HTTP response headers to return to the client.

Attributes
name (Required if statusCode is not specified)
> Header name.

value (Optional)
> HTTP header value.

statusCode (Required if name is not specified)
> Number; HTTP status code.

statusText (Optional)
> Explains status code.

Tag Chooser Dialog Box

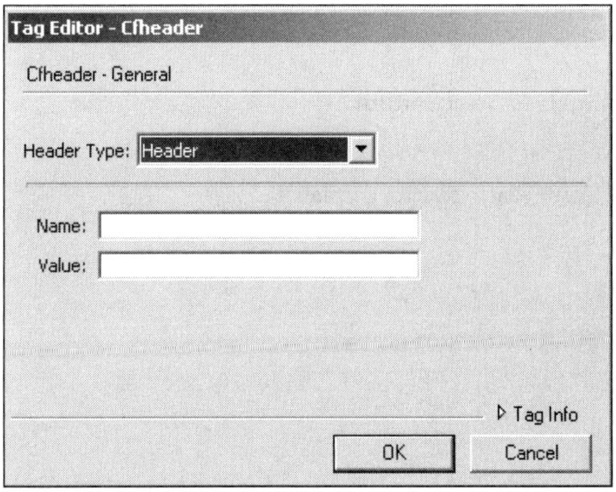

Figure B.21

CFOUTPUT

```
<cfoutput
query = "query_name"
group = "query_column"
groupCaseSensitive = "Yes" or "No"
startRow = "start_row"
maxRows = "max_rows_output">
</cfoutput>
```

Description

Displays the results of a database query or other operation.

Attributes

query (Optional)

Name of CFQUERY from which to draw data for output section.

group (Optional)

Query column to use when you group sets of records. Use this if you retrieved a recordset ordered on a query column. For example, if a recordset is ordered on Customer_ID in the CFQUERY tag, you can group the output on Customer_ID. Case-sensitive. Eliminates adjacent duplicates when data is sorted.

groupCaseSensitive (Optional)

Default: Yes

Boolean. Determines whether to group by case. To keep recordset intact, set to No.

startRow (Optional)

Default: 1

Row from which to start output.

maxRows (Optional)

Maximum number of rows to display.

Tag Chooser Dialog Box

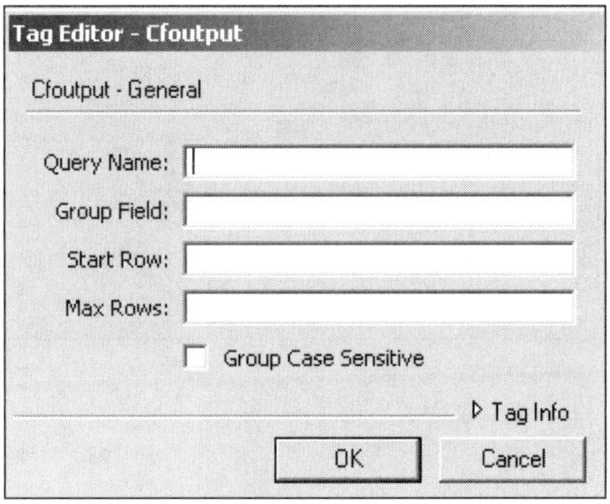

Figure B.22

CFPROCESSINGDIRECTIVE

```
<cfprocessingdirective
suppressWhiteSpace = "Yes" or "No"
pageEncoding = "page-encoding literal string">
CFML tags
</cfprocessingdirective>
```

Description

Determines whether to suppress output of extra whitespace and other output produced by CFML, within the tag scope. Used with applications that depend on the whitespace characteristics of their output stream.

Attributes

suppressWhiteSpace (Required)

Boolean. Determines whether to suppress whitespace and other output that is generated by CFML tags within a CFPROCESSINGDIRECTIVE block.

pageEncoding (Optional)

A string literal that specifies the character encoding to use to read the page. The value can be enclosed in single or double quotation marks, or no quotation marks.

Tag Chooser Dialog Box

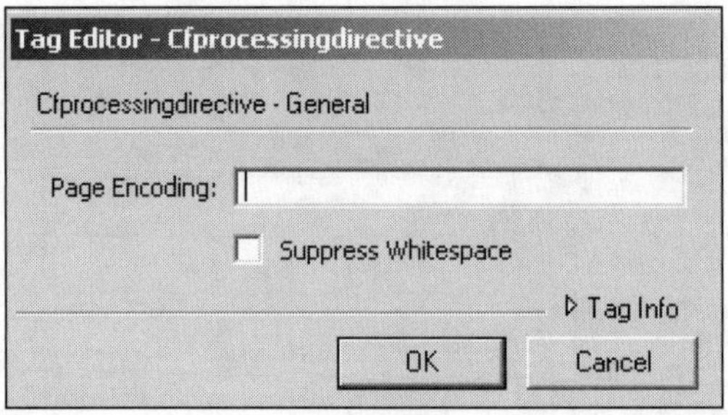

Tag Editor - Cfprocessingdirective

Cfprocessingdirective - General

Page Encoding: [   ]

☐ Suppress Whitespace

▷ Tag Info

[OK] [Cancel]

Figure B.23

CFTABLE

```
<cftable query = "query_name"
maxRows = "maxrows_table"
colSpacing = "number_of_spaces"
headerLines = "number_of_lines"
HTMLTable
border
colHeaders
startRow = "row_number">
...
</cftable>
```

Description

Builds a table in a ColdFusion page. This tag renders data as preformatted text, or, with the HTMLTable attribute, in an HTML table. If you don't want to write HTML table tag code, or if your data can be presented as preformatted text, use this tag.

Preformatted text (defined in HTML with the <PRE> and </PRE> tags) that displays text in a fixed-width font. It displays whitespace and line breaks exactly as they are written within the PRE tags. For more information, see an HTML reference guide.

Attributes

query (Required)

Name of CFQUERY from which to draw data.

maxRows (Optional)

Maximum number of rows to display in the table.

colSpacing (Optional)

Default: 2

Number of spaces between columns.

headerLines (Optional)

Default: 2

Number of lines to use for table header (the default leaves one line between the header and the first row of table).

HTMLTable (Optional)

Renders data in an HTML 3.0 table. If you use this attribute (regardless of its value), ColdFusion renders data in an HTML table.

border (Optional)

Displays border around table. If you use this attribute (regardless of its value), ColdFusion displays a border around the table. Use this only if you use the HTMLTable attribute.

colHeaders (Optional)

Displays column heads. If you use this attribute, you must also use the CFCOL tag header attribute to define them. If you use this attribute (regardless of its value), ColdFusion displays column heads.

startRow (Optional)

Default: 1

The query result row to put in the first table row.

Tag Chooser Dialog Box

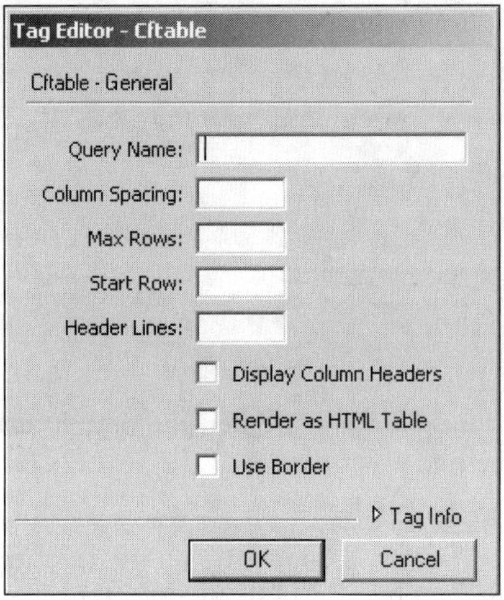

Figure B.24

Variable Manipulation Tags

CFCOOKIE

```
<cfcookie
name = "cookie_name"
value = "text"
expires = "period"
secure = "Yes" or "No"
path = "url"
domain = ".domain">
```

Description

Defines web browser cookie variables, including expiration and security options.

Attributes

`name` (Required)

Name of cookie variable.

`value` (Optional)

Value to assign to cookie variable.

`expires` (Optional)

Expiration date of cookie variable. Possible values can be:

A date (for example, 10/09/03).

A number of days (for example, 10 or 100).

`now`: Deletes cookie from client cookie.txt file.

`never`: Deletes cookie from client; writes cookie data to cookie.txt file.

`secure` (Optional)

If browser does not support Secure Sockets Layer (SSL) security, cookie is not sent.

`Yes`: Variable must be transmitted securely.

`path` (Optional)

URL within a domain to which the cookie applies; for example, `path = "/services/login"`. To specify multiple URLs, use multiple `CFCOOKIE` tags. If you specify `path`, you must also specify `domain`.

`domain` (Required)

If the `path` attribute is specified, `domain` must also be specified. This is the domain in which the cookie is valid and to which cookie content can be sent. It must start with a period. If the value is a subdomain, the valid domain is all domain names that end with the specified string. For a domain value that ends in a country code, the specification must contain at least three periods; for example, `.mongo.state.us`. For special top-level domains, two periods are required; for example, `.mgm.com`. Separate multiple entries with semicolons.

Tag Chooser Dialog Box

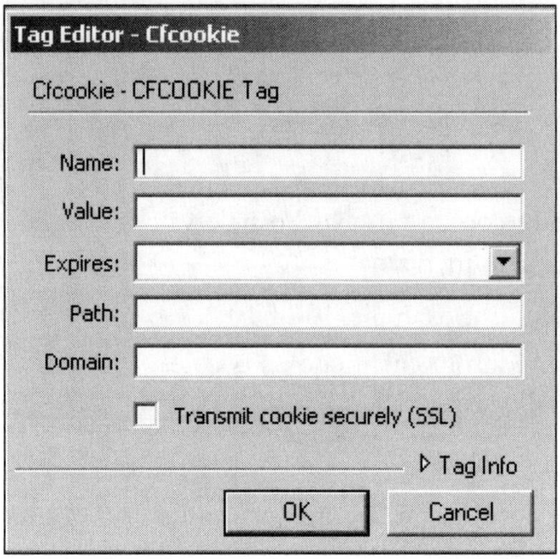

Figure B.25

CFPARAM

```
<cfparam name = "param_name"
type = "data_type"
default = "value">
```

Description

Tests for a parameter's existence, tests its data type, and, if a default value is not assigned, provides one.

Attributes

name (Required)
  Name of the parameter to test (such as Client.Email or Cookie.BackgroundColor). If omitted, and if the parameter does not exist, an error is thrown.

type (Optional)
  Possible types are any, array, binary, Boolean, date, numeric, query, string, struct, UUID, and variableName.

default (Optional)
  The value of the parameter if it does not exist.

Tag Chooser Dialog Box

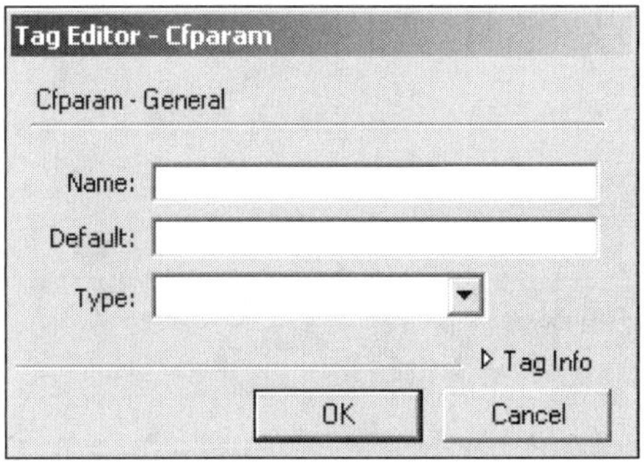

Figure B.26

CFSET

```
<cfset variable_name = expression>
```

Description

Defines a ColdFusion variable. If the variable exists, this tag sets it to the specified value.

Attributes

variable_name (Required)
   Variable

Data Flow and Control Tags

CFABORT

```
<cfabort showError = "error_message">
```

Description

Stops the processing of a ColdFusion page at the tag location. ColdFusion returns everything that was processed before the tag. The tag is often used with conditional logic to stop processing a page when a condition occurs.

Attributes

showError (Optional)
> Error to display, in a standard ColdFusion error page, when the tag executes.

Tag Chooser Dialog Box

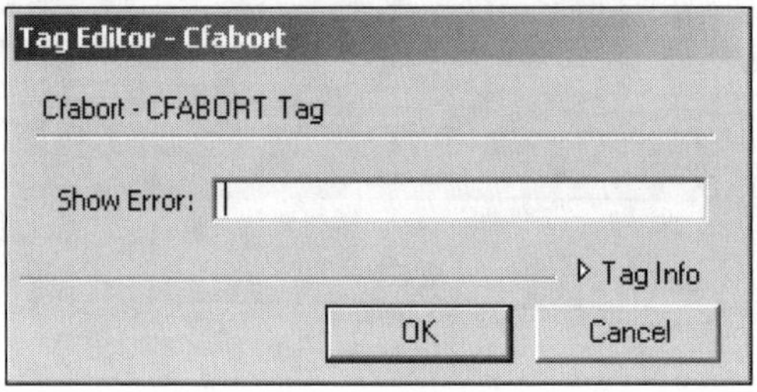

Figure B.27

CFBREAK

```
<cfbreak>
```

Description

Used to break out of a CFLOOP.

CFCASE

```
<cfcase action="action">
```

Description

Used with the CFSWITCH and CFDEFAULTCASE tags. For more information, see CFSWITCH.

Attributes

Value (Optional)
> One or more constant values that CFSWITCH compares to the expression (case-insensitive).

Delimiter (Optional)
> Character(s) that separates items in a list.

Tag Chooser Dialog Box

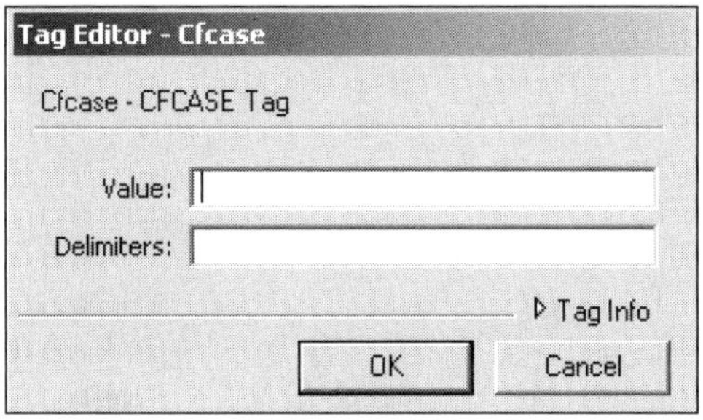

Figure B.28

CFCATCH

```
<cfcatch>
```

Description

Used with the CFTRY and CFFINALLY tags. For more information, see CFTRY and CFFINALLY.

Tag Chooser Dialog Box

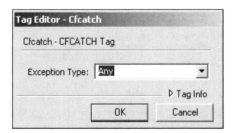

Figure B.29

CFDEFAULTCASE

```
<cfdefaultcase>
...
</cfdefaultcase>
```

Description

Used with the CFSWITCH and CFCASE tags to create a default action.

CFEXIT

```
<cfexit method = "method">
```

Description

This tag aborts processing of the currently executing CFML custom tag, exits the page within the currently executing CFML custom tag, or re-executes a section of code within the currently executing CFML custom tag.

Attributes

method (Optional)

Default: exittag

exittag: Aborts the processing of the currently executing tag.

exittemplate: Exits the page of the currently executing tag.

loop: Re-executes the body of the currently executing tag.

Tag Chooser Dialog Box

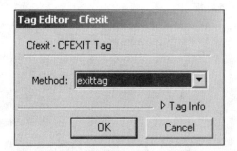

Figure B.30

CFIF/CFELSE/CFELSEIF

```
<cfif expression>
HTML and CFML tags
<cfelseif expression>
HTML and CFML tags
<cfelse>
HTML and CFML tags
</cfif>
```

Description

Creates simple and compound conditional statements in CFML. Tests an expression, variable, function return value, or string. Used, optionally, with the `CFELSE` and `CFELSEIF` tags.

For example: `<cfif "11/23/1998" GT "11/15/1998">`

CFLOCATION

```
<cflocation
url = "url"
addToken = "Yes" or "No">
```

Description

Stops page execution and opens a ColdFusion page or HTML file.

Attributes

`url` (Required)

URL of the HTML file or CFML page to open.

`addToken` (Optional)

`clientManagement` must be enabled.

`Yes`: Appends client variable information to URL.

Tag Chooser Dialog Box

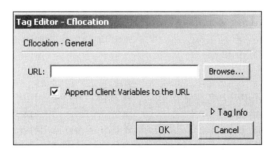

Figure B.31

CFLOOP

Index Loop

```
<cfloop index = "parameter_name"
from = "beginning_value"
to = "ending_value"
step = "increment">
...
HTML or CFML code to execute
...
```

Conditional Loop

```
<cfloop condition = "expression">
```

Query Loop

```
<cfloop query = "query_name"
startRow = "row_num"
endRow = "row_num">
```

List/File Loop

```
<cfloop index = "index_name"
list = "list_items"
delimiters = "item_delimiter">
```

COM Collection/Structure Loop

```
<cfloop collection = #variable#
item = "item">
```

Description

Looping is a programming technique that repeats a set of instructions or displays output repeatedly until one or more conditions are met.

An index loop repeats for a number of times that is determined by a numeric value. An index loop is also known as a FOR loop. A conditional loop repeats a block of code until a specified condition is no longer true. A conditional loop is also known as a WHERE loop. A query loop iterates through a recordset between specified row numbers. A list/file loop repeats through a list of values separated by a specified delimiter. A COM collection/structure loop repeats through a COM collection object or a structure by item.

Attributes

`index` (Required)

Index value for loop.

`from` (Required)

Beginning value of the index.

`to` (Required)

Ending value of the index.

`step` (Optional)

Default: 1

Step by which to increment or decrement the index value.

`condition` (Required)

Condition that controls the loop.

`query` (Required)

Query that controls the loop.

`startRow` (Optional)

First row of query that is included in the loop.

`endRow` (Optional)

Last row of query that is included in the loop.

`index` (Required)

In a list loop, the variable to receive the next list element.

`list` (Required)

A list, variable, or file name; contains a list.

`delimiters` (Optional)

Character(s) that separates items in a list.

Tag Chooser Dialog Box

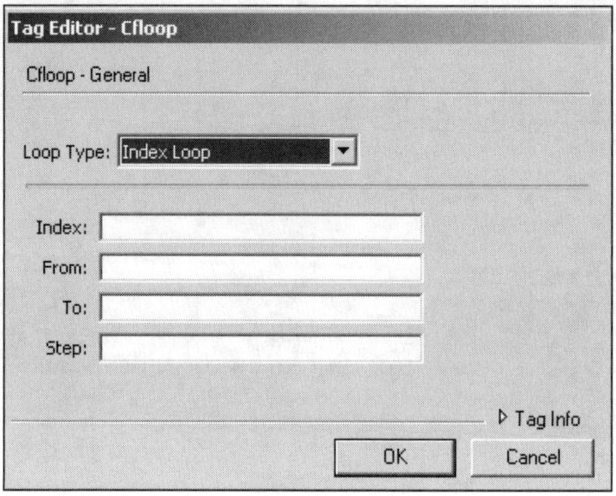

Figure B.32

CFRETHROW

```
<cfrethrow>
```

Description

Rethrows the currently active exception. Preserves the exception's `cfcatch.type` and `cfcatch.tagContext` variable values.

CFSCRIPT

```
<cfscript>
cfscript code goes here
</cfscript>
```

Description

Encloses a code block that contains CFSCRIPT statements.

CFSILENT

```
<cfsilent>
...
</cfsilent>
```

Description

Suppresses output produced by CFML within a tag's scope. This tag requires an end tag.

CFTRY

```
<cftry>
Add code here
<cfcatch type = "exceptiontype">
Exception processing code here
</cfcatch>
Optional: More cfcatch blocks here
</cftry>
```

Description

Used with one or more CFCATCH tags. Together, they catch and process exceptions in ColdFusion pages. Exceptions are events that disrupt the normal flow of instructions in a ColdFusion page, such as failed database operations, missing include files, and developer-specified events.

Attributes

type (Optional)

   Default: Any

   application: Catches application exceptions.

   database: Catches database exceptions.

   template: Catches ColdFusion page exceptions.

   security: Catches security exceptions.

   object: Catches object exceptions.

   missinginclude: Catches missing include file exceptions.

   expression: Catches expression exceptions.

   lock: Catches lock exceptions.

   custom_type: Catches developer-defined exceptions, defined in the CFTHROW tag.

   searchengine: Catches Verity search engine exceptions.

   any: Catches all exception types.

CFSWITCH

```
<cfswitch expression = "expression">
<cfcase value = "value" delimiters = "delimiters">
  HTML and CFML tags
</cfcase>
additional <cfcase></cfcase> tags
<cfdefaultcase>
  HTML and CFML tags
</cfdefaultcase>
</cfswitch>
```

Description

Evaluates a passed expression and passes control to the CFCASE tag that matches the expression result. You can, optionally, code a CFDEFAULTCASE tag, which receives control if there is no matching CFCASE tag value.

Attributes

expression (Required)

ColdFusion expression that yields a scalar value. ColdFusion converts integers, real numbers, Booleans, and dates to numeric values. For example, True, 1, and 1.0 are all equal.

value (Required)

One or more constant values that CFSWITCH compares to the expression (case-insensitive). If a value matches the expression, CFSWITCH executes the code between the CFCASE start and end tags. Duplicate value attributes cause a runtime error.

delimiters (Optional)

Default: , (comma)

Character that separates entries in a list of values.

Tag Chooser Dialog Box

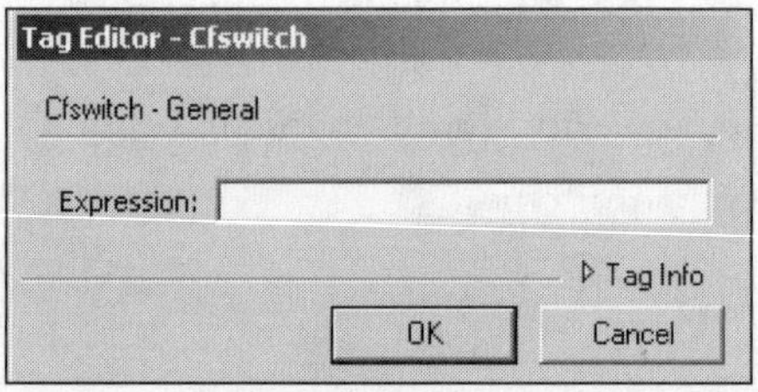

Figure B.33

CFTHROW

Syntax 1

```
<cfthrow
type = "exception_type"
message = "message"
detail = "detail_description"
errorCode = "error_code"
extendedInfo = "additional_information">
```

Syntax 2

```
<cfthrow object = #object_name#>
```

Description

Throws a developer-specified exception, which can be caught with a
CFCATCH tag.

Attributes

type (Optional)

> Default: Application
>
> A custom type.
>
> Application: Do not enter another predefined type; types are not generated
> by ColdFusion applications. If you specify Application, you need not
> specify a type for CFCATCH.

message (Optional)

> Message that describes the exception event.

detail (Optional)

> Description of the event. ColdFusion appends error position to the descrip-
> tion. The server uses this parameter if an error is not caught by your code.

errorCode (Optional)

> A custom error code that you supply.

extendedInfo (Optional)

> Additional information that you provide.

object (Optional)

> Requires the value of the CFOBJECT tag name attribute. Throws a Java excep-
> tion from a CFML tag. This attribute is mutually exclusive with all other
> attributes of this tag.

Tag Chooser Dialog Box

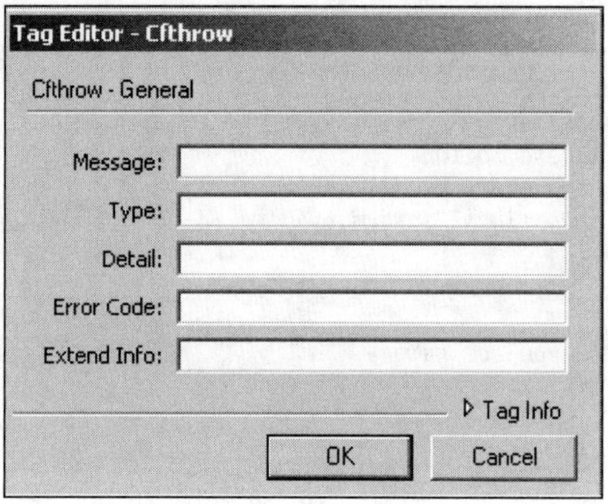

Figure B.34

Internet Protocol Tags

CFFTP

```
<cfftp action = "action"
  username = "name"
  password = "password"
  server = "server"
  timeout = "timeout in seconds"
  port = "port"
  connection = "name"
  proxyServer = "proxyserver"
  retryCount = "number"
  stopOnError = "Yes" or "No"
  passive = "Yes" or "No">
```

File and Directory Operations

```
<cfftp action = "action"
  username = "name"
  password = "password"
  name = "query_name"
  server = "server"
  ASCIIExtensionList = "extensions"
```

```
transferMode = "mode"
failIfExists = "Yes" or "No"
directory = "directory name"
localFile = "filename"
remoteFile = "filename"
item = "directory or file"
existing = "file or directory name"
new = "file or directory name"
proxyServer = "proxyserver"
passive = "Yes" or "No">
```

Description

Allows for the implementation of File Transfer Protocol (FTP) operations. Can be used to implement a connection to an FTP server, for connections caching, to implement file and directory operations, or to get results for a query.

Attributes

`action` (Required)

FTP operation to perform can be one of the following: `open`, `close`, `changedir`, `createDir`, `listDir`, `removeDir`, `getFile`, `putFile`, `rename`, `remove`, `getCurrentDir`, `getCurrentURL`, `existsDir`, `existsFile`, or `exists`.

`username` (Required if `action` = `"open"`)

Username to pass in the FTP operation.

If not using a cached connection, this tag is also required for directory and file commands.

`password` (Required if `action` = `"open"`)

Password to log in a user. If not using a cached connection, this tag is also required for directory and file commands.

`server` (Required if `action` = `"open"`)

FTP server to connect to; for example, `ftp.myserver.com`.

`timeout` (Optional)

Default: 30

Value in seconds for the timeout of all operations, including individual data request operations.

`port` (Optional)

Default: 21

Remote port to connect to.

connection (Optional)

Name of the FTP connection. Used to cache a new FTP connection or to reuse a connection. If you specify the username, password, and server attributes, and if no connection exists for them, ColdFusion creates one. Calls to CFFTP with the same connection name reuse the connection information.

proxyServer (Optional)

String. Name of proxy server (or servers) to use, if proxy access is specified.

retryCount (Optional)

Default: 1

Number of retries until failure is reported.

stopOnError (Optional)

Default: No

Yes: Halts processing and displays an appropriate error.

No: Populates these variables:

cfftp.succeeded: Yes or No.

cfftp.errorCode: Error number. See the IETF Network Working Group RFC 959: File Transfer Protocol (FTP): www.ietf.org/rfc/rfc0959.txt.

cfftp.errorText: Message text.

For conditional operations, use cfftp.errorCode. Do not use cfftp.errorText for this purpose.

passive (Optional)

Default: No

Yes: Enable passive mode.

name (Required if action = "listDir")

Query name of directory listing.

ASCIIExtensionList (Optional)

Delimited list of file extensions that force ASCII transfer mode, if transferMode = "auto". Possible values include txt, htm, html, cfm, cfml, shtm, shtml, css, asp, and asa.

transferMode (Optional)

Default: Auto

Options include ASCII FTP transfer mode, Binary FTP transfer mode, and Auto FTP transfer mode.

`failIfExists` (Optional)

> Default: `Yes`
>
> `Yes`: If a local file with the same name exists, `getFile` fails.

`directory` (Required if `action` = `"changedir/createDir/listDir/existsDir"`)
Directory on which to perform an operation.

`localFile` (Required if `action` = `"getFile/putFile"`)
Name of the file on the local file system.

`remoteFile` Required if `action` = `"getFile/putFile/existsFile"`)
Name of the file on the FTP server file system.

`item` (Required if `action` = `"exists/remove"`)
Object of these actions: file or directory.

`existing` (Required if `action` = `"rename"`)
Current name of the file or directory on the remote server.

`new` (Required if `action` = `"rename"`)
New name of the file or directory on the remote server

`proxyServer` (Optional)
String. Name of the proxy server(s) to use if proxy access is specified.

`passive` (Optional)

> Default: `No`
>
> `Yes`: Enable passive mode.

The following query objects are returned by `CFFTP` when `action` = `"listdir"`. Use the syntax *queryname.querycolumn* to access data.

`name`
Filename of the current element.

`path`
File path (without drive designation) of the current element.

`URL`
Complete URL for the current element (file or directory).

`length`
File size of the current element.

`lastModified`
Unformatted date/time value of the current element.

attributes
> String. Attributes of the current element: `normal` or `Directory`.

isDirectory
> Boolean. Determines whether object is a file or directory.

mode
> Octal string. Applies only to Solaris and HP-UX. Permissions.

Tag Chooser Dialog Box

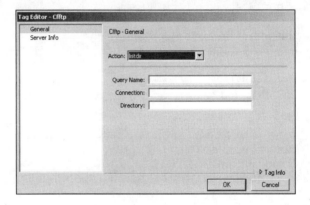

Figure B.35

CFHTTP

```
<cfhttp
url = "hostname"
port = "port_number"
method = "get"_or_"post"
username = "username"
password = "password"
name = "queryname"
columns = "query_columns"
firstrowasheaders = "yes" or "no"
path = "path"
file = "filename"
delimiter = "character"
textQualifier = "character"
resolveURL = "yes" or "no"
proxyServer = "hostname"
proxyPort = "port_number"
userAgent = "user_agent"
```

```
throwOnError = "yes" or "no"
redirect = "yes" or "no"
timeout = "timeout_period">
</cfhttp>
```

Description

Executes HTTP POST and GET operations on files. You can execute standard GET operations and create a query object from a text file. POST operations upload MIME file types to a server or post cookie, form field, URL, file, or CGI variables directly to a server.

Attributes

url (Required)

Default: http

Absolute URL of host name or IP address of server on which the file resides. URL must include protocol (HTTP or HTTPS) and hostname. It can contain a port number. Port number in this attribute overrides port value.

port (Optional)

Default: 80

Port number on server from which object is requested. When used with resolveURL, URLs of retrieved documents that specify a port number are automatically resolved to preserve links in the retrieved document. Port number in url attribute overrides this value.

method (Required)

get: Downloads text or binary file or creates a query from the contents of a text file.

post: Sends information to a server page or CGI program for processing. Requires a CFHTTPPARAM tag.

username (Optional)

When required by a server, a username.

password (Optional)

When required by a server, a password.

name (Optional)

Name to assign to a query if it is constructed from a file.

columns (Optional)

Column names for a query, when creating it as a result of a CFHTTP GET. By default, the first row of a text file is interpreted as column heads. If there are column heads in the text file from which the query is drawn, do not specify this attribute, except to overwrite them. If a duplicate column heading is encountered, ColdFusion appends an underscore to the name to make it unique. If there are no column headers in the text file, or to override those in the file, specify the columns attribute. ColdFusion never processes the first row of a file as data, even if you specify the columns attribute.

firstrowasheaders (Optional)

Default: yes

Determines how ColdFusion processes the first row of the query recordset.

yes: If the columns attribute is not specified, ColdFusion processes the data as column heads. If the columns attribute is specified, ColdFusion ignores this attribute.

no: If the columns attribute is not specified, processes as data, and generates column names; for example, column_1. If the columns attribute is specified, ColdFusion ignores this attribute.

path (Optional)

Path to directory in which to store the file. If path is not specified in POST or GET, a variable (cfhttp.fileContent) is created; you can use it to display the POST operation results in a CFOUTPUT tag.

file (Required if a POST operation and if path is specified)

Name of the file that is accessed. For GET operations, this defaults to the name specified in url. Enter path information in the path attribute.

delimiter (Required to create query)

Default: , (comma)

Options are tab or comma.

textQualifier (Required to create query)

Default: "" (double quotation mark)

Beginning and end of a column. Must be escaped when embedded in column. For example, if the qualifier is a double quotation mark, it is escaped as """". If there is no text qualifier in the file, specify " ".

resolveURL (Optional)

Default: No

For GET and POST.

Yes: The internal URLs in a page reference returned into the `fileContent` internal variable are fully resolved, including port number, so that links remain intact. The following HTML tags are resolved: `IMG SRC`, `A HREF`, `FORM ACTION`, `APPLET CODE`, `SCRIPT SRC`, `EMBED SRC`, `EMBED PLUGINSPACE`, `BODY BACKGROUND`, `FRAME SRC`, `BGSOUND SRC`, `OBJECT DATA`, `OBJECT CLASSID`, `OBJECT CODEBASE` and `OBJECT USEMAP`.

`proxyServer` (Optional)

Host name or IP address of a proxy server.

`proxyPort` (Optional)

Default: 80

Port number on proxy server from which object is requested. When used with `resolveURL`, the URLs of retrieved documents that specify a port number are automatically resolved to preserve links in the retrieved documents.

`userAgent` (Optional)

User agent request header.

`throwOnError` (Optional)

Default: `No`

Yes: Throw an exception that can be caught with the `CFTRY` and `CFCATCH` tags.

`redirect` (Optional)

Default: `Yes`

If `No`, and `throwOnError = "yes"`, then if `CFHTTP` fails, execution stops, and the status code and associated error message are returned in the variable `cfhttp.statuscode`. To determine where execution would have been redirected, use the variable `cfhttp.responseHeader[LOCATION]`. Up to four redirects will be followed on a request. After four, it works as if `redirect = "no"`.

Yes: Redirect execution.

No: Stop execution.

`timeout` (Optional)

Value, in seconds. When a URL timeout is specified in the browser, this setting takes precedence over the ColdFusion Administrator timeout, and ColdFusion uses the lesser of the URL timeout and the timeout passed in the `timeout` attribute, so that the request always times out before, or at the same time as, the page. If the URL timeout is not specified, ColdFusion uses the lesser of the Administrator timeout and the timeout passed in the timeout attribute. If the timeout is not set in any of these, ColdFusion waits indefinitely for the CFHTTP request to process.

Tag Chooser Dialog Box

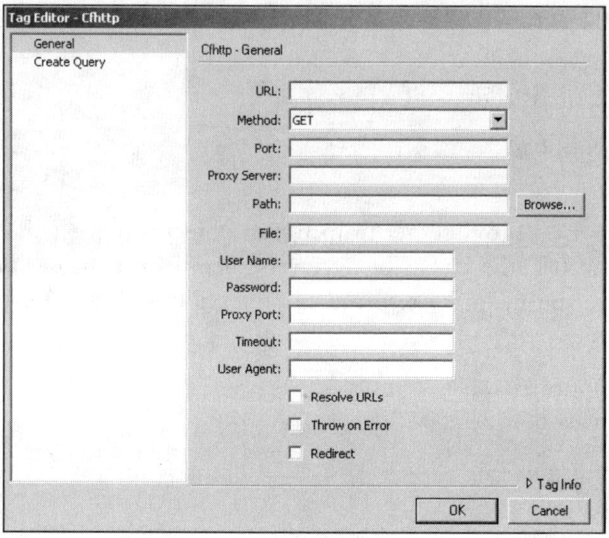

Figure B.36

CFHTTPPARAM

```
<cfhttpparam
name = "name"
type = "type"
value = "transaction type"
file = "filename">
```

Description

Required for a CFHTTP POST operation. Specifies parameters to build the operation.

Attributes

name (Required)
    Variable name for data that is passed.

type (Required)
    Transaction type: URL, FormField, Cookie, CGI, or File.

`value` (Optional if `type` = `"File"`)

Value of `URL`, `FormField`, `Cookie`, `File`, or `CGI` variables that are passed.

`file` (Required if `type` = `"File"`)

Filename.

Tag Chooser Dialog Box

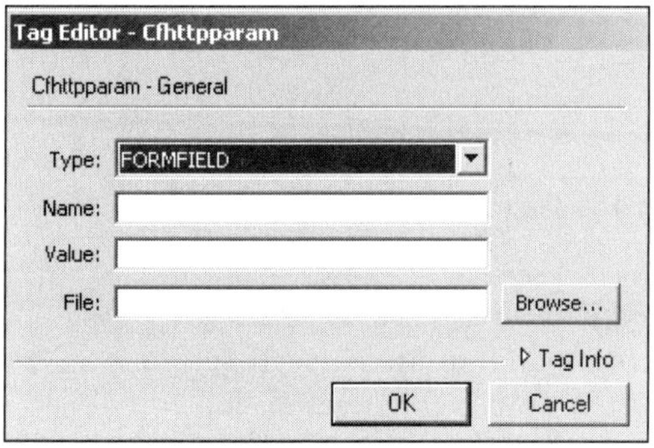

Figure B.37

CFLDAP

```
<cfldap server = "server_name"
port = "port_number"
username = "name"
password = "password"
action = "action"
name = "name"
timeout = "seconds"
maxRows = "number"
start = "distinguished_name"
scope = "scope"
attributes = "attribute, attribute"
filter = "filter"
sort = "attribute[, attribute]..."
sortControl = "nocase" and/or "desc" or "asc"
dn = "distinguished_name"
startRow - "row_number"
modifyType = "REPLACE" or "ADD" or "delete"
rebind = "Yes" or "No"
referral = "number_of_allowed_hops"
secure = "multi_field_security_string"
separator = "separator_character"
delimiter - "delimiter_character">
```

Description

Provides an interface to a Lightweight Directory Access Protocol (LDAP) directory server, such as the Netscape Directory Server.

Attributes

server (Required)

Host name or IP address of LDAP server.

port (Optional)

Default: 389

Port number.

username (Required if secure = "CFSSL_BASIC")

User ID.

password (Required if secure = "CFSSL_BASIC")

Password that corresponds to username. If secure = "CFSSL_BASIC", V2 encrypts the password before transmission.

action (Optional)

Default: query

query: Returns LDAP entry information only. Requires name, start, and attributes attributes.

add: Adds LDAP entries to the LDAP server. Requires the attributes attribute.

modify: Modifies LDAP entries, except the distinguished name dn attribute, on LDAP server. Requires dn. See modifyType attribute.

modifyDN: Modifies the distinguished name attribute for LDAP entries on the LDAP server. Requires dn.

delete: Deletes LDAP entries on an LDAP server. Requires dn.

name (Required if action = "Query")

Name of the LDAP query. The tag validates this value.

timeout (Optional)

Default: 60

Maximum length of time, in seconds, to wait for LDAP processing.

maxRows (Optional)

Maximum number of entries for LDAP queries.

start (Required if action = "Query")
Distinguished name of entry to be used to start a search.

scope (Optional)

Default: oneLevel

Scope of search, from entry specified in start attribute for action = "Query".

oneLevel: Entries one level below entry.

base: Only the entry.

subtree: Entry and all levels below it.

attributes (Required if action = "Query/Add/ModifyDN/Modify")
For queries, a comma-delimited list of attributes to return. For queries, to get all attributes, specify "*". For action = "add" or "modify", you can specify a list of update columns. Separate attributes with a semicolon. For action = "ModifyDN", ColdFusion passes attributes to the LDAP server without syntax checking.

filter (Optional)

"objectclass = *"

Search criteria for action = "query". List attributes in the form "(attribute operator value)". For example: "(sn = Smith)".

sort (Optional)
Attribute(s) by which to sort query results. Use a comma delimiter.

sortControl (Optional)

Default: asc

nocase: Case-insensitive sort.

asc: Ascending (A to Z) case-sensitive sort.

desc: Descending (Z to A) case-sensitive sort.

You can enter a combination of sort types; for example, sortControl = "nocase, asc".

dn (Required if action = "Add/ModifyDN/Modify/delete")
Distinguished name, for update action.

startRow (Optional)

Default: 1

Used with action = "query". First row of an LDAP query to insert into a ColdFusion query.

modifyType (Optional)

Default: replace

How to process an attribute in a multi-value list.

add: Appends the value to any attributes.

delete: Deletes the value from the set of attributes.

replace: Replaces the value with specified attributes.

You cannot add an attribute that is already present or that is empty.

rebind (Optional)

Default: No

Yes: Attempt to rebind referral callback and reissue query by referred address using original credentials.

No: Referred connections are anonymous.

referral (Optional)

Integer. Number of hops allowed in a referral. A value of 0 disables referred addresses for LDAP; no data is returned.

secure (Optional)

The security to employ, and the required information.

CFSSL_BASIC: Provides V2 SSL encryption and server authentication.

certificate_db: Certificate database file (in Netscape cert7.db format). Absolute path or simple filename. (See the Usage section.)

separator (Optional)

Default: , [comma]

Delimiter to separate attribute values of multi-value attributes. This is used by query, add, and modify actions, and by CFLDAP to output multi-value attributes. For example, if the separator is $ (dollar sign), the attributes attribute could be "objectclass = top$person", where the first value of objectclass is top, and the second value is person. This avoids confusion if values include commas.

delimiter (Optional)

Separator for attribute name-value pairs, if the attributes attribute specifies more than one item, it uses the semicolon delimiter. For example: mgrpms-grejecttext;lang-en. This is used by query, add, and modify actions, and by CFLDAP to output multi-value attributes. For example, if the delimiter is $ (dollar sign), you could specify this list of pairs with (e)Attributes "cn = Double Tree Inn$street = 1111 Elm;Suite 100.

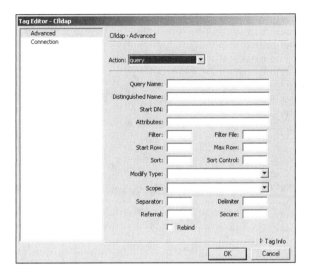

Figure B.38

CFMAIL

```
<cfmail to = "recipient"
from = "sender"
cc = "copy_to"
bcc = "blind_copy_to"
subject = "msg_subject"
type = "msg_type"
maxRows = "max_msgs"
MIMEAttach = "path"
query = "query_name"
group = "query_column"
groupCaseSensitive = "Yes" or "No"
startRow = "query_row"
server = "servername"
port = "port_ID"
mailerID = "headerid"
timeout = "seconds">
spoolEnable = "Yes" or "No">
...
</cfmail>
```

Description

Sends an email message that contains query output using an SMTP server.

Attributes

`to` (Required)

Message recipient name(s).

`from` (Required)

Email message sender.

`cc` (Optional)

Address(es) to which to copy the message.

`bcc` (Optional)

Address(es) to which to copy the message, without listing the receivers in the message header.

`subject` (Required)

Message subject; can be dynamically generated. For example, to send messages that give customers status updates, use "`Status of Order Number #Order_ID#`".

`type` (Optional)

Extended type attributes for a message. Informs the receiving email client that the message has embedded HTML tags to process. Used only by mail clients that support HTML.

`maxRows` (Optional)

Maximum number of messages to send.

`MIMEAttach` (Optional)

Path of file to attach to message. Attached file is MIME-encoded.

`query` (Optional)

Name of `CFQUERY` from which to draw data for message(s). Use this attribute to send more than one message, or to send query results within a message.

`group` (Optional)

Default: `CurrentRow`

Query column to use when you group sets of records to send as a message. For example, to send a set of billing statements to a customer, group on `Customer_ID`. This is case-sensitive. Eliminates adjacent duplicates when data is sorted by the specified field.

groupCaseSensitive (Optional)

Default: Yes

Boolean. Determines whether to consider case when grouping. If the query attribute specifies a query object that was generated by a case-insensitive SQL query, set this attribute to No to keep the recordset intact.

startRow (Optional)

Default: 1

Row in a query to start from.

server (Optional)

SMTP server address to use for sending messages. Server must be specified here or in the ColdFusion Administrator. A value here overrides the Administrator.

port (Optional)

Default: -1

TCP/IP port on which the SMTP server listens for requests. This is normally 25.

mailerID (Optional)

Default: ColdFusion Application Server

Mailer ID to be passed in X-Mailer SMTP header, which identifies the mailer application.

timeout (Optional)

Default: -1

Number of seconds to wait before timing out the connection to SMTP server.

spoolEnable (Optional)

Default: Yes

Yes: Saves a copy of the message until the sending operation is complete. May be slower than the No option.

No: Queues the message for sending, without storing a copy until the operation is complete.

Tag Chooser Dialog Box

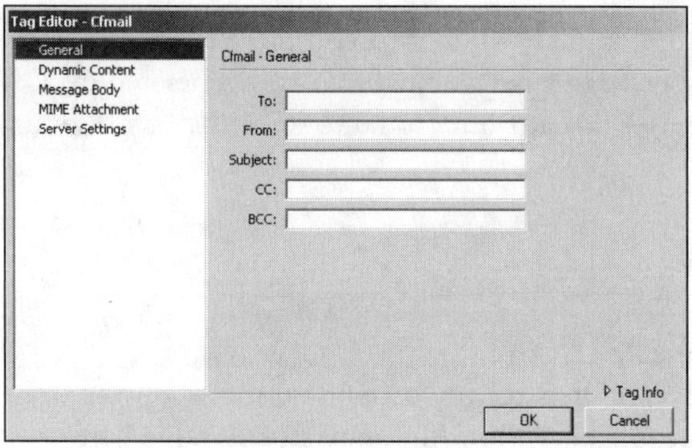

Figure B.39

CFMAILPARAM

```
<cfmail>
<cfmailparam  file = "file-name" >

or

<cfmailparam
name = "header-name"
value = "header-value" >

...

</cfmail>
```

Description

Attaches a file or adds a header to an email message. Used within the CFMAIL tag. You can use more than one CFMAILPARAM tag within a CFMAIL tag.

Attributes

file (Required if you do not specify the name attribute)
   Attaches a file to a message. Mutually exclusive with the name attribute.

name (Required if you do not specify the file attribute)
   Name of header; case-insensitive. Mutually exclusive with the file attribute.

value (Optional)
   Value of header.

Tag Chooser Dialog Box

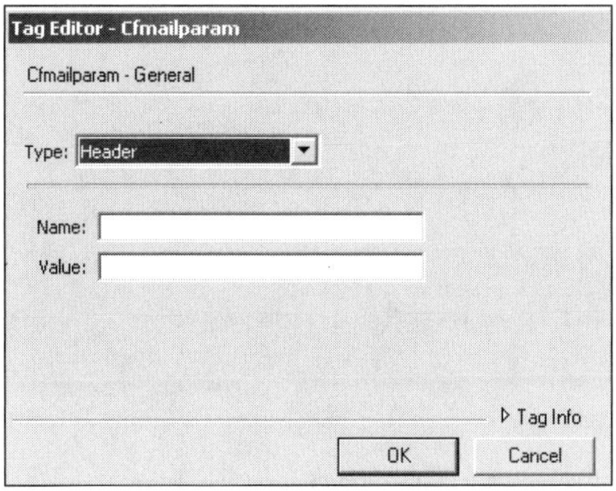

Figure B.40

CFPOP

```
<cfpop server = "servername"
port = "port_number"
username = "username"
password = "password"
action = "action"
name = "queryname"
messageNumber = "number"
uid = "number"
attachmentPath = "path"
timeout = "seconds"
maxRows = "number"
startRow = "number"
generateUniqueFilenames = "boolean">
```

Description

Retrieves and deletes email messages from a POP mail server.

Attributes

server (Required)

POP server identifier, which could be a host name, such as server.some-where.com, or an IP address, such as 192.1.2.225.

port (Optional)

Default: 110

POP port.

username (Optional)

Default: Anonymous

A username.

password (Optional)

Password that corresponds to the username.

action (Optional)

Default: getHeaderOnly

getHeaderOnly: Returns message header information only.

getAll: Returns message header information, message text, and attachments if attachmentPath is specified.

delete: Deletes messages on POP server.

name (Required if action = "getAll" or "getHeaderOnly")

Name for the index query.

messageNumber (Required if action = "delete")

Message number or comma-delimited list of message numbers to get. Applies to action = "getAll" and "getHeaderOnly". For these actions, if it is omitted, all messages on the server are returned. Invalid message numbers are ignored.

uid (Required if action = "delete")

UID(s) or a comma-delimited list of UIDs to retrieve. Applies to action = "getHeaderOnly" and action = "getAll". For these actions, if it is omitted, all messages on the server are returned. Invalid UIDs are ignored.

attachmentPath (Optional)

If action = "getAll", this allows attachments to be written to the directory. If this value is invalid, no attachment files are written to the server.

timeout (Optional)

Default: 60

Maximum time, in seconds, to wait for mail processing.

`maxRows` (Optional)

Default: 999999

Sets the number of messages returned, starting with the number in `startRow`. If `messageNumber` is specified, this attribute is ignored.

`startRow` (Optional)

Default: 1

First row number to get. If `messageNumber` is specified, this attribute is ignored.

`generateUniqueFilenames` (Optional)

Default: `No`

`Yes`: Generate unique filenames for files attached to an email message, to avoid naming conflicts when files are saved.

Tag Chooser Dialog Box

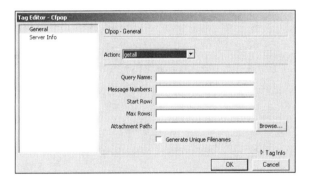

Figure B.41

File Management Tags

CFDIRECTORY

```
<cfdirectory
action = "directory action"
directory = "directory name"
name = "query name"
filter = "list filter"
mode = "permission"
sort = "sort specification"
newDirectory = "new directory name">
```

Description

Manages interactions with directories. This tag must be enabled in the ColdFusion Administrator in order for it to execute.

Attributes

action (Optional)

> Default: list

> list: Returns a query recordset of the files in the specified directory. Other commands are create, delete, and rename.

directory (Required)

> Absolute pathname of the directory against which to perform the action.

name (Required if action = "list")

> Name for the output recordset.

filter (Optional if action = "list")

> File extension filter applied to returned names, such as "*.cfm". One filter can be applied.

mode (Optional)

> Used with action = "create". This tag applies to only Solaris and HP-UX. Use in conjunction with octal values of the chmod command.

> 644: Assigns read/write permission to owner; read permission to group and other.

> 777: Assigns read/write/execute permission to all.

sort (Optional)

> Used if action = "list".

> Queries column(s) by which to sort directory listing.

newDirectory (Required if action = "rename")

> New name for the directory.

Tag Chooser Dialog Box

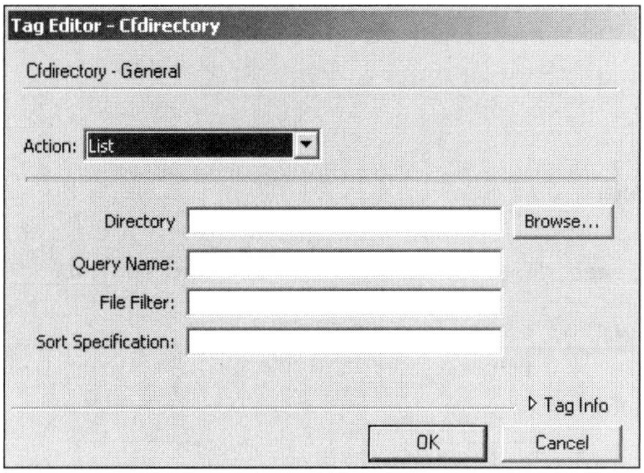

Figure B.42

CFFILE

```
<cffile action = "upload"
fileField = "formfield"
destination = "full_path_name"
nameConflict = "behavior"
accept = "mime_type/file_type"
mode = "permission"
attributes = "file",_"attribute"._or_"list">

<cffile action = "move/rename/copy/delete"
source = "full_path_name"
destination = "full_path_name"
mode = "mode"
attributes = "file_attributes_list"
charset = "charset_option">

<cffile action = "read/readBinary"
file = "full_path_name"
variable = "var_name"
encoding = "encoding_option"
charset = "charset_option">

<cffile action = "write/append"
file = "full_path_name"
output = "content"
mode = "permission"
addNewLine = "Yes" or "No"
attributes = "file_attributes list"
encoding = "encoding_option"
charset = "charset_option" >
```

Description

Manages interactions with files on the ColdFusion server. The action performed depends on the action attribute. This tag must be enabled in the ColdFusion Administrator in order to work.

Attributes

action (Required)

Type of file manipulation that the tag performs, including upload, move, rename, copy, read, delete, readBinary, write, and append.

fileField (Required)

Name of form field used to select the file. Do not use hash signs (#) to specify the field name.

destination (Required)

Absolute pathname of the directory or file on the web server. ColdFusion 5 and earlier: Trailing slash in directory path is required. ColdFusion MX: Trailing slash in directory path is optional. On Windows, use backward slashes; on Unix, use forward slashes.

nameConflict (Optional)

Default: Error

Action to take if filename is the same as that of a file in the directory.

Error: File is not saved. ColdFusion stops processing the page and returns an error.

Skip: File is not saved. This option permits custom behavior based on file properties.

Overwrite: Replaces file.

MakeUnique: Forms a unique filename for the upload; name is stored in the file object variable serverFile.

accept (Optional)

Limits MIME types. Comma-delimited list. For example, to permit JPEG and Microsoft Word file uploads: accept = "image/jpg, application/msword". The browser uses the file extension to determine the file type.

mode (Optional)

Applies only to Solaris and HP-UX. Permissions. Octal values of chmod command. Assigned to owner, group, and other, respectively. For example:

644: Assigns read/write permission to owner; read permission to group and other.

777: Assigns read/write/execute permission to all.

attributes (Optional)

One attribute (Windows) or a comma-delimited list of attributes (other platforms) to set on the file. If omitted, the file's attributes are maintained. Each value must be specified explicitly. For example, if you specify attributes = "readOnly", all other attributes are overwritten.

Options include ReadOnly, hidden, and normal. (If you use this option with other attributes, it is overridden by them.)

source (Required)

Absolute pathname of the file on the web server. On Windows, use backward slashes; on Unix, use forward slashes.

charset (Optional)

Default: ISO-8859-1

The Java character set name used for the file contents.

file (Required)

Absolute pathname of the file. On Windows, use backward slashes; on Unix, use forward slashes.

variable (Required)

Name of the variable to contain the contents of the text file.

encoding (Optional)

Default: -1

The character encoding of generated output. Any valid character encoding is usable.

output (Required)

Content of the file to be created.

addNewLine (Optional)

Default: Yes

Yes: Appends a newline character to text written to a file.

After a file upload is completed, you can get status information using file upload parameters. The status parameters use the CFFILE prefix; for example, CFFILE.clientDirectory. Status parameters can be used anywhere other ColdFusion parameters can be used.

`attemptedServerFile`
> Initial name. ColdFusion uses this when attempting to save a file.

`clientDirectory`
> Directory location of the file uploaded from the client's system.

`clientFile`
> Name of the file uploaded from the client's system.

`clientFileExt`
> Extension of the uploaded file on the client system (without a period).

`clientFileName`
> Name of the uploaded file on the client system (without an extension).

`contentSubType`
> MIME content subtype of the saved file.

`contentType`
> MIME content type of the saved file.

`dateLastAccessed`
> Date and time the uploaded file was last accessed.

`fileExisted`
> Whether the file already existed with the same path (`Yes` or `No`).

`fileSize`
> Size of the uploaded file.

`fileWasAppended`
> Whether ColdFusion appended uploaded the file to a file (`Yes` or `No`).

`fileWasOverwritten`
> Whether ColdFusion overwrote a file (`Yes` or `No`).

`fileWasRenamed`
> Whether the uploaded file is renamed to avoid a name conflict (`Yes` or `No`).

`fileWasSaved`
> Whether Cold Fusion saves a file (`Yes` or `No`).

`oldFileSize`
> Size of a file that was overwritten in the file upload operation.

`serverDirectory`
> Directory of the file saved on the server.

`serverFile`
Filename of the file saved on the server.

`serverFileExt`
Extension of the uploaded file on the server (without a period).

`serverFileName`
Name of the uploaded file on the server (without an extension).

`timeCreated`
Time the uploaded file was created.

`timeLastModified`
Date and time of the last modification to the uploaded file.

Tag Chooser Dialog Box

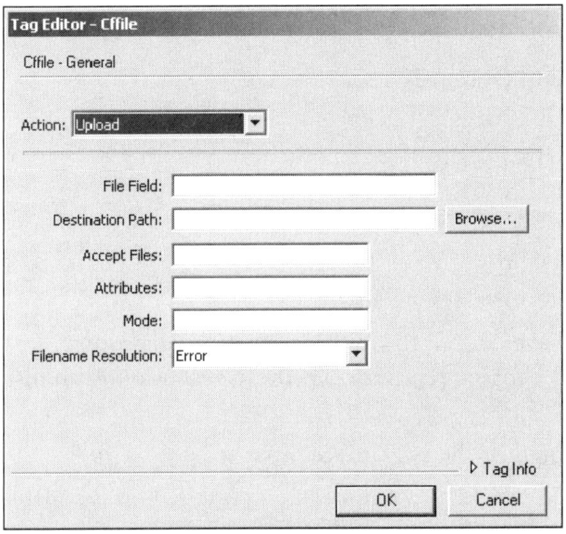

Figure B.43

Web Application Framework Tags

CFAPPLICATION

```
<cfapplication name = "application_name"
clientManagement = "Yes" or "No"
clientStorage = "datasource_name" or "Registry" or "Cookie"
```

```
setClientCookies = "Yes" or "No"
sessionManagement = "Yes" or "No"
sessionTimeout = #CreateTimeSpan(days, hours, minutes, seconds)#
applicationTimeout = #CreateTimeSpan(days, hours, minutes, seconds)#
setDomainCookies = "Yes" or "No">
```

Description

Defines the scope of a ColdFusion application; enables and disables storage of client variables; specifies the client variable storage mechanism; enables session variables; and sets application variable timeouts.

Server, Session, and Application scope variables are stored in memory as structures. You cannot access the UDF function scope as a structure.

Attributes

name (Required for Application and Session variables; Optional for Client variables)

Name of application, with a 64-character limit.

clientManagement_(Optional)

Default: No

Yes: Enables client variables.

clientStorage (Optional)

Default: registry

Defines where variables are stored.

datasource_name: Stored in ODBC or native data source. You must create a client variable storage repository in the ColdFusion Administrator, Variables page.

registry: Stored in the system Registry.

cookie: Stored on client computer in a cookie. This is scalable for a large number of clients. However, if the client disables cookies in the browser, client variables do not work.

setClientCookies (Optional)

Default: Yes

Yes: Enables client cookies.

No: ColdFusion does not automatically send CFID and CFTOKEN cookies to the client browser; you must manually code CFID and CFTOKEN on the URL for every page that uses Session or Client variables.

`sessionManagement`(Optional)

Default: No

Yes: Enables Session variables.

`sessionTimeout` (Optional)

Specified in the Variables page of the ColdFusion Administrator. Determines the lifespan of Session variables. Uses the `CreateTimeSpan` function and values in days, hours, minutes, and seconds, separated by commas.

`applicationTimeout` (Optional)

Specified in the Variables page of the ColdFusion Administrator. Determines the lifespan of Application variables. Uses the `CreateTimeSpan` function and values in days, hours, minutes, and seconds, separated by commas.

`setDomainCookies` (Optional)

Default: No

Yes: Sets `CFID` and `CFTOKEN` cookies for a domain (not a host). Required for applications running on clusters.

Tag Chooser Dialog Box

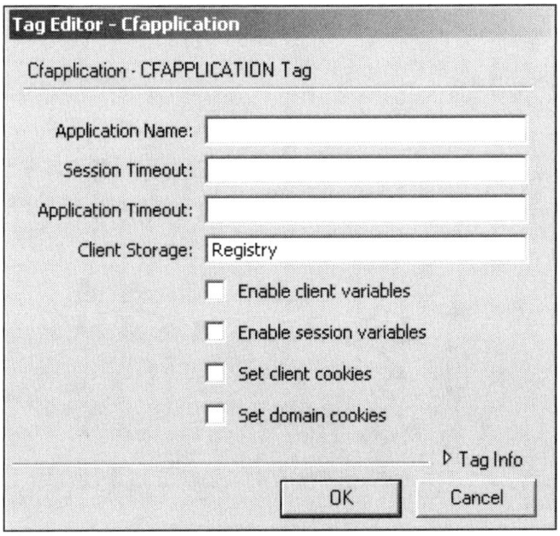

Figure B.44

CFERROR

```
<cferror type = "request" or "validation" or "exception"
template = "template_path"
mailTo = "email_address"
exception = "exception_type">
```

Description

Displays a custom HTML page when an error occurs. This lets you maintain a consistent look and feel among an application's functional and error pages.

Attributes

type (Required)

Type of error that the custom error page handles. Error types are application, database, template, security, object, missinginclude, expression, lock, custom_type, and any.

template (Required)

Relative path to the custom error page. (A ColdFusion page was formerly called a template.)

mailTo (Optional)

Email address to send exceptions to.

Tag Chooser Dialog Box

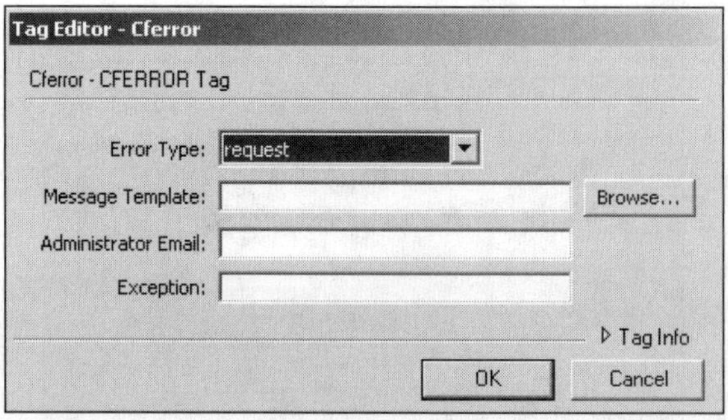

Figure B.45

Form Tags

CFAPPLET

```
<cfapplet appletSource = "applet_name"
name = "form_variable_name"
height = "height in pixels"
width = "width in pixels"
vSpace = "space_above_and_below_in_pixels"
hSpace = "space_on_each_side_in_pixels"
  align = "Left/Right/Bottom/Top/TextTop/Middle/AbsMiddle/
  /Baseline/AbsBottom"
notSupported = "message_to_display_for_nonJava_browser"
param_1 = "applet_parameter_name"
param_2 = "applet_parameter_name"
param_n = "applet_parameter_name">
```

Description

This tag references a registered custom Java applet. To register a Java applet, open the ColdFusion Administrator and click Java Applets.

Using this tag within a CFFORM tag is optional. If you use it within CFFORM, and the method attribute is defined in the Administrator, the return value is incorporated into the form.

Attributes

appletSource (Required)
Name of the registered applet.

name (Required)
Form variable name for the applet.

height (Optional)
Height of the applet, in pixels.

width (Optional)
Width of the applet, in pixels.

vSpace (Optional)
Space above and below the applet, in pixels.

hSpace (Optional)
Space on the left and right of the applet, in pixels.

align (Optional)
Alignment: Left, Right, Bottom, Top, TextTop, Middle, AbsMiddle, Baseline, AbsBottom

notSupported (Optional)

Text to display if a page that contains a Java applet-based CFFORM control is opened by a browser that does not support Java or has Java support disabled.

param_ n (Optional)

Registered parameter for the applet. Specify only to override values for the applet in the ColdFusion Administrator.

Tag Chooser Dialog Box

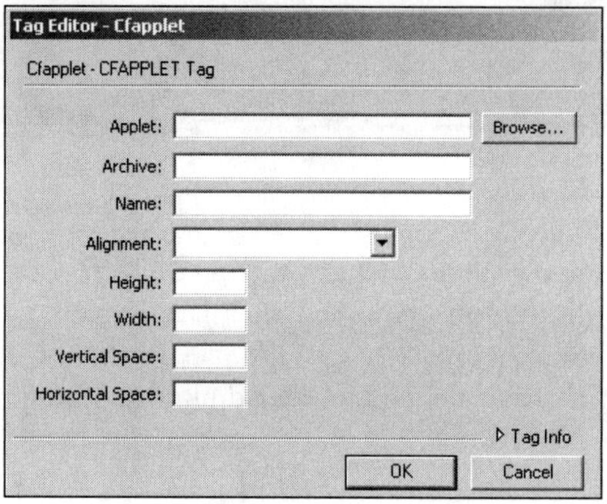

Figure B.46

CFFORM

```
<cfform name = "name"
action = "form_action"
preserveData = "Yes" or "No"
onSubmit = "javascript"
target = "window_name"
encType = "type"
passThrough = "HTML_attribute(s)"
codeBase = "URL"
archive = "URL" >
...
</cfform>
```

Description

Builds a form with CFML custom control tags. Use with such tags as CFINPUT, CFTEXTINPUT, CFSLIDER, CFTREE, and CFSELECT, to provide greater functionality.

Attributes

name (Optional)

A name for the form.

action (Optional)

Name of the ColdFusion page to execute when the form is submitted for processing.

preserveData (Optional)

Whether to override (preserve the display of) default data entered in controls in the action page display after the user submits the form.

onSubmit (Optional)

JavaScript function to execute after other input validation. Use to execute JavaScript for preprocessing data before the form is submitted.

target (Optional)

Window or frame to which form output is sent.

encType (Optional)

Default: *application/x-www-form-urlencoded*

MIME type to encode data sent by the POST method. I recommend that you accept the default. This attribute is included for compatibility with the HTML FORM tag.

passThrough (Optional)

For HTML attributes that are not supported by CFFORM. Attributes and values are passed to the HTML code that is generated for the tag.

codeBase (Optional)

Default: /CFIDE/classes/cf-j2re-win.cab

URL of downloadable JRE plug-in (for Internet Explorer only).

archive (Optional)

Default: /CFIDE/classes/CFJava2.jar

URL for downloadable Java classes for ColdFusion controls.

Tag Chooser Dialog Box

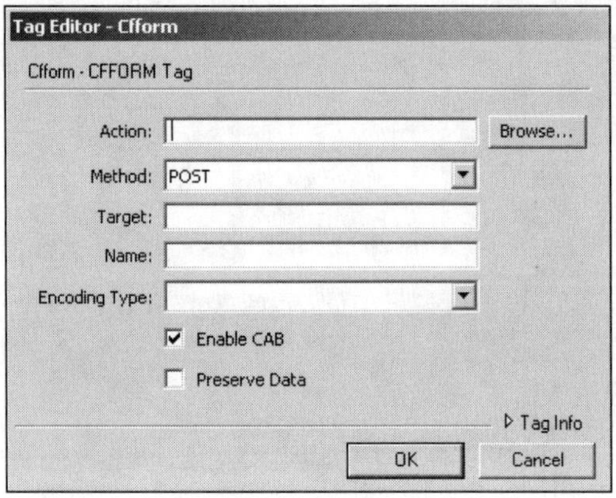

Figure B.47

CFGRID

```
<cfgrid name = "name"
height = "integer"
width = "integer"
autoWidth = "Yes" or "No"
vSpace = "integer"
hSpace = "integer"
align = "value"
query = "query_name"
insert = "Yes" or "No"
delete = "Yes" or "No"
sort = "Yes" or "No"
font = "column_font"
fontSize = "size"
italic = "Yes" or "No"
bold = "Yes" or "No"
textColor = "web color"
href = "URL"
hrefKey = "column_name"
target = "URL_target"
appendKey = "Yes" or "No"
highlightHref = "Yes" or "No"
onValidate = "javascript_function"
onError = "text"
gridDataAlign = "position"
gridLines = "Yes" or "No"
rowHeight = "pixels"
rowHeaders = "Yes" or "No"
rowHeaderAlign = "position"
```

```
rowHeaderFont = "font_name"
rowHeaderFontSize = "size"
rowHeaderItalic = "Yes" or "No"
rowHeaderBold = "Yes" or "No"
rowHeaderTextColor = "web color"
rowHeaderWidth = "col_width"
colHeaders = "Yes" or "No"
colHeaderAlign = "position"
colHeaderFont = "font_name"
colHeaderFontSize = "size"
colHeaderItalic = "Yes" or "No"
colHeaderBold = "Yes" or "No"
colHeaderTextColor = "web color"
bgColor = "web color"
selectColor = "web color"
selectMode = "mode"
maxRows = "number"
notSupported = "text"
pictureBar = "Yes" or "No"
insertButton = "text"
deleteButton = "text"
sortAscendingButton = "text"
sortDescendingButton = "text">
</cfgrid>
```

Description

Used within the CFFORM tag. Puts a grid control (a table of data) in a ColdFusion form. To specify column data, use the CFGRIDCOLUMN tag.

Attributes

name (Required)

Name of the grid element.

height (Optional)

Height of the grid control, in pixels.

width (Optional)

Width of the grid control, in pixels.

autoWidth (Optional)

Default: No

Yes: Sets column widths so that all columns display within the grid width.

No: Sets columns to equal widths. User can resize columns. Horizontal scroll bars are not available because if you specify a column width and set autoWidth = "Yes", ColdFusion sets to this width, if possible.

To render a grid, you must specify a value for one of these: CFGRIDCOLUMN width, CFGRID colheaders, or CFGRID autowidth.

vSpace (Optional)

Vertical space above and below the grid control, in pixels.

hSpace (Optional)

Horizontal space to the left and right of the grid control, in pixels.

align (Optional)

Alignment can be any of the following values: Top, Left, Bottom, Baseline, Texttop, Absbottom, Middle, Absmiddle, or Right.

query (Optional)

Name of the query associated with the grid control.

insert (Optional)

Default: No

Yes: User can insert row data in the grid. Takes effect only if selectmode="edit".

delete (Optional)

Default: No

Yes: User can delete row data from the grid. Takes effect only if selectmode="edit".

sort (Optional)

Default: No

Sort button performs simple text sort on the column. User can sort columns by clicking the column head.

Yes: Sort buttons display on the grid control.

font (Optional)

Font of column data in the grid control.

fontSize (Optional)

Size of text in the grid control, in points.

italic (Optional)

Default: No

Yes: Displays grid control text in italic.

bold (Optional)

Default: No

Yes. Displays grid control text in bold.

`textColor` (Optional)

Default: `Black`

Color of text in the grid control, as hex or web color.

`href` (Optional)

For a grid that is populated from a query, the URL to associate with the grid item or query column. If `href` is a query column, the query populates its value. If `href` is not a query column, it is processed as an HTML `href`.

`hrefKey` (Optional)

If the grid uses a query, this is the name of a query column. The column is the key, regardless of the `selectmode` value.

`target` (Optional)

Target of `href` URL.

`appendKey` (Optional)

Default: `Yes`

`Yes`: When used with `href`, this passes the query string value of the selected tree item in the URL to the application page in the `CFFORM action` attribute.

`highlightHref` (Optional)

Default: `Yes`

`Yes`: Highlights links associated with a `CFGRID` with an `href` attribute value.

`onValidate` (Optional)

A JavaScript function to validate user input. The form object, input object, and input object value are passed to `routine`, which returns `True` if validation succeeds; `False` otherwise.

`onError` (Optional)

A JavaScript function to execute if validation fails.

`gridDataAlign` (Optional)

Default: `Left`

Options are `Left`, `Right`, or `Center`.

`gridLines` (Optional)

Default: `Yes`

`Yes`: Enables row and column rules in the grid control.

`rowHeight` (Optional)

Minimum row height, in pixels, of the grid control. Used with `cfgridcolumn type = "Image"`. Defines space for graphics to display in a row.

`rowHeaders` (Optional)

Default: `Yes`

`Yes`: Displays a column of numeric row labels in the grid control.

`rowHeaderAlign` (Optional)

Default: `Left`

Options are `Left`, `Right`, or `Center`.

`rowHeaderFont` (Optional)

Row label font.

`rowHeaderFontSize` (Optional)

Row label text size in the grid control, in points.

`rowHeaderItalic` (Optional)

Default: `No`

`Yes`: Displays row label text in italic.

`rowHeaderBold` (Optional)

Default: `No`

`Yes`: Displays row label text in bold.

`rowHeaderTextColor` (Optional)

Default: `Black`

Text color of the grid control row headers.

`rowHeaderWidth` (Optional)

ColdFusion does not use this attribute. You can omit it.

`colHeaders` (Optional)

Default: `Yes`

`Yes`: Displays column headers in the grid control.

To render a grid, you must specify a value for one of these: `CFGRIDCOLUMN` width, `CFGRID` colheaders, or `CFGRID` autowidth.

`colHeaderAlign` (Optional)

Default: `Left`

Options are `Left`, `Right`, or `Center`.

`colHeaderFont` (Optional)

Font of column header in the grid control.

`colHeaderFontSize` (Optional)

Size of column header text in the grid control, in points.

`colHeaderItalic` (Optional)

Default: `No`

`Yes`: Displays column headers in italics.

`colHeaderBold` (Optional)

Default: `No`

`Yes`: Displays column headers in bold.

`colHeaderTextColor` (Optional)

Color of the grid control column headers.

`bgColor` (Optional)

Background color of the grid control.

`selectColor` (Optional)

Background color for a selected item.

`selectMode` (Optional)

Default: `Browse`

Selection mode for items in the grid control.

`Edit`: User can edit grid data. Selecting a cell opens the editor for the cell type.

`Single`: User selections are limited to the selected cell.

`Row`: User selections automatically extend to the row that contains the selected cell.

`Column`: User selections automatically extend to the column that contains the selected cell.

`Browse`: User can only browse grid data.

`maxRows` (Optional)

Maximum number of rows to display in the grid.

`notSupported` (Optional)

Text to display if the page that contains the Java applet-based `CFFORM` control is opened by a browser that does not support Java or has Java support disabled.

pictureBar (Optional)

Default: No

Yes: Images for Insert, Delete, and Sort buttons.

insertButton (Optional)

Default: Insert

Takes effect only if selectmode="edit".

deleteButton (Optional)

Default: Delete

Takes effect only if selectmode="edit".

sortAscendingButton (Optional)

Default: A -> Z

Sort button text.

sortDescendingButton (Optional)

Default: Z -> A

Sort button text.

Tag Chooser Dialog Box

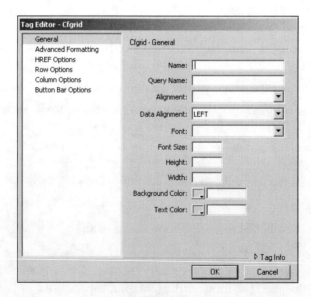

Figure B.48

CFGRIDCOLUMN

```
<cfgridcolumn name = "column_name"
header = "header"
width = "column_width"
font = "column_font"
fontSize = "size"
italic = "Yes" or "No"
bold = "Yes" or "No"
textColor = "web color" or "expression"
bgColor = "web color" or "expression"
href = "URL"
hrefKey = "column_name"
target = "URL_target"
select = "Yes" or "No"
display = "Yes" or "No"
type = "type"
headerFont = "font_name"
headerFontSize = "size"
headerItalic = "Yes" or "No"
headerBold = "Yes" or "No"
headerTextColor = "web color"
dataAlign = "position"
headerAlign = "position"
numberFormat = "format"
values = "Comma-separated strings and/or numeric range"
valuesDisplay = "Comma-separated strings and/or numeric range"
valuesDelimiter = "delimiter character">
```

Description

Used with the CFGRID tag, in a CFFORM tag. Use this tag to specify column data in a CFGRID control. The font and alignment attributes of CFGRIDCOLUMN override global font or alignment settings defined in CFGRID. For textColor and bgColor, expressions can be used to dynamically set colors. Syntax for an expression is as follows:

```
(CX operator string ? true_condition : false_condition)
```

Attributes

name (Required)

Name of the grid column element. If the grid uses a query, the column name must specify the name of a query column.

header (Optional)

Default: Yes

Column header text. Used only if CFGRID colHeaders = "Yes".

width (Optional)

Column head width.

Column width, in pixels. To render a grid, you must specify a value for one of these: CFGRIDCOLUMN width, CFGRID colheaders, or CFGRID autowidth.

font (Optional)

As specified by CFGRID.

Font of data in the column.

fontSize (Optional)

Size of text in the column.

italic (Optional)

Default: Yes. Displays grid control text in italics.

bold (Optional)

Default: Yes. Displays grid control text in bold.

textColor (Optional)

Color of the grid element text in the column, or an expression to manipulate color.

bgColor (Optional)

Color of the background of the grid column, or an expression to manipulate color.

href (Optional)

Relative or absolute URL to associate with a grid item.

hrefKey (Optional)

Name of the query column when the grid uses a query. Column becomes Key regardless of CFGRID selectmode value.

target (Optional)

Frame in which to open the link specified in href.

select (Optional)

Default: Yes. User can select the column in the grid control.

No: User cannot edit the column, regardless of CFGRID insert and delete values. If CFGRID selectMode = "Row" or "Browse", this value is ignored.

display (Optional)

Default: Yes

No: Hides the column.

`type` (Optional)

image: Grid displays an image that corresponds to the value in the column (a built-in ColdFusion image name, or an image in the cfide\classes directory or subdirectory referenced with a relative URL). If the image is larger than the column cell, it is clipped to fit. Built-in image names are as follows: `cd`, `computer`, `document`, `element`, `folder`, `floppy`, `fixed`, `remote`, `numeric` (user can sort grid data numerically), `boolean` (column displays as checkbox; if cell is editable, user can change checkmark), and `string_noCase` (user can sort grid data as case-insensitive text).

`headerFont` (Optional)

Column header font.

`headerFontSize` (Optional)

Column header text size, in pixels.

`headerItalic` (Optional)

Default: `Yes`. Displays the column header in italics.

`headerBold` (Optional)

Default: `Yes`. Displays the column header in bold.

`headerTextColor` (Optional)

Color of the grid control column header text.

Options: same as for `textColor` attribute.

`dataAlign` (Optional)

Column data alignment: `Left`, `Right`, or `Center`.

`headerAlign` (Optional)

Column header text alignment: `Left`, `Right`, or `Center`.

`numberFormat` (Optional)

Format for displaying numeric data in a grid. See "`numberFormat` Mask Characters."

`values` (Optional)

Formats cells in the column as drop-down list boxes. Allows for the specification of items in a drop-down list. Syntax used is `values = "grape, apple, orange, 1-10"`.

`valuesDisplay` (Optional)

Maps elements in the `values` attribute to string to display them in a drop-down list.

`valuesDelimiter` (Optional)

Default: , (comma)

Delimiter in `values` and `valuesDisplay` attributes.

Tag Chooser Dialog Box

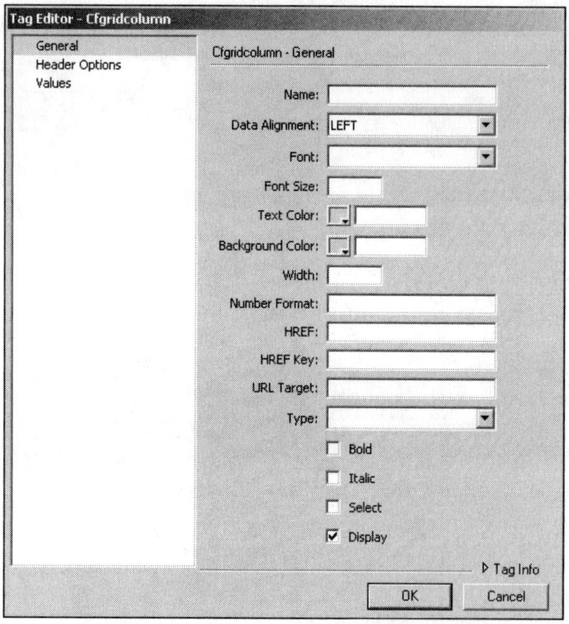

Figure B.49

CFGRIDROW

```
<cfgridrow data = "col1, col2, ...">
```

Description

Populates a grid that is constructed outside of a `CFQUERY` tag. This tag does not execute if the `query` attribute is specified in `CFGRID`.

Attributes

`data` (Required)

Delimited list of column values. If a value contains a comma, it must be escaped with another comma.

Tag Chooser Dialog Box

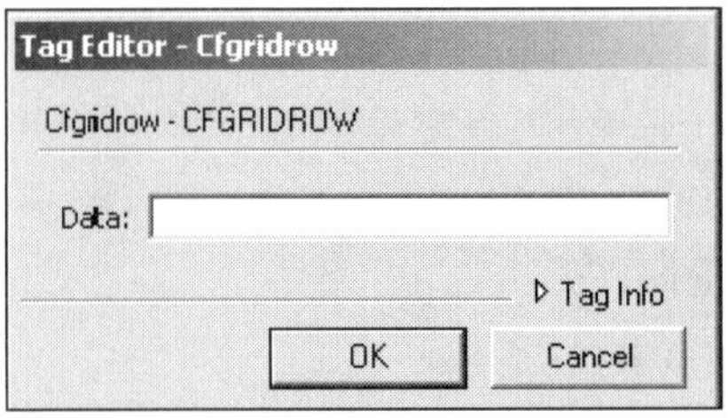

Figure B.50

CFGRIDUPDATE

```
<cfgridupdate
grid = "gridname"
dataSource = "data source name"
tableName = "table name"
username = "data source username"
password = "data source password"
tableOwner = "table owner"
tableQualifier = "qualifier"
keyOnly = "Yes" or "No">
```

Description

Used within a CFGRID tag. Updates data sources directly from the edited grid data. This tag provides a direct interface with your data source.

This tag applies delete row actions first, then insert row actions, then update row actions. If it encounters an error, it stops processing rows.

Attributes

grid (Required)

Name of CFGRID form element that is the source for the update action.

dataSource (Required)

Name of the data source for the update action.

tableName (Required)

Name of the table to update. For Oracle drivers, the entry must be upper-case. For Sybase drivers, the entry is case-sensitive—it must be the same case used when the table was created.

username (Optional)

Overrides the username value specified in ODBC setup.

password (Optional)

Overrides the password value specified in ODBC setup.

tableOwner (Optional)

Table owner, if supported.

tableQualifier (Optional)

Table qualifier, if supported. It is used for SQL Server and Oracle drivers to specify the name of database that contains the table.

Intersolv dBASE driver: Directory of DBF files.

Intersolv dBASE driver: Directory of DBF files.

keyOnly (Optional)

Default: No

Applies to the update action:

Yes: The WHERE criteria are limited to the key values.

No: The WHERE criteria include key values and the original values of changed fields.

Tag Chooser Dialog Box

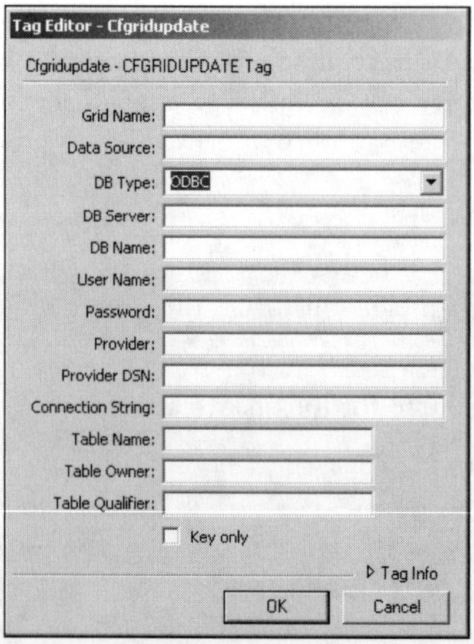

Figure B.51

CFINPUT

```
<cfinput type = "input_type"
name = "name"
value = "initial_value"
required = "Yes" or "No"
range = "min_value, max_value"
validate = "data_type"
onValidate = "javascript_function"
pattern = "regexp"
message = "validation_msg"
onError = "text"
size = "integer"
maxLength = "integer"
checked
passThrough = "HTML_attributes">
```

Description

Used within the CFFORM tag to place radio buttons, checkboxes, or text boxes on a form. Provides input validation for the specified control type.

Attributes

type (Optional)

Default: text

text: Creates a text box control.

radio: Creates a radio button control.

checkbox: Creates a checkbox control.

password: Creates a password entry control.

name (Required)
Name for form input element.

value (Required)
Initial value for form input element.

required (Optional)
Default: No

range (Optional)
Minimum and maximum value range, separated by a comma.
If type = "text" or "password", this applies only to numeric data.

validate (Optional)

Verifies a value's format:

date: U.S. date: mm/dd/yyyy.

eurodate: European date: dd/mm/yyyy.

time: Time: hh:mm:ss.

float: Floating point entry.

integer: Integer entry.

telephone: Telephone: ###-###-####. Separator: hyphen or blank. Area code and exchange must begin with a digit 1–9.

zipcode: (U.S. formats only) 5-digit: ##### or 9-digit: #####-####. Separator: hyphen or blank.

creditcard: Strips out blanks and dashes; uses the mod10 algorithm.

social_security_number: ###-##-####. Separator: hyphen or blank.

regular_expression: Matches input against a regular expression specified by the pattern attribute.

onValidate (Optional)

Custom JavaScript function to validate user input. The form object, input object, and input object values are passed to the routine, which should return True if validation succeeds, and False otherwise. If used, the validate attribute is ignored.

pattern (Required if validate = "regular_expression")

JavaScript regular expression pattern to validate input. Omit leading and trailing slashes.

message (Optional)

Message text to display if validation fails.

onError (Optional)

Custom JavaScript function to execute if validation fails.

size (Optional)

Size of input control. Ignored if type = "radio" or "checkbox".

maxLength (Optional)

Maximum length of text entered, if type = "Text" or "password".

checked (Optional)

Selects a control. No value is required. Applies if type = "radio" or "checkbox".

passThrough (Optional)

HTML attributes that are not supported by CFINPUT. If you specify an attribute and value, they are passed to the HTML code generated for the tag.

Tag Chooser Dialog Box

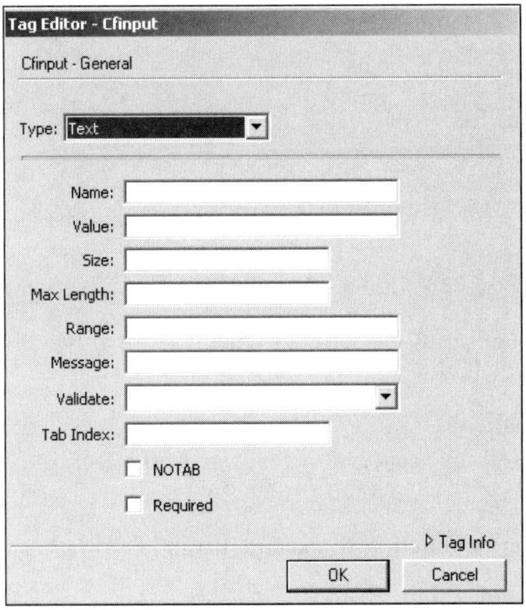

Figure B.52

CFSELECT

```
<cfselect name = "name"
required = "Yes" or "No"
message = "text"
onError = "text"
size = "integer"
multiple = "Yes" or "No"
query = "queryname"
selected = "column_value"
value = "text"
display = "text"
passThrough = "HTML_attributes">
</cfselect>
```

Description

Constructs a drop-down list box form control. Used within a CFFORM tag. You can populate the list from a query, or by using the HTML OPTION tag.

To ensure that a selected list box item persists across postbacks, use the CFFORM preserveData attribute with a list generated from a query. (This strategy works only with data that is populated from a query.)

Attributes

name (Required)
Name of the form.

size (Optional)
Number of entries in the drop-down list.

required (Optional)
Default: No

Yes: A list element must be selected when the form is submitted. Minimum size of the select box is 2.

message (Optional)
Message to display if required = "Yes" and no selection is made.

onError (Optional)
Custom JavaScript function to execute if validation fails.

multiple (Optional)
Default: No

Yes: Allow ability to select multiple elements in the drop-down list.

query (Optional)
Name of query to populate the drop-down list.

selected (Optional)
Value to display as preselected in the drop-down list. Must match an entry in the value attribute. This attribute applies only if list items are generated from a query.

value (Optional)
Query column value for the list element. Used with the query attribute.

display (Optional)
Value of the value attribute. Displays the query column and is used with the query attribute.

passThrough (Optional)

HTML attribute(s) that are not explicitly supported by CFSELECT. If you specify an attribute and its value, they are passed to HTML code that is generated for the CFSELECT tag.

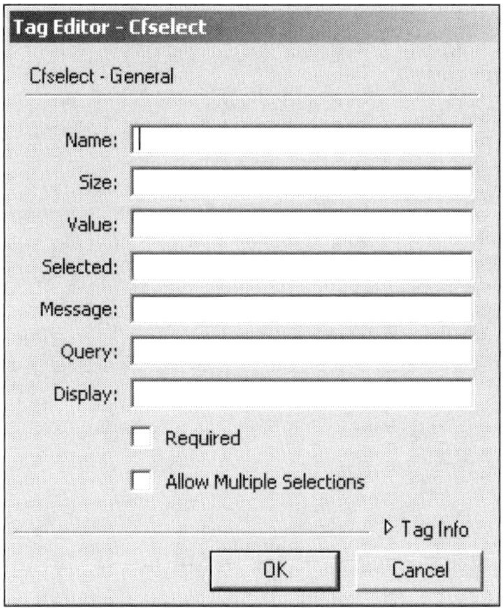

Figure B.53

CFSLIDER

```
<cfslider name = "name"
label = "text"
refreshLabel = "Yes" or "No"
range = "min_value, max_value"
scale = "uinteger"
value = "integer"
onValidate = "script_name"
message = "text"
onError = "text"
height = "integer"
width = "integer"
vSpace = "integer"
hSpace = "integer"
align = "alignment"
tickMarkMajor = "Yes" or "No"
tickMarkMinor = "Yes" or "No"
```

```
tickMarkImages = "URL1, URL2, URLn"
tickMarkLabels = "Yes" or "No" or "list"
lookAndFeel = "motif" or "windows" or "metal"
vertical = "Yes" or "No"
bgColor = "color"
textColor = "color"
font = "font_name"
fontSize = "integer"
italic = "Yes" or "No"
bold = "Yes" or "No"
notSupported = "text">
```

Description

Used within a CFFORM tag. Places a slider control, for selecting a numeric value from a range, in a ColdFusion form. The slider moves over the slider groove. As the user moves the slider, the current value displays.

Attributes

name (Required)

Name of the CFSLIDER control.

label (Optional)

Label to display with the control; for example, "Volume." This displays: "Volume %value%". To reference the value, use %value%. If %% is omitted, the slider value displays directly after the label.

refreshLabel (Optional)

Default: Yes

Yes: When the user moves the slider, the label is refreshed.

range (Optional)

Default: "0,100"

Numeric slider range values. Separate values with a comma.

scale (Optional)

Unsigned integer. Defines the slider scale, within a range. For example, if range = "0,1000" and scale = "100", the display values are: 0, 100, 200, 300, ... Signed and unsigned integers in ColdFusion are in the range 2,147,483,648 to 2,147,483,647.

value (Optional)

Minimum in range. Starting slider setting must be within the range values.

onValidate (Optional)

Custom JavaScript function to validate user input; in this case, a change to the default slider value. Specify only the function name.

message (Optional)

Message text to appear if validation fails.

onError (Optional)

Custom JavaScript function to execute if validation fails. Specify only the function name.

height (Optional)

Slider control height, in pixels.

width (Optional)

Slider control width, in pixels.

vSpace (Optional)

Vertical spacing above and below the slider, in pixels.

hSpace (Optional)

Horizontal spacing to the left and right of the slider, in pixels.

align (Optional)

Alignment of slider: top, left, bottom, baseline, texttop, absbottom, middle, absmiddle, or right.

tickMarkMajor (Optional)

Default: No

Yes: Render major tickmarks in slider scale.

No: No major tickmarks.

Major tickmarks display at intervals specified by the scale.

tickMarkMinor (Optional)

Default: No

Yes: Render minor tickmarks in slider scale.

No: No minor tickmarks.

Minor tickmarks display between major tickmarks.

tickMarkImages (Optional)

Comma-delimited list of URLs specifying images in the slider tickmark scale. If you do not specify enough values, the last value is repeated for the remaining tickmarks. If you specify too many values, extra values are ignored.

`tickMarkLabels` (Optional)

Default: `No`

`Yes`: Numeric tickmarks based on the value of the `range` and `scale` attributes.

`No`: Prevents label text from displaying.

Comma-delimited list of strings for tickmark labels; for example, "ten, twenty, thirty, forty." If you do not specify enough values, the last value is repeated for the remaining tickmarks. If you specify too many values, extra values are ignored.

`lookAndFeel` (Optional)

Default: `windows`

`motif`: Renders the slider using Motif style.

`windows`: Renders the slider using Windows style.

`metal`: Renders the slider using Java Swing style.

If the platform does not support your choice, the tag defaults to the platform's default style.

`vertical` (Optional)

Default: `No`

`Yes`: Renders the slider in the browser vertically. You must set the `width` and `height` attributes; ColdFusion does not automatically swap width and height values.

`No`: Renders the slider horizontally.

`bgColor` (Optional)

Background color of the slider label. For a hex value, use the form: `bgColor = "##xxxxxx"`, where x = 0–9 or A–F; use two hash marks or none.

`textColor` (Optional)

Options: Same as for `bgcolor` attribute.

`font` (Optional)

Font name for label text.

`fontSize` (Optional)

Font size for label text, in points.

`italic` (Optional)

Default: No

Yes: Italicizes label text.

No: Normal text.

`bold` (Optional)

Default: No

Yes: Bolds label text.

No: Normal text.

`notSupported` (Optional)

Text to display if a page that contains a Java applet-based `CFFORM` control is opened by a browser that does not support Java or has Java support disabled.

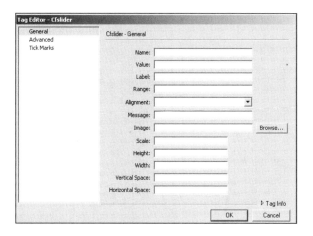

Figure B.54

CFTEXTINPUT

```
<cftextinput
name = "name"
value = "text"
required = "Yes" or "No"
range = "min_value, max_value"
validate = "data_type"
onValidate = "script_name"
message = "text"
onError = "text"
size = "integer"
font = "font_name"
```

```
fontSize = "integer"
italic = "Yes" or "No"
bold = "Yes" or "No"
height = "integer"
width = "integer"
vSpace = "integer"
hSpace = "integer"
align = "alignment"
bgColor = "color"
textColor = "color"
maxLength = "integer"
notSupported = "text">
```

Description

Puts a single-line text entry box in a CFFORM, and controls font characteristics.

Attributes

name (Required)
  Name for the CFTEXTINPUT control.

value (Optional)
  Initial value to display in the text control.

required (Optional)
  Default: No

  Yes: The user must enter or change text.

range= (Optional)
  Minimum-maximum value range, delimited by a comma. Valid only for numeric data.

validate (Optional)
  Validates to pre-set criteria embedded into CFTEXTINPUT.

onValidate (Optional)
  Custom JavaScript function to validate user input. The form object, input object, and input object value are passed to the routine, which should return True if validation succeeds; False otherwise. The validate attribute is ignored.

pattern (Required if validate = "regular_expression")
  JavaScript regular expression pattern to validate input. Omit leading and trailing slashes.

message (Optional)

Message text to display if validation fails.

onError (Optional)

Custom JavaScript function to execute if validation fails.

size (Optional)

Number of characters displayed before the horizontal scrollbar displays.

font (Optional)

Font name for the text.

fontSize (Optional)

Font size for text.

italic (Optional)

Default: No

Set text in italics.

bold (Optional)

Default: No

Set text in bold.

height (Optional)

Default: 40

Height of the control, in pixels.

width (Optional)

Width of the control, in pixels.

vSpace (Optional)

Vertical spacing of the control, in pixels.

hSpace (Optional)

Horizontal spacing of the control, in pixels.

align (Optional)

Alignment of the text entry box: Alignment: Left, Right, Bottom, Top, TextTop, Middle, AbsMiddle, Baseline, and AbsBottom.

bgColor (Optional)

Background color of the control.

textColor (Optional)

Text color for the control. Options: same as for the bgcolor attribute.

maxLength (Optional)

The maximum length of text entered.

notSupported (Optional)

Text to display if a page that contains a Java applet-based CFFORM control is opened by a browser that does not support Java, or has Java support disabled.

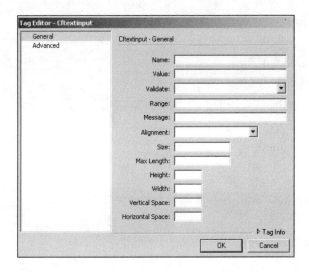

Figure B.55

CFTREE

```
<cftree name = "name"
required = "Yes" or "No"
delimiter = "delimiter"
completePath = "Yes" or "No"
appendKey = "Yes" or "No"
highlightHref = "Yes" or "No"
onValidate = "script_name"
message = "text"
onError = "text"
lookAndFeel = "motif" or "windows" or "metal"
font = "font"
fontSize = "size"
italic = "Yes" or "No"
bold = "Yes" or "No"
height = "integer"
width = "integer"
vSpace = "integer"
hSpace = "integer"
```

```
align = "alignment"
border = "Yes" or "No"
hScroll = "Yes" or "No"
vScroll = "Yes" or "No"
notSupported = "text">
</cftree>
```

Description

Inserts a tree control in a form. Validates user selections. Used within a CFTREE tag block. You can use a ColdFusion query to supply data to the tree.

Attributes

name (Required)

Name for the tree control.

required (Optional)

Default: No

Yes: User must select an item in the tree control.

delimiter (Optional)

Default: \\ (double slash).

Character to separate elements in the form variable path.

completePath (Optional)

Default: No

Tree name is returned as root.

Yes: Passes the root part of the treename.path form variable when CFTREE is submitted.

No, or omitted: Root level of the form variable is not passed; path value starts with the first node.

appendKey (Optional)

Default: Yes

Yes: When used with href, passes the CFTREEITEMKEY variable with the value of the selected tree item in the URL to the application page specified in the CFFORM action attribute.

highlightHref (Optional)

Default: Yes

Yes: Highlights links that are associated with a CFTREEITEM with a URL attribute value.

No: Disables highlights.

onValidate (Optional)

JavaScript function to validate user input. The form object, input object, and input object values are passed to the specified routine, which should return True if validation succeeds; False, otherwise.

message (Optional)

Message to display if validation fails.

onError (Optional)

JavaScript function to execute if validation fails.

lookAndFeel (Optional)

Default: windows

motif: Renders the slider in Motif style.

windows: Renders the slider in Windows style.

metal: Renders the slider in Java Swing style.

font (Optional)

Font name for the data in the tree control.

fontSize (Optional)

Font size for the text in the tree control, in points.

italic (Optional)

Default: No

Yes: Displays tree control text in italics.

bold (Optional)

Default: No

Yes: Displays tree control text in bold.

height (Optional)

Default: 320

Tree control height, in pixels.

width (Optional)

Default: 200

Tree control width, in pixels.

vSpace (Optional)

Vertical margin above and below the tree control, in pixels.

hSpace (Optional)

Horizontal spacing to the left and right of the tree control, in pixels.

align (Optional)

Alignment options: Left, Right, Bottom, Top, TextTop, Middle, AbsMiddle, Baseline, and AbsBottom.

border (Optional)

Default: Yes, creates a border.

hScroll (Optional)

Default: Yes

Yes: Permits horizontal scrolling.

vScroll (Optional)

Default: Yes

Yes: Permits vertical scrolling.

notSupported (Optional)

Message to display if the page that contains Java applet-based form control is opened by a browser that does not support Java, or has Java support disabled.

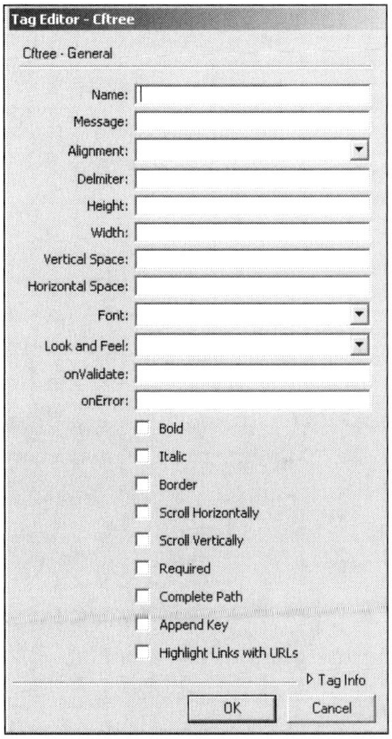

Figure B.56

CFTREEITEM

```
<cftreeitem
value = "text"
display = "text"
parent = "parent_name"
img = "filename"
imgopen = "filename"
href = "URL"
target = "URL_target"
query = "queryname"
queryAsRoot = "Yes" or "No"
expand = "Yes" or "No">
```

Description

Populates a form tree control, created with the CFTREE tag, with elements. To display icons, you can use the img values that ColdFusion provides, or reference your own icons.

Attributes

value (Required)

Value passed when CFFORM is submitted. When populating a tree with data from a CFQUERY, specify columns in a delimited list.

display (Optional)

Tree item label. When populating a tree with data from a query, specify names in a delimited list. For example, display = "dept_name,emp_name".

parent (Optional)

Value for the tree item parent.

img (Optional)

Image name, filename, or file URL for the tree item icon. You can specify a custom image. To do so, include the path and file extension; for example, img = "../images/page1.gif". To specify more than one image in a tree, or an image at the second or subsequent level, use commas to separate names, corresponding to level; for example, img = "folder,document" img = ",document" (example of second level).

imgopen (Optional)

Icon displayed with open tree item. You can specify the icon filename with a relative path. You can use a ColdFusion image.

href (Optional)

URL to associate with a tree item or query column for a tree that is populated from a query. If href is a query column, its value is the value populated by query. If href is not recognized as a query column, it is assumed that its text is an HTML href. When populating a tree with data from a query, hrefs can be specified in a delimited list.

target (Optional)

Target attribute of href URL. When populating a tree with data from a query, specify the target in a delimited list: target = "FRAME_BODY,_blank".

query (Optional)

Query name to generate data for the tree item.

queryAsRoot (Optional)

Defines a query as the root level. This avoids having to create another parent CFTREEITEM.

expand (Optional)

Default: Yes

Yes: Expands the tree to show tree item children.

No: Keeps the tree item collapsed.

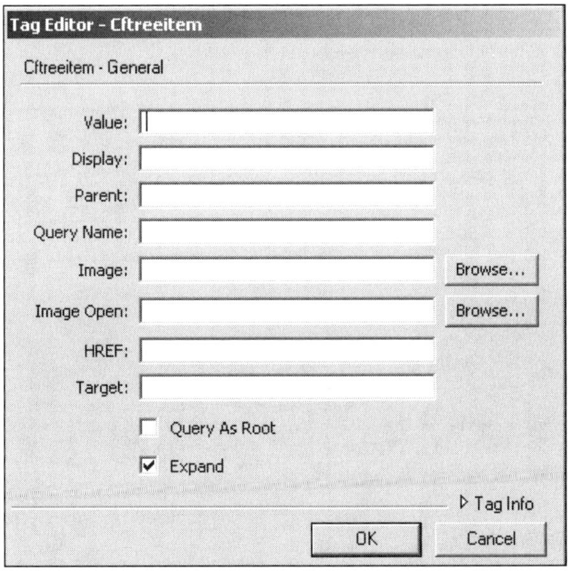

Figure B.57

Security Tags

CFLOGIN

```
<cflogin
idletimeout = "name"
applicationtoken = "token"
cookiedomain = "domain">
```

Description

A container for the code that authenticates the user. The body of this tag checks the user-provided ID and password against a data source, LDAP directory, or other repository of login identification. The body of this tag must include a CFLOGINUSER tag to establish the authenticated user's identity in ColdFusion.

Attributes

idletimout (Optional)
    Number of seconds for the login session to last before timing out.

applicationtoken (Optional)
    Application token to associate with login.

cookiedomain(Optional)
    Domain of cookie to use with login.

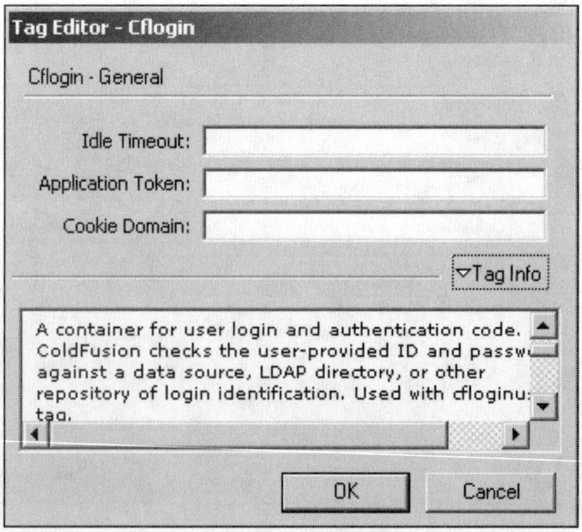

Figure B.58

CFLOGINUSER

```
<cfloginuser
name = "name"
password = "password"
roles = "roles">
```

Description

Identifies an authenticated user to ColdFusion. Specifies the user ID and roles. Used within a CFLOGIN tag.

Attributes

name (Required)
    User ID.

password (Required)
    Password.

roles (Optional)
    A comma-delimited list of role identifiers. ColdFusion processes spaces in a list element as part of the element.

Figure B.59

CFLOGOUT

```
<cflogout>
```

Description

Used inside of a CFLOGIN, this tag logs the current user out. Removes knowledge of the user ID and roles from the server. If you do not use this tag, the user is automatically logged out when the session ends.

Utility Tags

CFASSOCIATE

```
<cfassociate baseTag = "base_tag_name"
dataCollection = "collection_name">
```

Description

Allows subtag data to be saved with a base tag. Applies only to custom tags.

Attributes

BaseTag (Required)
  Base tag name.

DataCollection (Optional)
  Structure in which the base tag stores subtag data.

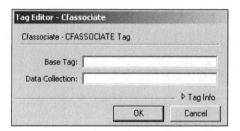

Figure B.60

CFCACHE

```
<cfcache action = "action"
username = "username"
password = "password"
protocol = "protocol_name"
directory = "directory_name_for_map_file"
cacheDirectory = "directory_name_for_cached_pages"
expireURL = "wildcarded_URL_reference"
port = "port_number">
```

Description

Stores a copy of a page on the server and/or client computer, to improve page rendering performance. To do this, the tag creates temporary files that contain the static HTML returned from a ColdFusion page.

Use this tag if it is not necessary to get dynamic content each time a user accesses a page.

You can use `CFCACHE` for simple URLs and URLs that contain URL parameters.

Attribute

`Action` (Optional)

> Default: `cache`
>
> `cache`: Server-side caching.
>
> `flush`: Refresh cached page. You can also specify the `directory` and `expireURL` attributes.
>
> `clientCache`: Browser caching.
>
> `optimal`: Optimal caching; combination of server-side and browser caching.

`username` (Optional)

> If required for basic authentication, a username.

`password` (Optional)

> If required for basic authentication, a password.

`protocol` (Optional)

> Default: `http://`
>
> Protocol used to create pages from the cache.

`directory` (Optional)

> Directory of the current page.
>
> Absolute directory path. Contains `cfcache.map` to use if `action = "flush"`.

`cacheDirectory` (Optional)

> Directory of the current page.
>
> Absolute path of the directory in which to cache pages.

`expireURL` (Optional)

> Flush all mappings.
>
> Used with `action = "flush"`. Takes a URL reference, including wildcards, that ColdFusion matches against all mappings in the `cfcache.map` file. For example: `"foo.cfm"` matches `"foo.cfm"`; `"fi.cfm?*"` matches `"fi.cfm?x = 5"` and `"fi.cfm?x = 9 "`.

port (Optional)

Default: 80

Port number of the web server from which a page is requested. Useful because CFCACHE calls CFHTTP. If the port is specified correctly in the internal call to CFHTTP, the URL of each retrieved document is resolved to preserve links.

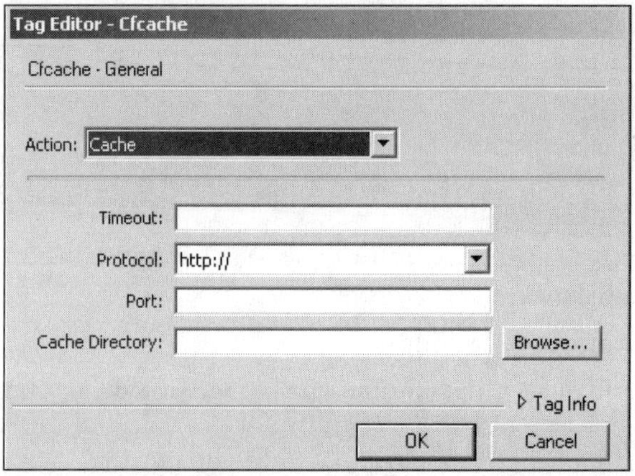

Figure B.61

CFDUMP

```
<cfdump var = #variable#
expand = "Yes or No">
```

Description

Outputs variables and their values. Useful for debugging. You can display the contents of simple and complex variables, objects, and components.

Attributes

var (Required)

Variable to display. Enclose a variable name in hash signs. These kinds of variables yield meaningful CFDUMP displays: array, CFC, Java object, simple, query, structure, UDF, wddx, and xml.

expand (Optional)

Default: Yes

Yes: In Internet Explorer and Mozilla, this automatically closes expanded views.

No: Leaves expanded views expanded.

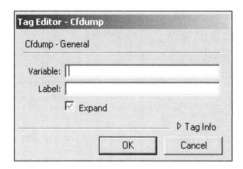

Figure B.62

CFEXECUTE

```
<cfexecute name = "ApplicationName"
arguments = "CommandLine Arguments"
outputFile = "Output file name"
timeout = "Timeout interval in seconds">
...
</cfexecute>
```

Description

Executes a ColdFusion developer-specified process on a server.

Attributes

name (Required)

Absolute path of the application to execute. On Windows, you must specify an extension; for example, C:\myapp.exe.

arguments (Optional)

Command-line variables passed to the application. If specified as a string, it is processed as follows:

Windows: Passed to process control subsystem for parsing.

Unix: Tokenized into an array of arguments. The default token separator is a space; you can delimit arguments that have embedded spaces with double quotation marks.

If passed as array, it is processed as follows:

Windows: Elements are concatenated into a string of tokens, separated by spaces.

Unix: Elements are copied into an array of `exec()` arguments.

outputFile (Optional)

File to direct program output to. If not specified, output is displayed on the page from which it was called.

timeout (Optional)

Default: 0

Length of time, in seconds, that the ColdFusion executing thread waits for a spawned process.

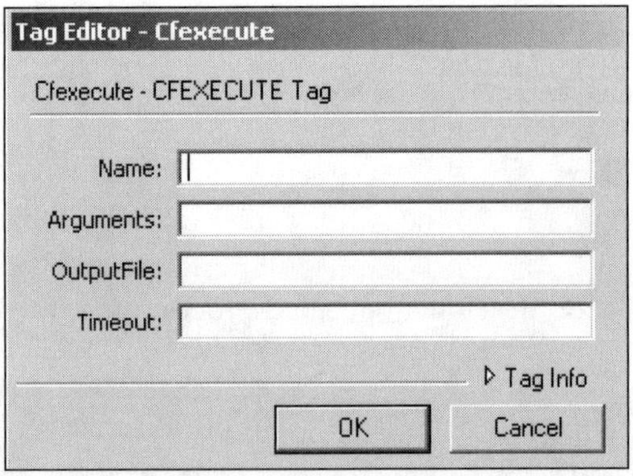

Figure B.63

CFFLUSH

```
<cfflush interval = "integer number of bytes">
```

Description

Flushes currently available data to the client. CFFLUSH cannot be used on the same page as CFLOCATION.

Attributes

interval (Optional)

Sets an integer that flushes output each time the set number of bytes becomes available. HTML headers and data that are already available when the tag is executed are omitted from the count.

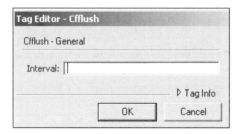

Figure B.64

CFHTMLHEAD

```
<cfhtmlhead text = "text">
```

Description

Writes text to the head section of a generated HTML page. It is useful for embedding JavaScript code, or putting other HTML tags, such as meta, link, title, or base, in an HTML page header.

Attributes

text (Required)

Text to add to the <head> area of an HTML page.

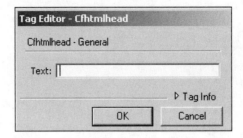

Figure B.65

CFINCLUDE

```
<cfinclude template = "template_name">
```

Description

Embeds references to ColdFusion pages in CFML. You can embed CFINCLUDE tags recursively. For another way to encapsulate CFML, see CFMODULE. (A ColdFusion page sometimes used to be called a ColdFusion template.)

Attributes

template (Required)
    A logical path to a ColdFusion page.

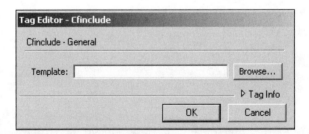

Figure B.66

CFLOCK

```
<cflock timeout = "timeout in seconds"
scope = "Application" or "Server" or "Session"
name = "lockname"
throwOnTimeout = "Yes" or "No"
type = "readOnly" or "exclusive ">
<!--- CFML to be synchronized --->
</cflock>
```

Description

Ensures the integrity of shared data. Instantiates the following kinds of locks:

- Exclusive: Allows single-thread access to the CFML constructs in its body. The tag body can be executed by one request at a time. No other requests can start executing within the tag while a request has an exclusive lock. ColdFusion issues exclusive locks on a first-come, first-served basis.

- Read-only: Allows multiple requests to access CFML constructs within the tag body concurrently. Uses a read-only lock only when shared data is read and not modified. If another request has an exclusive lock on shared data, the new request waits for the exclusive lock to be released.

Attributes

timeout (Required)

Maximum length of time, in seconds, to wait to obtain a lock. If the lock is obtained, tag execution continues. Otherwise, behavior depends on the throwOnTimeout attribute value.

scope (Optional)

Mutually exclusive with the name attribute. Choices are Application, Server, and Session.

name (Optional)

Lock name. Only one request can execute within this tag with a given name. Permits synchronizing access to resources from different parts of an application. Lock names are global to a ColdFusion server. They are shared among applications and user sessions, but not clustered servers. This is mutually exclusive with the scope attribute. It cannot be an empty string.

throwOnTimeout (Optional)

Default: Yes

How timeout conditions are handled.

Yes: Exception is generated for the timeout.

No: Execution continues past this tag.

type (Optional)

Default: exclusive

read-only: Lets more than one request read shared data.

exclusive: Lets one request read or write shared data.

Limit the scope of code that updates shared data structures, files, and CFXs. Exclusive locks are required to ensure the integrity of updates, but read-only locks are faster. In a performance-sensitive application, substitute read-only locks for exclusive locks where possible, such as when reading shared data.

Figure B.67

CFLOG

```
<cflog text = "text"
log = "log type"
file = "filename"
type = "message type"
thread = "yes"
date = "yes"
time = "yes"
application = "application name yes or no">
```

Description

Writes a message to a log file.

Attributes

`text` (Required)

Message text to log.

`log` (Optional)

If you omit the `file` attribute, this writes messages to the standard log file. This is ignored if you specify the `file` attribute.

`Application`: Writes to Application.log; normally used for application-specific messages.

`Scheduler`: Writes to Scheduler.log; normally used to log the execution of scheduled tasks.

`file` (Optional)

Message file. Specify only the main part of the filename. For example, to log to the Testing.log file, specify "Testing". The file must be located in the default log directory. You cannot specify a directory path. If the file does not exist, it is created automatically with the suffix .log.

`type` (Optional)

Default: Information

Type (severity) of the message: `Information`, `Warning`, `Error`, `Fatal Information`.

`thread` (Optional)

Default: `Yes`

A thread ID identifies that the internal service thread logged a message. Because a service thread normally services a CFML page request to completion, then moves on to the next queued request, the thread ID roughly indicates which request logged a message. This can help diagnose server activity patterns.

`Yes`: Log thread ID.

`No`: Deprecated. This option throws an error.

`dato` (Optional)

Default: `Yes`

`Yes`: Log the system date.

`No`: Deprecated. This option throws an error.

`time` (Optional)

Default: `Yes`

`Yes`: Log the system time.

`No`: Deprecated. This option throws an error.

`application` (Optional)

Default: `Yes`

`Yes`: Log application name, if it is specified in a `CFAPPLICATION` tag.

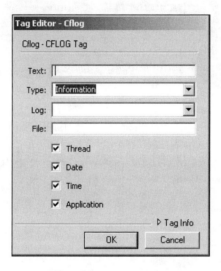

Figure B.68

CFMODULE

```
<cfmodule
template = "path"
name = "tag_name"
attributeCollection = "collection_structure"
attribute_name1 = "valuea"
attribute_name2 = "valueb"
...>
```

Description

Invokes a custom tag for use in ColdFusion application pages. This tag processes custom tag name conflicts.

Attributes

`template` (Required unless the `name` attribute is used)

Mutually exclusive with the `name` attribute. A path to the page that implements the tag.

Relative path: Expanded from the current page.

Absolute path: Expanded using ColdFusion mapping.

`name` (Required unless the `template` attribute is used)

Mutually exclusive with the `template` attribute. A custom tag name, in the form `Name.Name.Name....` Identifies the subdirectory, under the ColdFusion tag root directory, that contains the custom tag page. For example (Windows format): `<cfmodule name = macromedia.Forums40.GetUserOptions">`. This identifies the page GetUserOptions.cfm in the directory CustomTags\macromedia\Forums40 under the ColdFusion root directory.

`attributeCollection` (Optional)

A collection of key-value pairs that represent attribute names and values. You can specify multiple key-value pairs. You can specify this attribute only once.

`attribute_name` (Optional)

Attribute for a custom tag. You can include multiple instances of this attribute to specify the parameters of a custom tag.

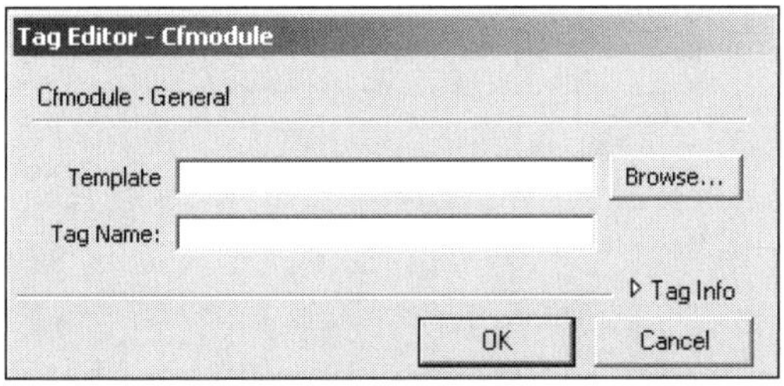

Figure B.69

CFREGISTRY

action = "getAll"

```
<cfregistry action = "getAll"
branch = "branch"
type = "data type"
name = "query name"
sort = "criteria">
```

action = "get"

```
<cfregistry action = "get"
branch = "branch"
entry = "key or value"
variable = "variable"
type = "data type">
```

action = "set"

```
<cfregistry action = "set"
  branch = "branch"
  entry = "key or value"
  type = "value type"
  value = "data">
```

action = "delete"

```
<cfregistry action = "delete"
  branch = "branch"
  entry = "key or value">
```

Description

This tag is deprecated for the Unix platform.

Reads, writes, and deletes keys and values in the system Registry. Provides persistent storage of client variables.

Attributes

action (Required)

Acceptable actions are getall, get, set, and delete.

branch (Required)

Name of a registry branch.

type (Optional)

Default: String

Data type of registry key.

`name` (Required)

Name of the recordset that will contain returned keys and values.

`sort` (Optional)

Default: `ASC`

Sorts query column data (case-insensitive). Sorts on `Entry`, `Type`, and `Value` columns as text. Can also be `DESC`. Specify a combination of columns from query output, in a comma-delimited list. For example, `sort = "value desc, entry asc"`.

`entry` (Required)

Registry value to access.

`variable` (Required)

Variable in which to put values.

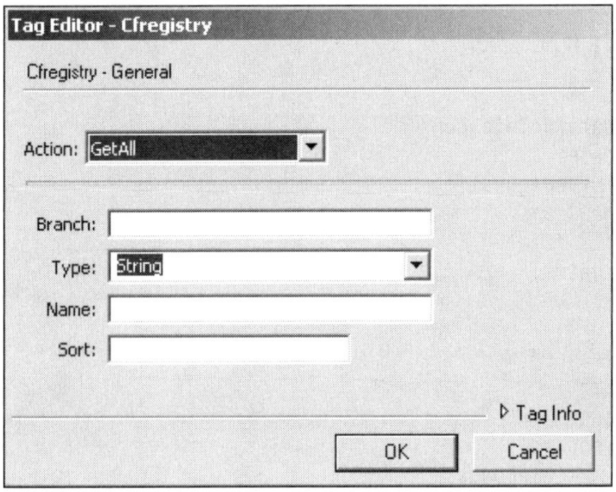

Figure B.70

CFSAVECONTENT

```
<cfsavecontent variable = "variable name">
content
</cfsavecontent>
```

Description

Saves everything in the body of the `CFSAVECONTENT` tag, including the results of evaluating expressions and executing custom tags, in the specified variable.

Attributes

variable (Required)

Name of the variable in which to save generated content within the tag.

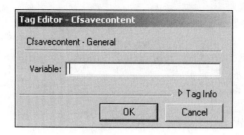

Figure B.71

CFSCHEDULE

```
<cfschedule
action = "update/delete/run"
task = "taskname"
operation = "HTTPRequest"
file = "filename"
path = "path_to_file"
startDate = "date"
startTime = "time"
url = "URL"
publish = "Yes" or "No"
endDate = "date"
endTime = "time"
interval = "seconds"
requestTimeOut = "seconds"
username = "username"
password = "password"
resolveURL = "Yes" or "No"
proxyServer = "hostname"
port = "port_number"
proxyPort = "port_number">
```

Description

Provides a programmatic interface to the ColdFusion scheduling engine. You can run a page at scheduled intervals, with the option to write out static HTML pages. This lets users access pages that publish data, such as reports, without waiting while a database transaction is performed to populate the page.

Information that the user supplies includes the scheduled ColdFusion page to execute, the time and frequency of execution, and whether to publish the task output. If the output is published, a path and file are specified.

Attributes

`action` (Required)

    `delete`: Deletes the task.

    `update`: Creates the task, if one does not exist.

    `run`: Executes the task.

`task` (Required)

    Name of the task.

`operation` (Required if `action` = `"update"`)

    Task that the scheduler performs. For static page generation, the only option is `HTTPRequest`.

`file` (Required if `publish` = `"Yes"`)

    Filename for the published file.

`path` (Required if `publish` = `"Yes"`)

    Path location for the published file.

`startDate` (Required if `action` = `"update"`)

    Date when task scheduling starts.

`startTime` (Required if `action` = `"update"`)

    Time when task scheduling starts (in seconds).

`url` (Required if `action` = `"update"`)

    URL to execute.

`publish` (Optional)

    Default: `No`

    `Yes`: Save the result to a file.

`endDate` (Optional)

    Date when the scheduled task ends.

`endTime` (Optional)

    Time when the scheduled task ends (in seconds).

interval (Required if action = "update")

Default: One hour

Interval at which task is scheduled. Options include seconds (minimum is 60), once, daily, weekly, and monthly.

requestTimeOut (Optional)

Customizes requestTimeOut for the task operation. Can be used to extend default timeout, for operations that require more time to execute.

username (Optional)

Username, if URL is protected.

password (Optional)

Password, if URL is protected.

proxyServer (Optional)

Host name or IP address of a proxy server.

resolveURL (Optional)

Default: No

Yes: Resolve links in the result page to absolute references.

port (Optional)

Default: 80

Server port number from which the task is scheduled. If resolveURL = "yes", retrieved document URLs that specify a port number are automatically resolved, to preserve links in the retrieved documents.

proxyPort (Optional)

Default: 80

Port number on proxy server from which the task is requested. When used with resolveURL, URLs of retrieved documents that specify a port number are automatically resolved, to preserve links in the retrieved documents.

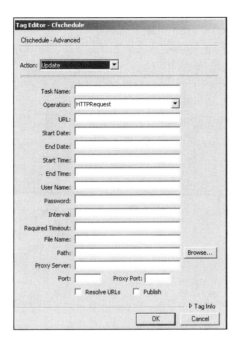

Figure B.72

CFSETTING

```
<cfsetting enableCFoutputOnly = "Yes" or "No"
showDebugOutput = "Yes" or "No"
requestTimeOut = "seconds">
```

Description

Controls aspects of page processing, such as the output of HTML code in pages.

Attributes

enableCFoutputOnly (Required)

Yes: Blocks output of HTML that is outside CFOUTPUT tags.

showDebugOutput (Optional)

Default: Yes

No: Suppresses debugging information that would otherwise display at the end of the generated page.

`RequestTimeout` (Optional)

Integer; number of seconds.

Time limit, after which ColdFusion processes the page as an unresponsive thread. Overrides the timeout set in the ColdFusion Administrator.

Figure B.73

CFTRACE

```
<cftrace
abort = "Yes or No"
category = "string"
inline = "Yes or No"
text = "string"
type = "format"
var = "variable_name">
</cftrace>
```

Description

Displays and logs debugging data about the state of an application at the time the CFTRACE tag executes. Tracks runtime logic flow, variable values, and execution time. Displays output on the application page or, in Dreamweaver 5 and later, in a Studio window. ColdFusion logs CFTRACE output to the file logs\cftrace.log, in the ColdFusion installation directory.

Attributes

`abort` (Optional)

Default: `No`

`Yes`: Calls `CFABORT` tag when the tag is executed.

`category` (Optional)

User-defined string for identifying trace groups.

`inline` (Optional)

Default: `No`

`Yes`: Flushes output to page as the tag executes. Within a `CFSILENT` tag, this option suppresses message display, but trace summary information is included in the debug output.

`text` (Optional)

User-defined string or simple variable. Outputs to the `CFLOG` text attribute.

`type` (Optional)

Default: Information

Output format. Outputs to the `CFLOG type` attribute. Possible types are Information, Warning, Error, and Fatal Information.

`var` (Optional)

The name of one simple or complex variable to display. A complex variable, such as a structure, is displayed in `CFDUMP` format. Useful for displaying a temporary value, or a value that does not display on any CFM page.

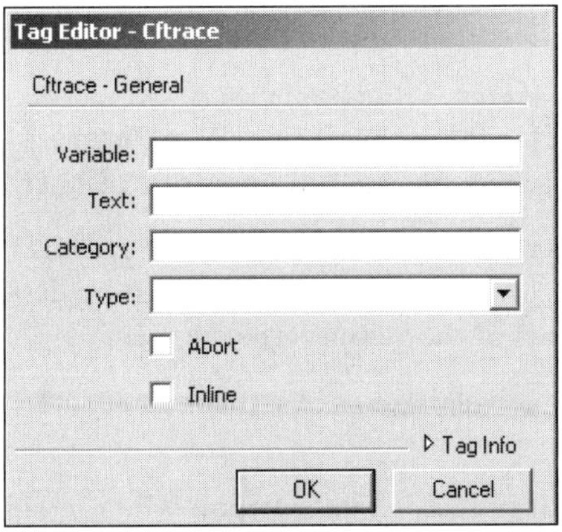

Figure B.74

CFWDDX

```
<cfwddx action = "action"
input = "input data"
output = "result variable name"
topLevelVariable = "top level variable name for javascript"
useTimeZoneInfo = "Yes" or "No"
validate = "Yes" or "No" >
```

Description

Serializes and deserializes CFML data structures to the XML-based WDDX
format. The WDDX is an XML vocabulary for describing complex data structures in a standard, generic way. Implementing it lets you use the HTTP protocol to exchange information among application server platforms, application
servers, and browsers.

This tag generates JavaScript statements to instantiate JavaScript objects
equivalent to the contents of a WDDX packet or CFML data structure. It
interoperates with Unicode.

Attributes

action (Required)

cfml2wddx: Serialize CFML to WDDX.

wddx2cfml: Deserialize WDDX to CFML.

cfml2js: Serialize CFML to JavaScript.

wddx2js: Deserialize WDDX to JavaScript.

input (Required)
A value to process.

output (Required if action = "wddx2cfml")
Name of the variable for output. If action = "WDDX2JS" or "CFML2JS", and
this attribute is omitted, the result is output in an HTML stream.

TopLevelVariable (Required if action = "wddx2js/cfml2js")
Name of the top-level JavaScript object created by deserialization. The
object is an instance of the WddxRecordset object.

useTimeZoneInfo (Optional)

Default: Yes

Whether to output time-zone information when serializing CFML to
WDDX.

Yes: The hour-minute offset, represented in ISO8601 format, is output.

No: The local time is output.

`validate` (Optional)

Default: No

Applies if `action` = `"wddx2cfml/wddx2js"`.

Yes: Validates WDDX input with an XML parser using WDDX DTD. If parser processes the input without error, the packet is deserialized. Otherwise, an error is thrown.

No: No input validation.

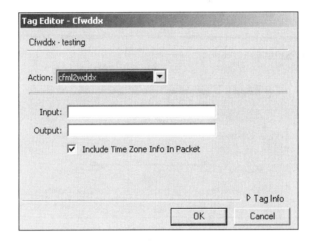

Figure B.75

External System Tags

CFIMPORT

```
<cfimport
taglib = "taglib-location"
prefix = "custom"
webservice = "URL"/>
```

Description

Copies a Java Server Page (JSP) tag library into a CFML page. A JSP tag library is a packaged set of tag handlers that conform to the JSP 1.1 tag extension API.

Attributes

taglib (Required)

Tag library URI, such as a URL path to a JAR in a web application (/WEB-INF/lib/sometags.jar) or a path to the tag library descriptor (/sometags.tld).

prefix (Required)

Prefix by which to access imported JSP tags on the CFML page. To import tags directly, specify an empty value, "". Use this to create server-side versions of common HTML tags.

webservice (Optional)

URL of a WSDL file.

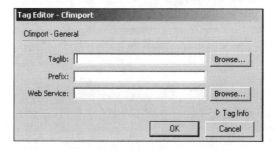

Figure B.76

CFOBJECT

action = *"com"*

```
<cfobject
  type = "com"
  action = "action"
  class = "program_ID"
  name = "text"
  context = "context"
  server = "server_name">
```

action = *"component"*

```
<cfobject
  type = "component"
  name = "variable name"
  component = "component name">
```

```
action = "corba"

  <cfobject
    type = "corba"
    context = "context"
    class = "file or naming service"
    name = "text"
    locale = "type-value arguments">
```

```
action = "java"

  <cfobject
    type = "Java"
    action = "Create"
    class = "Java class"
    name = "object name">
```

```
action = "webservice"

  <cfobject
    webservice= "http://....?wsdl" or "name set in Administrator"
    name = "myobjectname">
```

Description

Used to create and manipulate COM objects, ColdFusion components, web service objects, and Java and Enterprise JavaBeans. This can also be used to call a method on a registered CORBA object.

This tag may be disabled under ColdFusion Basic Security, in the ColdFusion Administrator. On Unix, this tag does not support COM objects.

Attributes

cfobject type = "com"

action (Required)

create: Instantiates a COM object (typically a DLL) before invoking methods or properties.

connect: Connects to a COM object (typically an EXE) running on the server.

class (Required)

Component ProgID for the object to invoke.

name (Required)

String; name for the instantiated component.

context (Optional)

Possible contexts are InProc, Local, and Remote.

On Windows: If not specified, this tag uses the Registry setting. Server required if context = "Remote".

cfobject type = "component"

name (Required)
String; name for the instantiated component.

component (Required)
Name of component to instantiate.

cfobject type = "corba"

context (Required)

IOR: ColdFusion uses Interoperable Object Reference (IOR) to access a CORBA server.

NameService: ColdFusion uses naming service to access a server. This option is valid only with the InitialContext of a VisiBroker orb.

class (Required)

If context = "IOR", the name of the file that contains a string-formatted version of IOR. ColdFusion must be able to read this file.

If context = "NameService", the period-delimited naming context for the naming service; for example IBM.Dept.Doc.empobject.

name (Required)
String; name for the instantiated component. An application uses it to reference the CORBA object's methods and attributes.

Locale (Optional)
Sets arguments for a call to init_orb. Use of this attribute is specific to VisiBroker orbs. It is available in C++, Version 3.2. The value must be in the form locale = " -ORBagentAddr 199.99.129.33 -ORBagentPort 19000". Each type-value pair must start with a hyphen.

cfobject type = "java"

action (Required)
Create: Creates a Java or WebLogic Environment object.

class (Required)
Java class.

name (Required)
    String; name for the instantiated component.

cfobject type = "webservice"

Webservice (Required)
    URI of web service.

action (Required)
class (Required)
name (Required)

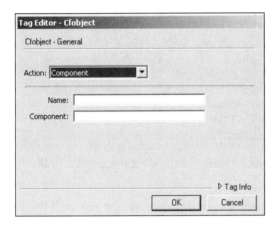

Figure B.77

CFREPORT

```
<cfreport report = "report_path"
dataSource = "ds_name"
type = "type"
timeout = "number of seconds"
orderBy = "result_order"
username = "username"
password = "password"
formula = "formula">
</cfreport>
```

Description

Runs a predefined Crystal Reports report. Applies only to Windows systems. Uses the CFCRYSTAL.exe file to generate reports. Sets parameters in the Crystal Reports engine according to its attribute values.

Attributes

`datasource` (Optional)

Name of the registered ODBC or native data source.

`type` (Optional)

Default: `standard`

Possible types are `standard`, `netscape`, and `microsoft`.

`timeout` (Optional)

Maximum time, in seconds, in which a connection must be made to a Crystal Report

`report` (Required)

Report path. Stores Crystal Reports files in the same directories as ColdFusion page files.

`orderBy` (Optional)

Orders results according to your specifications.

`username` (Optional)

Username required for entry into database where the report is created. Overrides default settings for the data source in ColdFusion Administrator.

`password` (Optional)

Password that corresponds to the username required for database access. Overrides the default settings for the data source in the ColdFusion Administrator.

`formula` (Optional)

One or more named formulas. Terminate each formula with a semicolon. Use the format `formula = "formulaname1 = 'formula1';formulaname2 = 'formula2';"`. If you use a semicolon in a formula, you must escape it by typing it twice (`;;`); for example, `formula = "Name1 = 'Val_1a;;Val_1b'; Name2 = 'Val2';"`.

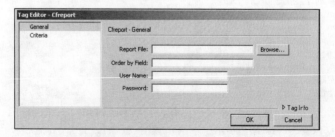

Figure B.78

CFXML

```
<CFXML
variable="xmlVarName"
caseSensitive="yes" or "no">
```

Description

Creates a ColdFusion XML document object that contains the markup in the tag body. This tag can include XML and CFML tags. ColdFusion processes the CFML code in the tag body, then assigns the resulting text to an XML document object variable.

Attributes

variable

The name of an XML variable.

caseSensitive (Optional)

Default: no

yes: Maintains the case of document elements and attributes.

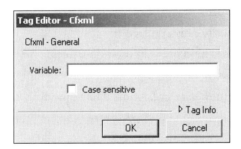

Figure B.79

CFCOLLECTION

```
<cfcollection
action = "action"
collection = "collection name"
path = "path_of_verity_directory"
language = "language"
name = "queryname">
```

Description

Creates and administers collections returned by a search engine. An internal collection can be created either with the CFCOLLECTION tag or in the ColdFusion Administrator, which calls the CFCOLLECTION tag. An external collection can be created using a native Verity indexing tool, such as Vspider or MKVDK.

Attributes

action (Optional)

Default: list

create: Creates and maps a directory for a collection, composed of the path attribute value and the collection attribute value.

repair: Fixes data corruption in a collection. You must permit the repair operation to complete before another action on the collection begins.

delete: Deletes a map to a collection.

optimize: Optimizes the structure and contents of a collection for searching; recovers space.

list: Gets the attributes of one or more collections; one row per collection.

collection (Required)

This tag automatically maps collections.

A collection name. The name can include spaces.

path (Required if action = "create")

Absolute path to the Verity collection. The value to provide depends on the action attribute. If action = create, provide the directory path to the collection.

language (Optional)

Default: English

Other languages can be used, but this requires the appropriate (European or Asian) Verity Locales language pack.

name (Required if action = "list")

Name for the query results returned by the list action.

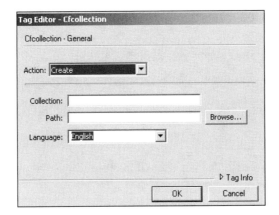

Figure B.80

CFINDEX

```
<cfindex
collection = "collection_name"
action = "action"
type = "type"
title = "title"
key = "ID"
body = "body"
custom1 = "custom_value"
custom2 = "custom_value"
URLpath = "URL"
extensions = "file_extensions"
query = "query_name"
recurse = "Yes" or "No"
language = "language">
```

Description

Populates collections with indexed data. A collection must be created before it can be populated. An internal collection can be created with either the CFCOLLECTION tag or the ColdFusion Administrator. An external collection can be created using a native Verity indexing tool, such as Vspider or MKVDK.

Attributes

collection (Required)

Collection name, or, for unregistered collections, an absolute path; for example, collection = "e:\collections\personnel".

action (Optional)

update: Updates a collection and adds a key to the index. I recommend that you avoid using the **CFLOCK** tag with this option; see the Usage section.

delete: Deletes data in the entities specified by the **type** attribute.

purge: Deletes all keys from a collection.

refresh: Purges a collection, then updates it.

type (Optional)

custom, if query attribute is specified; **file**, otherwise.

file: Using the **key** attribute value of the query result as input, applies the action to filenames or file paths.

path: Using the **key** attribute value of the query result as input, applies the action to filenames or file paths that pass the extensions filter.

custom: If **action** = "update" or "delete", this applies the action to custom entities in query results.

title (Required if **type** = "Custom")

Title for collection. Query column name for type and a valid query name. Permits searching collections by title or displaying a separate title from the key.

key (Required if **action** = "update/delete/refresh")

Default: (empty string)

If **type** = "file" or **type** = "path", the absolute path.

If **type** = "custom", a query column name (typically, the primary key column name).

If **type** = any other value, a query column name.

This attribute is required for the actions listed unless you intend for its value to be an empty string.

body (Required if **type** = "custom")

ASCII text to index.

Query column name(s), if name is specified in the query. You can specify columns in a delimited list.

custom1 (Optional)

Custom field in which you can store data during an indexing operation. Specify a query column name for **type**, and a query name.

custom2 (Optional)

Usage is the same as for **custom1**.

URLpath (Optional)

If type="file" or "path", specifies the URL path. When the collection is searched with CFSEARCH, this pathname is prefixed to filenames and returned as the url attribute.

extensions (Optional)

Default: HTM, HTML, CFM, CFML, DBM, DBML

Delimited list of file extensions that ColdFusion uses to index files. If type = "Path" . "*.", this returns files with no extension. For example, the following code returns files with a listed extension or no extension: extensions = ".htm, .html, .cfm, .cfml, "*.".

query (Optional)

Query against which the collection is generated.

recurse (Optional)

Default: No

Yes: If type = "path", directories below the path specified in the key are included in the indexing operation.

language (Optional)

Default: English

If a language other than English is selected, it requires the appropriate (European or Asian) Verity Locales language pack.

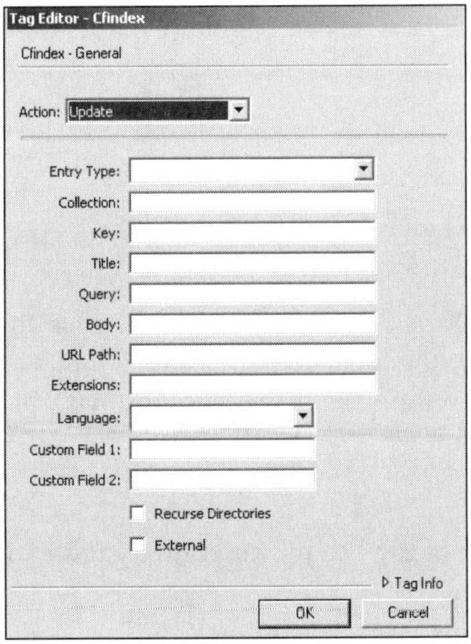

Figure B.81

CFSEARCH

```
<cfsearch name = "search_name"
collection = "collection_name"
type = "criteria"
criteria = "search_expression"
maxRows = "number"
startRow = "row_number"
language = "language">
```

Description

Executes a search against data that is indexed in a Verity collection. This tag and the CFINDEX tag encapsulate the Verity indexing and searching utilities.

A collection must be created and indexed before this tag can return search results.

Attributes

name (Required)

Name of the search query. For a registered collection, specify the collection name. For an unregistered collection, specify an absolute path.

collection (Required)

Path(s) and/or registered collection name(s). Registered names are listed in the ColdFusion Administrator, Verity Collections, and Verity Server pages. To specify multiple collections, use a comma-delimited list; for example, CFUSER, e:\collections\personnel. If you specify multiple collections, all must be registered by one search engine (ColdFusion or K2Server).

type (Optional)

Default: simple

simple: STEM and MANY operators are used.

explicit: Operators must be invoked explicitly.

criteria (Optional)

Search criteria. Follows the syntax rules of the type attribute. If you pass a mixed-case entry in this attribute, the search is case-sensitive. If you pass all uppercase or all lowercase, the search is case-insensitive.

maxRows (Optional)

Default: All

Maximum number of rows to return in query results, placed within double quotation marks.

`startRow` (Optional)

    Default: 1

    First row number to get.

`language` (Optional)

    Default: `English`

    For languages other than English you must install the appropriate ColdFusion International Verity language pack.

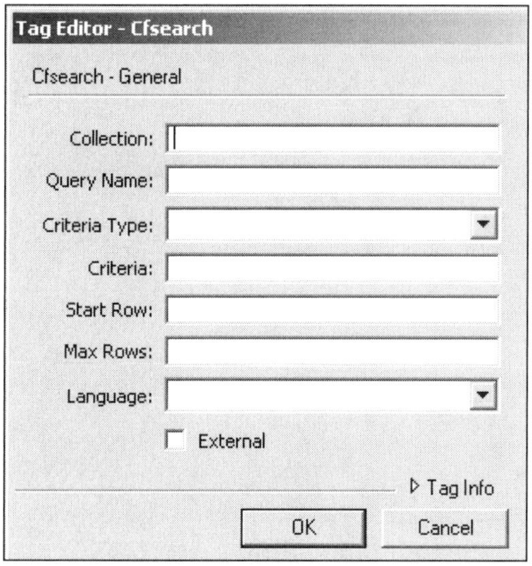

Figure B.82

C

Dreamweaver MX Keyboard Shortcuts

THIS APPENDIX CONTAINS THE WINDOWS AND MACINTOSH keyboard shortcuts for Dreamweaver MX, using the Macromedia Standard keyboard shortcut set. You can choose different shortcut sets or create new ones using the Keyboard Shortcuts dialog box. To open the Keyboard Shortcuts dialog box in Dreamweaver, select the Edit menu, Keyboard Shortcuts.

For more information about creating custom keyboard shortcuts, see Chapter 22, "Customizing Dreamweaver for ColdFusion Development."

The keyboard shortcuts in this chapter are abbreviated. The following list describes the abbreviations:

- CTRL—Ctrl key on PC
- CMMD—Command key on Macintosh
- Ins—Insert key on PC and Macintosh
- Del—Delete key on PC and Macintosh
- Bksp—Backspace key on PC and Macintosh

The keyboard shortcuts are organized into basic, code editing, site panel, and visual design view shortcuts.

> **Exporting HTML Shortcuts**
> To export an HTML copy of a Dreamweaver keyboard shortcut set, open the Keyboard Shortcuts dialog box and click the Export as HTML button.

Dreamweaver MX Keyboard Shortcuts

Table C.1 lists the basic Dreamweaver MX keyboard shortcuts for both the Windows and Macintosh platforms.

Table C.1 **Dreamweaver MX Basic Keyboard Shortcuts**

Description	Windows Shortcut	Macintosh Shortcut
New File	CTRL+N	CMMD+N
Open File	CTRL+O	CMMD+O
Open in Frame	CTRL+Shift+O	CMMD+Shift+O
Close File	CTRL+W	CMMD+W
Save File	CTRL+S	CMMD+S
Save As	CTRL+Shift+S	CMMD+Shift+S
Check Links	Shift+F8	Shift+F8
Undo	CTRL+Z	CMMD+Z
Redo	CTRL+Y	CMMD+Y
Cut	CTRL+X	CMMD+X
Paste	CTRL+V	CMMD+V
Copy	CTRL+C	CMMD+C
Select All	CTRL+A	CMMD+A
Find	CTRL+F	CMMD+F
Find Again	F3	F3
Switch Views	CTRL+`	CMMD+`
Bold	CTRL+B	CMMD+B
Italic	CTRL+I	CMMD+I
Refresh Design View	F5	F5
Live Data View	CTRL+Shift+R	CMMD+Shift+R
Head Content	CTRL+Shift+W	CMMD+Shift+W
Server Debug	CTRL+Shift+G	CMMD+Shift+G
Next Document	CTRL+Tab	CMMD+Tab
Previous Document	CTRL+Shift+Tab	CMMD+Shift+Tab

Description	Windows Shortcut	Macintosh Shortcut
Open Using Dreamweaver Help	F1	F1
Open Using ColdFusion Help	CTRL+F1	CMMD+F1
Open Reference	Panel	Shift+F1

Table C.2 lists the Dreamweaver MX code-editing keyboard shortcuts for both the Windows and Macintosh platforms.

Table C.2 **Dreamweaver MX Code Editing Keyboard Shortcuts**

Description	Windows Shortcut	Macintosh Shortcut
Toggle Breakpoint	CTRL+Alt+B	CMMD+OPT+B
Copy HTML	CTRL+Shift+C	CMMD+Shift+C
Paste HTML	CTRL+Shift+V	CMMD+Shift+V
Select Parent Tag	CTRL+[	CMMD+[
Select Child Tag	CTRL+]	CMMD+]
Go to Line	CTRL+G	CMMD+G
Show Code Hints	CTRL+Space	CMMD+Space
Indent Code	CTRL+Shift+>	CMMD+Shift+>
Outdent Code	CTRL+Shift+<	CMMD+Shift+<
Print Code	CTRL+P	CMMD+P
Delete Word Left	CTRL+Bksp	CMMD+Bksp
Delete Word Right	CTRL+Del	CMMD+Del
Select Line Up	Shift+Up Arrow	Shift+Up Arrow
Select Line Down	Shift+Down Arrow	Shift+Down Arrow
Character Select Left	Shift+Left Arrow	Shift+Left Arrow
Character Select Right	Shift+Right Arrow	Shift+Right Arrow
Select to Page Up	Shift+PageUp	Shift+PageUp
Select to Page Down	Shift+PageDown	Shift+PageDown
Move Word Left	CTRL+Left Arrow	CMMD+Left Arrow
Move Word Right	CTRL+Right Arrow	CMMD+Right Arrow
Select Word Left	CTRL+Shift+Left Arrow	CMMD+Shift+Left Arrow
Select Word Right	CTRL+Shift+Right Arrow	CTRL+Shift+Right Arrow

continues

Table C.2   **Continued**

Description	Windows Shortcut	Macintosh Shortcut
Move to Line Start	HOME	HOME
Move to Line End	END	END
Select to Start of Line	Shift+HOME	Shift+HOME
Select to End of Line	Shift+END	Shift+END
Select to Start of File	CTRL+Shift+HOME	CMMD+Shift+HOME
Select to End of File	CTRL+Shift+END	CMMD+Shift+END

Table C.3 lists the Dreamweaver MX site panel keyboard shortcuts for both the Windows and Macintosh platforms.

Table C.3   **Dreamweaver MX Site Panel Keyboard Shortcuts**

Description	Windows Shortcut	Macintosh Shortcut
Open Site Files	F8	F8
Open Site Map	Alt+F8	OPT+F8
Refresh Site Files	F5	F5
Create New Site File	CTRL+Shift+N	CMMD+Shift+N
Create New Site Folder	CTRL+Alt+Shift+N	CTRL+Alt+Shift+N
Refresh Local Site	Shift+F5	Shift+F5
Refresh Remote Site	Alt+F5	OPT+F5
View Site Map as Root	CTRL+Shift+R	CMMD+Shift+R
Link to New File in Site Map	CTRL+Shift+N	CMMD+Shift+N
Get File from Remote Server	CTRL+Shift+D	CMMD+Shift+D
Put File from Remote Server	CTRL+Shift+U	CMMD+Shift+U
Check File into Source Control	CTRL+Alt+Shift+U	CMMD+Alt+Shift+U
Check Out from Source Control	CTRL+Alt+Shift+D	CMMD+OPT+Shift+D
Search Results	CTRL+Shift+F	CMMD+Shift+F
Validate Results	CTRL+Shift+F7	CMMD+Shift+F7

Description	Windows Shortcut	Macintosh Shortcut
Target Browser Check	CTRL+Shift+F8	CMMD+Shift+F8
Link Checker	CTRL+Shift+F9	CMMD+Shift+F9
Site Reports	CTRL+Shift+F10	CMMD+Shift+F10
FTP Log	CTRL+Shift+F11	CMMD+Shift+F11

Table C.4 lists the Dreamweaver MX visual design view keyboard shortcuts for both the Windows and Macintosh platforms.

Table C.4 **Dreamweaver MX Visual Design View Keyboard Shortcuts**

Description	Windows Shortcut	Macintosh Shortcut
Hide All Visual Aids	CTRL+Shift+I	CMMD+Shift+I
Show Rulers	CTRL+Alt+R	CMMD+OPT+R
Show Grid	CTRL+Alt+G	CMMD+OPT+G
Snap to Grid	CTRL+Alt+Shift+G	CMMD+OPT+Shift+G
Play Plugin	CTRL+Alt+P	CMMD+OPT+P
Stop Plugin	CTRL+Alt+X	CMMD+OPT+X
Play All Plugins	CTRL+Alt+Shift+P	CMMD+OPT+Shift+P
Stop All Plugins	CTRL+Alt+Shift+X	CMMD+OPT+Shift+X
Show Panels	F4	F4
Insert Tag	CTRL+E	CMMD+E
Insert Image	CTRL+Alt+I	CMMD+OPT+I
Insert Flash movie	CTRL+Alt+F	CMMD+OPT+F
Insert Shockwave movie	CTRL+Alt+D	CMMD+OPT+D
Insert Table	CTRL+Alt+T	CMMD+OPT+T
Insert Editable Region Object	CTRL+Alt+V	CMMD+OPT+V
Insert Named Anchor	CTRL+Alt+A	CMMD+OPT+A
Insert Line Break	Shift+Return	Shift+Return
Insert Non-Breaking Space	CTRL+Shift+Space	CMMD+Shift+Space
Modify Page Properties	CTRL+J	CMMD+J
Modify Selection Properties	CTRL+Shift+J	CMMD+Shift+J

continues

Table C.4 **Continued**

Description	Windows Shortcut	Macintosh Shortcut
Quick Tag Editor	CTRL+T	CMMD+T
Insert Link	CTRL+L	CMMD+L
Delete Link	CTRL+Shift+L	CMMD+Shift+L
Select All Table Rows	CTRL+A	CMMD+A
Merge Cells	CTRL+Alt+M	CMMD+OPT+M
Split Cells	CTRL+Alt+S	CMMD+OPT+S
Insert Row	CTRL+M	CMMD+M
Insert Column	CTRL+Shift+A	CMMD+Shift+A
Delete Row	CTRL+Shift+M	CMMD+Shift+M
Delete Column	CTRL+Shift+-	CMMD+Shift+-
Increase Row Span	CTRL+Shift+]	CMMD+Shift+]
Decrease Row Span	CTRL+Shift+[	CMMD+Shift+[
Align Left	CTRL+Shift+1	CMMD+Shift+1
Align Right	CTRL+Shift+3	CMMD+Shift+3
Align Top	CTRL+Shift+4	CMMD+Shift+4
Align Bottom	CTRL+Shift+6	CMMD+Shift+6
Make Same Height	CTRL+Shift+7	CMMD+Shift+7
Make Same Width	CTRL+Shift+9	CMMD+Shift+9
Add Object to Library	CTRL+Shift+B	CMMD+Shift+B
Add Object to Timeline	CTRL+Alt+Shift+T	CMMD+OPT+Shift+T
Add Keyframe to Timeline	F6	F6
Indent Text	CTRL+Alt+]	CMMD+OPT+]
Outdent Text	CTRL+Alt+[	CMMD+Alt+[
Set Paragraph Format to None	CTRL+0	CMMD+0
Set Paragraph Format to Paragraph	CTRL+Shift+P	CMMD+Shift+P
Set Paragraph Format to Header 1	CTRL+Shift+1	CMMD+Shift+1
Set Paragraph Format to Header 2	CTRL+Shift+2	CMMD+Shift+2

Description	Windows Shortcut	Macintosh Shortcut
Set Paragraph Format to Header 3	CTRL+Shift+3	CMMD+Shift+3
Set Paragraph Format to Header 4	CTRL+Shift+4	CMMD+Shift+4
Set Paragraph Format to Header 5	CTRL+Shift+5	CMMD+Shift+5
Set Paragraph Format to Header 6	CTRL+Shift+6	CMMD+Shift+6
Align Paragraph Left	CTRL+Alt+Shift+L	CMMD+Alt+Shift+L
Align Paragraph Right	CTRL+Alt+Shift+R	CMMD+Alt+Shift+R
Align Paragraph Center	CTRL+Alt+Shift+C	CMMD+Alt+Shift+C
Align Paragraph Justify	CTRL+Alt+Shift+J	CMMD+Alt+Shift+J
Edit CSS Style Sheet	CTRL+Shift+E	CMMD+Shift+E
Check Spelling	Shift+F7	Shift+F7
Start Recording Commands	CTRL+Shift+X	CMMD+Shift+X
Open Insert Panel	CTRL+F2	CMMD+F2
Open Preferences Dialog	CTRL+U	CMMD+U
Open Properties Panel	CTRL+F3	CMMD+F3
Open Answers Panel	Alt+F1	OPT+F1
Open CSS Styles Panel	Shift+F11	Shift+F11
Open HTML Styles Panel	CTRL+F11	CMMD+F11
Open Behaviors	Shift+F3	Shift+F3
Open Tag Inspector	F9	F9
Open Snippets Panel	Shift+F9	Shift+F9
Open Reference Panel	Shift+F1	Shift+F1
Open Databases Panel	CTRL+Shift+F10	CMMD+Shift+F10

continues

Table C.4 **Continued**

Description	Windows Shortcut	Macintosh Shortcut
Open Bindings Panel	CTRL+F10	CMMD+F10
Open Server Behaviors Panel	CTRL+F9	CMMD+F9
Open Components Panel	CTRL+F7	CMMD+F7
Open Site Panel	F8	F8
Open Assets Panel	F11	F11
Open Code Inspector Panel	F10	F10
Open Frames Panel	Shift+F2	Shift+F2
Open History Panel	Shift+F10	Shift+F10
Open Layers Panel	F2	F2
Open SiteSpring Panel	F7	F7
Open Timelines Panel	Alt+F9	OPT+F9
Show All Panels	F4	F4

Index

C

VOICES THAT MATTER

HOW TO CONTACT US

VISIT OUR WEB SITE

WWW.NEWRIDERS.COM

On our web site, you'll find information about our other books, authors, tables of contents, and book errata. You will also find information about book registration and how to purchase our books, both domestically and internationally.

EMAIL US

Contact us at: **nrfeedback@newriders.com**

- If you have comments or questions about this book
- To report errors that you have found in this book
- If you have a book proposal to submit or are interested in writing for New Riders
- If you are an expert in a computer topic or technology and are interested in being a technical editor who reviews manuscripts for technical accuracy

Contact us at: **nreducation@newriders.com**

- If you are an instructor from an educational institution who wants to preview New Riders books for classroom use. Email should include your name, title, school, department, address, phone number, office days/hours, text in use, and enrollment, along with your request for desk/examination copies and/or additional information.

Contact us at: **nrmedia@newriders.com**

- If you are a member of the media who is interested in reviewing copies of New Riders books. Send your name, mailing address, and email address, along with the name of the publication or web site you work for.

BULK PURCHASES/CORPORATE SALES

The publisher offers discounts on this book when ordered in quantity for bulk purchases and special sales. For sales within the U.S., please contact: Corporate and Government Sales (800) 382-3419 or **corpsales@pearsontechgroup.com**. Outside of the U.S., please contact: International Sales (317) 581-3793 or **international@pearsontechgroup.com**.

WRITE TO US

New Riders Publishing
201 W. 103rd St.
Indianapolis, IN 46290-1097

CALL/FAX US

Toll-free (800) 571-5840
If outside U.S. (317) 581-3500
Ask for New Riders
FAX: (317) 581-4663

New Riders

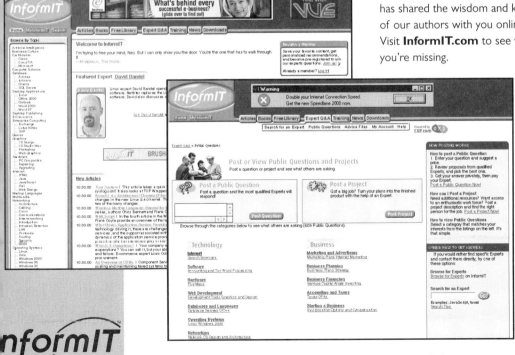

DREAMWEAVER MX

Inside Dreamweaver MX
073571181X
Laura Gutman,
Patty Ayers,
Donald S. Booth
US$44.99

**Dreamweaver MX
Web Development**
0735713081
Drew McLellan
US$45.00

Dreamweaver MX Magic
0735711798
Brad Halstead,
Sean Nicholson, et al.
US$39.99

**Joseph Lowery's Beyond
Dreamweaver**
0735712778
Joseph Lowery
US$45.00

**eLearning with
Dreamweaver MX:
Building Online
Learning Applications**
0735712743
Betsy Bruce
US$45.00

**Dreamweaver MX
Extensions**
0735711828
Laura Gutman
US$39.99

Dreamweaver MX Templates
0735713197
Brad Halstead
Murray Summers
US$29.99
Available October 2002

Dreamweaver MX Killer Tips
0735713022
Joseph Lowery
US$39.99
Available January 2003

New Riders

VOICES
THAT MATTER™

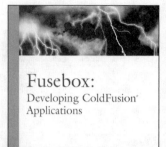

Colophon

The image of a dramatic evening thunderstorm on this book's cover was captured by Don Ferrell (PhotoDisc). The lightning storm photo is part of a compilation of photographs of the elements of Earth, wind, fire, and water.

This book was written and edited in Microsoft Word, and laid out in QuarkXPress. The font used for the body text is Bembo and Mono. It was printed on 50# Husky Offset Smooth paper at VonHoffmann Inc. in Owensville, Missouri. Prepress consisted of PostScript computer-to-plate technology (filmless process). The cover was printed at Moore Langen Printing in Terre Haute, Indiana, on 12 pt., coated on one side.